THE POLITICAL ECONOMY

OF THE LABOUR MOVEMENT

IN ST. VINCENT

AND THE GRENADINES

The Political Economy of the Labour Movement
in St. Vincent and the Grenadines

©2019 Ralph E. Gonsalves

Printed in the United States

ISBN# 9781091563797

This is the fifth volume in a series entitled *Caribbean Ideas*
published by Strategy Forum, Inc.
Kingstown, St. Vincent and the Grenadines

Other titles in the series include
The Case for Caribbean Reparatory Justice
Our Caribbean Civilisation and Its Political Prospects
Our Caribbean and Global Insecurity
Globalised. Climatised. Stigmatised.

The Political Economy

of the Labour Movement

in St. Vincent

and the Grenadines

Ralph E. Gonsalves

DEDICATION

To my dear friend, comrade, and working class fighter for justice, Caspar London, who left us too soon;

and

To the working people of St. Vincent and the Grenadines, the Caribbean and the world.

CONTENTS

Abbreviations..9

Preface... 13

  I. Background and Setting 17

     Geography, Demography and Political History:
     A Brief Overview.. 17

     The Impact of the Evolving Political Economy..................... 28

     Cultural Pluralism, Classes & Social Stratification
     in the Evolving Political Economy 50

     The Conceptual Frame of the Labour Movement
     and Trade Unions 54

  II. The 1935 Uprising and Its Significance on Political
     and Trade Union Development... 61

     The Uprising Itself 61

     The Significance of the Uprising
     to the Working People 66

  III.   The Emergence of Trade Unionism 1945-1957 75

     Political Unionism Defined 75

     Political Unionism Emerges 77

     Activism in the Labour Movement
     and Electoral Battles, 1951-1957 86

  IV. Political Unionism: PPP–FIAWU (1957-1963):
     First Years in Government... 113

   V. Political Unionism, 1963-1969: Challenges
     and Consolidation.. 139

     The Challenges to the PPP-FIAWU Nexus: 1963-1966....... 139

     The Decline of the PPP, The Consolidation of SVLP,
     Conflicts In CTAWU: 1966-1969...................................... 153

  VI. The Road to Independence: 1969-1979............................. 161

Political Defiance to SVLP Dominance...161

SVLP Returns Ascendant Amidst Political and
   Trade Union Challenges 174

VII.   A Post-Independence Review of the Political Economy
       of the Labour Movement 1980-2018...191

The Exhaustion, Decline and Defeat
   of the Labour Government, 1980-1984 191

NDP Ascendant, Its Counter-Revolution Unfolds,
   "Labour" Forces Regroup: July 1984 – February 1994.............205

Decline of NDP, Popular Resistance, And Resurgent Labour:
   February 1994-2000 217

Labour Returns United as ULP Government:
   March 2001-2018, Thus Far 225

Summary Review of Achievements of Labour, 2001-2018 238

Summation of the Condition of Progressive Politics
   & the Labour Movement in the Post-1979 Period 248

VIII.   Two Final Notes on Leadership and Women.................................257
       Leadership in the Labour Movement and
       the Nation: 1935-2018 257

Women in Politics, Trade Unionism and the
   Political Economy: 1951-2018 283

IX.   Summation and Concluding Reflections on the
       Labour Movement..311

Bibliography 335

General Index 341

Name Index 349

ABBREVIATIONS

ACLM	Antigua-Caribbean Liberation Movement
ACS	Association of Caribbean States
ALBA	Bolivarian Alternative for Our Americas
BLAC	Black Liberation Action Committee
CARICOM	Caribbean Community
CDB	Caribbean Development Bank
CCL	Caribbean Congress of Labour
CSA	Civil Service Association
CELAC	Community of States of Latin America and the Caribbean
CTAWU	Commercial Technical and Allied Workers' Union
DFM	Democratic Freedom Movement
DRP	Democratic Republican Party
EFP	Education Forum of the People
FIAWU	Federated Industrial and Agricultural Workers' Union
FNWU	Farmers and National Workers' Union
GP	Green Party
MNU	Movement for National Unity
MSP	Mitchell-Sylvester Party
NCDD	National Committee in Defence of Democracy
NDP	New Democratic Party

NFU	National Farmers' Union
NIC	National Independence Committee
NWM	National Workers' Movement
NUPW	National Union of Progressive Workers
OBCA	Organisation for Black Cultural Awareness
ODD	Organisation in Defence of Democracy
OECS	Organisation of Eastern Caribbean States
PDM	People's Democratic Movement
PDP	People's Democratic Party
PPM	People's Progressive Movement
PPP	People's Political Party
PSU	Public Service Union
PWP	People's Working Party
SCOPE	Standing Conference of Opposition Parties of the Eastern Caribbean
SVEEA	St. Vincent Employers' and Employees' Association
SVEF	St. Vincent Employers' Federation
SVFL	St. Vincent Federation of Labour
SVGA	St. Vincent Growers' Association
SVGTU	St. Vincent and the Grenadines Teachers' Union
SVGWU	St. Vincent General Workers' Union
SVGLP	St. Vincent and the Grenadines Labour Party
SVLP	St. Vincent Labour Party
SVLOA	St. Vincent Land Owners' Association
SVNM	St. Vincent National Movement
SVPCU	St. Vincent Peasant Cultivators' Union

SVGRA	St. Vincent Representative Government Association
SSTA	St. Vincent Secondary Teachers' Association
SVGTU	St. Vincent and the Grenadines Teachers' Union
SVTUC	St. Vincent Trade Union Congress
SVUWU	St. Vincent United Workers' Union
SVWA	St. Vincent Workingmen's Association
SVWU	St. Vincent Workers' Union
TWA	Trinidad Workingmen's Association
ULP	Unity Labour Party
UPM	United People's Movement
UWI	University of the West Indies
UWPRU	United Workers, Peasants, and Ratepayers' Union
WAPU	Workers and Peasants' Union
YSG	Young Socialist Group
YULIMO	Youlou United Liberation Movement

Currency

BWI $ = British West Indian Dollar (BWI $4.80 = 1pound sterling)

EC $ = Eastern Caribbean Dollar (EC $2.70 = US $1)

PREFACE

I decided to write this book for three main reasons: First, to provide the working people, nationally, regionally and globally, especially the young, with a coherent understanding and explanation of the history and political economy of the labour movement in St. Vincent and the Grenadines; secondly, to correct the many prejudices and anti-worker biases of the bourgeois and neo-liberal perspectives in their telling of the story of the labour movement in this country; and thirdly, to reaffirm yet again that the understanding and an explanation of a country's political economy in the epoch of capitalism, can be best pursued through a thorough examination of its labour movement and the working people who constitute it.

In his preface to *The Black Jacobins*, C.L.R. James offers an insight into the profundity and explanatory power of an historical materialist analysis of the political economy, inclusive of the national, class, ethnic, and gender struggles of ordinary men and women in life, living, production, and reproduction, thus:

> *The writing of history becomes ever more difficult. The power of god or the weakness of man, Christianity or the divine right of kings to govern wrong, can easily be made responsible for the downfall of states or the birth of new societies. Such elementary conceptions lend themselves willingly to narrative treatment and from Tacitus to Mc Caulay, from Thucydides to Green, the traditionally famous historians have been more artist than scientist; they wrote so well because they saw so little.*

To see much more we must dig deeper, examine the real material world and its contradictions therein, analyse the realities of the human condition historically and comparatively, and draw conclusions therefrom methodically and scientifically. It is so easy to write with cleverness and superficiality of the complexities of the labour movement by stylising facts in search of a theory of explanation; doing so without getting to the pith and substance which undergird, and ultimately determine, the activities of men, women, and their leaders in the ebb and flow of the political economy and its historical evolution or alterations. Indeed, often, too, bourgeois historians over-emphasise the actions of leaders but pay little attention to followers; such an exercise is not without interest or meaning but it is often misleading and contrived.

James himself reminds us that:

> Great men make history, but only such history as it is possible for them to make. Their freedom of achievement is limited by the necessities of their environment. To portray the limits of those necessities and the realisation, complete or partial, of all the possibilities, that is the true business of the historian.

Leaders are important but without the understanding and explanation of their circumstances, the analysis is deficient.

In 1971, at the age of twenty-five years, I completed the research and writing for a thesis in partial fulfilment of my Master of Science (MSc) Degree in Government from the University of the West Indies (UWI), Mona, Jamaica. The thesis was entitled *The Role of Labour in the Political Process of St. Vincent, 1935-1970.* Some of the material in this book on that earlier period has come from the research conducted by me nearly 50 years ago. Much additional research has since been done for that period, and beyond; the analysis offered here has had the benefit of a greater maturity and understanding.

The coverage of the political economy of the labour movement for the post-1970 years up to the present time (2019) has posed a challenge for objective scholarship because I have been a major participant in the nationalist, anti-imperialist, socialist-oriented, and advanced social democratic work of the labour movement over most of those years. Indeed, I mark the period of my serious political activism from October 16, 1968, when as the leader of the university students in Jamaica, I led a huge mass protest of students and sections of the general public against the action of the then government of Jamaica in banning the revolutionary activist and intellectual, Walter Rodney of Guyana, from re-entering Jamaica on his return from a Black Writers' Conference in Montreal, Canada; Rodney was, at the time, a Lecturer at UWI in the Department of History. The protesters in the demonstration suffered rough repression at the hands of the Jamaican security forces.

By 1975, I became a member of the socialist Youlou United Liberation Movement (YULIMO) of St. Vincent and the Grenadines. In September 1979

I was in the leadership of the United People's Movement (UPM) and a candidate in the general elections of December 1979. Since then until 2015, I contested every single general election — nine in all — in St. Vincent and the Grenadines, first as the Political Leader of the Movement of National Unity (MNU) — 1984 to 1994 — and later, from December 1998 as the Political Leader of the Unity Labour Party (ULP). Since February 1994 until now I have been the elected parliamentary representative for North Central Windward. I became Leader of the Opposition in October 1999 and Prime Minister in March 2001, a position I have been occupying, unbroken, since then. All throughout these years I have been thus attached to the labour movement and progressive politics. I am a "labour" man; and I defend and promote always the interests of the working people.

Thus, in the post-1970 period, I have written as participant, eye-witness, and ear-witness. I have brought to bear, accordingly, all the benefits and burdens of the activist and observer in the metaphoric political ring to the business of analysing the political economy of the labour movement as it has evolved.

In the text which follows, in respect of the references to me and my role as researcher or participant, I have written in the third person. I have done so because this book is not an autobiography; I consider that the narrative runs smoother in the third person.

One other stylistic matter: St. Vincent and the Grenadines became independent on October 27, 1979. Prior to that date, the country's name was "St. Vincent". Thus, I have used both names, reflective of the colonial and post-colonial periods as the circumstances have admitted.

I have sought to write this book as an integrated, composite whole. At the same time, though, I have made every effort to facilitate those readers who may wish to read separate chapters not necessarily in their chronological sequences, yet permit them to have a flavour of the whole. The reader is the judge as to my success in this regard.

I am deeply indebted to my Executive Secretary, Mrs. Angie Jackson, and St. Vincent and the Grenadines' Ambassador to the United Nations, Ms. Rhonda King, for their respective roles in the preparation and publication of this book. My wife, Eloise, and my son Camillo, have been helpful to me in my writing of this book. I thank them, and others unnamed, for their support.

I am dedicating this book to my fallen comrade and friend, Caspar London, a socialist activist and trade unionist, whose death has been an enduring loss to me, and moreso to the poor and working people of St. Vincent and the Grenadines and the world. Working people in St. Vincent and the Grenadines do not yet know the fullness of their loss.

February 2019
St. Vincent and the Grenadines

CHAPTER I

BACKGROUND AND SETTING

GEOGRAPHY, DEMOGRAPHY AND POLITICAL HISTORY: A BRIEF OVERVIEW

St. Vincent and the Grenadines is a vulnerable, multi-island, developing, independent country in the Caribbean. It secured its independence from Britain on October 27, 1979, after over 200 years of British over-rule. Its landscape amounts to 150 square miles and its seascape admeasures approximately 11,000 square nautical miles. The largest and most populous of the islands is St. Vincent, which accounts for a land area of 133 square miles and some 99,000 persons or 91 percent of the entire country's total population of almost 110,000, according to the 2012 Population Census. The island-chain which makes up St. Vincent and the Grenadines is comprised of 32 islands and islets, of which only nine are populated. Apart from St. Vincent, the following are populated: Young Island, Bequia, Mustique, Canouan, Mayreau, Palm Island, Petit St. Vincent, and Union Island. The chain of islands which runs south from Bequia to Union Island is collectively called "the Grenadines".

St. Vincent is a rugged, mountainous, tropical island of volcanic origin, lush vegetation, and with an average annual rainfall of 100 inches; it is possessed of many rivers and streams. The Grenadine islands are of coral formation with white-sand beaches, but with no rivers and much less rainfall than on St. Vincent. The seas around St. Vincent and the Grenadines are clean and beautiful; they are rich with marine life, including abundant fish, lobster, and conch. St. Vincent and the Grenadines is prone to natural disasters: Hurricanes, storms, landslides, and volcanic eruptions; its last truly cataclysmic eruption was in 1902. In this era of adverse climate change, the problematic weather and climatic events have been unfamiliar and unprecedented; there is urgency for adaptation and mitigation responses in the building of resilience.

To the north, the nearest neighbour of St. Vincent and the Grenadines is St. Lucia, some 21 miles separating their closest points of contact; to the immediate south, at an even closer distance, is Grenada; and Barbados is the nearest neighbour to the east, 100 miles away.

European contact with St. Vincent and the Grenadines occurred sometime between the late 15th and early 16th centuries. However, European conquest and settlement did not take place until after 1763 when, at the Treaty of Paris, Britain was allocated suzerainty over St. Vincent and the Grenadines in the general carve-up, between France and Britain, of several territories in the Eastern Caribbean. Between early European contact and the post-1763 British settlement, European adventurers of one sort or another, mainly under official British or French over-lordship, established here and there in St. Vincent and the Grenadines a tenuous occupation of limited parcels of land. Indeed, when the British settlers arrived in the immediate aftermath of the Treaty of Paris, they met a significant number of Frenchmen and women (over 1,000) and African slaves (under 3,000) on about 3,000 acres of land on the western side of St. Vincent.

In fact, the French farmers occupied the land with the "de facto" permission of the indigenous people, the Callinago and the Garifuna, who owned all the land in common in St. Vincent and the Grenadines in a communal way of life, but with an authority structure headed by their Paramount Chief. And despite Franco-British agreement at the Treaty of Paris, France had not quite abandoned their interest in St. Vincent and the Grenadines, in pursuance of which the French dislodged, temporarily, Britain's control in the four-year period, 1779-1783.

Before European contact with St. Vincent and the Grenadines (which was alternatively known, natively, as Youlou and the Begos or Yuremein or Hairouna), the indigenous population called themselves Callinagoes ("the peaceful ones") although they were labelled as Caribs ("the warlike ones") by the Europeans. Over time the Callinagoes mated with Africans (runaway slaves from Barbados, slaves from a shipwreck off St. Vincent in the 1670s, and African slaves brought by French occupiers). The offspring of the conjoined Callinagoes and Africans became known as Garifuna. The British began making a distinction between "Yellow Caribs" (the Callinagoes) and "Black Caribs" (the Garifuna). The British sought to divide and rule them on the basis of ethnic identification. They feigned a preference for "the Yellow Caribs" whom they thought were more accommodating to their colonial over-rule.

By the 1780s, the indigenous population of St. Vincent and the Grenadines was estimated at just below 10,000, most of whom were Garifuna. Indeed, the Chief with whom the British were compelled to do business was Joseph Chatoyer, Paramount Chief of the Garifuna People.

Relations between the British and the indigenous people soured badly after the British formally declared, in 1764, that all the land in St. Vincent and the Grenadines belonged legally to the British Crown. There then ensued a bitter series of battles, skirmishes, and prolonged wars in which the Callinago and Garifuna people resisted British ownership and control of their country. At the core of these conflicts were two issues: Land ownership and the right to self-determination. As oppressed peoples the world over have done historically, the Callinago and Garifuna fought for the land which belonged to them and for the right to govern themselves as they saw fit.

Thus, between 1764 and 1795, the Garifuna-led guerrilla campaign ensued against the British, interspersed by occasional treaties and peace offerings which were repeatedly broken by the British. In 1795, in the last of the sustained wars, Chatoyer was ambushed and killed; the indigenous patriots were defeated by overwhelming force and the more advanced war technology of the British.

Swiftly, the British embarked on a genocidal putsch against the Callinago and Garifuna. In the process, over 5,000 of them were forcibly transported to the offshore island of Balliceaux. After six months there, a lack of food and water and elementary sanitary facilities caused the death of over one-half of that number. The 2,026 survivors were then exiled to Roatan Island in the Bay of Honduras. From this sturdy, resilient group of Garifuna, their descendants can now be found in Belize, Honduras, Nicaragua, Guatemala, and further afield in the United States of America, especially in sections of New York and California.

Meanwhile, in St. Vincent and the Grenadines, by 1800, the Callinago and Garifuna were deprived by the British of all their land save and except for 238 acres in the difficult and relatively unproductive terrain on the north-east of St. Vincent. They were also deprived of the legal right to own land. They had become the conquered remnants of a proud and independent people in their own nation. In 2002, the Unity Labour Party government proclaimed the Right Excellent Joseph Chatoyer, Paramount Chief of the Garifuna People, as the country's first, and so far only, National Hero on account of his extraordinary deeds in fighting British colonialism in the interest of his people.

British colonialism, in the wake of its assumption of suzerainty of St. Vincent and the Grenadines in 1763, established, among other things, a plantation economy producing mainly sugar, and based on African slave labour. Between 1764 and 1807 when the British slave trade was abolished, the records show that 55,562 African slaves disembarked in St. Vincent and the Grenadines. At slavery's end, Emancipation Day August 01, 1838, there were some 22,250 registered slaves; there was a very high attrition rate among them due to the savagery of slavery.

The need for labour to man the colonial plantation economy and its external mercantile capitalist linkages caused the British government in the post-emancipation period to recruit, first, indentured labourers from Portugal's Madeira, then indentured "free" African labourers from West Africa, and finally indentured labourers from India. The Portuguese indentured labourers/servants from Madeira, numbering just over 2,000, were brought between November 1845 and 1852; slightly over 1,000 indentured "free" Africans were brought in the late 1840s and early 1850s; and the Indian indentured labourers, numbering approximately 2,500, came between 1861 and 1880.

Save and except for a few years of itinerant French rule in the late 1770s to early 1780s (1779 – 1783), St. Vincent and the Grenadines was under British suzerainty from 1763 until internal self-government in 1969 and full constitutional independence on October 27, 1979.

Two hundred or so years of British colonialism in St. Vincent and the Grenadines demand reflections on colonialism generally, and more specifically a colonialism imposed by a mercantile capitalist Britain which, in the nineteenth century, evolved into industrial capitalism, then into monopoly capitalism as the twentieth century approached.

The Martinican poet, philosopher, and politician, Aimé Césaire, in an essay originally published in 1955 entitled *"Discourse on Colonialism"* (republished in 2000 by *Monthly Review Press*) sagely advises that:

> *No one colonizes innocently, that no one colonises with impunity either; that a nation which colonizes, that a civilization which justifies colonization — and therefore force — is already a sick civilisation, a civilisation which is morally diseased, which irresistibly, progressing from one consequence to another, one denial to another... Colonisation: bridgehead in a campaign to civilise barbarism from which there may emerge at any moment the negation of civilisation, pure and simple.*

The effect of colonialism is to change the coloniser and the colonised. Césaire correctly insists that:

> *Colonisation...dehumanizes even the most civilized man;*
> *that the colonial enterprise, colonial conquest, which is*
> *based on contempt for the native and justified by that*
> *contempt, inevitably tends to change him who undertakes*
> *it; that the colonizer, who in order to ease his conscience*
> *gets into the habit of seeing the other man as* an animal,
> *accustoms himself to treating him like an animal, and*
> *tends objectively to transform* himself *into an animal.*
> *It is this result, this boomerang effect of colonization....*

At its core, colonisation always is about sucking resources from the colony to be benefit of the colonisers and the colonising State. Yet, the colonisers speak of progress in the colonies. Césaire answers this colonial "justification" thus:

> *Security? Culture? The rule of law? In the meantime,*
> *I look around and wherever there are colonizers face to*
> *face, I see force, brutality, cruelty, sadism, conflict, and,*
> *in a parody of education, the hasty manufacture of a*
> *few thousand subordinate functionaries, 'boys', artisans,*
> *office clerks, and interpreters necessary for the smooth*
> *operation of business.*

More profoundly, Césaire succinctly advises:

> *....Colonization='thingification'.... They talk about pro-*
> *gress, about 'achievements'.... I am talking about societies*
> *drained of their essence, cultures trampled underfoot,*
> *institutions undermined, lands confiscated, religions*
> *smashed, magnificent artistic creations destroyed, ex-*
> *traordinary* possibilities *wiped out.*
>
> *....I am talking about natural economies that have been*
> *disrupted — harmonious and viable economies adapted*
> *to the indigenous population — about food crops de-*
> *stroyed, malnutrition permanently introduced, agricul-*
> *tural development oriented solely toward the benefit of*
> *the metropolitan countries; about the looting of products,*
> *the looting of raw materials.*

This was colonisation in the Caribbean; it was so, too, in Africa about which Walter Rodney wrote so compellingly in his 1973 classic, *How Europe Underdeveloped Africa.*

The colonial State established in St. Vincent and the Grenadines was an external imposition by the colonising power, Britain. It did not arise from any pre-existing class struggle in the colony to hold class antagonisms in check. Pre-colonial St. Vincent was a classless society of indigenous people who lived in communion with one other with an authority structure to serve communal needs, not to acquire new means of holding down and exploiting an oppressed class. The colonial state in St. Vincent and the Grenadines was set up to serve first and foremost the economic and political interests of the British ruling class and the capitalist state in Britain, and at the first remove the planter-merchant elite of British stock who for fortune and adventure set up business in St. Vincent and the Grenadines. It was designed to rule over the indigenous people and African slaves during an imposed slavery and later, the working people after emancipation, within an evolving capitalism. In the formative sixty years of British colonialism, the accomplished Vincentian historian, Dr. Bernard Marshall, has told this story very well in his book, published in 2007, entitled *Slavery, Law and Society in the British Windward Islands, 1763 – 1823.*

The colonial state over the historical period (1763 to the onset of independence in 1979) assumed different political forms with varying levels of unrepresentative and representative governments and devolutions to local authority centres.

Between 1763 and the introduction of universal adult suffrage in 1951, there were in St. Vincent and the Grenadines various models of unrepresentative, gubernatorial governance under British colonial hegemony. At first there was, what historians have called, the Old Representative System (ORS) of government with an elected Assembly based on a very limited franchise of the planter-merchant elite, a nominated Council, and a virtually all-powerful Governor appointed by the British government. The ORS was a kind of miniature, pale imitation, of the Commons, Lords, and Crown in the mother country, Britain. For various reasons, the ORS gave way over time to a Pure Crown Colony System of Government in which the Governor was advised legislatively through a Council consisting of officials and nominated members appointed by the Crown. Indeed, between 1867 and 1925 when the Pure Crown Colony System of Government operated there were no elections, not even on the basis of a limited franchise. Between 1925 and 1935, a Modified Crown Colony System was set up in which the Legislative Council consisted of officials, nominated members, and four representatives, elected on a limited property-owning franchise. The Executive Council remained in the hands of the colonial officials under the Governor or Administrator.

After the popular anti-colonial uprising of October 21, 1935, the franchise was liberalised in 1936 to accommodate more popular voices in the legislature, but still under colonial gubernatorial control and dominance. Gradual changes occurred in the post-1936 period without altering the substance of governance until universal adult suffrage (one person, one vote, for those 21 years and over) was introduced for the 1951 general elections.

Universal adult suffrage, however, did not alter colonial control in the legislature since the officials, nominated members, and the presiding Administrator, representing the Governor — then resident in Grenada — were able to out-vote the eight elected legislators. In 1951, the eight members of the legislature were all elected on the platform of the anti-colonial and reformist Eighth Army of Liberation. They were swiftly split in two under the rubric "Big Four" and "Little Four" — the former more accommodating to colonialism, the latter more militant.

In 1954, an embryonic Ministerial Committee system was introduced; and in 1957, a fuller Ministerial system but still under the executive leadership of the Colonial Administrator who acted for the Governor. In 1960, a Chief Minister was appointed; he headed the Executive Council (an embryonic Cabinet) for the first time but the Colonial Administrator still retained responsibility for the public service and the Police; the Governor held, always, certain "reserve powers"; Britain, too, had responsibility for the country's foreign affairs. The majority party had control of the Legislative Council – the law-making body; after passage of the Bills the Colonial Governor or Administrator was required to assent to them before they became law.

In 1969, St. Vincent and the Grenadines became a self-governing country in association with Britain. The Chief Minister became the Premier and a fully-fledged Cabinet was established with responsibility for all internal affairs. Britain retained control of defence and foreign affairs of St. Vincent and the Grenadines.

In 1979, St. Vincent and the Grenadines became an independent nation. The Premier was replaced by a Prime Minister. A unicameral legislature evolved containing 13 elected members; four Senators appointed by the largely ceremonial Head of State, the Governor General, on the advice of the Prime Minister; two senators appointed by the Governor-General on the advice of the Leader of the Opposition; and an Attorney General who may be a public servant, or a political appointee from among the elected members or senators. The House of Assembly is presided over by a Speaker, someone from outside the regular membership of the House but elected by the members of the House of Assembly. For the 1989 general elections, the number of elected members was increased to fifteen.

The 1979 Constitution is of a liberal democratic type. It offers protection of an individual's fundamental rights and freedoms. It provides for an independent judiciary; and it contains important provisions for an independent Public Service Commission, Police Service Commission, Director of Audit, Director of Public Prosecutions, and an impartial public service. Checks and balances abound in the Constitution, though, in its operation, the Constitution permits substantially Cabinet, and even Prime Ministerial, government. An effort to provide a root-and-branch democratisation of a proposed republican Constitution was defeated in a popular referendum in November 2009.

The state apparatus in the post-1979 period has frequently displayed a relative autonomy of the major contending classes internally, though still constrained by them and, more so, by monopoly capitalism externally. This relative autonomy of the state has been occasioned by a complex of factors, including particularly the relatively undeveloped nature of the contending class, their "class balance," the gubernatorial inheritance from the colonial state, the seeming all-class embrace of the nation, the requisites of electoral democracy, and the social democratic offerings of the state.

Over the historical sweep of colonial rule in St Vincent and the Grenadines from 1763 to the anti-colonial uprising of October 1935, both resistance and accommodation to colonialism were evident from those who were subject peoples. The Callinago-Garifuna struggles against colonial domination and land-grabbing by the British were at the core of popular resistance between 1763 and 1800. Throughout slavery, African slaves engaged in various forms of resistance, from lethargic labour to indigenous religious worship and the battle for an autonomous cultural space for the folk, and to isolated anti-slavery skirmishes. In the post-emancipation period in the 19th century among the highlights of anti-colonial resistance were the strike — withdrawal of labour — in 1848, the peasant and worker protests of 1862, and the resistance of Indian indentured labourers centred at Argyle in the early 1860s to the terms of their indentureship and their social condition.

In the post-1918 World War, and before October 1935, organised stirrings for self-government and popular regional representation, and regional integration of a democratic kind, arose in the form of the St. Vincent Representative Government Association and a branch of the Universal Negro Improvement Association of Marcus Mosiah Garvey.

The anti-colonial uprising of October 21, 1935, mistakenly referred to as "the 1935 riots" by some historians, ushered in the commencement of the social democratic revolution in St. Vincent and the Grenadines, a process which is well-advanced but still incomplete. George Augustus Mc Intosh emerged out of this cauldron of anti-colonial struggles as the dominant figure in the labour movement and politics until the on-rush of a more ostensibly militant political grouping, the Eighth Army of Liberation, to contest the 1951 general elections under universal adult suffrage. Out of the 1935 Uprising sprung the mass-based St. Vincent Workingmen's Association (SVWA) and an inchoate political organisation, the St. Vincent Labour Party (SVLP).

Between 1951 and 2019, the working people, the peasantry, and progressive elements of the national bourgeoisie, the middle class, professionals of one kind or another, small business operators, through their respective organisations including trade unions, have struggled to obtain socio-economic and political space to advance their interests and those of the nation. Political parties have emerged to represent various interests and what they perceived to be national interests. Various popularly-elected governments have been: In the colonial period, Ebenezer Joshua's People's Political Party (PPP) (1957-1967); Milton Cato's St. Vincent Labour Party (SVLP) (1967-1972); James Mitchell – PPP Coalition (1972-1974); Cato's SVLP (1974-1989); Since independence, Cato's SVLP (1979-1984); Mitchell's New Democratic Party (NDP) (1984-2001); and Ralph Gonsalves' Unity Labour Party (ULP) (2001-2019, thus far). Between 1957 and 2019, all these governments, save and except Mitchell's NDP (1984-2001), have sought, in one measure or the other, to advance the social democratic revolution within the capitalist mode of production and its external monopoly capitalist linkages. Mitchell's NDP represented a counter-revolution to social democracy; Gonsalves' ULP has fashioned the most advanced form of social democracy, nationalism and anti-imperialism.

Throughout colonial rule in St. Vincent and the Grenadines, colonial Britain framed its strategy of domination based on military strength, economic power, religion (Anglicanism and to a lesser extent Methodism and Roman Catholicism), concentrated political and judicial authority systems, and cultural hegemony. Colonialism's tactics were varied: Divide the subject peoples and rule them; violence and genocide; slavery and indentureship; concentration of ownership of land and commerce in a few reliable hands; direct or indirect colonial over-rule, in various forms; the promotion of the false idea of the cultural superiority of British values and institutions, and the fallacy of an alleged inferiority of non-white peoples; wage exploitation of labour in the post-emancipation period; and the use of the Police Force, the military, and the judicial system to enforce colonial order. In the early decades of the 20th century, colonialism introduced and consolidated *limited* secondary education for the brightest handful of colonials who were being prepared to man the institutions of state in tandem with colonialism; introduced, too, was elemental telecommunications through a British company, Cable and Wireless Limited. International banking was done through Barclays Bank; later Canadian commercial banks arrived. In the 1970s a National Commercial Bank was established and regional commercial banks entered the domestic financial market.

In the early 20th century an indigenous domestic savings bank, the Agricultural Credit and Loan Bank was founded. In the 1940s, another indigenous domestic bank, the St. Vincent Cooperative Bank, known popularly as the "Penny Bank" was set up. So, too, was the indigenous St. Vincent Building and Loan Association.

The strength of a consolidated British colonialism over time in St. Vincent and the Grenadines engendered the belief among the subject people that it was futile to confront head-on the colonial hegemon. So, subject peoples accommodated themselves to colonialism and sought to advance their interests through negotiation, quiet resentment, and occasional outbursts of isolated protests or even fewer uprisings.

Each time British colonialism felt threatened in St. Vincent and the Grenadines or in its neighbouring Caribbean possessions, it provided "the stick", the coercive arm of the colonial apparatus, and "the carrot" of possible amelioration. Oft-times, circumstances — economic and socio-political — in Britain itself conspired to presage some change, ameliorative or otherwise.

Examples abound: The genocidal war against the Callinago and Garifuna and the consolidation of British political and juridical institutions; the focussed organisation of African slavery in St. Vincent and the Grenadines after 1763 and then the abolition of the slave trade in 1807; the harsh condition of slavery for 70 years (1764 to 1834) followed by a marginally less harsh 4-year apprenticeship period leading to the formal emancipation of slaves in 1838; internal reorganisation of indebted estates under the Encumbered Estates Acts of the 1850s consequent upon a slump in the sugar economy; the introduction of indentured labour, first from Madeira and then "free" Africans, and later from India, to ease the labour shortage in the 1840s and early 1850s, and between the 1860s and 1881; the dissolution of the Old Representative System (ORS) of Government in 1867 until 1925, in line with colonialism's earlier dissolution of the ORS in Jamaica consequent upon the Morant Bay Rebellion of 1865, to keep other emergent economic and political elites out of the elected legislature, albeit on a very restrictive franchise; the appointment of the Royal Commission in 1896 to address popular demands for land reform; the appointment of the Wood Commission in 1922 to examine and report upon the demand in the British colonies in the Caribbean for greater popular representation in the legislature; the appointment of the Fergusson-Orr Commission in the early 1930s to consider regional integration; the appointment of the Orde Browne Commission in 1937 to report on labour conditions; the appointment of the Moyne Commission in 1938 to report upon the socio-economic and political conditions in the British Caribbean consequent upon the spate of anti-colonial uprisings in the region between 1935 and 1938; the limited liberalisation of the Constitution of St. Vincent and the Grenadines in 1936 following upon the 1935 Uprising; the further constitutional liberalisation after 1945 leading to universal adult suffrage in 1951 in St. Vincent and the Grenadines following the publication of the report of the Moyne Commission in 1945; the establishment of the Labour Department and a limited Social Welfarism after, respectively, the 1935 Uprising and the setting up of the Colonial Welfare and Development Agency at the Colonial Office in Britain in the 1940s; and the gradual process of constitutional decolonisation between universal adult suffrage of 1951 and formal independence in 1979.

For our current analytic purposes, several salient features of the history of St. Vincent and the Grenadines stand out, including the ultimate historical determinant of the successive dominant modes of production of slavery and capitalism; the tradition of both resistance and accommodation to colonialism by subject peoples; the shaping of an "authoritarian personality" of the planter-merchant elite and subject peoples by slavery, indentureship, and colonialism, an ill-formed personality-type which oscillates between submission and aggression and which, over time, has been tempered, muted, or cleansed through appropriate education (religious or otherwise) and political consciousness; the evolution of a planter-merchant elite which was overwhelmingly crass, materialistic, devoid of intellect or uplifting culture, stuffed with racism, colonial mimicry, and backwardness; the evolution of a matrifocal family structure in a wider society which was nevertheless conditioned and underpinned by a patriarchy which adversely undermined equality and stability in gender and power relations to the disadvantage of women and society as a whole; the prolonged time taken for the establishment and consolidation of British colonial rule in St. Vincent and the Grenadines, occurring only after over 30 years of protracted war against them by the Callinago and Garifuna, a set of historical circumstances not evident anywhere else in the Anglo-Caribbean; the settled consensus in the latter half of the 20th century that political change is preferable in the Anglo-Caribbean context through consensual and peaceful parliamentary means, even though from time-to-time occasional protests or bouts of political disorder have occurred; a comparatively shorter period of organised slavery in St. Vincent and the Grenadines (74 years from 1764 to 1838) than in all other former British colonies in the Caribbean including St. Kitts, Barbados, Antigua, and Jamaica; a current population mix derived largely from the progeny of the Callinago/Garifuna, the descendants of migrants, free and unfree, who hailed from Anglo-Saxon Europe, Africa, Madeira, and Asia, and recent arrivants from the Middle East and China; a general bundle of impactful issues touching and concerning race, class, gender, culture and their evolution through a special set of historical circumstances under colonialism and a parliamentary democracy of limitations and possibilities, determined ultimately by successive dominant modes of production of slavery and capitalism, in a particular geographic setting; and a State apparatus which still bears the imprint of a colonial gubernatorial governance, inclusive of its tendency to be "autonomous" or unyoked from any fully-formed national economic class, yet constrained by, and objectively connected to, monopoly capitalism globally.

It is to some of these salient historical features that we now turn as further context for our study of trade unions and their political nexus within an evolving political economy.

THE IMPACT OF THE EVOLVING POLITICAL ECONOMY

The study of the political economy of a society embraces an analysis of the interplay of economic, political, socio-cultural, ideational factors, formal and informal institutions in all their many-sided inter-connectedness, contradictions, alterations, and change over time. Explicitly, the study of political economy recognises real flesh-and-blood people behind seemingly abstract analytic categories; and its studies them in their multiple relations in the mode of production and the wider social formation. So, for example, the academic discipline of economics, simpliciter, focusses in the aggregate economy on salaries and wages, rents and profits, money and taxation. Political economy, on the other hand, insists on interrogating the real individuals behind of, or connected to, these seemingly abstract economic categories. Thus, behind wages and salaries there are workers; rents and profits are the domain of landlords/renters and entrepreneurs/capitalists respectively; and money and taxation are the immediate business of those who manage or direct the relevant apparatuses of the State, which in a competitive democracy are overseen by representatives elected by the people. Thus, the economic, socio-cultural and political behaviour, including the multiple interactions, of all these real flesh-and-blood actors in the political economy, come to the fore for study, understanding, and explanation.

At the core of the science of political economy is the understanding and explanation of the economic, and consequentially socio-political relations between people engaged in the production and distribution of the material means of life and living at different stages of social development.

As in other areas of the social sciences, there are significantly different approaches (in addition to minor, specific conceptual frames) to the analytic field of political economy. For our purposes, there are three: 1) An ideational focus which masks the essence of the functioning of the political economy, and abstracts in a static and mechanistic, as distinct from a dialectical way, aggregate economic or behavioural categories, without getting to the structural bases of the relevant phenomena. This approach is favoured by most defenders of the status quo, and is decidedly bourgeois in the contemporary period; 2) an existential frame which highlights an especial individual human essence in the functioning of the political economy; in this way socio-economic and political causation are largely down-played and patterns of activities beyond the existential essence of the individual are not identified and analysed; and 3) a sophisticated dialectical and historical materialist approach grounded in the actual condition of the political economy (economy, polity, socio-cultural nexus, ideas, and institutions), so as to better observe and explain the real world in its changing or altered circumstances. The dialectical materialist approach, as applied to the actual historical and contemporary realities, which takes its guidance originally from the writings of Karl Marx and Frederick Engels, and refined subsequently by like-minded scholars, appears to be the most useful of the explanatory approaches, but without necessarily adopting the attendant perspective (or even baggage) of its broad, prophetic hypotheses of the future ordering of societies generally or of a small, underdeveloped one like St. Vincent and the Grenadines on the periphery, relatively-speaking, of monopoly capitalism.

In his *Preface to a Contribution to the Critique of Political Economy*, published in 1859, Karl Marx laid down the theoretical frame of the dialectical and historical materialist approach to the study of political economy in the oft-quoted passage:

The general result at which I arrived and which...served as a guiding thread for my studies, can be briefly formulated as follows: In the social production of their life, men enter into definite relations that are indispensable and independent of their will, relations of production which correspond to a definite stage of development of their material production constitutes the economic structure of society, the real foundation, on which rises a legal and political superstructure and to which correspond definite forms of social consciousness. The mode of production of material life conditions the social, political, and intellectual life process in general. It is not the consciousness of men that determines their being, but, on the contrary, their social being that determines their consciousness. At a certain stage of their development, the material productive forces of society come into conflict with the existing relations of production, or — what is but a legal expression of the same thing — with the property relations within it which they have been at work hitherto. From forms of development of the productive forces these relations turn into fetters. Then begins an epoch of social revolution. With the change of the economic foundation the entire immense superstructure is more or less rapidly transformed.

This preferred theoretical framework for the understanding and explanation of the political economy has often been caricatured by its critics as limited, limiting, and erroneous in its alleged one-dimensional economic determinism. But it is this caricature, and the misrepresentations, which are wrong and misleading. Frederick Engels himself has had to address precisely this issue many years after the death of Karl Marx.

In an insightful letter to J. Bloch in September, 1890, Engels wrote:

According to the materialist conception of history, the ultimately *determining element in history is the production and reproduction of real life. More than this neither Marx nor I have ever asserted. Hence if somebody twists this into saying that the economic element is the* only *determining one, he transforms that proposition into a meaningless, abstract, senseless phrase. The economic situation is the basis, but the various elements of the superstructure — the political forms of the class struggle and its results, to wit: constitutions established by the victorious class after a successful battle, etc., juridical forms, and even the reflexes of these actual struggles in the brains of the participants, political, juristic, philosophical theories, religious views and their further development into systems of dogmas — also exercise their influence upon the course of historical struggles and in many cases preponderate in determining their form. There is an interaction of all these elements in which, amid all the endless host of accidents (that is, of things and events whose inner inter-connection is so remote or so impossible of proof that we can regard it as non-existent, as negligible), the economic movement finally asserts itself as necessary. Otherwise the application of the theory to any period of history would be easier than the solution of a simple equation of the first degree.*

Engels further elaborated as follows:

We make our history ourselves, but in the first place, under definite assumptions and conditions. Among these the economic ones are ultimately decisive. But the political ones, etc. and indeed even the traditions which haunt human minds also play a part, although not the decisive one.... History is made in such a way that the final result always arises from conflicts between many individual wills, of which each in turn has been made what it is by a host of particular conditions of life. Thus there are innumerable intersecting forces, an infinite series of parallelograms of forces which give rise to one resultant — the historical event.

Over the period from European contact with St. Vincent and the Grenadines in the late 15th to early 16th centuries, and particularly after the organised colonial settlement in 1763, to today, there have been successive *dominant* modes of production (slavery and then capitalism) which have been the ultimate determining element in the shaping of the contours, and events, in the historical evolution of St. Vincent and the Grenadines. These *dominant* modes of production have possessed within each of them real flesh-and-blood people aggregated in classes and ethnic-racial-cultural groups which in their actual struggles in life, production, and reproduction, have imposed or fashioned particular political forms, juridical systems, and coercive apparatuses of the State system. In the society as a whole these *dominant* modes of production have correspondingly engendered or shaped the particular social arrangements or institutions, ideas, philosophical theories, religious beliefs, dogmas, and various cultural practices. Indeed, amidst all these "intersecting forces, an infinite series of parallelograms of forces", including actions resulting from a multitude of individual wills of ordinary persons and leaders and a "host of accidents", one or other bundle of forces may preponderate in determining the form, and content, of the political struggle. In the history of St. Vincent and the Grenadines, for example, ethnicity-racial-cultural matrices have preponderated at critical junctures and have infused the society's tapestry, life, gender relations, production, and reproduction; oft-times, ethnic or racial *identifications* have masked a more fundamental class struggle.

From time immemorial, human beings, in their interaction with nature, have had to provide themselves with the material requisites for subsistence, life, and living such as food, clothing, shelter, and material comforts. Material production has always been — and still is — the basis of human existence. As history evolves, this material production undergoes changes or alterations and develops its forms and means. The *basis* of history, not the totality of history, are successive modes of production.

In the historical materialist understanding of political economy, the *mode of production* is fundamental. The mode of production has two aspects: the *productive forces* and the *relations of production*. The productive forces consist of *labour* and the material *means of production* which category includes the *objects of labour* and the *means of labour*. Labour is the first and most important purposeful activity of human beings focussed on the production of the necessities and requisites of subsistence, life and living. Human beings do not find all that they need to live and develop from nature alone; they are required to produce many things, and services, from their interaction with nature, their physical environment. In the process, the skills, knowledge, abilities of human beings are advanced for life, living, production, and reproduction. The objects of labour are to be found in nature — land, rivers, seas, air — and extracted from nature for production; as technology and knowledge expand, new objects of nature are discovered for human beings' production and consumption. The means of labour are the things which human beings use upon the objects of labour: the means of labour include tools, computers, roads, airports, ports, buildings that are needed for labour, in its interface with nature, for the production process.

The second aspect of the mode of production are the relations of production; in the process of production people act on nature, and at the same time enter into definite relations with each other. Marx outlined this with clarity in his 1849 publication, entitled *Wage Labour and Capital*, thus:

> *In production, men not only act on nature but also on one another. They produce only by cooperating in a certain way and mutually exchanging their activities. In order to produce, they enter into definite connections and relations with one another and only within these social connections and relations does their action on nature, does production, take place....These social relations into which producers enter with one another, the conditions under which they exchange their activities and participate in the whole act of production, will naturally vary according to the character of the means of production.*

Accordingly, within a mode of production, class struggles, infused with ethnic-racial dimensions and structure, and gender-family relations, in the historical context of St. Vincent and the Grenadines, have occurred. Out of these struggles, a *superstructure* of political institutions, juridical systems, coercive state mechanisms, ideas, laws, religious beliefs, and an assortment of cultural practices have been, and are being, fashioned. In an endless way, the interactions between the productive forces and the relations of production, in the mode of production, and the superstructure, which together constitute a particular *social formation (socio-economic formation)*, take place.

Alterations or changes in the mode of production and within the superstructure occur in their multiple inter-connections; indeed, in one way or another, everything is always changing, always moving. These changes or alterations take place as a consequence of the conflicts or contradictions arising from the material order of life, living, and production; these contradictions play themselves out, dialectically, through the activities of real flesh-and-blood people individually, and collectively in groups or classes. The dialectic "laws" of constant change, through opposites and the unity of opposites in the socio-economic formation, are observed historically. In a nutshell, all this constitutes the dialectical materialist conception of the political economy which, as applied to history, is historical materialism.

For completeness, it is important to note that besides the production of material goods for subsistence, life, and living, is the reproduction of human beings and the use of labour *outside* of the production process. The processes of reproduction of life and the utilisation of "non-production" labour occurs through the family or familial relationships. The use of "non-productive" family labour, though separate from the productive process, is certainly linked to it or in supportive facilitation of it; invariably this family labour is unpaid but necessary and desirable in socio-economic terms. The family, critically, plays a vital role, too, in ethical, legal, educational, and spiritual relations which influence behaviour and society. The family itself, and gender relations within it, have evolved over time; both the family and gender relations have been shaped by successive modes of production and their internal alterations; they have impacted trade unionism and politics which impacts will be explored in the on-going narrative.

Historically, in the pre-Columbian era in St. Vincent and the Grenadines, there was a communal mode of production of the indigenous people — the Callinago and the Garifuna. European conquest and settlement imposed, in the post-1763 period up to 1838, a *dominant* slave mode of production (black African slaves and British/European masters), but with external exchange relations of British/European capitalism, mercantilist at first, then industrial capitalism. After the formal emancipation of slaves in 1838, capitalism emerged as the *dominant* mode of production; from 1838 until today, *dominant* capitalism has assumed different forms, determined primarily by the evolution of global capitalism from industrial capitalism to monopoly capitalism (a merger of industrial and finance capital) which itself has, in accordance with its own dynamics, altered itself. In the period 1838 to the mid-1960s or thereabouts, the plantation economy of the pre-capitalist era held sway but with huge modifications as the economy, society, and polity underwent profound alterations in an evolving monopoly capitalism externally and its knock-on national linkages. Thereafter, the ghost of the plantation system has haunted, and still haunts, life, production and reproduction in St. Vincent and the Grenadines.

Throughout history in St. Vincent and the Grenadines, alongside the successive *dominant* modes of production have existed sub-ordinate or subsidiary modes, the principal of which has been the small trading and small-scale producing modes of production, including small-scale retail trading, small farming and subsistence or artisanal fishing, and the like. The subsidiary modes of production have accorded much space for people's sustainable livelihoods but have always been shaped by the *dominant* modes of production and their alterations. The evolution of, and shifts in, actual economic activities within the succeeding modes of production have demonstrated human beings' quest, in their interface with nature and their material surroundings, to advance their lives, production and reproduction. Individual families, including, significantly, the women within them, have played, and do play critical economic roles in these subsidiary modes of production. Within them family labour has been vital. These economic activities need to be traced and detailed; so, too, the essential demographics.

The export economy of St. Vincent and the Grenadines, from 1763 up until the latter part of the last decade of the twentieth century — in the middle of the 1990s — was dominated by agriculture. Four crops constituted, at various historical periods, the core of the agricultural sector: sugar, arrowroot, cotton, and bananas. Minor crops of significance have been root crops (yam, dasheen, sweet potatoes, tannia, eddoes, cassava), coconuts, cocoa, coffee, fruits, vegetables, spices. Animal husbandry has been supportive in the rearing of sheep, goats, pigs, and cattle. Fishing, largely artisanal, mainly for domestic consumption, has been an important industry in particular communities of St. Vincent and the Grenadines.

From the mid-1990s tourism, in tandem with assorted services (banking, insurance, professional services), has been the mainstay of the export economy; three-quarters of the overall national economy are now accounted for in services, mainly tourism. The national economy has been transformed from a goods-based economy to a services-based one. To be sure agriculture, fishing, and small light manufacturing create much value-added and jobs, but services are dominant. The development of the air transport, cruise ship facilities, and the revolution in information technology — critical elements in the altered productive forces — have facilitated the increasing dominance of the tourism industry, which has, in turn, affected the economy, production relations and politics.

The nature and character of the national economy, the crops cultivated, the diversification into tourism, ownership of land and other resources, and the extent of the state and private sectors, have had major causal impacts on politics and trade unionism in St. Vincent and the Grenadines. All these considerations need to be explored so as to enhance a proper understanding and explanation of the political economy of the labour movement.

The sugar economy and slavery were introduced into St. Vincent after the British assumed suzerainty in 1763 at the conclusion of the Seven Years' War with France. Between 1764 and 1807 — the date of the abolition of the British slave trade in the West Indies and Africa — 55,562 African slaves were forcibly brought to St. Vincent; this number is 6,614 less than the 62,176 Africans who were forcibly embarked on the ships sailing from West Africa.

The initial steps to sugar cane cultivation and the production of sugar and molasses in St. Vincent involved: 1) the declaration that all the land, which was held in common by the indigenous Callinago and Garifuna people, belonged to the British Crown; 2) the limiting of the sale of the land in fee simple to British subjects only; 3) the granting of permission to 1,300 French settlers and their 2,700 slaves to remain on the property which they occupied in 1763, for a maximum of forty years with leasehold rights only; 4) the importation of enslaved Africans to provide the labour to cultivate sugar cane; 5) the restriction of lands sold to no more than single parcels of 500 acres; 6) the introduction of the sugar-cane plants, machinery, and skilled personnel necessary for the sugar industry; 7) and the swift and firm establishment of the authority of the colonial State.

The British, in introducing a sugar industry in St. Vincent, applied all their knowledge and experiences gained from the mature, West Indian sugar economies, especially, Jamaica, Barbados, Antigua, and St. Kitts.

Sugar production in 1766 amounted to 35 tons; by 1770, it rose to 1,930 tons. Throughout the 1790s, total sugar production in St. Vincent fluctuated between 3,130 tons in 1774 to 2,049 tons in 1779. The French recapture of St. Vincent between 1779 and 1783 affected sugar production adversely, and there were no exports to Britain in those years. Thereafter, the intensification of the anti-colonial guerrilla war against the British, led by the Garifuna, crippled sugar cane cultivation and the production of sugar. Cane fields were burnt and sugar mills destroyed by the Garifuna. The conflict culminated in epic battles, between the Garifuna and the British. The Garifuna were defeated and their chief, Joseph Chatoyer was killed. Large scale genocide was committed against the native peoples. Forced transfer to the inhospitable island of Balliceaux (part of St. Vincent), and then enforced exile of the survivors to Roatan Island in the Bay of Honduras, completed Britain's colonial triumph in St. Vincent. Conquest was consolidated, and ordered settlement was achieved by 1800.

After 1800, sugar production was stabilised, reaching its peak in 1828. In 1807, sugar production was 11,200 tons; in 1820, sugar production slipped to 10,834 tons, but rose to 14,403 tons in 1828. Then it declined by one-third over the next five years.

The period 1839 to 1902 witnessed further decline in the sugar industry until its collapse by 1902. The causal factors for all this were labour supply problems; challenges in the world sugar market; financial problems for sugar planters; mismanagement, inefficiencies, and un-competitiveness; and adverse weather events such as a major hurricane in 1898, and the volcanic eruption in 1902. In this period African slavery formally ended and indentured labourers were introduced: 2,100 from Madeira between 1845 and 1850; 1,036 "liberated" Africans between 1846 and 1862; and 2,429 East Indians between 1861 and 1880.

In 1840, sugar production was 6,900 tons; it increased to 8,829 tons in 1852 and dropped sharply to 4,906 tons in 1855. A resurgent period came between 1865 and 1878. Thereafter a terminal decline set in. Between 1883 and 1892 sugar production declined by 58 percent; in 1902 sugar production was down to a paltry 262 tones, caused by sharp decline annually in the 19 years since beet sugar had flooded the market in Britain. By 1892, arrowroot had already outpaced sugar as the main export commodity. Between 1902 and 1963, according to Joseph Spinelli in his *Land Use and Population in St. Vincent, 1763 – 1960* (Ph.D. Thesis, University of Florida, 1973, unpublished):

> *Vincentian sugar production was, in fact, subsidised by the British government, with output fluctuating according to the demand for St. Vincent's other primary products — arrowroot, cotton, and bananas.*

During the first World War, sugar production limped along with a short-term stimulus of a price increase in the British market. In 1926, the sugar industry was revived. It produced semi-refined sugar ("dark crystals") and molasses syrup through a single, modern factory at Mt. Bentinck; it continued in this state until 1962 when it was closed, ostensibly because of a two-week strike by workers, but in reality because of its inefficiency, lack of market competitiveness, diminishing supplies of sugar cane, and its marginal financial viability.

The sugar industry was revived briefly in 1979 by the State under the government headed by Milton Cato's SVLP. This revival lasted until 1985 when it was finally closed by the successor government of James Mitchell's NDP which insisted that it was uneconomical and a drain on the government's resources.

The second major agricultural crop over the historical period has been arrowroot from which a starch is produced. This commodity has been more closely identified with St. Vincent than any other. Before European contact, conquest, settlement, the Callinago and the Garifuna cultivated arrowroot for food and medicine.

The estates, devoted primarily to sugar cane cultivation, engaged in growing arrowroot, particularly after 1838, on marginal lands unsuited for sugar cane. After emancipation, a number of ex-slaves who became small farmers, cultivated arrowroot for commercial purposes. Between 1831 and 1838, the average annual production of arrowroot starch was 3,200 pounds; by the end of 1834 it was 25,600 pounds. The average annual production for the "apprenticeship" years (1834–1838) was over 37,000 pounds. In 1851, the production of arrowroot starch reached 315,000 pounds. By 1859, according to William G. Sewell in his book, *The Ordeal of Free Labour in the British West Indies*, the sugar dominance was being challenged by small cultivators producing arrowroot. By 1877, exports of arrowroot starch accounted for 23 percent of total exports; and by 1879, arrowroot starch provided 52 percent of export earnings, the first time since 1763 that another export crop exceeded sugar's export earnings.

Prior to the 1898 hurricane, there were nearly as many estate arrowroot mills as sugar mills. In 1892 there were 61 sugar mills on estates compared to 33 arrowroot mills producing starch; in 1896, there were 54 sugar mills and 50 arrowroot mills. Small proprietors also had arrowroot mills scattered across St. Vincent. Arrowroot assisted in consolidating and strengthening the peasantry. The sugar and arrowroot mills contributed to the technological development of the country, the acquisition of technical skills by sections of the population, the development of the productive forces, and alterations in the social organisation of labour.

Up to the early 1920s, between 50 percent and 70 percent of the annual output of arrowroot starch was sold to the unstable British market. In 1924, this shifted with a large order for starch from the United States of America — a first time large order therefrom. In 1923, the arrowroot starch exported to the USA amounted to 62,852 pounds; in 1924, arrowroot starch exports to the USA jumped to 367,843 pounds or 13 percent of the total annual supply. By 1927, 1.8 million pounds were sold to the USA and 1.3 million pounds to Britain; but by 1930, the arrowroot starch exports to the USA amounted to 1.98 million pounds, and to Britain, 1.01 million pounds. In 1940, total arrowroot starch exports were 9.7 million pounds which fell and stabilised at around 7.5 million pounds between 1950 and 1960. By that time the estates produced 80 percent of arrowroot and the peasant cultivators, 20 percent. In 1951, arrowroot starch accounted for 51 percent of total exports of St. Vincent.

So significant had arrowroot production become by the third decade of the twentieth century that on December 23, 1930, the government created a statutory body, the St. Vincent Arrowroot Growers' Association, to provide for systematic marketing of the starch which henceforth was to be exported only through the Association. The Association, however, relied too much on one buyer in the USA and that eventually contributed to the decline of the industry. This fact coupled with the alternative land use for a more lucrative agricultural crop, bananas, reduced arrowroot cultivation.

In 1964, the largest American purchaser cut back on its purchases of arrowroot starch and plunged the arrowroot industry into a tailspin. C.I. Martin tells the story in his thesis, *Role of Government in the Agricultural Development of St. Vincent* (Unpublished MSc Thesis, UWI, St. Augustine, Trinidad and Tobago, 1967). Substitute starches from potato and corn were utilised instead. Issues of price, quality, and the stability and dependability of supply occasioned market difficulties for arrowroot producers. The loss of the principal purchaser in the USA placed the Association in a downward spiral: It continued to purchase the producers' arrowroot starch which gave rise to a stockpile, undermining the sale price and further weakening the Association's finances. The knock-on effects were unemployment, reduced farmers' incomes, and falling supplies.

Between then and now — 2019 — the arrowroot industry has remained precariously poised. The industry has one factory, state-owned, which operates inefficiently and produces low quality starch. Annual production of starch is around 200,000 pounds; the arrowroot is grown largely in the north-east of St. Vincent by small farmers on predominantly marginal land. Stockpiling still takes place in the absence of secured markets at a competitive price. There are active plans to build a modern factory so as to put the industry on a sounder footing. The government of St. Vincent and the Grenadines and WINFRESH, a regional producer and marketing company for agricultural products, including bananas, which is owned principally by the four governments of the Windward Islands, are in an advanced discussion for a joint venture in the arrowroot industry. The government of India has approved a grant to St. Vincent and the Grenadines of US $1.1 million to modernise the industry, including the building of a modern arrowroot factory. But reaping arrowroot manually, through the use of a hoe, is an arduous, metaphorically back-breaking task in the context of a social aversion by agricultural workers to dig arrowroot. Repeated attempts at mechanised harvesting have failed due to the terrain of the land and the nature of the arrowroot rhizome.

A third agricultural crop in much of the recorded history of St. Vincent, which evolved from a minor status after 1763 into a major crop in the early to mid-twentieth century, was cotton. Prior to the British conquest and the commencement of settlement in 1763, the French farmers on the western side of St. Vincent, and other farmers in the dry Grenadine islands, grew cotton. Thereafter, cotton, particularly the Marie Galante type, was prevalent mainly in the Grenadines. Marie Galante cotton was not a major export crop.

The Sea Island variety of cotton became a significant crop early in the twentieth century within a relatively short period of time. Indeed, St. Vincent became famous for long staple (fibre) luxury cotton. In the 1902 – 1903 cotton season, Sea Island Cotton was introduced on an experimental basis in St. Vincent. Within ten years, the acreage devoted to the Sea Island Cotton had grown to 5,068 acres, thus according it a significant place in the economy. In 1905, the government, sensing the potential in Sea Island Cotton, set up a St. Vincent Cotton Growers' Association to steer the industry and to market the cotton.

Between 1912 and 1920, cotton had its ups and downs, but by 1920, the acreage under cotton amounted to 6,453. In that year, export income from Sea Island Cotton was 60 percent of total exports. By 1939 – 1940, the acreage under Sea Island Cotton had declined to 5,486 acres; within five years, 1944 – 1949, there was a further decrease in acreage to 2,312 or a drop of 58 percent. Un-competitiveness, disease, and alternative use for the land, precipitated this decline.

Immediately after the Second World War, cotton production fell further, but a sharp rise in price occasioned a temporary rebound of the industry in the 1949 to 1952 period with an average annual production of 387,000 pounds per year — a commendable level of output even though it was below the 534,000 pounds per year between 1935 and 1940. By 1959, cotton's death knell was sounded. Market conditions, substitute products, technological alterations, the destruction by fire of the St. Vincent Government's Cotton Ginnery, and the transfer of cotton lands to bananas, all combined to bring to an end the cotton industry. Between 1958-1959 and 1960-1961 cotton seasons, the acreage under cotton dropped by 90 percent, from 2,100 acres to 220 acres. The failure and/or refusal of the government to rebuild the ginnery prompted the growers, including the estates, to give up on cotton cultivation and to turn more assuredly to bananas.

In the competitive use, in the mid-1950s for limited land for respective crops, Spinelli offered a summation of an economic rationale as follows:

> *Using 1954 prices, it has been shown that* one acre
> of land *under various crops yields a* gross income *as*

*follows: (1) Bananas, £92 (sterling); (2) Arrowroot,
£63; (3) Sugar Cane, £54; Cotton, £40; and (5) Coconuts (copra), £40. When net profit is considered,
however, the order of profitability (excluding bananas)
is as follows: (1) Cotton, £20 (sterling); (2) Coconuts,
£20; (3) Arrowroot, £15; (4) Sugar Cane, £10. The
order of importance must be according to the gross
income per acre, because most of the small growers do
not price their labour or that of the members of their
family. They are concerned with the largest lump cash
payment at the time of sale.*

The fourth major agricultural crop in St. Vincent, particularly between 1955 and 2000, has been bananas. In the early twentieth century bananas were cultivated but not to a large extent; the peak, prior to the 1950s, was in 1937 when 1,100 acres were planted, largely of the "Gros Michel" variety; by 1940, cultivation of bananas had fallen to a mere 300 acres.

The modern banana industry took off in the mid-1950s with the "Lacatan" variety of banana. A Dutch-owned shipper and marketer, Geest Industries Limited, agreed in 1954 to purchase the total available export supply of bananas from St. Vincent. One of the contractual provisions was that the management and purchase arrangements for the industry be conducted through an organisation of banana growers. Thus was formed the St. Vincent Banana Growers' Association, which in concert with other similar organisations in the other Windward Islands (Dominica, Grenada, and St. Lucia), established the Windward Islands Banana Growers' Association (WINBAN). Geest Industries traded with all these banana-producing islands. The bananas were sold to the United Kingdom market under subsidised preferential market arrangements. Swiftly in St. Vincent, 4,600 acres were under banana cultivation in 1956; by 1960, banana production covered 6,300 acres. As a percentage of total exports, bananas accounted for 1.3 percent in 1954; by 1959, banana exports were 48.3 percent of St. Vincent's total exports in value.

The banana lift-off in St. Vincent was as a small farmer crop. In 1958, 85 percent of the growers farmed less than five acres of land; their holdings accounted for 36 percent of banana acreage and 33 percent of total production. The larger farmers were more efficient but the life-blood and base of the industry were small farmers.

Banana production grew to such an extent that by 1992, over 10,000 acres were under bananas with export earnings, from 78,000 tons of bananas, in excess of EC $100 million or 80 percent of raw commodity exports. Britain's entry into the European Union (EU) Single Market in 1992, caused a new banana trading regime to be put in place from July 01, 1993, with some reduced market preferences and enhanced market standards. Challenges to the EU banana marketing regime came repeatedly over the next few years from the USA (which grew no bananas but was the home to the banana marketing giants, Chiquita, Dole, and Del Monte) and Ecuador, a major Latin American banana producer. These challenges were made to the World Trade Organisation (WTO) which handed down rulings which slashed the market preferences for Caribbean (Windward Islands, Jamaica, and Belize) bananas. The upshot of all this was a gradual diminution of the market preferences to the point of extinction. At the same time, the market standards became more onerous and expensive. Uncompetitive farmers slowly exited banana production. By 2001, under 12,000 tons of banana were exported to the United Kingdom. Currently, the export market is a small regional market in Trinidad and Barbados; by 2017, no bananas were exported to the United Kingdom and actual production has fallen significantly. Even the regional market is becoming challenging for Windward Islands' producers given competition from Suriname and Costa Rica.

The ups and downs of minor crops paralleled the production of major crops (sugar, arrowroot, cotton, bananas) at various periods, historically.

Currently, there is a revival of cocoa and coffee production, both driven by foreign investors. The St. Vincent Cocoa Company, owned by a British–born investor who is a naturalised citizen of St. Vincent and the Grenadines, grows cocoa itself and purchases from small farmers. The Cocoa Company is today the largest single employer of labour in agriculture with 250 employees; it exports the raw materials as premium island cocoa, but it also produces its own chocolate bars. Overall, the cocoa industry employs some 350 persons. A few dozen small farmers are in cocoa cultivation. The total acreage currently under cocoa production is 500, the bulk of which is under fee simple ownership or leasehold by the Cocoa Company. The coffee revival lags behind that of cocoa but it is very much on stream. Root crops, fruits, vegetables, spices, and animal husbandry complete the make up the mix of agricultural production.

Most of agriculture in St. Vincent and the Grenadines is undertaken by small farmers. From the late 1960s into the 1980s, the former plantations were sub-divided and sold by the planters themselves or through a land reform process engineered by successive governments.

There is one crop, cannabis, (marijuana/ganja) which, since the 1970s, has been cultivated illegally, but it has provided a livelihood for small farmers, particularly in the north west and north east areas of St. Vincent. It has been grown largely on state-owned lands above the 1,000-feet contour. It has been produced for the local and regional markets, primarily.

Much of the cannabis cultivation has been damaging to the forests in that the trees are chopped down to make available the land for the growing of cannabis. This damaging environmental practice has been a cause of natural disasters — landslides and blockage of rivers and bridges — during heavy rainfalls.

There are no credible estimates of the value of the illegal cannabis cultivation but it is reasonably assessed to amount to several millions of dollars.

Currently, the ULP government is been actively pursuing a medical cannabis industry. Recently, in late 2018, it secured passage through Parliament of the Medical Cannabis Industry Bill which envisages, among other things, the regulation of medical cannabis for domestic consumption and export.

Except for the period 1951-1962, when Joshua's Federated Industrial Agricultural Workers' Union (FIAWU) attempted seriously, but without a sustained success, to organise the agricultural workers in trade unions, there has been little effort at trade unionism in the agricultural sector. Two other episodic attempts were made to do so: Calder Williams in North Leeward (Richmond Vale Estate) with the Workers' and Peasants' Union, and Caspar London of the National Union of Progressive Workers (NUPM) at Orange Hill Estates, both in the mid-to-late 1970s. It has been quite challenging to organise agricultural workers in St. Vincent and the Grenadines in trade unions.

The Gross Domestic Product (GDP) in current prices in 2017 shows that the agriculture sector contributed EC (Eastern Caribbean) $137.6 million to the economy [US $1 = EC $2.70]. Of this sum, bananas now account (in EC $) for a mere $1.4 million; other crops, $115.9 million; livestock, $19.5 million; and forestry, $0.9 million. Agriculture contributes 7.0 percent of GDP at market prices which in total amounts to EC $2.19 billion.

Other important sectors, in terms of value at market prices in current prices (in EC $) are as follows: Fishing, $10 million; manufacturing, $101.7 million; hotels and restaurants, $36.9 million; transportation and storage, $250.3 million; wholesale and retail, $230 million; construction $142.4 million; electricity and water, $69 million; financial intermediation, $122.1 million; real estate, renting and business activities, $260.9 million; public administration, $223.5 million; education, $103.8 million; health and social work, $56.8 million; and other community, social, and personal services, $32.6 million. The bulk of trade union membership comes from workers in public administration, banking and finance, education, air transportation, ports, electricity, telecommunications, water and health services, and manufacturing.

Across the economic sectors, tourism and allied services contribute some $300 million in export earnings. There are approximately 2,400 rooms available in hotels, guest houses, and apartments for tourists. The single largest tourism plants are at Mustique and Canouan in the Grenadines, and Buccament Resorts which is closed temporarily. Most of the other hotel operations are small, family-owned hotels. Room expansion is taking place as a consequence of the official thrust in tourism in the wake of the opening on February 14, 2017, of the country's first international airport, the Argyle International Airport (AIA). There is very little trade union presence among the workers in the hotel and tourism sector.

The light manufacturing sector took off in St. Vincent under the "industrialisation-by-invitation" policy of the SVLP government in the late 1960s and the expansion and consolidation thereafter by successive governments. The main locus of manufacturing is the Campden Park Industrial Estate. Among the major manufacturing commodities produced at Campden Park and elsewhere are: flour, rice, animal feed; rum, beer, stout, beverages; galvanised sheetings, windows and doors; plastics and pvc commodities; boxes and containers; peanuts, plantain chips, peppers, jams, jellies; an assortment of rums; arrowroot and cassava starches; bottled water and fruit drinks; coconut water and chocolate bars; clothing and apparel; and moringa and other "bush teas". Trade union members have been drawn from the workers at the main manufacturing enterprises.

The economically-active producers, the "labour force", according to the last Population Census in 2012, numbered 52,014 of which 40,821 were employed and 11,193 unemployed. The comparative numbers in the 2001 Census were: the labour force, 44,984 persons of which 35,588 were employed and 9,396 unemployed. The size of the labour force increased by 7,030 between 2001 and 2012 although the actual population overall increased by only 969! The substantial answer to this seeming paradox lies in the internal alterations of the demographics: the older segments (over-55) who are looking for work and able to work increased significantly between 2001 and 2012.

In 2001, the over-55 -year olds in the labour force numbered 3,770; in 2012, this category in the labour force had increased to 7,654 or an increase of 3,884 or 103 percent! The actual number of over-55-year olds who were employed in 2001 was 3,391; in 2012, the comparable number was 6,657, an increase of 3,266 or 96.3 percent. The overall increase in the number of employed persons in 2012 over 2001 was 5,233. The increase in the retirement age from 55 years to 60 years is clearly being impactful. Challenges accordingly arise from these statistical facts from several standpoints, for the present and future developments and alterations in the political economy.

The statistics of the National Insurance Services (NIS), which are a proxy for employment data, show that active registrants at the NIS (employees and self-employeds) increased from 30,373 in 2000 to 40,728 in 2018. The time series data reveal an increased number of active registrants between 2001 and 2008, then a decline between 2009 to 2011 reflecting the impact of the global economic meltdown of that period, and a pick-up thereafter as a consequence of moderate economic recovery. Active registrants, generally, are approximately 15-20 percent below persons in actual employment, since many such persons are not actually registered at the NIS.

By industry, in 2012 the largest employers of labour were wholesale and Retail, 6,882 (16.9 percent of labour force); public administration and defence, 3,976 (9.7 percent); education, 3,168 (7.8 percent);; agriculture, 4.808 (11.8 percent); manufacturing, 2,061 (5.1 percent); construction, 4,750 (11.6 percent); transportation, 3,096 (7.6 percent); accommodation and food service activities, 3,022 (7.4 percent); activities of households as employers, 1,964 (4.8 percent); human health and social work, 1,398 (3.4 percent).

By sector, in 2012 the main employers were private businesses, 18,659 persons (45.7 percent of employed persons totally); the State sector (local, central government, State enterprises), 10,412 persons (25.5 percent); self-employeds, 7,850 (19.2 percent); and private homes, 1,973 (4.8 percent)

The single largest employer of labour is the State/government sector with 10,412 persons in the aggregate; next is the Mustique Company with 1,300 employees, followed by the Canouan Developers with over 1,100 employees. Some 2,500 Vincentians are employed on cruise ships but these persons are not adequately covered by the census. But the largest groups of employers, in the aggregate, are the multiplicity of small-and-medium-sized private sector businesses or enterprises, as reflected in the aggregate numbers, by sector, referenced earlier.

All these employees constitute the "raw material" of the labour movement. Clearly, though, the trade unions have challenges in organising, for various reasons, the bulk of these employees. The trade unions in 2018 had as their members almost one-fifth (20 percent) of the employed labour force but of the total labour force (employed and unemployed) the percentage of trade union membership falls to approximately 15 percent.

The revolution in information technology has seen a growth in telecommunications and the creation of other information technology and computer products or services. The revolution in information technology, inclusive of internet facilities, mobile telephones, and social media platforms, have impacted significantly the production, trade, and commerce in goods and services; it has also profoundly influenced politics and the labour movement in the evolving 21st century. Similarly, there is a growth in renewable energy products including solar energy for individual homes and the national grid itself.

The economic shift from plantation agriculture to small-farming agriculture has impacted politics and trade unionism immensely. Undoubtedly, this shift helped to undercut the populist politics of Ebenezer Joshua's PPP and its trade union arm, the FIAWU. This factor and the diversification of the economy into services and manufacturing have provided economic bases for more modernising political parties and trade unions in the period after Joshua's hey-day from 1951 to 1972. This economic shift aided the rise and consolidation of the popular appeal of the SVLP between 1961 and 1984. The NDP's pledges to modernise the state administration, to advance the services sector, including tourism, more assuredly, while revitalising small-scale agriculture, aided its ascendancy. But its limited material successes, its philosophical and programmatic limitations, and its stalling or reversal of the social democratic revolution opened the way in the late 20th and early 21st centuries for the ULP to become ascendant in new circumstances. Importantly, too, the ULP's profound commitment to advancing social democracy, reducing poverty, implementing an education revolution, building a competitive post-colonial economy, and opposing neo-liberalism and the "Washington Consensus" positively endeared it to the people. The NDP's counter-revolution to the social democratic revolution built by the labour movement (inclusive of the PPP and SVLP governments) had, in time, demonstrated its failure and dead-end socio-political praxis of a pristine "free enterprise" and anti-national neo-liberalism.

The advances in education, particularly after the post-2001 Education Revolution, and the spread of the global revolution in information communication technology, have altered the nature and content of politics and trade

unionism, even though it is the on-going global struggle, and its national oı.
shoot, between capital and labour which continues to fashion the contours of
the political economy itself. This struggle is many-sided at the global, regional,
national and local levels. Integral to this struggle are cross-cutting factors of
ethnicity, gender, and other identities which provide complexities in the actual
realities which are being analysed and explained.

The demography of the country underpins, too, the political economy
of the labour movement and forms part of, and impacts, the matrices of the
productive forces and production relations.

When Britain assumed suzerainty of St. Vincent in 1763, there were an
estimated 10,000 Callinago and Garifuna people. Between then and the sub-
duing of the native population through war, genocide, and forced exile, over
one-half of the Callinago and Garifuna people were killed or removed from
St. Vincent. As was hitherto indicated, between 1764 and 1807 (the end of the
British trade in African slaves) 55,562 enslaved Africans were landed in St.
Vincent. In 1838, the last full year of slavery, there were 22,250 slaves. There
was clearly a huge attrition in the slave population due to the higher mortality
of an aging male population without a sufficient reproduction to compensate
for deaths and the periodic manumission of the elderly and infirm from the
slave registers. Spinelli discusses this quite well in his 1973 doctoral thesis,
Land Use and Population in St. Vincent, 1763-1960.

Between 1844 and 1881, Madeiran Portuguese, Liberated Africans, and
East Indians totalling 5,575 were brought to St. Vincent as indentured servants.

The period 1881 to 1931 was one of multiple natural disasters and harsh
economic dislocation. In the 1890s, over 60 percent of the working population
was unemployed; in the hurricane of 1898 there were 298 deaths and extensive
damage and destruction to buildings, physical infrastructure, sugar mills and
arrowroot mills; in 1902, the volcanic eruption caused the death of an estimated
2,000 persons; the sugar industry collapsed after 1881; in 1926, another terrible
hurricane struck; and in 1929-1931, the massive world economic depression
caused further economic ruin in St. Vincent. These factors contributed to significant emigration of Vincentians, particularly to other Caribbean countries.

Indeed, between 1891 and 1911, the annual rate of net migration was
minus 18.89 per thousand persons, the highest ever recorded by any official
census; the actual net migration in raw numbers was minus 15,667 persons.
So, although the natural increase of the population between 1891 and 1911

amounted to 16,490, because of the size of the net migration, the actual increase in population in that twenty-year period was a mere 823 persons. Between 1911 and 1921, the population increased from 41,877 to 44,447: The natural increase of 8,160 was offset by a new outflow of 5,590 persons. Between 1921 to 1931, the population increased by 3,514 growing from 44,447 in 1921 to 47,961 in 1931. In this period emigration slowed markedly.

In the fifty-year period (1881 to 1931), the population increased absolutely from 40,548 to 47,961, an increase of 7,413 persons. But, the natural increase of the population (births minus deaths) was 40,420; so, massive outward migration in this fifty-year period ensured a relatively small increase in the actual population.

Between 1931 and 1960, St. Vincent's population experienced its most rapid annual rate of growth in its census history from 1844. The rate of growth of the population was a whopping 1.72 percent per year over those twenty-nine years. High fertility rates combined with declining mortality accounted for the growth of the population from 47,961 persons in 1931 to 79,948 in 1960, an increase of 31,987. Not even significant migration could contain sufficiently the natural increase. For example, between 1947 and 1959, the natural increase amounted to 28,000 and net migration was -11,220; net migration thus reduced the natural population increase by 40 percent. Without emigration, the population would have doubled in seventeen years.

Over the next 52 years (1960-2012), the population increased to 109,991 or an increase of 30,043. The data show that the most rapid average *annual increase* was in the inter-censal period 1950-1960 of 1,307 persons and in the inter-censal period 1970-1980 of 1,090 persons. In the two most recent inter-censal periods 1991-2001 and 2001-2012, the *average annual increases* were comparatively low, with increases in the number of persons being 142 and 88 respectively. In fact these latter 21 years have seen the *lowest average annual increase* since the 1891-1911 inter-censorial years.

From 1991, the average annual increase in the population of St. Vincent and the Grenadines started to diminish sharply: In 1980, the population stood at 97,845; it grew between then and 1991 to 107,598. Between 1991 and 2001, the population increased to 109,022; by 2012, the population edged up to 109,991 or by an absolute increase of 969 persons over the eleven-year period 2001 – 2012. The rate of increase of the population between 2001 and 2012 was the lowest since 1911.

During the most recent inter-censal period 2001-2012, a total of 4,851 persons migrated, 45 percent or 2,182 of whom migrated for reason of employment; 28.5 percent (1,380 persons) emigrated because of family reunification; 613 emigrated as students; and 72 persons emigrated for medical purposes. Emigration continues to be important to the political economy of St. Vincent and the Grenadines.

St. Vincent and the Grenadines has been a country pre-dominantly of African descent since enslaved Africans were brought to the country in 1764. According to the 2012 Population and Housing Census, the ethnic distribution of the population is as follows: African descent, 71.2 percent; mixed (mainly African ad-mixed with other ethnicities), 23.0 percent; indigenous, 3.3 percent; East Indian, 1.1 percent; Caucasian, 0.8 percent; Portuguese, 0.7 percent; other, 0.2 percent.

From the latter half of the nineteenth century until today, two relevant features of the population must be noted: the population is young; and migration overseas has been an important avenue for people's search for employment and educational opportunities. In the 2012 population census, the 0 − 14 years age cohort was 17.6 percent of the total population; and the 15 − 19 year-old age group was 9.07 percent of the total population; thus the under-19 year old population exceeds one quarter of the population. Recently, in 2012, the 45- 64 years age cohort accounted for 20.9 percent of the population; and the over 65-year age group in 2012 was 9.1 percent of the population; these numbers point to an aging population also. Significant emigration has taken place to Canada, USA, Britain, and other Caribbean countries over the last 130 years or so.

These bundles of demographic facts have influenced life, production, and reproduction; politics and trade unionism; and overall, the political economy of the labour movement.

The political expressions of the State and non-State entities, including trade unions, have been ultimately determined by the evolving character and condition of the successive *dominant* modes of production. In the period 1763 − 1951, colonialism imposed varying governing political arrangements in which popular democratic content was lacking or minimal. In 1951, colonialism conceded a popular franchise of universal adult suffrage but within an extant political context of colonial rule. From 1951 onwards, in gradual stages, political authority devolved to popularly-elected parliamentary representatives until internal self-government in 1969, which in 1979 matured into formal political independence. At each stage of the political evolution, the nature of the *dominant* mode of production and its external linkages were fundamental to the overall political economy.

Of fundamental importance specifically to trade unionism was, too, the nature and character of the emergence and evolution of the capitalist mode of production. Trade unions were not possible in St. Vincent and the Grenadines before the rise of capitalism in 1838; before then the slave mode of production utilised slave labour, not wage labour, pre-dominantly. The emergence of capitalism internally after the emancipation of slaves offered the possibility of the laying of the basis of a working class and trade unionism. But trade unionism did not emerge in the immediate years after the formal abolition of slavery for a number of reasons; and its elemental development in the early three or four decades of the 20th century was profoundly constrained. Shortly, I shall sketch the framework of the development of trade unionism. First, I shall explore, in outline, the impactful ethnic-racial-cultural factors in the evolving political economy.

CULTURAL PLURALISM, CLASSES AND SOCIAL STRATIFICATION IN THE EVOLVING POLITICAL ECONOMY

During slavery, and for much of the 19th century after the emancipation of the slaves in 1838, St. Vincent and the Grenadines, in sociological terms, was a more or less classic "plural society" in the sense that each racial or cultural section had its own relatively distinct pattern of socio-cultural integration. The social structure was like a pyramid: a small ethnic group of white Anglo-Saxons at the top who owned the bulk of the productive land and commercial enterprises or who occupied the senior positions in the colonial state apparatus; below this narrow ethnic/racial/class section at the top was a slightly broader band of Caucasian technicians, estate overseers and business managers, smaller property-owners, and the more privileged persons of mixed blood — the progeny of white parents and those of other ethnicities; and at the bottom of the pyramid, a large mass of African slaves and the dispossessed Callinago and Garifuna people. After Emancipation up to the end of Indian indentured labour in 1881, this bottom rung of the pyramid contained the ex-slaves, "free" Africans, indentured labourers (Madeiran and Indian), and other unskilled workers, including from the declining population of Callinago and Garifuna.

This plural society, in which race and class were almost completely coterminous, was held together centrally by the following: colonial domination generally; the enforced acceptance by substantial, if not overwhelming, numbers of the subject people that Anglo-Saxon race, culture and, social and political institutions were superior to those of other ethnicities and civilisations; the nature of the plantation economy and its external capitalist linkages; and the authoritarian presence of the colonial state machinery, including its coercive arm and the judicial system.

Each of the ethnic/racial/culture sections in the plural society had its own relatively distinct pattern of socio-cultural integration through the particular institutions of the economy, politics and public administration, religion, family, and associational or socio-cultural groupings.

Over time, the plural society evolved into a socially stratified society with a core of values shared across the various ethnic, class or social groupings in which the hitherto distinct institutional patterns of socio-cultural integration had become diffused into a modified whole. The distinct pluralities, over time, broke down and gave way to a greater heterogeneity or even homogeneity, though with class stratification and socio-cultural differentiations; over time, ethnic considerations dissolved into a much less social significance. Still, residues of ethnic identifications have occasioned dissonance in social relations and public discourse; in particular circumstances they have assumed prominence. Through the fever of history, contemporary Vincentian society has become unified around a core of shared social and democratic values even though social stratification is grounded on the bases of class, incomes, socio-cultural orientations, ethnic identification, and one's role in the social organisation of labour.

The evolution, consolidation, expansion of capitalism and its alterations, from the post-emancipation into the 20th and early 21st centuries, have been fundamental in the process of the societal metamorphosis from a culturally-plural society to a stratified class-based society though with an increasingly creolised or home-grown cultural outlook.

Particularly since the 1960s, Vincentian society has become increasingly creolised and heterogeneous, if not homogeneous, though stratified on class bases but with residual ethnic identification. Among the major factors engendering increasing homogeneity and creolisation have been the following: the pervasive development of modern capitalism; the processes of enhanced political democracy and decolonisation; the rise of a unified nationhood; the widespread availability of education; the modernisation of the society and increased cultural globalisation; the decentralisation of religious worship and the spread of non-traditional religious denominations; the spread of modern telecommunications and the ease of travel overseas; and the force of biology in the mixing of the races or ethnicities. The institutions of the economy, family, school, church, popular culture, mass media, modern communications, the trade union, and political party, have all played critical roles in the process of enhanced homogeneity and creolisation.

The system of social stratification which has evolved in St. Vincent and the Grenadines evidences a class-based society, criss-crossed by ethnic and gender identities, and status; these are, in turn, influenced by face-to-face relations in a small society and the requisites of a liberal-democratic order.

Fundamentally, classes are defined by their respective relationships to the means of production (means of labour and the objects of labour) and their definite relations of production within the production process. These production relations and the productive forces (labour and the means of production) constitute the particular mode of production which is the ultimate determinant of the contours of the society, its institutions, and their functioning. The members of particular classes have perceptions or a consciousness of their common interest; that class consciousness may manifest itself at different levels, as a partial consciousness or a class "in itself" or a total consciousness of a class "for itself".

Marx in *The Eighteenth Brumaire of Louis Napoleon* first published in 1852, encapsulates the real essence of the nature of classes and their actions, thus:

> *In so far as millions of families live under economic conditions of existence that separate their mode of life, their interests, and their culture from those of other classes, and put them in hostile opposition to the latter, they form a class. In so far as there is merely a local interconnection --- and the identity of their interests begets no community, no national bond and no political organisation among them, they do not form a class. They are consequently incapable of enforcing their class interests in their own name.*

V.I. Lenin offered in his monograph, *A Great Beginning*, written in 1919, a summary and apt definition of classes, thus:

> *[Classes are] large groups of people differing from each other by the place they occupy in a historically determined system of social production, by their relation (in most cases fixed and formulated in law) to the means of production, by their role in the social organisation*

> *of labour, and consequently, by the dimensions of the*
> *share of social wealth of which they dispose and the*
> *mode of acquiring it.*

The successive modes of production in St. Vincent and the Grenadines — communal, slave, and capitalist — have determined the social formations at various historical stages in the country's evolution or development. In the pre-Columbian society, property was held in common, communally, and thus classes did not exist. When the slave mode of production, through enslaved Africans, was imposed (long after the demise of classical slavery in Europe) by European mercantilist, and emergent industrial, capitalism, two major classes arose: the white slave-owners and the black slaves. The emancipation of the slaves in 1838 gave rise to "free labour" within an evolving capitalist mode of production which today is shaped by global monopoly capitalism.

Accordingly, the class configuration in contemporary Vincentian society is manifested in its complexities as follows: An underclass, mainly unemployed, which has the hustling traits of the "lumpen-proletariat"; the working class who sell their labour power for wages; a small group of part-workers, part-peasants, part small traders who engage in own-account activities, a kind of "semi-proletariat" allied to the working class and are often indistinguishable from them; a varied group which can best be described by the catch-all category of the "petit bourgeoisie" and which class includes professionals of one kind or another, the broad group of national political elites, the salaried middle-strata, the middle-level farmers, middle-level shopkeepers, and the like; and a numerically very small economically dominant-class of big businessmen/women (local and foreign), and a handful of dominant political and bureaucratic elites who command the citadels of State power.

The fluidity of the undeveloped capitalist mode of production in St. Vincent and the Grenadines indicates that classes are in the process of formation and alteration without the rigidities of the class structure of a mature capitalist society such as Britain, with its aristocratic underpinnings and residues. This fluidity also means that in each of the broad class categories, there is not a homogeneity or an absolute coincidence of interests of the members of particular classes. Further, status, in the sense of social estimation of honour, intrudes and complicates matters. Further complexities arise with the political-bureaucratic grouping which drives the central apparatuses of the State and who derive their position in the social organisation of labour from their formal role in the State machinery. Identities of an ethnic or gender nature may, occasionally, intrude in the system of social stratification. At the same time, there has grown up a basic core of shared values between all the classes or groups derived from their common feeling of national belonging and their commitment to an evolving Caribbean civilisation, inclusive of its Vincentian component.

Yet, despite the commonalities, the material interests of the various classes manifest themselves in class struggles, whether muted or aggressive, organised or disorganised. The history of St. Vincent and the Grenadines is replete with all this, and more. These struggles of real flesh-and-blood people within the mode of production, provide the fundamental impetus for change, socio-economic and political alterations.

The history of the Caribbean, including St. Vincent and the Grenadines, has fashioned a legitimate and distinct island or seaboard civilisation which is possessed of a trajectory for further development and ennoblement. Metaphorically, our Caribbean can be seen as a coherent symphony but with occasional dissonance: We are the songs of the indigenous people (Callinago, Garifuna, Amerindian); we are the rhythm of Africa, the melody of Europe, the chords of Asia, and the home-grown lyrics of the Caribbean. This Caribbean civilisation has adopted, adapted, and created civilised norms, structures, and institutions in an especial landscape and seascape. Within it, though, classes exist, and class struggles at varying levels of intensity are a constant central feature of the political economy.

THE CONCEPTUAL FRAME OF THE LABOUR MOVEMENT AND TRADE UNIONS

A labour movement focusses on the mobilisation and organisation of those who sell their labour power for wages, namely workers, in their own interest and that of the society as a whole. A labour movement usually consists of two constellations: Formally organised and registered trade unions; and a broader set of like-minded, labour-connected entities, including political parties with a "labour" base, and civil society organisations, which have as their focus the upliftment of "labour" and the working people.

Trade unions are essentially structured organisations of workers established for the central purpose of acting as bargaining agents for workers in their respective employment units in order to secure wage increases, improved conditions of work, or other such workplace benefits. Trade unions also function as advocacy groupings to push for, through legislative or other lawful means, the attainment of enhanced economic, social, and political benefits principally for their members.

The Trade Unions and Trade Disputes Act [Chapter 216 of the Laws of St. Vincent and the Grenadines] which was passed in 1950, and is still the subsisting relevant law, defines a trade union as:

> *Any combination whether temporary or permanent, the principal purposes of which are, under its constitution, regulation of the relations between workmen and masters, or between workmen and workmen, or between masters and masters, whether such combination would or would not, if this Act had not been enacted, have been deemed to have been an unlawful combination by reason of some one or more of its purposes being in restraint of trade.*

Legally, therefore, an employers' organisation can be registered as a trade union. And, indeed, some have done so in St. Vincent and the Grenadines. But for our purposes, we restrict our understanding of trade unions in the normal accepted sense in modern industrial relations as organisations of which the members are workers, not employers.

Historically, the origins and development of trade unions in St. Vincent and the Grenadines, the wider Caribbean, or indeed in any other country, cannot be understood outside the context of the rise of capitalism and its evolution or development. Both processes are bound up inextricably. In St. Vincent and the Grenadines and the Caribbean, trade unionism is based on the working class and that class arose historically for the first time under capitalism.

Prior to 1838 in St. Vincent and the rest of the English-speaking Caribbean, there were no trade unions simply because under the then prevailing dominant mode of production, slavery, there was no working class. Slavery did not recognise workers; the productive labour was provided by slaves who were viewed legally, and in production, as "chattels", not persons. The selling of labour power for wages was not integral to slavery; there was no freedom for slaves to contract with the owners of capital, the slave-owners, to sell their labour power.

When slavery ended in 1838, the capitalist mode of production was ushered in, slowly at first but more fully later, as its mercantile capitalist links internationally metamorphosed into monopoly capitalism with binding ties to industrial and finance capital globally. These material advances coupled with the removal of certain legal and political constraints on the development of capitalism fuelled the growth of the forces and buttressed the altered production relations of post-slavery capitalism, out of which a working class was formed and gradually developed, and which provided the membership base for trade unions.

However, although capitalism sprung up in the immediate post-1838 epoch, trade unions did not arise in St. Vincent and the Grenadines or other British Caribbean colonies until the first two and three decades of the twentieth century, and did not form the centre of the industrial relations scene until after the mid-1930s. Why?

First, during the first fifty, sixty or more years after the abolition of slavery, the size of the working class was small due to the underdeveloped nature of capitalism. Secondly, and perhaps more importantly, the working class was inexperienced as a class and thus was unable, or insufficiently prepared, to form trade unions or demand trade union rights. Moreover, legal and political restrictions were imposed on workers to organise industrially or politically. Further, in the formative years of trade unionism, intra-union conflicts, inter-union schisms, a lack of internal union democracy, and insufficient attention to members' material condition retarded trade union development.

These factors combined to delay the growth of trade unionism in the British Caribbean colonies. Among the first workers' organisations to emerge, though not as legally registered trade unions, were the Artisans Union in Jamaica in the 1880s and the Trinidad Workingmen's Association in Trinidad and Tobago shortly after the end of the First World War in 1918. The first legally registered trade union was the Jamaica Longshoremen's Union (No.1) which registered under the 1919 Trade Unions Ordinance in that country. This was the first piece of legislation of this kind anywhere in the British Caribbean that removed legal restraints on the right to organise trade unions.

During the next twenty years, other British Caribbean colonies enacted similar trade union legislation, though with limitations: Trinidad, St. Vincent and St. Lucia in 1933; the Leeward Islands (Antigua, St. Kitts and Montserrat) in 1931 and 1939; Grenada in 1934; and Barbados in 1939.

The legal right to organise trade unions was essential to the growth of trade unionism. So, too, were the changes in the political sphere: the development of political parties, and the drive towards constitutional decolonisation. But these factors, although influential in spurring trade union development, were themselves the results of the development of capitalism and its contradictions internally, the crisis of international capitalism globally in the 1929-31 period, and the impact of the struggles of the international working class movement especially in the Soviet Union, Britain, the United States of America, Latin America, Africa, and Asia.

The period of the 1930s was indeed the watershed for the West Indian, including the Vincentian, trade union movement. It represented a break with the earlier period in which trade unionism was growing patchily with a few members; it was now becoming a genuine mass movement of working people and their social allies. The uprisings across the Caribbean region in the 1930s, and other workers' struggles of that period, were largely and immediately responsible for this development.

The harsh socio-economic conditions and the undemocratic system of colonial governance were the contexts for these uprisings in St. Vincent, Jamaica, and St. Kitts in 1935; in Barbados and Trinidad in 1937; in Jamaica again in 1938. Protests and other forms of workers' struggle occurred and intensified in Antigua, Dominica, Grenada, and St. Lucia. After these events, the process of change, albeit gradual and measured, commenced in the social and political arrangements in the West Indies. Over the next four or so decades, the accumulated changes grew to be significant. Out of these popular stirrings of the working people and their social allies, a veritable social democratic revolution was initiated and consolidated; its full development and maturation is yet to be completed or attained.

Emerging from the popular uprisings and other workers' struggles were a number of trade unions and political organisations often with the same leadership, thus giving birth to the phenomenon of political unionism which persisted in a pristine form up to the early 1970s, and later in a more diluted way.

In St. Vincent, the St. Vincent Workingmen's Association (SVWA) and the St. Vincent Labour Party were formed in 1935, more or less simultaneously, with emphasis on the former, under the leadership of George Augustus Mc Intosh. However, the SVMA was not registered as a trade union; in 1945, a specific workers' offshoot was created as the St. Vincent General Workers' Union, and became formally registered as a trade union. An almost identical trade union-political party nexus was fashioned in almost every territory in the West Indies from the late 1930s into the early 1950s, and consolidated into the 1970s. Thereafter, a more "economistic" and less political brand of trade unionism developed even though political activism remained an aspect of trade unions' functioning in their quest to promote and defend their members' interests.

From the formation and registration of the first trade union nearly 75 years ago until the present time (2019), trade unions have found themselves in a structurally ambivalent position within an evolving capitalist mode of production whereby they are creatures of this specific mode of production — they are part of it — yet they represent labour which is objectively opposed to capital. Two progressive options have faced them: 1) straddle the pull of conflicting forces (labour and capital), improve their members' material circumstances, and prod a reformation of the capitalist mode of production; or 2) in alliance with political forces dedicated to socialism or socialist orientation (non-capitalist path), seek to break out of the very conflicting forces in the class interest of the working people.

Trade unions, by themselves, cannot lead the process of making fundamental alterations to capitalism and build a transition to socialism or effect its realisation. That mission has historically been entrusted to an appropriate political party, grounded in the working people but with relevant class alliances across the board. But the historic mission appears unavailable or highly problematic to any political party in any small Caribbean country like St. Vincent and the Grenadines in the grip of global monopoly capitalism and its geographic proximity to an imperial United States of America.

Even in the most propitious circumstances of the existence of a strong socialist bloc headed by the former Soviet Union, even Cuba, the largest and most populous island in the Caribbean, found it extremely problematic and challenging to build a prosperous, socialist society in the period 1959 to 1991; at the latter date, the Soviet Union collapsed and, in turn, the similarly nominal socialist countries in Eastern Europe. After the demise of the Soviet Union, Cuba had to endure a "special period" of profound adjustment for approximately ten years; thereafter, it has had to make relevant amendments to its socialist model, which admittedly has shown remarkable resilience though stuffed with weaknesses and limitations amidst its amazing strengths and, as yet, unrealised possibilities.

Grenada, roughly the physical size and population like St. Vincent and the Grenadines, sought to establish the basis for a "non-capitalist", not socialist, path to development between March 1979 and October 1983, with the support of Cuba and the world socialist bloc; the collapse of the People's Revolutionary Government (PRG) brought that uneven, though promising, experiment to an end.

Without the solidarity support of a strong socialist presence, globally, the offering of socialism in St. Vincent and the Grenadines or any other similar-placed small island developing country is most unlikely to get off the ground. Given these countries' objective condition (small size, scarcity of material resources, extreme vulnerability, undeveloped political base, geographic location in the orbit of American imperialism, the extant external linkages to monopoly capitalism), the socialist, or radical non-capitalist, option is realistically, a non-starter. A creative, advanced social democracy through parliamentary means, combining accommodation and resistance to monopoly capitalism, is a promising framework for a compelling developmental strategy with appropriate external links.

That being the case, trade unions have been left with the possible alternative of improving their members' material circumstances and, in concert with their political allies, engaging with a process of reforming capitalism through the praxis of advanced social democracy, regionalism and nationalism, and anti-imperialism, and alignments and actions against neo-liberalism.

Of course, some trade union leaders have unfortunately chosen the unwise path of embracing modern capitalism, imperialism, and neo-liberalism which are diametrically opposed to the interests of the members of the unions. Such trade union leaders are wrong in their conclusion that working people's organisations in concert with the appropriate political and social allies, locally and globally, cannot find the space in the extant political economy to exploit the possibilities and push the boundaries of the limitations therein to enhance immensely working people's benefits at the workplace and in a wider and advanced social democracy in the society. A much better world is surely possible! But some trade union leaders, stuffed with personal vanities, vainglorious ambitions, and an undeveloped political consciousness, unfortunately embrace neo-liberalism and a subservience to monopoly capitalism. Inevitably, these trade union leaders isolate themselves from progressive political and social alliances and lose their members' trust as they opportunistically seek support and succour from the very political forces and economic interests which have an agenda to stall or even subvert an alive social democracy which serves the working people and nation well.

CHAPTER II

THE 1935 UPRISING AND ITS SIGNIFICANCE ON POLITICAL AND TRADE UNION DEVELOPMENT

THE UPRISING ITSELF

On October 21, 1935, the working people embarked upon a spontaneous, popular uprising in St. Vincent against colonial governance and harsh socio-economic conditions. This uprising was centred in Kingstown but working people (workers and peasants) as far to the northeast as Georgetown (22 miles from Kingstown), and to the north-west at Chateaubelair (22 miles from Kingstown), also protested. The uprising lasted for less than one day in Kingstown but resistance to the colonial authorities continued for a further two days in Stubbs, Byera, and Campden Park.

The origins of the uprising, as distinct from the actual event which sparked it, were traceable to the socio-economic conditions which existed in this British colony up to 1935. The litany of the people's woes included very low wages; rampant unemployment; deplorably bad housing; minimal educational opportunities; abysmally poor health services; ameliorative social legislation marginal or absent; non-existent representation of, for, and by the mass of the people; economic exploitation of the non-organised and leaderless black masses by a minority, wealthy white group; and political oppression under a "Crown Colony" system of colonialism. One hundred and seventy-two years of colonial subjugation, slavery, indentureship, post-emancipation and contemporary neglect had accumulated to push the people to a spontaneous uprising.

But a spark was needed to ignite the people to rebellion. The actual event which occasioned the uprising itself was increased taxation. The colonial, and oligarchic Legislative Council met on October 21, 1935, to approve an imposition of increased taxation by way of an amendment to the Customs Duties

Ordinance; the working people resisted in an uprising. The working people were being asked to pay more for spirits, cigarettes, matches, and fuel. In the absence of any counter-balancing initiatives in their favour, the people rose up against the colonial government and their own material plight. Prior to the actual uprising, the working people had earlier consulted the acknowledged leader of a growing mass movement, George Augustus Mc Intosh, on a course of action. Mc Intosh petitioned the Governor, Sir Selwyn Grier, for the withdrawal of the tax increases but the Governor was unyielding in his response. Mc Intosh urged the working people to be peaceful but once the masses were on the move spontaneously, riotous activity was inevitable.

The original protesters who assembled in-front of the building — "the Court House" — which housed the Legislative Council, were mainly women, armed with sticks. They were shortly joined by a contingent of some 200 persons, mainly men, armed with stones, sledge hammers, cutlasses, knives, and sticks. Their demands were reflected in the slogans: "We can't stand any more duties on food and clothing"; "We have no work to do"; "We are hungry"; "Something will happen in town today if we are not satisfied".

The Governor hastily adjourned the meeting of the Legislative Council. He falsely claimed that the additional duties were put only on commodities which were not used by economically-disadvantaged persons. The working people responded: the Attorney-General was punched by one who alleged that the official had kicked him; the Governor received minor cuts in the melee; a few cars of Government officials were damaged; the Court House windows were smashed; the Prisons, nearby to the Court House, were broken into and several prisoners were released.

Around Kingstown, many business places were broken into, including that of F.A. Corea and Company, the principal shareholder of which was a member of the wealthy planter-merchant elite and a legislator. Meanwhile, the Governor had been personally directing operations of the police. The Riot Act was read. The crowd at Corea's was fired on; one person was killed and several others injured. To supplement the Police Force, the Governor called on volunteers and "law-abiding citizens".

As the uprising spread to the rural areas, roads were blocked and the rudimentary telephone facilities were damaged. It was reported that the protesters "invaded the homes of wealthy people, treating them with scorn and contempt". In response, the Governor ordered that the police and volunteers be placed at strategic points like the Cable and Wireless premises, the port, and the electricity plant.

The official line, adopted to discredit the participants in this uprising, was to suggest that these persons were plain "rioters". And in the words of the Governor, were "a gang of men — and women" who could not claim to be "genuine workers at all"; he insisted that "few genuine workers and peasants on estates were affected". The America Press went further, depicting "the rioters" as a "pack of savages". Both officialdom and their supportive press were wrong: The participants in the uprising were in the main responsible working people who had been pushed beyond reasonable limits in an extant condition of socio-economic and political oppression.

It is problematic to isolate precisely who were the real leaders of the 1935 uprising. This is attributable, in part, to the fact that the uprising was unplanned, entirely spontaneous. Research indicates that in Kingstown, "Sheriff" Lewis and Bertha Mutt, both working class people, were prominent. In the rural areas, local leaders from the working people emerged as focal points for the instigation of the protests. The St. Vincent Representative Government Association (SVRGA), a grouping comprised mainly of middle-class political activists, and the major leaders within it, played compromising and ambiguous roles. Officially, the SVRGA distanced itself from the uprising. Of these leaders, George Mc Intosh was the most sympathetic to the protesters' grievances and understood their action, although he was not supportive of their methods. As Gordon Lewis remarked in his book *The Growth of the Modern West Indies*, Mc Intosh "for all his defiant radicalism was certainly no Leninist insurrectionist"; his radicalism seemed to have been "a combination of borrowed [British] Labour Party rhetoric and domestic social paternalism" couched within the framework of British parliamentary democracy and its attendant constitutional/legal focus.

Indeed, on October 29, 1935, at a meeting of the Kingstown Board of which he was a member, Mc Intosh moved a resolution which was unanimously accepted, conveying the Town Board's "deep regret" about the "riots" and congratulating the Government on "the stand taken in suppressing the disorder". Publicly, in September 1936, Mc Intosh urged a working class rally to reclaim "the good name that was lost to St. Vincent since 21 October 1935".

From the beginning, all informed persons, except the colonial authorities, knew that Mc Intosh did not promote, direct or support the uprising and its riotous off-shoots. Yet, he was arrested on November 23, 1935, on a criminal charge of treason-felony for his alleged agitational role in the uprising. On December 11, 1935, Mc Intosh was discharged from custody after a five-day Preliminary Inquiry at the Magistrate's Court; the presiding Magistrate, after hearing testimony from nineteen witnesses, concluded that he found "no thread of incriminating evidence" against Mc Intosh to justify sending the matter for trial on indictment at the Criminal Assizes.

The bizarre prosecution of Mc Intosh reflected colonialism's incomprehension of the protests. They could not accept that people, hitherto docile, rose up spontaneously without the malevolent guidance of some person or persons. So, the regime chose Mc Intosh and assigned him the mantle of agitator and instigator. It was a convenient but false thesis; the colonialists were in denial.

Before the uprising had subsided, the colonial government embarked on a robust response to maintain colonial order, and rounded up dozens of alleged perpetrators and conspirators; they detained most of them. At first, the spontaneity of the uprising caught the police off-guard. Swiftly, though, the Governor took control of directing the police's operations, recruited local volunteers to assist, summoned supporting police personnel from neighbouring islands, and alerted the British warship, the H.M.S Challenger which arrived in St. Vincent by midnight of October 21, 1935. The government was in full repressive mode.

In his address, at the close of the meeting of the Legislative Council on October 28, 1935, the Governor stressed that he hoped that "the arrival of the H.M.S Challenger was an object lesson to lawless individuals". In his stern address, he refused to indicate when the state of emergency imposed on October 22, 1935, would be lifted; in the event, the emergency lasted for another three weeks. Further, the Governor announced his intention to introduce legislation to accord greater powers to the government to deal with "those who make it their business to foment trouble". He warned, too, that he was not prepared to permit further abuse of the liberty of the press and speech. Meanwhile he imposed a censorship of the press. So tough was the pertinent legislation that the Secretary of State in Britain, on being questioned about this muzzling ordinance in the House of Commons, agreed with its objectives but pledged to consider reducing the penalties which in certain cases, he admitted, appeared to be "excessive". Four years later, the ordinance was repealed.

The colonial governor's response to the uprising evidenced a lack of understanding of its causes. In his address at Kingstown's Carnegie Library on October 28, 1935, the Governor, Sir Selwyn Grier, listed three possible causes of what he called "the riots": 1) the introduction of the measure on customs duties which he insisted was wrongly characterised by the public; 2) overcharging by shopkeepers; and 3) racial antagonism engendered by the Italian-Abyssinian (Ethiopian) War. He failed to acknowledge the underlying colonial neglect of

St. Vincent over the years and the extremely harsh conditions of life for people. Clearly, the Governor was out-of-touch with economic realities on the ground or blinded by colonial arrogance and ruling class disdain for people's suffering.

So, instead of leading a sensible discussion on the causes of the uprising, the Governor imposed censorship of the news. Instead of seeing the participants in the uprising as bona fide working people with real grievances, he saw them as criminals; he thus had seventy of them arrested, many of whom were charged, found guilty, and imprisoned for terms between five and forty years; a number of them were shipped off to Grenada; subsequently their sentences were commuted after a few years. The colonial regime even trumped up the ludicrous and unsustainable charge of treason-felony against Mc Intosh. Scapegoating Mc Intosh failed miserably!

The "unthinking" and repressive nature of colonialism when on the defensive has been repeatedly analysed comparatively, by distinguished scholars. This irrationality was evident in the immediate aftermath of the 1935 uprising. Unnecessarily, the colonial government made George Mc Intosh a martyr and unwittingly confirmed him as the veritable tribune of the people.

The spontaneity of the uprising reflected the unorganised, and disorganised, state of the working people. The very spontaneity was indicative of the working people's undeveloped political consciousness, lack of effective leadership, and absence of a well-thought out political programme beyond a demand for socio-economic conditions to improve within a vaguely-reformed colonial system. These weaknesses, and more, of the unplanned uprising made it much easier for colonialism to suppress it and subdue the popular forces.

Concomitantly, these very weaknesses of a lack of organisation and spontaneity meant that the working people's struggles were to be easily taken off the streets to the conference table by middle-class constitutionalists, honest and reform-minded patriots, but who themselves frowned upon non-legal methods and who themselves embraced a supine gradualism in their challenge to colonial over-rule. The path of the social democratic revolution, not only in St. Vincent and the Grenadines but also elsewhere in the English-speaking Caribbean, was thus set for a gradualist, step-by-step constitutional decolonisation predicated upon a notion of "fitness to rule". British colonialism and the West Indian reformists differed substantially on the content of governance reforms and the time-table for their achievement, but they were in lock-step, more or less, on the requisite of orderly change and the need for a demonstration of responsibility and readiness of "the natives" to occupy the citadels of authority in the Westminster-Whitehall model or close variants thereof.

The alternatives of the Haitian and Russian Revolutions over a hundred years apart between the late 18th and early 20th centuries, frightened West Indian colonials, the general public and leaders alike, into accepting, albeit with amendments, the colonial prescription towards self-government and socio-economic amelioration. Later, the Cuban Revolution of 1959, the Bolivarian Republic of Venezuela and 21st century "socialism" reinforced, similarly, this ideological predisposition, even in an age of rampaging monopoly capitalism, neo-liberalism, and unbalanced globalisation that gravely disadvantage peripheral nations and peoples. So, the popular, progressive forces have had to arrive at a carefully nuanced reform agenda of resistance and accommodation, in the people's interest, as the prevailing circumstances admitted.

THE SIGNIFICANCE OF THE UPRISING TO THE WORKING PEOPLE

In terms of immediate material gains for the working people, the 1935 uprising was not successful. The demands for a rescinding of the imposition of increased customs duties went unheeded by the colonial government; the popular clamour for an overall amelioration of the socio-economic condition for the working people received no official listening ear, at least not in the immediate aftermath of the uprising. Possible ameliorative work was certainly postponed. Immediately, there were arrests, court trials, increased police surveillance, curtailment of a "free press", and additional prison accommodation.

However, the 1935 uprising in St. Vincent and similar uprisings across the West Indies in the 1930s succeeded in lifting working people's consciousness of the possibilities of a different, better way. Further, where petitions, largely submissive and grovelling by subject peoples in St. Vincent for almost 100 years after the emancipation of slaves in 1838, had had little impact on colonial thinking, the anti-colonial uprisings in concert with other global events caused colonialism to rethink its over-rule and time-table for decolonisation. In short, the uprisings forced colonialism to listen, and eventually to amend somewhat its ways.

Politically, on the ground in St. Vincent, the more progressive popular leaders, especially George Mc Intosh, began in earnest to channel the increasing anti-colonial fervour of the working people into relevant organisations to represent popular interests. Thus, Mc Intosh led the formation of the St. Vincent Workingmen's Association (SVWA), and its political affiliate the St. Vincent Labour Party (SVLP), the former being the more effective instrument of popular mobilisation.

The SVWA, with Mc Intosh as its President, was registered as a limited liability company and not as a trade union. The leadership of the SVWA reasoned that the Trade Union Ordinance of 1933 was an inadequate law for the regulation of trade unions, especially since it did not provide for peaceful picketing or immunity for a union against actions in tort (civil court actions against a union). Interestingly, the British Labour Party had earlier advised the Trinidad Workingmen's Association (TWA) not to register as a trade union under a similar law on account of its very limitations. It is probable that Captain Cipriani, leader of the TWA, had so advised Mc Intosh, since there was ongoing contact between them. Later, in 1939, Sir Walter Citrine of the British Trade Union Congress tendered similar advice to the SVWA.

By the end of its first month of operation, following its formation on March 2, 1936, the SVWA recorded an increase in membership from 480 to 4,000 with branch representation in ninety-seven villages and towns. This was quite an extraordinary achievement in mass mobilisation and organisation. The SVMA's main aims were to protect the working class, encourage thrift, and provide financial assistance in times of distress; it was, in part, mutual benefit and cooperative society. By 1944, it had established a Penny Savings Department of the Association.

The SVLP was set up as the formal political vehicle to push for constitutional advance, to offer candidates for elections under liberalised constitutional arrangements, and to provide political representation for the working people, in and out of the Legislative Council and the Kingstown Board. In the first general elections in 1936 under a mildly-reformed constitution, the SVLP's popular leaders, Mc Intosh, Ebenezer Duncan, and St. Clair Bonadie were elected to the legislature under a liberalised, but still restricted, franchise. Ebenezer Duncan had been for several years the Secretary of the SVGRA and editor and proprietor of a weekly newspaper, *The Investigator*, and St. Clair Bonadie was the editor and proprietor of a progressive newspaper, *The Times*. Mc Intosh, a druggist by profession, with his own drug store, was a long-standing member of the Kingstown Board; he was the acknowledged leader of the working people and possessed of a deeply-felt anti-colonial and socialist orientation. The profound nexus, organisationally and in leadership, between the SVWA and SVLP laid the ground work for the growth of political trade unionism in the country. The SVWA, though, provided the solid mass base for the SVLP's political operations.

The robust organisational work of the working people in the SVWA and SVLP prompted the employees, including the planters, into similar action in defence of their class interests. In 1937, the St. Vincent Employers' and Employees Association (SVEEA) was formed, and registered as a Friendly Society, emphasising, unconvincingly, that politics was not its chief concern. Nevertheless, it attempted to counter the influence of the SVWA-SVLP combination. For example, in a by-election for the North Windward District in 1939, Percy Stephens of the SVWA defeated Frank Child, a well-liked planter, of the SVEEA by a margin of 143 to 122 votes. In 1939, a potentially formidable counter to the SVWA, the St. Vincent Land Owners Association (SVLOA) was formed. St. Vincent was then a planter-dominated agricultural economy. One hundred and thirty-five estates controlled over two-thirds of the arable, agricultural land. The originators of the SVLOA were William Hadley and J. Punnett who respectively controlled for their families 3,472 acres of land in eleven estates and 3,171 acres in eight estates.

After the repressive, coercive dust of the immediate post-uprising period had settled in colonialism's favour, it set about to introduce a number of limited measures designed to induce the working people into believing that the colonial masters had their interest at heart. It was the classic response of colonialism: Impose social and political order, as never before, after any protest or uprising; and then when the storm is settled on colonialism's own terms, initiate a few ameliorative measures to assist in maintaining the calm.

Part of the region-wide response of British colonialism to the anti-colonial uprisings of 1935-1937, was to dispatch a Royal Commission to the West Indies in 1937. This Commission, headed by Major G. St. J. Orde Browne, issued its report in 1939 under the title *Labour Conditions in the West Indies* (Command Paper, HMSO, 6070). While Major Orde Browne's Commission was conducting his investigations and preparing its report, the people of Jamaica launched their massive anti-colonial uprising in 1938. This popular uprising prompted British colonialism to send another Royal Commission, with a more wide-ranging mandate, including that of constitutional liberalisation, under Lord Moyne in 1938-39, prior to the outbreak of the Second World War in 1939. After the War, in 1945, Lord Moyne reported under the rubric, *West India Royal Commission 1938-1939* (Command Paper 6607, HMSO, 1945).

In St. Vincent, the colonial administration began its limited piece-meal changes in the post-1935 period, on labour-related issues in 1937. In that year, it increased minimum wages under the Labour (Minimum Wages) Ordinance of 1934 to one shilling and two pence (1s.2d.) for men and ten pence (10d.) for women, per day of eight hours minimum, but not more than nine hours; the two pence increase in wages was the first for nearly 100 years. In the same year, the old Masters and Servants Act, which contained penal sanctions for offences arising out of labour contracts, was repealed. In its place was enacted the Employers and Servants Ordinance which also prescribed the manner and time of payment of wages; this Ordinance prescribed that "labourers' wages shall be paid in money only and at intervals not exceeding a fortnight"; hitherto employers, especially planters, often paid their workers partly in kind. In October 1937, a Labour Commissioner was appointed to ensure the proper working of the Minimum Wage Ordnance and to look generally into the conditions of labour. In 1939, the Trade Unions (Amendment) Ordinance was passed providing for peaceful picketing; and in that year, a limited Workmen's Compensation Ordinance was adopted after languishing in the Committee stage of the Legislature since 1934. In 1940, a basic Factories Ordinance "providing for the safe-guarding against accidents of workers employed in or about the factories" was passed; the main factories at the time were arrowroot factories, the sugar factory, the cotton ginnery, and two soft-drinks factories. Also enacted in 1940 was the Trade Disputes (Arbitration and Inquiry) Ordinance which provided for "the settlement of trade disputes by arbitration tribunals and for the appointment of Boards of Inquiry to investigate the cause and circumstances of existing or apprehended disputes."

In 1942, the colonial government, in seeking to establish an institutional framework for labour, passed the Department of Labour Ordinance which made a statutory provision for the setting up of a Department of Labour and a Labour Advisory Board. This Ordinance also repealed the Labour (Minimum Wage) Ordinance of 1934 and its amendments and conferred on the Governor-in-Council powers to make orders pertaining to conditions of labour in any industry or occupation with a view to stabilise or improve working conditions. In 1943, the very important Trade Unions (Amendment) Ordinance was passed. This made provision for "immunity from criminal and civil proceedings of persons who combine to do certain acts in furtherance of a trade dispute". In the same year, an Order was issued entitled the Department of Labour (Powers and Duties of Labour Commission) Order, which among other things, conferred statutory powers on the Labour Commissioner to deal with matters affecting all classes of workers, instead of agricultural workers only, as hitherto.

Despite this flurry of legislative attempts to ameliorate the condition of working people's lives, their conditions remained virtually the same. For instance, the Colonial Administrator proudly proclaimed in December 1934 that wages, on the average, increased by 43 percent over the pre-war wage rates; that the increase for road workers was 56 percent and for the categories of labour between 20 and 40 percent over the same period. However, what the Administrator failed to state was that the cost of living outstripped, by far, the wage increases: In 1943, the cost of living index had risen to 185 from the base year of 100 in 1939.

Further, although there were wage increases in 1937, the Labour Commissioner in 1938 informed the Moyne Commission that the employers were giving bigger tasks since the passage of the Minimum Wage Ordinance in 1934, and that they had withdrawn certain material privileges normally allowed to estate workers. So, in practical terms, the planters preferred to allocate "task work" rather than daily paid work and proceeded to make larger those task requirements; and estate-workers' privileges such as the usual temporary grant of small parcels of land to preferred workers as "yam piece" and permission for grazing of workers' personal livestock on estates, were increasingly denied. These anti-worker actions by planters in the post-1935 Uprising period were almost identical to the planters' material responses to the workers' strike in Mt. Bentinck in 1862.

The planter-merchant elite were wholly short-sighted in their opposition to even the most minimal reform or ameliorative measures; they lacked the requisite vision to see the challenges to the extant political economy. Economically-dominant elites across history, and particularly those in the West Indies with little cultural sophistication or any history of profound ideational reflections, invariably miss the significance of impending or prospective changes in the following: production relations: the development of the productive forces, including technological alterations; governance arrangements; and the extent and content of social and political discourses. The planter-merchant elite in St. Vincent, and the rest of the Caribbean, saw none of these likely alterations internally, regionally, and globally. And if they did see any of them, they did not comprehend their significance. Indeed, the colonial authorities grounded in the strategic perspective of a changing imperialism, were more alert to the changes ahead, but even they were unable to bring themselves to accommodate those changes, save and except in limited and narrow ways.

The planter-merchant elite felt themselves safe and cocooned perhaps as the proverbial sardines in a tin: Their workers' wages were low and the conditions of work deplorable; the working people were not organised and their consciousness as workers, and as a class, was low; preferential treatment was enjoyed in the British market for uncompetitive agricultural products; taxation and other demands upon the ruling economic elites from the colonial state was limited; the colonial legislative and executive machinery strongly represented the class interests of the planters and merchants; social status, based on economic power and ethnic solidarity, of these elites was assured within a veritable plantation economy and society with all the residues from the mid-nineteenth century; and the properties and persons of the ruling class were amply protected by the coercive arm of the state locally and the military might of the British Empire externally.

The planter-merchant elite in St. Vincent were oblivious to what loomed ahead. Little would they have considered that within 30 years of the 1935 uprising that the uncompetitive sugar industry run by the plantocracy would be dead, and that it would flounder in its re-incarnation under state ownership in the early 1980s. They would never have envisaged that within forty years, plantation agriculture would be rendered wholly uncompetitive and unsustainable and the plantations sold off either by way of sub-division to small farmers and the children of former estate workers or as failed ventures to the State. Neither the planter-merchant elite nor the immediate political successors to colonialism foresaw revolutionary developments, and profound contradictions within monopoly capitalism itself and the widespread adoption of trade liberalisation. And it was not until very late, too, that the planter-merchant elite contemplated the extent and meaning of nationalism, anti-colonialism, constitutional decolonisation, and political independence at home and in colonial territories abroad. Indeed, up to 1960 or thereabouts, the planer-merchant elite of the long colonial era did not see that their demise was shortly upon them!

Thus, in abject myopia, in 1938 Frank Child, a large estate-owner at Grand Sable, opposed an unambiguous call for sensible land reform by way of Land Settlement involving the State and estate workers, by the West Indian Congress at a meeting in Trinidad. Child had attended this meeting on behalf of the St. Vincent Chamber — an organisation of merchants and planters; on instruction from his organisation, Child instead proposed merely an examination of the question where it may be found "necessary and practicable". The planters were unable to grasp any of the significant socio-economic changes which loomed ahead and which would bring their long era of dominance to a close.

Even the colonial authorities were ahead of the planter-merchant elite on minimalist land reform. After all, in 1896, the British government appointed a West India Royal Commission to examine, among other things, the land-owning system and to recommend possible changes. Following its 1897 Report, small farmer holdings arose in several parts of St. Vincent including in areas such as Park Hill, Three Rivers, and South Rivers. Further, in the 1940s, the colonial government in St. Vincent, at the urging of Mc Intosh, established a Land Settlement Estate Scheme at Richmond and Wallilabou in the north west of St. Vincent.

The representatives of labour in the Legislative Council in the immediate post-1935 period made a series of reforming proposals: Land Settlement, increased wages, improved conditions of work, better health and educational facilities, constitutional liberalisation, and regional integration. The mildly-reformed legislature of 1936 up to the period of universal adult suffrage in 1951, afforded little authority to the elected representatives who were still elected on a restrictive property franchise.

In 1946, Mc Intosh hailed as a "great experiment" the decision of the colonial regime to purchase 4,669 acres of land at Richmond at a cost of 60,000 pounds sterling, on which to settle working class people. Mc Intosh's enthusiasm for this colonial initiative as a move away from "land monopoly" was misplaced, and premature, since no further land reform measure was again instituted by the colonial government in St. Vincent. Indeed, when Mc Intosh called in 1947 for Land Settlement arrangements on the Windward side of the island, the government baulked; and when he similarly called in the legislature for a "nationalisation of land and industry", the colonial government evasively replied that "it is difficult and complicated" and thus must be referred to the British Secretary of State for the Colonies. On November 21, 1949, Mc Intosh pushed his case further in the Legislative Council by insisting that: "Socialism is the only way that we can hope to oust this capitalist system and bring people up to a decent standard of living."

On December 12, 1949, in the legislature, George Mc Intosh levelled one of his strongest attacks on the colonial system of the day, claiming that Britain noticed St. Vincent because "we had a riot" and that he feared "the result of another".

The colonial government's response to Mc Intosh's representations was basically three-fold: 1) Attack the functioning of the SVMA; 2) seek to divide the leadership of the working-class movement; and 3) implement, in a watered-down fashion, some of the working people's demands, and so co-opt some of those ideas. Examples abound of colonialism's machinations against the SVWA and Mc Intosh. For instance, in 1937, the Colonial Administrator, Alban Wright, in feigning interest in the working people and at the same time attempting to create divisions in the labour movement, preoccupied himself in exposing alleged inefficiencies and even financial improprieties in the SVWA; this was a constant theme of the colonial authorities. Further, the colonial regime sought to divide the leadership of the SVWA-SVLP by expressing, publicly, preferences for the more moderate and vacillating members of the leadership, and denouncing Mc Intosh as an extreme socialist and a fellow-traveller of communism. Even Mc Intosh's close colleagues disapproved of the prominent placement of a photograph of Joseph Stalin, the leader of the Soviet Union, in his drug store; Mc Intosh appreciated the exemplary leadership of Stalin and the sacrifices of the Soviet people (25 million of whom died in the Second World War) in the global struggle against Adolph Hitler, Nazism and fascism.

Arguably, the most significant results from the standpoints of working people's politics and trade unionism of the 1935 uprising and subsequent political activities in the decade thereafter by the working people, were the growing political consciousness of the working class and their organisation into the SVWA-SVLP nexus. It is clear that the working people were concerned about forging a unity among themselves to combat the colonial regime and the planter-merchant elite. The enthusiastic support for the SVMA is evidence of this. Less than one full year after its formation, the SVWA boasted a membership of 4,000 in 97 villages and towns. Similarly, the people's organisation into numerous Friendly Societies provided further testimony of their determination to find solutions through the solidarity of collective efforts. Additionally, on the estates, it was reported that the workers were less submissive than hitherto; they were more demanding of their rights; and political agitation on the estates, increased.

In short, the worker no longer saw him- or herself as subservient to "Massa"; the workers were prepared to challenge authority more than ever, even though they were still in a weakened position objectively. In "An Open Letter" from George Mc Intosh to the workers published in *The Times* (December 09, 1939), he wrote simply: "The scales are falling off the eyes of a good many of our working class." That perhaps was the matter of the most lasting significance of the 1935 uprising for the working people.

Still, colonialism was keen to ensure that the workers' militancy was restrained and to use their own representatives to assist in this restraint. In the immediate aftermath of the 1935 uprising, in an instructive address in the Legislative Council, the Governor, Sir Selwyn Grier asserted:

> *I must assume therefore that there is a section of the community, which is not represented here — and that it would be of great advantage to the Administration if men could be found to represent it...who are prepared to cooperate with the Administrator.*

Colonialism's quest to find accommodating men, and women, who claim to represent the people's interest, to cooperate with it, had long been central to its strategic approach. This line was similarly articulated before 1935, and after, by every Royal Commission to have visited the West Indies. It is still the approach of neocolonialism and imperialism! Unfortunately, too many representatives of the people in government and in opposition, in the contemporary period have no proper appreciation of the strategic approach, in all its amendments and metaphoric sugar-coating, of neocolonialism, monopoly capitalism, and their associated political hegemony.

CHAPTER III

THE EMERGENCE OF TRADE UNIONISM 1945-1957

POLITICAL UNIONISM DEFINED

The first political linkages in St. Vincent and the Grenadines between a workers' organisation, the SVMA, and a political entity, the SVLP, were fashioned in the immediate aftermath of the 1935 uprising. The dating of the first clear emergence of political unionism, however, is surely 1945 when the St. Vincent General Workers' Union (SVGWU), and the St. Vincent Peasant Cultivators' Union (SVPCU), both "labour" arms of the SVLP, were formally registered as trade unions. The SVGWU drew its core membership from the SVWA which continued to function as a benevolent or mutual assistance society, a small savings mechanism, and an advocacy group for working people's interests.

This emergence of political unionism in 1945 and its growth from the 1950s to the early 1970s in varying forms, was to dominate that period of Vincentian trade unionism.

The main indices or characteristics of a pristine political unionism can be summarised as follows: 1) The continuous effort invested in day-to-day political activities; 2) the great importance attached to political affiliations and objectives; and 3) the virtually complete integration, in an organisational sense, of the trade union and political party, often both with the same leadership.

Political unionism and economic unionism are, conceptually, polar opposites. However, in practical terms, political unionism and economic unionism are not mutually exclusive means of action and may often alternate in the activities in this or that union; at given times, one of these two forms of unionism may preponderate over the other.

Accordingly, it is useful to construct a continuum with the "ideal" types of political unionism and economic unionism at opposite ends of the continuum. By way of example, trade unions in socialist Cuba will be found at the political unionism end of the spectrum and the economic unionism of capitalist United States of America at the other end.

Between these two extreme ends of the spectrum are a number of broad variations manifesting themselves in terms of organisation, objectives, and actual activities in their economic or political emphases.

Vincentian trade unions have exhibited from the early years of the 1940s until the early 1970s a marked tendency towards political unionism, though not of the type which is integrated politically within a juridically-ordained, one-party State, as in the case of Cuba. The political unionism in St. Vincent has been shaped by the very milieu from which the unions have emerged and have been consolidated. First, the small size, territory and population, of the country, and the nature of the economy, are crucial in this regard. The scarcity of leaders, due to population size and a paucity of leadership skills, has meant that most of the trade union leaders have invariably been leaders, or closely-linked to leaders, within the political parties, at least up to the early 1970s. Further, the small size of the economy has inevitably drawn it into the realm of political and State activity. A scarcity of material resources in a society generally, gives rise to an abundance of politics in the acquisition and distribution of these resources; conversely, an abundance of material resources tends to lead to a scarcity of politics in the ownership, management, and distribution of these very resources.

It is evident that the kind of economic unionism present in advanced capitalist countries like the United States of America requires a significantly large economic base coupled to an economic system which is mainly in private hands. That kind of territorial base is absent in St. Vincent and the Grenadines, where huge chunks of its economic activities have been under the ownership, direction, or facilitation of the State. Further, it is one of the recognised prerequisites of economic unionism, that in countries where it is found both the number and the percentage of unemployed persons should be at the lowest possible level; in St. Vincent and the Grenadines, unemployment has been historically high subsequent to the abolition of slavery in 1838; indeed, the economy of St. Vincent and the Grenadines has had the challenge of a limited absorptive capacity of labour. Such a condition facilitates political unionism, particularly in a competitive political environment.

In St. Vincent and the Grenadines, as in numerous developing countries, the central government and state enterprises are the single largest employers of labour. Although, cumulatively, the private sector has been the largest employer of labour, there is no single private sector employer which comes close to providing the aggregate employment of the State sector. Further, in small economies like St. Vincent and the Grenadines, a situation has existed whereby State-private sector contractual relationships effectively give the government a significant leverage in the private sector as well. Accordingly, in this milieu, those who man the apparatuses of the State have been in a position to influence markedly the livelihoods of large sections of the labour force. In this context, opportunities exist for those who occupy the leading positions in the machinery of the State to exercise patronage and manipulative levers, if they choose to do so. All these factors have, historically, given rise to political unionism.

In colonial St. Vincent, the non-political brand of "responsible trade unionism" which the British Administrators sought to impose did not fall on fertile ground due to the nature and size of the country's economy, and the consequential politics. The basic fact is that the character and type of the labour movement was fashioned by the economy and polity; political unionism triumphed because it was moulded by the local circumstances. In practical terms, too, the nationalist, anti-colonial struggles were inextricably inter-connected with the fight of the working people for material upliftment. British colonialism's preference for a non-political brand of trade unionism was itself an ideological statement in favour of an artificial separation of politics and trade unionism for the benefit of colonialism's continued over-rule. So, political unionism arose as a product from the structural foundations of the economy, society and politics. The political unionism which emerged in colonial St. Vincent represented the struggle of the working people to achieve not only a higher standard of material living, but also to reform and participate in the political system to secure those material gains and a more participatory democracy.

POLITICAL UNIONISM EMERGES

The period from 1945 to adult suffrage in 1951 saw the registration of three working people's unions: the St. Vincent Peasant Cultivators' Union (SVPCU) in 1945; the St. Vincent General Workers' Union (SVGWU) in 1945; and the United Workers, Peasants, and Ratepayers' Union (UWPRU) in 1951. The potentially powerful employers' union, the St. Vincent Growers' Union (SVGU) was formally registered in 1946. The SVPCU and the SVGWU were formed under the leadership of George Mc Intosh and Ebenezer Duncan, who were President-General and Secretary respectively of both organisations. It was the intention of these officers who also led the SVLP and the historically important SVWA, to organise and mobilise the workers and peasants separately in two trade union entities rather than under one umbrella as was done through the SVWA. Still, the clear plan was that both the SVGWU and the SVPCU would be linked organisationally, and with a nexus to the political party led by Mc Intosh and Duncan.

The main objects of the SVPCU were grounded in commercial, social and political concerns: 1) To maintain equitable prices of produce for peasants and to ensure suitable markets; 2) to obtain through arbitration, collective bargaining between employers and employees; 3) to further political objects affecting peasant cultivation; 4) to engage in participatory businesses; and 5) to provide a number of benefits such as legal, and funeral expenses, and sickness benefits.

Of much broader scope was the SVGWU, a "blanket union" that sought to organise all workers irrespective of their trade or employment. It marked the beginning of "pure" blanket trade unionism as an organisational form in St. Vincent, although it had a forerunner in the working people's organisation, the SVWA, which was not registered as a trade union. The objects of the SVGWU centred on improving wages, conditions of work, employment, social services for workers, and political advocacy on issues touching and concerning workers.

These two trade unions, the SVPCU and the SVGWU, were active, particularly on political matters relating to their members' interests, up to the general elections of 1951, the first held under universal adult suffrage. In those elections, the team led by George Mc Intosh was soundly defeated by the more militant Eighth Army of Liberation under the leadership of George Hamilton Charles, and Ebenezer Theodore Joshua. After 1951, both the SVPCU and the SVGWU faded; by 1956, they were defunct.

One significant feature of both the SVPCU and the SVGWU was their recognition of the importance of both the peasantry and the wage-earners as political bases for the SVLP in competitive electoral politics. To be sure, such bases were of relevance to the great push forward by Mc Intosh and his progressive colleagues for land settlement, wage increases, increased employment, and universal adult suffrage. The unions conjoined material considerations with the overtly political.

One of the first collective agreements, labelled a "trade agreement" by the Labour Department, was concluded between the bakeries in Kingstown and the SVGWU in 1946. This agreement covered wages and working conditions of bakers as well as a disputes-settlement procedure.

By 1947, two years after the formation of these two unions, there was solid growth in their membership: 758 in the case of the SVGWU; 224 in the SVPCU. It is to be noted that, according to the 1946 Population Census, the total population of St. Vincent was 61,600, of whom 22,691 were gainfully employed; the largest employer by economic sector was agriculture which employed 11,299 persons. Despite the growth in union membership, the numbers were still quite small; trade unionism was still in its infancy.

The St. Vincent Growers' Union, despite its early attempt to combat the rise of the Workers' and Peasants' Unions, failed to attract peasants to its cause and remained largely as an organisation representing the narrow class interests of the planters; its membership stood at 50. Within a year of its registration in 1946, the Growers' Union effectively folded. Even at its dissolution in 1947 at Park Hill, a rural peasant village, the large growers were still so intent on laying a foundation for a future alliance with peasant cultivators that it was decided to revive the former Credit Society of Park Hill as a move in that direction. Nothing tangible ever came of this proposed revival: There was no political appetite among the peasantry to join forces with the planters, even though the peasants themselves were uncertain about hitching their wagon to the political juggernaut of the SVWA-SVLP-SVGWU nexus, which focused mainly on the concerns of urban workers, and at the first remove, agricultural workers, and at the second remove, peasants.

At the same time, the labour movement pushed for representation of "labour" on the Executive Council of the colonial government in accordance with the recommendation of the Moyne Commission in 1945. The representatives of labour in the Legislative Council had come to realise that in order to exercise influence meaningfully on government's policy, they would require, at the very least, to sit on the Executive Council which had been, from time immemorial, the preserve of the colonial officials and the nominated representatives of the planter-merchant elite; it never, since 1763, contained a representative who spoke for labour. Both *The Times* and *The Investigator* newspapers, edited respectively by St. Clair Bonadie and Ebenezer Duncan of the SVWA-SVLP combination, also campaigned for "labour" membership of the Executive Council.

In October 1946, general elections were held, again on a restricted property franchise although more liberalised than in the 1925 to 1936 era. All the working people's organisations — the SVLP, the SVWA, SVGWU, and the SVPCU — together with the two pro-labour newspapers, mobilised in quest of winning all five electoral districts — four on St. Vincent itself and one in the Grenadines.

Despite some dissonance arising largely from personality squabbles, and candidate-selection, particularly in the Leeward and South Windward districts, labour faced the general elections in opposition to the common foe of the plant-er-merchant elite who were tacitly supported by the colonial regime. In the event, the "labour" candidates won the four seats on mainland St. Vincent, but the standard-bearer of "labour" was unsuccessful, yet again, in the Grenadines.

The results of the election showed labour's dominance. George Mc Intosh was returned unopposed in Kingstown; in North Windward, Ebenezer Duncan defeated the planter and President of the Growers' Union, Eric Hadley with s score of 762 votes to 472 votes; in the Leeward district, Edmund Joachim of the SVLP defeated Herbert Davis by a margin of 421 votes to 367 votes; in South Windward, there was a tie between St. Clair Bonadie of the SVLP and Julian Baynes (Independent) with 153 votes each, with Alphaeus Allen trailing on 46 votes — the legislature resolved the contest in favour of Bonadie; and in the Grenadines, Syl De Freitas, a merchant, (94 votes) defeated Sidney Mc Intosh, a businessman on the SVLP ticket (73 votes).

The acknowledged labour leader, George Mc Intosh, was at the pinnacle of his political career. In the build-up to the 1946 general elections, the plant-er-merchant elite had boasted that they had a "trump card" to run against Mc Intosh in Kingstown. In the event, they were unable to persuade anyone to be foolhardy enough to contest the seat against Mc Intosh; so, the "hero" of the working people was returned unopposed.

The defeat of the political cause of the planter-merchant elite in the 1946 general elections, even on a restricted property franchise, prompted them to take petty retaliatory action on the estates and in the merchant businesses, against the working people, even though huge numbers of them were not eligible voters. The planter-merchant elite were becoming apprehensive of what they perceived as on-rushing dangers of a growing wave of popular democracy regionally. For example, in Jamaica in 1944, the labour movement organised, under the leadership of Alexander Bustamante, through a nexus between the Jamaica Labour Party and the Bustamante Industrial Trade Union, swept the polls, conducted for the first time under the system of universal adult suffrage.

So, too, did the Barbados Labour Party and the labour movement in Trinidad make electoral advances in Barbados and Trinidad. All over the region, the social democratic revolution was advancing through the efforts of the working people themselves.

Yet, the increased apprehension of the planter-merchant elite did not cause them to think strategically. Instead of an accommodation to popular democratic changes and an adaptation to alterations in a modernising capitalism globally, the planter-merchant elite remained stuck in the old modes of thought and functioning of the ancien regime. As Gordon Lewis noted in *The Growth of the Modern West Indies*, the local plantocracy was rooted, too, in "technological conservatism". So, they resisted changes in the political economy but their resistance was doomed to fail. They did not as yet realise that it was not possible for them to rule much longer in the old way; and they, dinosaur-like, were as a class, incapable of altering the socio-economic model of the plantation system or to fashion a new way in which to rule.

The economic inefficiency of the planter-merchant elite in St. Vincent was authoritatively assessed in 1947 by an expert, Dr. A.L. Jolly in his "Preliminary Examination of the Economic and Fiscal Structure in St. Vincent" published in *A Plan of Development for the Colony of St. Vincent*, edited by Bernard Gibbs. Jolly observed that the "glaring economic defect of West Indian populations" was deficient entrepreneurial ability, so that there was:

> *...too little competition between managers of agricultural and industrial enterprise and too much competition among the wage earning labourers. As a result, the earnings are high in relation to the services they render in making their business ever more efficient, as judged by European standards; the wages of the workers judged by the same standards are low for their services in sweat and toil.*

This was true of the sugar industry, and the arrowroot industry, which was in the ascendancy in the 1940s. In the case of the arrowroot industry, a number of critical observations from the Robinson Report of 1944 and other reports, onwards, detailed the structural and managerial inefficiencies, but hardly anything was done to implement the sensible recommendations for improvement. This failure and/or refusal to reform, improve, or alter these structural and managerial efficiencies was, in the words of Gordon Lewis,

> *...largely because the people who suffered most under the system, that is, the class of small peasant growers, were not the people who had the most influence on the structure*

of the industry, the strategic directive group being, in
fact, inadequately educated planters and planters' sons,
with very little, if any, training in tropical agriculture
and whose lifestyle is that of the idle rich.

The electoral success in 1946 of the Mc Intosh-led labour movement papered over its weaknesses and limitations. The consciousness of the working people, as a class, though growing, was still undeveloped and uneven. Estate life was perennially difficult for the working people who were subject to severe material deprivation, routine indignities, and humiliations as a consequence of the plantation system and colonial over-rule. Existence for the poor and workers in urban centres was no better, and arguably worse. These objective, harsh conditions of life of the workers both dulled their inclination for political organisation and activity and, at the same time, outraged their humanity and sense of fairness. They oscillated between submissiveness and aggression to "massa". Religious dogma induced them to alternating bouts of an acceptance of their lot and political quietism, on the one hand, and a determination, on the other, to act in solidarity with those of their class to better their individual and collective lives, materially. Quality leadership and sound organisation were required but they were in short supply.

By 1948, of the working people's organisations, only the SVGWU was fully functional; the SVWA was a shadow of its former self; the SVLP had become virtually non-existent. In 1948, the SVGWU reported officially a membership of 1,209, an increase over the preceding year; the bulk of the membership was drawn from manual workers (592) and artisans and craftsmen (250).

The virtual collapse of the peasants' union (SVPCU) was attributable to the marked individualism of the peasantry, the spatial difficulty in organising them, and the weaknesses of the union leadership. The leaders of the SVPCU were by socialisation and residence, urban-centred; the peasants were not their natural constituency; and all this showed in the leadership's infrequent articulation of the peasants' causes such as the demand for more cultivable lands, easier credit, and better market facilities. These factors effectively held back the growth and development of the SVPCU.

Meanwhile, the day-to-day struggles between labour and capital continued, occasioning worker disruptions and even "wild-cat" strikes. For example, in 1949 the male workers employed at the St. Vincent Cooperative Arrowroot Association went on strike for higher wages while their trade union leaders were negotiating for pay increases. It was only after the Association had sought the help of the Labour Department that the workers resumed work with the promise of a satisfactory settlement. The workers actually took matters into their own hands; they appeared impatient with the pace of the union-management talks, and withdrew their labour without their union's approval.

Criticisms of the way the labour leaders were exercising their role were appearing frequently in the newspapers, especially *The Vincentian*, owned by the planter-merchant elite, which had emerged to challenge the two labour-supportive newspapers, *The Times* and *The Investigator*. In November 1948, for example, there appeared a letter written by a correspondent and social activist, Sidney King, which posed the question: "Labour Party labouring or having a Party?" In the circumstances, the critique was not far-fetched or without some foundation. The letter-writer's central complaint was "the lack of power shown by the Labour Party in labour matters, is something all workers must be cross about;" the letter bemoaned the parlous condition of the workers and was a call for a more focussed, and intense, labour activism.

Still, the Colonial Administrator appeared oblivious to the impoverished and dire condition of the working people. Perhaps the seemingly lacklustre performance of labour's representatives emboldened him to advise the SVGWU in 1949 of the need to hold wage demands in abeyance because of the devaluation of sterling currency. The Administrator, in his 1950 budget speech, bemoaned the government's budgetary deficit of BWI $129,801, or in excess of EC $7 million in today's values. At the same time the Growers' Union/Planters' Association publicly objected to any increased taxation on the productive sector.

The burden of an increasing cost of living weighed heavily upon the working people: By the end of 1951, the consumer price index had jumped sharply to 264 over the base year (100) of 1939.

Meanwhile, the lethargy of the colonial government in implementing ostensibly ameliorative social legislation was troubling. For example, the Factory Legislation adopted in 1943 was not put into effect until 1947; the Labour Advisory Board which was set up to advise the government on labour matters, met infrequently — only three times in 1948. Inexplicably, the colonial government stone-walled and resisted Mc Intosh's reasonable demand to have the minutes of these meetings published.

By 1951, there were signs that George Mc Intosh's influence and popular support was waning. From a membership of 1,161 members at December 31, 1949, the numerical strength of his SVGWU had fallen to a mere 500 in

1951. Organisationally, the union was in a ramshackle condition; and its earlier promise of enhanced material benefits for the workers was not realised.

By 1951, too, the working people's support was substantially won over by the rapid rise of George Hamilton Charles and his United Workers, Peasants, and Ratepayers Unions (UWPRU). In its first year of operation, the UWPRU enrolled, according to the 1951 Colonial Office Annual Report, some 8,000 members, large numbers of whom were originally members of Mc Intosh's SVWA-SVPCU-SVLP combination. Workers' increasing disillusionment with Mc Intosh's leadership and the rise of a new brand of anti-colonial and working-class militancy by Charles and supportive leaders such as Ebenezer Theodore Joshua, propelled UWPRU into the people's consciousness.

Before Mc Intosh's demise as the popular leader, he assisted the passage of an important piece of trade union legislation. In April 1950, the Trade Unions and Trade Disputes Ordinance was enacted; it provided for the regulation of trade unions and trade disputes. It repealed the first Trade Union Ordinance of 1933 and its amendments in 1939, 1940, and 1943.

The legislative reform process for trade unions was, more or less, in lock-step with the constitutional and political initiative of ushering in universal adult suffrage for the next general elections which were due in 1951. The British Secretary of State for the Colonies had earlier announced this measure of democratic enlargement through universal adult suffrage *subject* to a simple literacy test. He had requested the local legislature to propose the nature of the literacy test and to examine the arrangements for monetary deposits which electoral candidates were required to make.

Accordingly, a Select Committee of the Legislative Council was established to consider the constitutional reform proposals centred on universal adult suffrage. The minutes of the Legislative Committee makes interesting reading. On August 11, 1949, George Mc Intosh proposed, in committee, a motion to delete the literacy test proviso; the motion was carried five votes to three. Those voting in the affirmative were the elected "labour" members: Mc Intosh, Ebenezer Duncan, Edmund Joachim, and St. Clair Bonadie, plus a nominated member, O.D. Brisbane, a liberal-minded businessman; voting against were E.A.C. Hughes, a lawyer, and William Hadley, both nominated members, and Sylvester De Freitas, an entrepreneur who represented the Grenadines. The officials in the legislature did not vote on this matter. Hughes' argument against Mc Intosh's motion was entirely technical; he insisted that the matter which the Secretary of State had referred to the legislature was not the issue of the literacy test but *the form* of a literacy test.

As regards the matter of deposit requirements and property/income qualifications for election candidates, the "labour" representatives of Mc Intosh, Bonadie, Joachim, and Duncan were in favour of the complete removal of both property and income qualifications for candidates and an increase in the deposit on a candidate's nomination; Hughes, Hadley, De Freitas, and Brisbane voted against. These latter four legislators proposed instead a reduction of the property and income qualification by fifty percent for the candidates, and leaving the deposit at the same level as before; this proposal did not receive the support of the "labour" legislators.

In the event, the secretary of state resolved the issues by the ordering of no literacy test for voters and the removal of income and property qualifications, with an increase in deposits, for the election candidates. In short, he accepted the recommendations of the "labour" representatives.

As the 1951 general elections loomed, political activism heightened competitively. Ahead lay a definitive contest for the political leadership of the national labour movement between the organisations under the leadership of George Mc Intosh, on the one hand, and those under George Charles and Ebenezer Joshua, on the other hand.

Charles and Joshua, president-general and treasurer, respectively, of the UWPRU had recently returned from Trinidad where they had gained experience over several years in the practical school of Uriah "Buzz" Butler's mass politics which possessed a message shaped by "God, Marx, and the British Empire" — to use Gordon Lewis' telling phrase. Indeed, Joshua had contested the 1950 general elections in Trinidad on the ticket of Butler's political party but he lost to Roy Joseph in a constituency in southern Trinidad. Charles returned to St. Vincent ahead of Joshua, and both did so to contest the 1951 elections under the popular franchise.

Swiftly, Charles launched his UWPRU in January 1951 to secure a labour base on which to compete effectively against Mc Intosh and his multiplicity of working people organisations which had arisen in the aftermath of the 1935 uprising. The very name which Charles selected for his union was reflective of a strategy to organise the workers and peasants under his conjoined, and evolving, union/political umbrella. The aim of this blanket union was "to secure the complete organisation of all workers employed in any institution, trade and industry in the colony." as outlined in "The Rules for Registration of UWPRU". The UWPRU's objects were similar to those of Mc Intosh's SVGWU particularly in respect of wages, conditions of work, sickness and death benefits, and the establishment of participatory businesses. The supreme authority of the union was vested in an annual conference of delegates elected by the branches and, subject to that authority, the union was constitutionally structured to be governed by an executive committee. In reality, though, it was Charles who controlled, directed, and made the decisions for the union.

A significant and innovative aspect of this union, in the landscape of trade unionism in St. Vincent, was the establishment of a political fund to be used for political activities. The details relevant to the operation of such a fund under the trade union law, were required to be submitted to the Registrar of Trade Unions.

The aim to set up such a political fund was indicative of the UWPRU's intention to gear up for political activity. At the same time, though, the official scrutiny of that fund by the Registrar meant that colonialism was concerned that a check be maintained to ensure that workers' monies were not excessively used or misused for political purposes; this reflected, in part, colonialism's disdain for, or a reluctance in any embrace of, political unionism.

Indeed, in 1954, the colonial government amended the 1950 Trade Unions and Trade Disputes Ordinance to restrict the use of trade union funds for certain political purposes; the amendment called for specific approval of the political objects to be funded by a resolution of the members of the union in a secret ballot or otherwise specifically included in the rules of the union approved by the Registrar. It is ironic that the British sought to restrict political funding by a trade union when the British Labour Party was heavily supported financially by individual unions and the Trade Union Congress in Britain. Undoubtedly, colonialism considered that a unity of trade union and political forces posed a danger to the colonial administration and its continuance.

With the advent of universal adult suffrage and the further liberalisation of the constitution, the trade union/political party linkages became the norm. In a competitive political environment, with the prospect of enhanced devolved authority to elected representatives, the political stakes increased; the political competition thus intensified, in practice.

ACTIVISM IN THE LABOUR MOVEMENT
AND ELECTORAL BATTLES, 1951-1957

On January 12, 1951, the UWPRU was formally registered as a trade union. On October 15, 1951, general elections were held to elect representatives for the eight constituencies: seven on mainland St. Vincent; and one in the

Grenadines. Between both dates, a ten-month period, the UWPRU was very active as a trade union and politically.

The phenomenal growth of the UWPRU can be gauged from the fact that in its first twelve months of operation, it achieved a membership of 8,000. This was an extraordinary accomplishment when it is considered that the total population of St. Vincent, according to the 1946 Census, for persons aged between 15 and 64 years was only 27,000: 21,580 in the age cohort 15-44 years; and 5,510 in the age cohort 45-64 years.

The veritable political earthquake of the UWPRU in its first twelve functional months was comparatively more impressive than the impactful presence of Mc Intosh's SVWA in the immediate aftermath of the 1935 uprising. In its first twelve months of operation the SVWA recorded a membership of 4,000; the UWPRU chalked up twice as many members in a similar time period.

A significant number of the UWPRU's organisers in the villages and towns were schooled in the trade union and political networks of the 1935-1951 period. Several of them had had experience, too, of trade union and political activism in neighbouring islands, especially Trinidad and Tobago. Most of the members of the UWPRU were wage-earners in agriculture and workers in the urban areas. Interestingly, in official communications, the grassroots organisers of the UWPRU went out of their way to emphasise their primary interest in trade unionism and not in politics. So, for example, in statements to the registrar of trade unions in 1951, foundation members such as Thaddeus Parris, Clive Richardson, Eli Cuffy, all of Evesham, and George Samuel of Brighton, expressed their central commitment to trade unionism and not politics. More than likely, these statements were meant to impress British officialdom, which frowned upon the mixing of trade unionism and politics, and not necessarily an affirmation of any political quietism.

The formal elaboration of a democratic organisational structure contained in the Rules of UWPRU masked its oligarchic operations, with George Charles as the principal maker of important decisions. The decentralised branch structure of the union facilitated the collection of union dues and political mobilisation rather than the building of effective, democratic, trade unionism. As the events unfolded, the UWPRU flourished as a mass organisation when George Charles' political stocks were in the ascendancy; when Charles' political popularity waned, the UWPRU faltered. So, in 1951 there were forty branches of the UWPRU; thereafter it went into decline: thirty branches in 1952, seventeen in 1953, two in 1954, and none in 1956 when its registration as a trade union was cancelled by the registrar of trade unions. The ups and downs of the UWPRU correlated with the political ascendancy and demise of George Charles.

Still, we ought not to fall into the error of explaining Charles' rise and fall by focussing simply on his "personality". Undoubtedly, he received working people's support because he and his union actually convinced the working people that it was better to join this more dynamic and militant representative vehicle than to remain tied to Mc Intosh's union-political combination which had grown stale and inadequate. A vacuum in the organisational nexus of trade unionism and politics had arisen; Charles took advantage of this. His flamboyant political style, his rhetoric, his stronger anti-colonial message, his sharper blasts against the planter-merchant elite, caused the working people to rally to him and his trade union. However, when it soon became clear that Charles and the UWPRU were unable to provide the requisite leadership in securing benefits for the working people either through the trade union or the legislature, his political stocks eroded to the extent that in his third electoral outing in 1957, after personal victories in the 1951 and 1954 elections, he lost his Central Windward constituency.

Nevertheless, at 34 years of age, in 1951, before his fairly rapid fall from political grace, George Charles seemed supreme among the working people's leaders. The contemporary newspaper report (*The Vincentian*, May 5, 1951) of the UWPRU's first May Day celebration in 1951 gives a flavour of this. Charles had invited the Colonial Administrator, the Labour Commissioner, Ministers of Religion, and his constellation of subordinate leaders to enunciate the necessity and desirability of proper trade unions and a progressive path forward for the working people. At a gathering of over two thousand persons — impressive mobilisation in an age of a paucity of road transportation — Charles appeared, according to *The Vincentian*:

> *In a very dynamic style, he took a bible and swore to be*
> *faithful to the union, promising never to let them down.*

Charles' messianic approach to leadership had been evidently learnt from Tubal Uriah "Buzz" Butler of Trinidad; it was an approach which was to infuse much of trade union-political leadership for the next twenty or so years until the fading of Ebenezer Joshua after 1972.

The ascendancy of Charles and the UWPRU, including Ebenezer Joshua and the formidable Herman Young, reflected a growing union-political strug-gle in the wider labour movement between these new "arrivants" of younger men and the old guard of George Mc Intosh, Ebenezer Duncan, and St. Clair

Bonadie. The small size of the country and the immediacy of sharp inter-per-sonal rivalries added to the objective political differences between the labour stalwarts of the post-1935 period and the new militants who were gearing up to mobilise for the breaking-down of the proverbial walls of a colonial Jericho.

In a caustic letter to *The Vincentian* newspaper of June 16, 1951, Mc Intosh attacked the UWPRU as consisting of "mis-leaders" who "have sprung up to traverse the road prepared by us". This was a constant refrain of Mc Intosh and his supporters in the SVWA-SVLP. But the old guard was no electoral match for the more militant, younger men who, relying on the political base of the UWPRU fashioned an electoral vehicle for the general elections of October 1951 called the Eighth Army of Liberation — borrowing the lustre of Field Marshall Montgomery's "Eighth Army" in the recently-concluded Second World War, and coinciding with the eight legislative seats on offer in the general elections.

The sixty-five year old Mc Intosh went down in ignominious defeat in his traditional Kingstown stronghold to an "Eighth Army" newcomer, Rudolph Baynes, by 1,065 votes (48.9 percent) to 861 (39.5 percent); an independent candidate, Dr. Frank Ellis garnered 252 votes. Five years earlier, Mc Intosh so completely ruled the political roost in Kingstown that he was returned unopposed in the 1946 general elections under a restrictive franchise. George Charles was victorious in the Central Windward constituency with 76.9 percent of the votes cast; Ebenezer Joshua won with 63.4 percent of the votes cast in the North Windward constituency. The other victorious "Eighth Army" candidates were: Sam Slater in the North Leeward constituency with 1,794 votes (62 percent of votes cast); Herman Young in South Leeward with 2,106 votes (89.7 percent of votes cast); Evans Morgan in South Windward with 1,834 votes (85 percent of votes cast); Julian Baynes in St. George with 1,726 votes (81 percent of the votes cast); and Clive Tannis in the Grenadines with 813 votes (54 percent of the votes cast). Former SVMA-SVLP legislators, Edmund Joachim and St. Clair Bonadie went down in defeat respectively in North Leeward with 1,093 votes (37.8 percent) and St. George with 314 votes (14.7 percent). The very expanded, universal franchise for which Mc Intosh and his colleagues had agitated became the very mechanism which delivered their political defeat.

The clean sweep of all eight seats by the Eighth Army of Liberation was both wide and deep. In three of the seats (South Leeward, South Windward and St. George) the Eighth Army candidates won in each seat with over 80 percent of the votes cast; in one other constituency, Central Windward, the victory was attained with over 75 percent of the votes; in each of two constituencies (North Windward and North Leeward), there were victories by in excess of 60 percent of the votes cast; and in two other seats there were victories by 54 percent in the Grenadines; and 48.9 percent in Kingstown in a three-way contest, one of the defeated contestants being the titan, George Mc Intosh. In total, 12,544 electors, or 70.35 percent of the valid votes cast, voted for the candidates of the Eighth Army. This was truly impressive!

As an electoral machine, the Eighth Army was little more than a loose coalition of individual office-seekers who exploited an emerging political vacuum and were possessed of an inchoate message around anti-colonial, anti-planter rhetoric and minimalist working people's demands. However, their political freshness, their energy, their sharper militant tone, their robust political style, and appealing message, struck a responsive chord in a hopeful people with a growing but still undeveloped level of working people's political consciousness.

Voting turnout in this first election under universal adult suffrage was at the commendable level of almost seventy percent (69.7 percent) of the registered voters. Of the 27,409 registered votes, 19,110 voted but 1,278 of the ballots were rejected as "spoilt".

Unfortunately, the unity of the Eighth Army, so impressively displayed and supported popularly in the 1951 general elections, was shortly to be shattered. Before the election celebrations had been fully exhausted, the Eighth Army experienced a disastrous, divisive split between the so-called "Big Four" (Ebenezer Joshua, Rudolph Baynes, Julian Baynes, and Sam Slater) and the "Little Four" (George Charles, Herman Young, Evans Morgan, and Clive Tannis). Joshua and Charles emerged as leaders of the respective factions.

The split was made easy precisely because the Eighth Army was a loose coalition of individualists with no coherent ideology, save that of a vague anti-colonialism and a limited working people's agenda. The desire for office was the major cementing force. In that context, petty intrigue, ambitions, and personality clashes easily engendered, and exaggerated, divisiveness. More than one of them thought that they were leadership material; and it had become evident to many, if not most, of them that George Charles was not the best possible popular leader on offer.

One version of the immediate reason for the split reflected both the political immaturity of the outfit and the existence of contrasting ideas or approaches to tackle the colonial administration. In an interview with the author two decades or so later, on September 9, 1970, Herman Young considered that the "Big Four" were much too concerned with opposing the colonial order and insufficiently alert to the possibility of winning benefits for the people through cooperation with it. The actual precipitation of the break, Young claimed, was when the "Big Four" opted for an election victory celebration at Julian Baynes' residence while the "Little Four" accepted the invitation for the one at Government House — the Colonial Administrator's official residence.

However, in the author's interviews with Ebenezer Joshua on July 29th and August 6th, 1970, Joshua stressed, in the main, the differences between Charles and himself which went beyond, but included, their strategic and tactical approaches to colonialism. Joshua insisted that he had urged Charles to organise a bona fide political party and to keep the UWPRU separate, though allied to it. According to Joshua, Charles refused and advised him (Joshua) to form his own party. Almost a year later, on January 03, 1952, Joshua obliged by forming the People's Political Party (PPP). Joshua contended that only a well-organised party could provide a broad enough base of mass mobilisation, beyond a trade union, to confront the colonial government and the plantocracy — the two major enemies of the working people identified by Joshua.

In the author's interviews with Joshua, it was clear that he was contemptuous of Charles' leadership ability. He plainly stated that "Charles failed because of his stupidity". Joshua realised during the 1951 election campaign that Charles had an abundance of flamboyance and little substance. Joshua felt, too, that there was a popular acknowledgement of his own leadership skills, and large numbers saw him as the "de facto" leader. Undoubtedly, Joshua had distinguished himself as being possessed of considerable dynamism, superb oratical skills, and a greater clarity of ideas. At 43 years of age, Joshua appeared more thoughtful and mature than Charles; there was undoubted attraction of Joshua to the working people. In all, Joshua was simply not prepared to be led anymore by Charles.

So, by early January 1952, in less than three months after the general elections of October 1951, Joshua formed his PPP. His next organisational task was to establish an affiliated union. In April 1952, Joshua caused to be registered the Federated Industrial and Agricultural Workers' Union (FIAWU) with himself as President and Julian Baynes of the "Big Four" as his deputy.

While Charles and his "Little Four" were focussing on cooperating with the colonial government in the Legislative Council (which comprised the Administrator, two officials, three nominated members, and the eight elected members), Joshua was criss-crossing the country organising the PPP and the FIAWU. Meanwhile, Joshua, still nominally the Treasurer of the UWPRU, set about discrediting Charles and his inability to account for union funds. Joshua issued a financial statement of the UWPRU showing a BWI $5,000 deficit in that union's finances. Charles countered that the financial report was false. The Registrar of Trade Unions, in accordance with the law, appointed an auditor to examine and report upon the UWPRU's finances; the auditor revealed that the sum of $2,045.19 was unaccounted for. The auditor found that the accounting systems and the handling of the union's finances were unsatisfactory. In addition, many members of the union submitted complaints to the Registrar alleging a failure of the union to pay the death benefits which had become due.

The matter of the alleged financial improprieties and laxity in the UWPRU and Charles' role therein became public issues. At first, the acting Colonial Administrator, Bernard Gibbs, contrived to delay or avoid the publication of the report of the Registrar-appointed auditor. After all, Charles had been working hand-in-glove with the Colonial Administrator, so a favour of sorts was due him; or at least so it appeared to the public.

In March 1952, public pressure mounted on Acting Administrator Gibbs to publish the auditor's report. Joshua and his colleagues in the "Big Four" were milking the issue for all that it was worth to the political discomfort of Charles. In this period, *The Vincentian* newspaper, in an editorial, demanded the publication of the auditor's report; public-spirited citizens and political activists such as R.N. Eustace, Ebenezer Joshua and Rudolph Baynes wrote to the Registrar, requesting copies of the report; and the leaders of the PPP were addressing the issue in their public meetings. On March 12, 1952, the Registrar wrote to the Acting Administrator and urged upon him a further direction because "he cannot put off Joshua any longer." Just over a week later, the Registrar was again communicating to the Acting Administrator that he had been vilified by Joshua in public meetings on March 16th and March 20th, 1952, for withholding the auditor's report. Gibbs was still unmoved. In a letter dated April 3, 1952 in response to one from a member of the UWPRU, Alexander Ince of Kingstown who had requested the auditor's report and appropriate action, the Acting Administrator excused his failure to take action on the ground that if he did "it would be interpreted as an attack on trade unionism especially at this stage in St. Vincent." Gibbs advised individuals to take their own legal action if they so desired.

On May 2, 1952, when the "Big Four" in the Legislative Council called for a full-scale enquiry into the financial state of Charles' union, the "Little Four" together with Gibbs, who used his casting vote, rejected the motion. This gave further credence that the "Little Four", having sold out to the colonial administration, were now being assisted in the protection of Charles by the Acting Administrator himself.

The "Little Four" were now facing a wave of public hostility. In September 1952, Charles and his colleague, Evans Morgan, left a public meeting in Kingstown under police protection, after being threatened by hostile crowds. This period marked the beginning of Charles' decline and the political ascendancy of Ebenezer Joshua.

From the moment that Joshua was elected to the legislature in the 1951 elections, he embarked therein upon a programme of radical attacks against colonialism, the plantocracy, and their political allies, while at the same time championing the cause of the working people.

On November 1, 1951, at his very first meeting of the Legislative Council, Joshua critiqued the Governor for referring to St. Vincent as part of the free world because the "four freedoms" were still denied colonial peoples. When the Governor found it expedient to use his over-riding powers to veto some decisions of the Legislative Council, Joshua warned the country of the dangers of colonialism's undemocratic authoritarianism. On the floor of the legislature, Joshua led his colleagues from "the Big Four" in their repeated calls for better distribution of land, lower land prices, increased minimum wages, and meaningful liberalisation of constitutional governance to accord substantial devolved authority to the elected representatives. Meanwhile Charles and the "Little Four" compromised with, and provided ongoing legislative support to, the colonial government. Colonialism was effectively dividing the working people's movement, and gaining for itself a measure of political comfort. In the process, Charles was slowly digging his own political grave and ceding the dominant leadership of the labour movement to Joshua.

The registration of Joshua's FIAWU in April 1952, provided an institutional conduit through which to channel practical day-to-day grievances of the working people. The FIAWU's structure and objects were similar to those of the UWPRU but Joshua's focussed pro-worker endeavours caused a strengthening of the FIAWU. By 1953, the FIAWU had a membership of 2,500, the largest of any union in St. Vincent. The UWPRU was in decline but still boasted a membership of 1,100; and Mc Intosh's SVGWU was virtually defunct with a membership of fifty. The other registered trade union, the Teachers' Association, had a membership of 300.

The rapid fall in the membership of the UWPRU from the giddy heights of 8,000 in 1951 to roughly one-eighth thereof by 1953 was dramatic. Charles and his colleagues only had themselves to blame. The UWPRU failed to win for the workers any substantial material benefits. Moreover, in the legislature, they became pre-occupied with the embrace of colonialism's legislative and administrative agenda.

At the same time, Joshua was making a considerable effort in extending the reach of the FIAWU and strengthening its organisation, especially in Kingstown, in the sugar belt in Central Windward and North Windward, and on the Land Settlement Estates in North Leeward, particularly at Richmond. At the Mt. Bentinck sugar estates and factory, the FIAWU was demanding recognition as a bargaining agent for the workers. In Kingstown, Joshua and his FIAWU were similarly engaged on behalf of the stevedores, port workers and the employees at the electricity plant. Relentlessly, all over the country, Joshua was seeking ways and means to advance the cause of the workers, while Charles seemed prepared to rest on his 1951 laurels and cooperate with colonialism; thus he lost much support.

A significant administrative development arose out of the saga surrounding the financial accounting of the UWPRU. In late 1952, the acting Administrator Gibbs sought to exercise some control over future registrations of trade unions. On November 11, 1952, Gibbs wrote the registrar of trade unions advising that on no account must he register a new trade union without first consulting the labour commissioner and until he had secured a covering authority from the Administrator. It is arguable that Gibbs was acting outside of the Trade Union and Trade Disputes Ordinance of 1950 which had specifically accorded the registrar the sole right to register trade unions. Interestingly, there was no adverse public commentary on Gibbs' apparent abuse of his executive authority; in all probability, Gibbs' executive diktat to the registrar was kept as a closely-guarded secret, buried in the registrar's files.

Although the 1951 constitution did not transfer much authority to the elected members — they were not a majority on the executive council — it did prove a useful legislative forum from which the ills or shortcomings of the system could be exposed and limited reforms or improvements effected. Joshua clearly recognised these possibilities for the working people's advance, even as he was aware of the legislature's profound limitations to achieve real change for the better for the workers. In the midst of the political manoeuvrings, the ongoing class struggle ensued daily between the working people, on the one hand, and the planter-merchant elite, on the other, buttressed by a colonial state. Over the next few years, 1952-1957, the colonial regime in tandem with the plantocracy, the merchants, the pro-regime and compromising labour leaders, sought to put various forms of pressure on Joshua and the PPP-FIAWU link-up. The state apparatus, including the police, the legal system, and the colonial bureaucracy, was utilised to blunt the political agenda of Joshua.

On July 31, 1952, for example, Joshua's parliamentary colleagues voted to oust him from the executive council, ostensibly on the ground that his behaviour was inimical to good government. Herman Young and Clive Tannis, in the Legislative Council, moved and seconded the motion for Joshua's ouster. The ouster motion was based on Joshua's alleged unjustified public attacks on the legislators and his exposure of the positions that they had adopted within the confines of the executive council. This was primarily an attempt to discredit Joshua for an offence which, in its essence, was a breach of his "oath of secrecy" in his revelation of information to the public of the deliberations of the executive council. Shortly after Joshua's removal from the executive council, he was reinstated when it was recognised that the requisite two-thirds majority for expulsion had not been obtained.

Since 1951, Joshua and the workers on the sugar estates and at the sugar factory were conjoined in a battle with the plantocracy over elemental worker demands for improved wages, working conditions, and trade union recognition. In 1951, he had led the workers in a minor work stoppage at the Mt. Bentinck Estates in support of a claim for higher wages; he was at the time the treasurer of UWPRU. The Labour Department had intervened and the matter was "amicably settled" in the words of the *Colonial Office Annual Report*, 1951. Mt. Bentinck Estates were at the core of the sugar industry; it was also where the sole sugar factory was located. It was, too, a populous community, part of the conurbation of Georgetown — the country's second major town. It was the alive heartland of Joshua's political base; he was the elected representative for that area since the general elections of October 15, 1951, part of his North Windward electoral constituency.

By 1952, Joshua had organised his own trade union. On December 5, 1952, the fight for the FIAWU to be recognised by the Mt. Bentinck Estates as the bargaining agent for the factory and agricultural workers, began in earnest. On that day, the union made the following demands: 1) A 30 percent wage increase; 2) the institution of a close shop system to include all workers in the bargaining unit; 3) trade union recognition; 4) time-and-a-half pay for work done on Sundays and public holidays; 5) gratuity for workers based on the number of days worked per year; and 6) compensation for workers as laid down in the Workmen Compensation Ordinance. These demands were neither radical nor unreasonable. The management of the Mt. Bentinck Estates ignored the workers' demands as set out in the union's letter of December 5, 1952, which had also indicated the union's willingness to allow the labour commissioner to examine its membership register for the purpose of ascertaining the union's majority support for recognition. The Labour Department did not respond either.

Nine days later, on December 14, 1952, the FIAWU reiterated, by letter, its position. Again, there was silence from the estates' management and the labour commissioner. It was clear that Joshua had exposed the nature of "plantocratic" rule and its linkage with the colonial administration. It was the first time in the history of the colony that the basis of the sugar barons' hegemony had been so questioned and confronted. Six days later, on December 20, 1952, Joshua was arrested on charges of sedition and creating public mischief. In early 1953, a second charge of sedition was added. The former charge of sedition related to a speech, alleged to have been made by Joshua, claiming that "legislators of the colony were treacherously plotting with the police to oppress the working class." On the second charge of sedition, Joshua was accused by the police to have said that "the Administrator and every policeman were instructed to fabricate statements" against him. The charge of public mischief revolved around a speech which Joshua was purported to have made to the effect that "the police were scheming politically and storing up a veritable arsenal to shoot down people." Joshua was found guilty and fined $100; and a two-year bond to hold the peace was also imposed on him. Predictably, he appealed the decision, first to the Windward and Leeward Islands Court of Appeal, which upheld the conviction. Then he further appealed to the Privy Council in Britain which squashed the decisions of the lower courts. It is hardly too much to suggest that the legal attack on Joshua amounted to an effort by the colonial administration in St. Vincent to weaken the labour movement and anti-colonial political activities by attempting to silence the most militant leader of the working people.

But Joshua was not to be silenced. Riding a wave of working class support, in February 1953 he again called out the workers at Mt. Bentinck Estates to strike in support of their on-going demands from 1952. Forty cane cutters and one hundred and thirty factory workers responded to his call and went on strike in support of his demands. It was only after a 10 percent wage increase was granted that the workers returned to their jobs, following a stoppage of two weeks. Numerous acts of disturbance had taken place during the strike period and a potentially explosive situation still existed, even after the settlement.

Colonel A.H. Jenkins, chief of police, reported acts of violence at political meetings in the Georgetown area — capital of the then North Windward constituency. Jenkins claimed that a member of the legislative and executive councils (obviously referring to Joshua) had slandered him in the discharge of his duties. On March 5, 1952, Joshua informed the Legislative Council that the police were intimidating his constituents with rifles and warned that police harassment might well result in further acts of violence. In January 1954, the cane-cutters at Mt. Bentinck again went on strike for more wages; a further wage increase of 10 percent was granted but not before more acts of violence had occurred. Meanwhile, the question of union recognition was still pending. In the same year, Joshua also directed his followers at the government's Land Settlement Estates, on the north-western or North Leeward side of St. Vincent, to strike for increased wages for reaping arrowroot; the upshot was an increase of 5 cents per basket of arrowroot dug, from 25 cents to 30 cents per basket. The brutal exploitation which existed on the sugar and arrowroot estates was highlighted in a memorandum of the FIAWU to the Jolly Commission in its 1955 *Report of the Commission of Enquiry on the Sugar Industry of St. Vincent.*

As Joshua's political profile was enhanced and support for the PPP-FIAWU nexus grew, not only the planters and colonial government took aim against him. His more compromising, erstwhile labour leaders sought to use their presence in the Legislative Council, with the support of the nominated and official members of the legislature, to cut him down, politically. So, on April 1, 1954, Charles successfully proposed a motion in the Legislative Council to have Joshua's election to the executive council revoked. Charles' basic case was grounded in anti-communist, cold war hysteria: that Joshua was an international communist and "an enemy of the Commonwealth way of life by reason of his attendance at a conference in Vienna dominated by Russia;" and that the FIAWU, as an affiliate of the communist-dominated World Federation of Trade Unions (WFTU), was thus enjoined to participate in global subversive activities. With the 1954 general elections a few months away, Charles' opportunistic attack on Joshua in the legislature was a crude attempt to tarnish him in the eyes of the working people, and so weaken him. The problem was, though, that Charles' credibility was sinking fast; it was his mass base which was eroding rapidly; chicanery in the legislature by him against Joshua with "plantocratic" and colonialism's support was to no avail.

Joshua was not to be forced on the defensive. His working people radicalism, his class battle against the planter-merchant elite, and his anti-colonialism, grew sharper. Joshua was organising, mobilising, educating and agitating the working people all over St. Vincent, particularly on the estates and among the working class in Kingstown. Still, the labour movement was divided and the PPP had not yet gained the overwhelming national support of the kind which the Eighth Army of Liberation had garnered three years earlier. The middle class, important politically though numerically small, identified primarily with the colonial status quo; influential teachers and public servants saw Joshua as nothing more than a trade union and political demagogue.

In July 1954, the colonial administration's ineptness and undemocratic ethos gave Joshua an opportunity to burnish his image among teachers and the middle class. Some of the more progressive teachers had remembered that it was Joshua who had assisted them in 1952 by having the Teachers' Association registered as a trade union. Foolishly, the colonial administration transferred a headteacher, the president of the teachers' association, the highly-respected Thomas M. Saunders, for a speech which he made. Saunders was formally charged, administratively, by the colonial government for: 1) insulting the education officer by deliberately leaving him out of a vote of thanks; and 2) airing in public some grievances of teachers about which the Colonial Administrator had no prior official knowledge. Joshua seized on the issue with gusto and held several public meetings in defence of Saunders against the unjustifiable punishment of the transfer. Joshua's activism on the issue turned the matter into a "cause célèbre" and thus fuelled wide public protest against colonialism's folly in its attempt to muzzle a headteacher and union leader on account of trifles.

On August 2, 1954, general elections were held for eight representatives to the Legislative Council. These elections were noteworthy for the following: 1) This was the last election foray of the veteran, 68-year old George Mc Intosh, who contested the Kingstown seat as an independent candidate in a losing cause by coming third in a three-man contest with 24 percent of the valid votes cast; so, too, was St. Clair Bonadie, who lost in South Leeward with 17 percent of the votes; 2) for the first time since 1936, the SVWA-SVLP combination did not field a single candidate under their banner; 3) the Eighth Army did not field any candidate; that electoral vehicle had ceased to exist; it was a one-election phenomenon in 1951; 4) Joshua's PPP was the only political party to field candidates; it did so in all eight seats; 5) the PPP candidates, in total, polled 6,193 votes or 40 percent of the 15,501 votes which were validly cast; for this effort, the PPP won three seats (Joshua in North Windward, Herman Young in South Leeward and Edmund Joachim in North Leeward — there was a by-election in that constituency and Samuel Slater reversed his defeat in the general elections); 6) seven of the eight representatives from 1951 were returned in the general elections; Slater was returned in a by-election; all except Joshua and Young (who both won as PPP candidates) gained victories as independent candidates; 7) in all, there were 27 candidates, 19 of whom were "independents" and eight were from the PPP; 8) five of the elected represent-atives, all as "Independents" were returned with majorities below 50 percent of the valid votes cast in contests with multiple candidates; the other three elected representatives from the PPP won with majorities ranging between 50.8 percent to 82.8 percent; 9) fewer persons voted in 1954 than in 1951: 15,501 in 1954 and 18,219 in 1951 cast valid ballots; the percentage turnout of registered votes fell to 59 percent in 1954 compared to 70 percent in 1951; 10) a woman, Floris Simmonds, in the Grenadines contested elections — an historic first for a female candidate; she garnered 7 percent of the votes.

From the 1954 general elections, Ebenezer Joshua was confirmed as the foremost national political leader with the sole organised political party, the PPP, and the undoubted leader of the labour movement. In his North Wind-ward constituency he won 79 percent of the valid votes cast; only his fellow PPP standard-bearer Herman Young in South Leeward secured a higher per-centage vote, 82.8 percent, but Joshua secured the largest number of votes, 1,614 to Young's 1,420; the PPP's Joachim won 1,515 votes or 50.8 percent in North Leeward.

The individual performances from others of the defunct Eighth Army paled in comparison to the election results for Joshua and Young. These per-formances, in summary, were as follows: 1) George Charles in Central Wind-ward, 44 percent of the votes validly cast; 2) Rudolph Baynes in Kingstown, 43 percent of the votes; 3) Julian Baynes in St. George, 33 percent of the votes; and 4) Clive Tannis in the Grenadines, 42 percent of the votes, beating Cyril Mitchell by 23 votes; and Levi Latham in South Windward, who had earlier won a by-election in that constituency due to the resignation , and migration overseas, of Evans Morgan, was returned with 46 percent of the votes.

Although, the PPP's performance in the 1954 elections was commend-able, there was still much work to be done for the Joshua-led PPP-FIAWU combination to become dominant. The loss of Edmund Joachim's seat in a by-election to Sam Slater in North Leeward was a temporary set-back for the PPP. Similarly, the mercurial meanderings and political gymnastics of Herman Young in South Leeward were to cause him to cease his alliance with Joshua's PPP. Thus, in the immediate post-1954 legislature, Joshua was again standing largely alone. Apart from his strong personal base in North Windward and North Leeward, there was still much political ground to cover. In Kingstown, the PPP candidate in the 1954 elections secured a second-place to Rudolph

Baynes with 33 percent of the votes. In St. George, the PPP candidate, Conrad Forbes, secured a third-place with 26 percent of the votes; in Central Windward, the PPP candidate, Charles Griffith, placed second to George Charles, in a five-man race, with 21 percent of the vote; in South Windward, the PPP candidate was clobbered in a five-way race; and in the Grenadines, the PPP candidate, Gabriel Forde, placed third in a four-man contest with 10 percent of the votes.

In several constituencies, the PPP had poor quality candidates. The 1954 general elections, however, saw the first female candidate in St. Vincent; the path-breaker was Floris Simmonds, an Independent candidate in the Grenadines who received 84 votes, or 7 percent of the valid votes cast. Between then and the 2015 general elections, over a spread of 17 general elections, there have been only 32 female candidates, a mere 13 of whom were fielded by major political parties. It is a matter on which there will be further discussion in this volume.

Despite Joshua's relative isolation in the immediate post-1954 Legislative Council, the general elections showed that his PPP-FIAWU represented, though unevenly, the major political force of the working people on the ground. He was possessed of a significant, and growing, base upon which to build dominance in the labour movement and national politics.

Shortly after the 1954 general elections, Joshua was to renew the trade union battle with the planters. In the period 1954 to 1956, Joshua widened his organisational effort to embrace all 16 estates in North and Central Windward (Fancy, Owia, Orange Hill, Waterloo, Tourama, Lot 14, Rabacca, Mt. Bentinck, Grand Sable, Mt. William, Gorse, Colonarie, Belle Vue, Mt. Grennan, Sans Souci, and Union) amounting to over 10,000 acres of land. Mt. Bentinck Estates, though, were still his primary target. His electoral performance in North Windward in 1954 had seen an increase and consolidation of his support from his 1951 electoral score of 63 percent of the votes to 79 percent. His residence in Georgetown, close to Mt. Bentinck, placed him in daily contact with the workers on the estates there.

In late January 1955 there was a general stoppage of work at Mt. Bentinck Estates. On behalf of the FIAWU, Joshua informed the management by letter, on February 1, 1955, of this occurrence and called for union recognition and collective bargaining status. For over two years since the FIAWU had originally written Mt. Bentinck Estates on December 5, 1952, the management, with the connivance of the colonial government, had been stalling. Finally, on February 3, 1955, the management replied to Joshua's latest missive with an equivocating stance that "the question of the recognition of your union can only be considered if and when you can establish that the majority of the sugar workers...are members of your union." On February 4, 1955, as Joshua had indicated two years earlier, he replied that he was prepared to submit to the Labour Department his union lists to show that FIAWU controlled 75 percent of the workers if Mt. Bentinck Estates also submitted their workers' list for cross-checking. The management obliged but FIAWU failed to do so despite several reminders.

The FIAWU's tactical non-submission of its membership lists at Mt. Bentinck Estates arose seemingly from four considerations: 1) The management's knowledge of the workers who were enrolled as members of the union raised workers' fears of victimisation, and perhaps dismissal; 2) Joshua did not trust the Labour Department to be impartial in the discharge of its statutory duties; 3) Joshua was convinced that the management and shareholders had no intention to recognise the union through the normal industrial relations processes; and 4) the union leadership was satisfied that only strikes, work stoppages, mass pressure, and political strength would bring the management and shareholders to the bargaining table.

So, the FIAWU-PPP ramped up their on-the-ground agitation for several months focussing on immediate material demands. On December 10, 1955, the FIAWU circulated a document to the owners of all the estates in North Windward, including at Mt. Bentinck, and adjacent ones in Central Windward, with a list of worker demands relating to increased wages, improved conditions of work, the illegal employment of juveniles, and union recognition. Only Mt. Bentinck Estates replied. On December 19, 1955, the union again made its demands. The management of Mt. Bentinck Estates answered evasively. It claimed that the business was burdened with high capital expenditure costs due to the modernisation of the sugar factory; and that it was awaiting the *Report of the Commission of Enquiry into Wages and Other Conditions of Employment of Agricultural Workers in St. Vincent*, headed by Sir Clement Malone, which was due in early 1956.

The management's submission about the capital costs of factory modernisation was intended to deflect the union's wages demands, because, objectively, as the Jolly Report of April 1955 on the sugar industry had pointed out, *"the improvement was made without any real deprivation of the shareholders"*. In fact, the increased capital costs were borne by the workers, the peasants who supplied sugar cane, and the Government which gave Mt. Bentinck Estates a guaranteed production subsidy. As the Jolly Report explained, the shareholders found it convenient to plough back into the business some of its profits in capital expenditure, because if it had declared more than eight percent dividends, in all probability the government subsidy would have been withdrawn.

Between December 19, 1955, and the beginning of March 1956, none of the union's wage claims and other demands was met. Interestingly, the Malone Report on agricultural wages was published in January 1956, but the estates were still unmoved.

Meanwhile, Joshua was focussed in seeking to strengthen his political position. At the meeting of the Legislative Council on November 3, 1956, in attempting to forge better linkages between the labour movement and the peasantry, Joshua moved a motion, successfully, which called on the government to protect the farmers and workers, who were land tenants, from arbitrary dispossession by landlords. In the legislature, he was building solid ties with Sam Slater and Levi Latham who were very supportive of him on a number of motions concerning the betterment of the working people. Julian Baynes, who had earlier been a supporter of Joshua, distanced himself from Joshua due to personality differences; Baynes moved swiftly to the St. Vincent Labour Party, formed in 1955 under the leadership of Robert Milton Cato, an accomplished lawyer and public personality.

Political figures, established and aspiring, were already positioning themselves, from early 1956, for the 1957 general elections. These elections were due to take place under reformed constitutional arrangements which would provide for an embryonic ministerial system and therefore greater devolved authority to the popularly-elected representatives.

So, on March 8, 1956, in the self-proclaimed gradualist "preparation" of local leaders for Westminster-style democracy, typical of British colonialism, the authorities in "the mother country" directed the introduction of the ministerial system of government in a minimalist form. The elected representatives, more favoured by the colonial administration, namely, George Charles, Herman Young, Rudolph Baynes, and Clive Tannis, were appointed as ministers, having served as veritable apprentices in the pre-ministerial "committee system". These hand-picked legislators, who were now fully entrenched in the colonial system, found themselves not only in opposition to Joshua but increasingly in opposition, however articulated, to much of the legitimate demands of the labour movement. On March 28, 1956, Joshua was to denounce them in the legislature as "agents of the Crown".

While the quartet of legislators (Charles, Rudolph Baynes, Young, and Tannis) preoccupied themselves, in tandem with the colonial officials under the Administrator, with the elemental public administration of the colonial system through the restrictive, embryonic ministerial system, Ebenezer Joshua and his PPP-FIAWU political machine were at work on the ground. Accordingly, he promptly issued in early March 1956, a summary of workers' demands on the North Windward estates as follows: 1) The institution of collective bargaining; 2) "that the principles of trade unionism be accepted as the only decent means of fair play and moral justice for workers in the employment of the Mt. Bentinck Estates and kindred ones"; 3) a 30 percent wage increase; and 4) backpay from 1952.

The owners of the estates did not budge at all. They had never truly embraced the idea of the unionisation of their workers; colonialism's formal legislative imprimatur of trade unions from the minimalist framework of 1933 to a modern and relevant regulatory system, formally adopted in 1950, had yet to prompt or sway the planters to embrace trade unionism as a worthwhile feature of industrial relations between management and workers. Indeed, if any confirmation was needed of this, E.A.C. Hughes, a distinguished lawyer and a then director of Mt. Bentinck Estates, admitted to the author in an interview on September 1, 1970, that "the attitudes of the employers then, like several now, was an unenlightened one." He expressed the view that the shareholders of Mt. Bentinck Estates were opposed to trade unionism because they felt that it meant increased wages and a probable loss in profits for them. In all likelihood, too, their sense of class superiority made them bristle at the thought that they had to negotiate wages with workers whom they were "favouring" with jobs; probably, also, ethnic considerations and the whole weight of dead generations of the plantocracy weighed heavily on their brains and their emotions.

On March 11, 1956, Joshua called out the workers on all eleven North Windward estates on strike in relation to the earlier demands. Within one week, the estate workers other than those at Mt. Bentinck and the five "Orange Hill" estates (Rabacca, Tourama, Lot 14, Waterloo, and Orange Hill) were back at work. From March 11, 1956 until May 19, 1956 — over two months — the workers at the "Orange Hill" estates and both factory and estate workers at Mt. Bentinck remained on strike; the militancy of the workers centred at Mt. Bentinck. It was the largest and most eventful strike in the history of St. Vincent.

One thousand labourers on all eleven estates participated in the earlier period of the strike; the bulk were from the "Orange Hill" estates and Mt. Bentinck. Violence featured prominently in the strike and was widespread in North and Central Windward. Indeed, in some areas, many workers were forced to withdraw their labour involuntarily because of the violence. According to contemporaneous reports, the police both initiated violence and responded to worker-instigated violence. Joshua alleged in the Legislative Council both on March 28, 1956, and June 06, 1956, that the police under the leadership of Colonel Sydney Anderson, chief of police, over-reacted to what was initially a peaceful strike action; he insisted that the peaceful picketers were beaten by the police for absolutely no lawful reason.

Two weeks or so into the strike, on March 24, 1956, the Labour Commissioner, in attempting to settle the dispute, informed the FIAWU that on the issue of union recognition, the management of Mt. Bentinck Estates would concede only if they could ascertain the union's strength at the workplace through an examination of the membership register. The Labour Commissioner claimed that Mt. Bentinck Estates had informed him that:

> *The continuous incitement of workers to strike without making prior demands, and the repeated vilification and abuse of the Company's officers...are not calculated to impress the Company with that stability and responsibility of the union which is so essential to good labour relations."*

Clearly, it was not true that the FIAWU had not made "prior demands"; these were made with regularity since 1952. In a special meeting of the legislature, on March 28, 1956, summoned to discuss the strike, Joshua criticised the labour commissioner as "weak and vacillating!" Moreover, he accused the Colonial Administrator of "cunning tricks dating back to 1952 to deny workers of trade union rights". He contended also that the violence which occurred was triggered by the Chief of Police, Colonel Anderson, who had attempted to interrupt a political meeting at Georgetown while Mrs. Ivy Joshua (wife of Ebenezer Joshua) was urging people to keep the peace. In Joshua's words: "Anderson came to the area as if he were drugged with morphine, armed with a platoon of men with fixed bayonets and rifles, terrorising people." The labour leader accused the planters of wanting to take his people back to slavery. Charles, once a trade unionist, but now in opposition to Joshua and the workers, argued in the legislature, on the same day — March 28th — that if the workers "do not want to work, they should behave themselves, go home and do not cause trouble." It was evident that this once progressive leader had been won over to the side of the ruling class, perhaps through the glittering mirage of his embryonic ministerial office.

The Administrator, recognising both the gravity of the situation and the failure of the labour commissioner as interlocutor, took on the official role of mediator. On April 16, 1956, the Administrator issued proposals agreed to by all parties for settlement of the dispute. The crux of the proposals revolved around three issues: 1) that the union arrange for an immediate start-up of work as is necessary for preliminary factory work, and that the company agree not to lock-out these workers; 2) that the company submit a list of its employees; and 3) the FIAWU forward the register of its unionised members employed by the company.

In keeping with these proposals, Joshua immediately called the relevant section of the workers for work resumption at the factory. On April 18, 1956 E.A.C. Hughes, a director and lawyer of the company, wrote to the Administrator informing him that "no further discussion can be contemplated until there was a complete return of workers." The management had thus breached the faith; the Mt. Bentinck Estates also claimed that although the agreement document was negotiated, it was not ratified. Instead of a partial return of workers as originally proposed, Mt. Bentinck Estates demanded a full resumption. On April 25, 1956, the FIAWU called on Mt. Bentinck Estates to clarify their position in forty-eight hours or else face a reinstitution of strike action. The estates ignored the strike ultimatum.

On May 3, 1956, the company closed its factory and threatened to terminate operations for the year 1956. A day later, Hughes, in a letter to the Administrator, outlined three conditions for the resumption of operations: 1) the crop will commence as soon as practicable on "Malone wages"; 2) the FIAWU will give the Administrator an unconditional written guarantee that there will be no further stoppage of work by either field or factory workers for the current crop; and 3) the advance payment to sugar cane farmers will be reduced to BWI $9.00 per ton of cane, due to the expected adverse production yield because of the delay in harvesting. The management was taking a very tough stance so as to force the strike-weary workers back to work.

A number of issues arises from the proposals negotiated by the Administrator on April 16, 1956, their subsequent rejection by the estates' management, and the counter proposals of May 4, 1956. First, it appears as though Joshua was eager for a settlement from which he could salvage some sort of victory. The alternative was to keep the strike going in the context of uncertainty as to whether the strikers could have held out much longer. The Administrator's proposals were clearly favourable to the management in that the substantial questions of a wage increase and back-pay from 1952 were not included, while the union had to ensure the return of the factory workers. All that the management was required to do was to submit its list of workers as a prelude to a possible recognition of the workers.

The rejection of the Administrator's pro-management proposals by the Mt. Bentinck Estates indicated their desire to humiliate Joshua, for this was in fact the only reasonable inference to be made from its own counter-proposals. To suggest that a trade union give a written "blank cheque" of no-strike for the remainder of the sugar-cane season was to take away from the union its only credible weapon against management abuses. In addition, to reduce the advanced price of the sugar-cane paid by the Mt. Bentinck factory to farmers, mainly peasants, as a result of the workers' strike, was an attempt to drive a wedge between peasants and workers, a prospect Joshua was anxious to avoid.

Thus, on May 11, 1956, Joshua wrote to the Governor of the Windward Islands, resident in Grenada and who possessed constitutional authority over the Colonial Administrator in St. Vincent, requesting a meeting. On May 12th, the reply came that such a meeting was not possible "until your union makes it clear publicly that it disassociates itself entirely from acts of violence which are taking place in the Georgetown and Mt. Bentinck areas." The government was also adopting a tough line, having recognised that a significant number of workers were anxious to get back to work. In fact many workers had already returned to work on some of the estates. In a profound sense Joshua was boxed in politically. It would have been politically damaging for him to denounce any union activities which allegedly occasioned the violence. The strike, already two months in duration, was sapping the political energy and meagre resources of workers who were unaccustomed to such prolonged and intense political actions. Thus, recognising the inability of his union and its members to hold out much longer, he made a defiant concession, from a weakened position, by way of a circular from the FIAWU to the workers on May 12, 1956, urging them to resume work if they were willing to do so, on the condition of no victimisation. One week later, there was full resumption at Mt. Bentinck, and the most eventful strike in the history of the colony had ended.

On the said May 12, 1956, the planters' press, *The Vincentian*, ramped up its critique of Joshua. In a sharp denunciation of political unionism, this newspaper editorialised, hysterically, that the admixture of trade unionism and politics was a more serious threat than communism. So consumed with anti-Joshua bile was the editor of the planters' mouth-piece that he offered no reflection of the danger to the working people of a state apparatus doing the bidding of the planter-merchant elite and colonialism in concert with some legislators who strayed from representing their own constituents' interests. The editorial labelled the FIAWU deceitful, when in fact the estate-owners who were employing deceit, chicanery, and hypocrisy in their continued sub-jection of working people.

Having been pressured into directing the striking workers back to work, Joshua sought on June 7, 1956, in the Legislative Council, to regain the initiative by calling for the adoption of a motion to institute a commission of enquiry into the strike. With the support of only Julian Baynes, Samuel Slater, and Levi Latham, his motion was rejected by the combined majority of three nominated members, two officials, and George Charles and Clive Tannis; the two other elected legislators and members of the Executive Council, Rudolph Baynes and Herman Young, were absent — out of the country. Such a commission, undoubtedly, would have probed into police violence and more generally, the circumstances of the strike.

Joshua was resolved that out of any setbacks in the legislature and in his union battles, he would seek to advance the workers' cause always. He was not daunted; he continued to thunder in the legislature, to organise and mobilise on the ground. On November 1, 1956, in the Legislative Council, he advertised his political strength: "I am not here in this Council to represent a handful of people. I am a leader of labour and hope to be a leader of socialism."

Joshua was consolidating his political work nationally, especially in cer-tain critical areas of North Windward, North Leeward, Central Windward, South Windward, St. George, Kingstown, and even in the Grenadines. His FIAWU in 1956 pushed for recognition as the workers' bargaining agent at the electricity plant in Kingstown, and threatened to strike if the manage-ment refused to comply. Promptly, the management informed the workers of the penal section of the Public Utility Ordinance which prescribed a fine of BWI $100.00 or a maximum term of imprisonment of three months or both, should a strike occur without adequate formal notice. A mere suggestion of a strike at the electricity plant brought the police at the plant to interrogate and intimidate workers. In the legislature on November 1, 1956, Joshua sought unsuccessfully to garner support for the repeal of the penal section of the said Ordinance. The political strategy of Joshua was clear: Build support, politically, nation-wide; strengthen the PPP-FIAWU in, and around, the rural estates;

fortify support in Kingstown and command vital services such as electricity and the Kingstown port.

The militant activism of Joshua's PPP-FIAWU inspired workers to promote and defend their interests, even where the FIAWU was not providing leadership. Accordingly, before the end of 1956 a number of relatively minor industrial disputes arose. For example, there was a stoppage of work at the Cane Grove estate for better conditions of work which lasted for eight days, involving eighty workers; the workers resumed work only after an agreement was signed between the estate management and the workers' representatives. In neighbouring Peniston, the workers on the estate there went on a one-day strike in connection with task-work which they considered too onerous, and back-pay as recommended by the Malone Report. Here, the workers pressed their case without a recognised leader; it was only after the estate management reduced the task-work and agreed to pay the back-pay that the workers returned to work. In Kingstown, the employees at the planters' press, The Vincentian Publishing Company, and the waterfront workers went on strike for increased wages. At the hydro-electric plant, the workers demanded increased wages, but as employees in an essential service, their case was put before an arbitration tribunal.

It was not only the unskilled and semi-skilled workers who engaged in industrial action; the teachers also did. In early October, 1956, four hundred and forty-five primary school teachers went on a three-week strike in support of claim for higher wages.

With so much dissension in the colony, the *ancien regime* appeared unable to tackle the extant problems of poverty, unemployment, low productivity, economic malaise, an oppressive plantation system, poor housing and health facilities, restricted educational opportunities, terrible physical infrastructure, and an unrepresentative system of government; it offered, too, no credible hope for the future. The colonial Governor, Administrator, and the co-opted ministerial occupants from among the elected legislators were essentially marking time. The budget of October 1956 came and went without popular expectation or hope of any significant improvement.

But before the end of 1956, the colonial regime had one repressive loose-end to tie up with a silly prosecution of Joshua before the law courts. On the very day that the strike at Mt. Bentinck Estates ended on May 19, 1956, the police had raided Joshua's premises and seized a bundle of magazines and newspapers which the government considered to be "subversive" and thus prohibited; they also took away personal documents of Joshua. Among the seized literature were *The Soviet Weekly, For A Lasting Peace, Thunder* (a publication of the People's Progressive Party (PPP) led by Cheddi Jagan in British Guiana), and *Caribbean News,* which Joshua dubbed as "reactionary". In November 1956, Joshua was found guilty of having prohibited literature in his possession and was fined £50 sterling. He appealed; in July 1957, he won his appeal.

As the year 1957 opened, political aspirants were preparing themselves for the impending general elections which were later held on September 12, 1957. Shortly before the general elections, Herman Young and George Charles launched the People's Liberation Movement (PLM) under the former's leadership.

In these elections, three parties contested: the PPP under Joshua's leadership; the St. Vincent Labour Party (SVLP), founded in 1955, and led by Milton Cato; and the PLM led by Herman Young. The PPP contested all eight seats; the SVLP contests six seats; and the PLM, five seats. There were five independent candidates, one each in five constituencies.

There were several interesting electoral contests in particular constituencies. In Central Windward, Joshua decided to take on Charles, his political nemesis after the 1951 general elections onwards. Joshua decided to leave his safe North Windward seat for his wife, Ivy Joshua, who contested for the first time. In South Leeward, two political leaders clashed: Herman Young of the PLM and the 42-year old lawyer, Milton Cato of the SVLP. In Kingstown, a youthful land surveyor, Stinson Campbell, with much political promise, ran on the PPP ticket against the stalwart, Rudolph Baynes of the SVLP who had subjected the titan, George Mc Intosh, to electoral defeats in the 1951 and 1954 elections.

Of interest, too, in the 1957 general elections were the defeat of incumbents from 1951 to 1954: Rudolph Baynes in Kingstown, Julian Baynes in St. George, and George Charles in Central Windward. The other five incumbents won: Joshua in Central Windward, Samuel Slater (Independent) in North Leeward, Herman Young in South Leeward, Levi Latham (on the PPP ticket) in South Windward, and Clive Tannis (Independent) in the Grenadines. The new elected representatives were: Ivy Joshua (PPP) in North Windward, Afflick Haynes (PPP) in St. George, and Stinson Campbell (PPP) in Kingstown.

In Central Windward, Joshua defeated Charles by a majority of 1,618 votes (or 61 percent of the votes) to 896 votes (34 percent). In a three-way fight in South Leeward, Herman Young (1,151 votes or 41 percent) triumphed over Milton Cato (723 votes or 30 percent) and George King of the PPP (568 votes or 23 percent). In Kingstown, Campbell garnered 1,698 votes (62 percent) to Baynes' 1031 votes (38 percent); and in North Windward, Ivy Joshua scored the highest absolute number of votes, 2,223 and the highest percentage, 83.5 percent, of votes of any candidate in the 1957 general elections. She thus became the first woman to be elected as a parliamentary representative in the history of St. Vincent and the Grenadines.

At the general level, the elections' results in 1957 showed that the incumbent legislators who stood askance from Joshua and the popular working people's struggles in the 1954-1957 period performed worse in their constituencies than in 1954. Let us take some critical examples: Charles' percentage vote fell in Central Windward from 44 percent in 1954 to 34 percent in 1957; Young's share of the vote in South Leeward declined sharply from 83 percent in 1954 to 47 percent in 1957; Samuel Slater's vote in North Leeward fell from the 1954 by-election of 52 percent to 43 percent in 1957. Julian Baynes' vote in St. George in 1954 remained basically the same in 1957: 33 percent and 36 percent respectively. Only Clive Tannis of the anti-Joshua group increased significantly his percentage vote in the Grenadines from 42 percent of the valid votes cast in 1954 to 57 percent in 1957, reflective, in part, of the political peculiarities of the Grenadines.

On the other hand, the sole incumbent elected representative, who stayed in solidarity with Joshua, Levi Latham in South Windward, enhanced his electoral performance from 46 percent of the vote in 1954 to 55 percent in 1957 on a PPP ticket. The new-comers who were elected on the PPP ticket did quite well.

Overall, the 1957 general elections were a huge success for Joshua's PPP. In 1954, the PPP had secured 40 percent of the popular vote (6,193 votes) with three seats (Young deserted shortly thereafter; and Joachim in North Leeward lost by way of a by-election). In 1957, PPP won 49 percent of the vote (9,836 votes) and five seats. Joshua was thus called upon to form the government under the ministerial system and took the main ministerial position for elected legislators at the time, the Ministry of Trade and Production. The portfolios of finance, the police, and the public service were still in the hands of colonial officialdom under the Administrator and Governor; the British government retained responsibility for defence and foreign affairs.

In its first electoral outing, the SVLP under Milton Cato secured the second highest aggregate number of votes in the 1957 elections: 3,912 votes or 19.4 percent, but it won no seats. Its best performing candidate was the redoubtable entrepreneur, Edmund Joachim in North Leeward, with 1,134 votes or 38 percent of the valid votes cast; Joachim had been the PPP's candidate in that constituency in 1954. The second best performer was Rudolph Baynes in Kingstown with a score of 1,031 votes or 38 percent. Cato, himself, with 723 votes (30 percent), lost to Herman Young in South Leeward. Shortly after the elections, Young effectively folded up his PLM, which won, in the aggregate 3,029 votes or some 15 percent, of the votes, and joined Cato's SVLP as its deputy political leader. Latham also soon left the PPP and joined the SVLP. Two victorious candidates in 1957 on independent tickets, Slater and Tannis, were to join the PPP in the 1957-1961 period. In total, independent candidates won 3,332 votes (15 percent) in the 1957 general elections.

The maturation of the competitive political system was in evidence by the time of the 1957 elections. In the 1951 elections, there was an electoral umbrella called the Eighth Army of Liberation which was a convenient banner for a group of young anti-colonial personalities. The Eighth Army quickly fell apart. In the 1954 general elections, the PPP was the only political party, having been formed in early 1952; it survived and prospered by the 1957 general elections. The PLM was hastily gathered as an electoral vehicle for the 1957 electoral contest but it soon fell apart. The SVLP, a moderate social democratic organisation, founded in 1955, built itself slowly over two years to become by 1957 the second most populous party in the country. The 1957 general elections, and the events following, placed the SVLP under Cato's leadership on the path to be the major political competitor to the PPP.

Cato, one of the central founders of the SVLP in 1955, was born in 1915 in St. Vincent; he was educated at the St. Vincent Boys' Grammar School from 1928 to 1933. From his early years he evinced an interest in law and articled to a barrister/solicitor in Kingstown. Before he commenced his formal study of law in 1945 at the Middle Temple Inn of Court in London, he joined the First Canadian Army; he attained the rank of sergeant and saw active service in Europe. In 1948, Cato was called to the bar at Middle Temple in London. On his return to St. Vincent and the Grenadines, he opened his private law practice and involved himself in many civic and sporting entities before taking the political plunge in national politics in 1955 with the formation of the SVLP. He became chairman of the Kingstown Town Board in 1953 and was a member thereof from 1955 to 1959. From very early, a strong personality, measured and patriotic shone through, grounded in a love for people. For the next 27 years until his retirement from active politics in 1984 he was a towering figure in Vincentian politics and the major political rival in the 1957-1974 period to Ebenezer Joshua.

CHAPTER IV

POLITICAL UNIONISM: PPP–FIAWU (1957-1963) FIRST YEARS IN GOVERNMENT

Joshua's emergence as the leader of the popularly-elected members of a colonial government which had them in a veritable political straight-jacket, posed for him the problem of reconciling conflicting demands and balancing criss-crossing pressures in this peculiar political system. There were high expectations from his supporters but he knew that he was possessed of little actual governmental power, constitutional authority, or access to resources to deliver material benefits for them. To be sure, he had a measure of authority but that was not consistent with his obligations to be responsive to his people; he would often, if not inevitably, be held responsible for the colonial government's acts or omissions and be blamed when things go awry or wrong but not acclaimed for that which was commendable, even if he were the principal architect of the good.

It is not often appreciated today, and perhaps even less then, that Joshua's elected team had no real decision-making authority in the portfolios of finance, the public service, police, defence, and external affairs. At the Executive Council he and his political colleagues could persuade the Administrator and officials, he could petition the Governor or the British Secretary of State for the Colonies on this or that matter from his perch as the popularly-elected leader, but he was essentially, at times, supplicant, interlocutor, advocate. Admittedly, he and his colleagues were adorned with ministerial oversight or portfolio allocations of trade and production, education, health, social services, communications and works, but they had little means with which to effect meaningful accomplishments for their constituents and the nation as a whole.

Joshua, therefore, devised a fascinating "modus operandi" of being in government and in opposition, at the same time, as it conveniently or appropriately suited him. This was almost a species of political schizophrenia which popularly-elected leaders in executive positions had to endure in British colonial regimes in their evolution or transition to responsible ministerial government under internal self-government or formal constitutional independence. Joshua had many examples to learn from in the historical experiences of Jamaica, Trinidad and Tobago, Barbados, and British Guiana, and from the contemporary political evolutions in the neighbouring Windward and Leeward Islands. Undoubtedly, the experience of British Guiana would have been fresh in his mind: In 1953, the British Government suspended the constitution of British Guiana and reverted to direct colonial rule when the popularly-elected government of Cheddi Jagan's People's Progressive Party (PPP) — fraternal party of Joshua's PPP — ran afoul of the colonial strictures in its pursuance of a radical reformist and nationalist agenda. Later, in 1962, Joshua would also have had cause to mull over the fate of the populist Eric Gairy in Grenada when his government, within the constitutional frame of colonial containment, was removed, also by way of a suspension of the constitution, albeit for different reasons than in British Guiana. Joshua, thus, throughout his stint as popular leader in an Executive, within a colonial regime, from 1957 to 1967, under various forms of constitutional liberalisation, resolved to thread carefully while always pushing the boundaries of his colonial straight-jacket.

Joshua and his ministerial colleagues had to manoeuvre themselves, too, within a colonial state machinery which had its own ethos, ideology, routinization and rationalisation, conservatism, and arcane practices rooted in the realism and traditions of colonial power. Undergirding all this were the strength of British imperialism, the monopoly capitalist system, and their linkages with the local planter-merchant elite.

At the inter-personal level within the colonial bureaucracy, the civil service — from the Colonial Administrator down to the local bureaucrats — were anxious not to have any of their authority eroded by a political and trade union demagogue — the terms in which they saw Joshua. The state functionaries represented interests to which Joshua and the working class were historically opposed. Yet due to the limiting nature of the constitutional arrangements and the under-developed, though growing, political consciousness and organisational coherence of the working people, Joshua was constrained to acquiesce in many of the decisions, approaches, and demands of the colonial bureaucracy.

Tactical manoeuvring in, or strategic acquiescence to, or even agreement with, the colonial state by Joshua and his colleagues were ways to find political space in quest of achieving gains, however limited or partial, for their constituents. Oft-times they found it necessary, prudent, or even expedient to oppose the colonial apparatus in order to sustain, credibly, their links with the working people.

Electoral promises by Joshua and his PPP were not easy to be fulfilled. To begin with, some of the promises of dramatic improvements in job creation and wages, education, health, housing, and physical infrastructure, water and electricity, were far-fetched. But even modest enhancements were constrained not only by the nature of the state apparatuses themselves but also on account of the undeveloped nature of the economy, the plantation system, production and exchange relations, and the scarcity of resources. Given Joshua's history of denouncing both the colonial administrators and the planter-merchant elite, he was viewed with grave suspicion by those with whom he felt obliged to fashion a productive relationship in order to deliver practical, uplifting results for his people. It was a political tight-rope to walk; it required immense political skill, judgment, clarity of purpose, and organisational solidarity, with and among the working people, to make sustainable advances.

In attempting, for example, to provide jobs for his supporters, Joshua utilised whatever flexibility was available at the Public Works Department and other state agencies. But this approach, which oft-times meant a manipulation of the colonial bureaucracy and re-channelling of resources towards the working people, brought Joshua in conflict with the civil service. The civil service responded, from time-to-time, by "sabotaging" him. Joshua, on the other had "terrorised" them verbally in the public square, particularly in the Kingstown Market Square at his regular Wednesday night public meetings.

The concepts of civil servants' "sabotage" of popular labour leaders in government and the verbal "terror" in response on the political hustings were first introduced into the literature on Caribbean politics by Professor Archibald Singham in his 1968 classic, *The Hero and the Crowd in a Colonial Polity*, in which he analysed, among other things, the perennial conflicts between Eric Gairy and the public servants in colonial Grenada in the 1950s and 1960s. "Sabotage" involved, among other things, procrastination and undue delays in accomplishing tasks, frequent shifting of personnel including at the populist leader's ministerial office, withholding or denying information, misleading the government minister, and actually "losing" or hiding files. Verbal "terror" was overblown, and often unfair or inaccurate, critique of this or that senior or junior public servant whom the populist leader considered to be deserving of his public wrath; sometimes this verbal "terror" was contrived, or even hypocritical, for effect upon those who were listening. In a small, face-to-face society like St. Vincent, public servants and their families would thus suffer verbal abuse in public places, from the leader's political supporters. It was unpleasant and wrong all-around; it was very debilitating to public administration, social and inter-personal relations among persons who were all nationals of St. Vincent. Meanwhile, colonialism still ruled the political roost even as the people bickered and quarrelled unnecessarily among themselves to their own detriment. These problems inhered in the task of a working people's leader seeking to grapple not only with bureaucratic complexities but also with the multiple contradictions which faced him as a member of the Executive Council and a holder of ministerial office in the colonial state. Such problems were to remain constant, at varying levels of intensity, throughout Joshua's tenure in office, 1957 to 1967.

Ostensibly, due to the pressure of governmental work, Joshua resigned as President-General of the FIAWU within months of becoming a minister of government. He was replaced by Rennie Small, with Joshua's nephew, Leroy Commissiong, as Secretary-General. Joshua took for himself the position of Deputy President-General of his union. In an interview with the author on August 06, 1970, Joshua asserted that he had recognised that a conflict of interest would likely result if he maintained both his ministerial and union leadership roles. It is unlikely that Joshua had imbibed the colonial doctrine of the necessity and desirability of a separation of trade unionism and politics. In all probability, it was one of Joshua's tactical manoeuvres in his interface with the colonial state apparatus.

Despite his relinquishing of the top spot, formally, in the FIAWU, Joshua's influence in the union remained supreme. On February 11, 1958, the first test of Joshua's potentially "conflicting roles" came to a head when the FIAWU's members who were working at the Kingstown Banana Depot went on strike for higher wages. Joshua, as Minister of Trade, Production and Labour intervened to settle the dispute. *The Vincentian* of February 15, 1958, reported the he was "most helpful in arranging a settlement".

By 1958, the FIAWU was the largest and most influential trade union in St. Vincent with a membership of 2,780, centred mainly in the Kingstown, Chateaubelair-Richmond, and Georgetown areas. At Mt. Bentinck Estates Company Limited, in 1958, the FIAWU was finally recognised as the bargaining agent for the estate and factory workers. This recognition came on March 3, 1958, with little trade union pressure. Evidently, the governmental linkage of the PPP-FIAWU persuaded the management and shareholders to recognise the union. E.A.C. Hughes, a senior director of the company, informed the author in an interview on September 16, 1970, that had union recognition not been accorded, economic concessions of significance to the company granted by the government, including a subsidy, were in possible jeopardy of being withdrawn. The pre-1957 issue of ascertaining the extent of union membership among the company's workers as a necessary prerequisite to union recognition was discarded or ignored by the company's shareholders. To the owners of Mr. Bentinck Estates, the political strength of Joshua and the influence of his governmental authority were highly persuasive or even conclusive in 1957 in their decision-making, even as the two-month strike in 1956 by Joshua's FIAWU was of little moment! Interesting lessons were being taught to, but not necessarily learnt by, the leadership of the working people.

Shortly after the September 1957 general elections, Herman Young's PLM and Milton Cato's SVLP were moving towards an amalgamation of their political forces. In those elections, the SVLP and PLM candidates won, in the aggregate, 6,941 votes or 34.5 percent of the valid votes cast, with the SVLP winning 19.4 percent of this total and the PLM 15.06 percent. The PLM won one seat; and the SVLP won none. It surely could not have been lost on Herman Young in South Leeward that he won with only 47 percent of the vote in a three-way fight; and Cato of the SVLP on his first electoral outing got 30 percent of the vote. A joinder of both in South Leeward would put Young in an impregnable position. Twenty-two years later, on August 27, 1970, in an interview with the author, Young averred that, in the merger between PLM and SVLP, it was decided to retain the name SVLP for the united party because the psychological value of the word "labour" could be easily exploited at the polls. But the party had no "labour" arm or trade union wing.

The truth is that the core leadership of the SVLP was mainly middle-class, drawn from the professions and business with no links to trade unions. Still, it had a social democratic outlook lodged philosophically in a frame of a mixed economy led by a vibrant private sector. Cato's SVLP was a party of modernisation and reform; it was keen on orderly constitutional advance of a liberal-democratic cast; it was nationalist and regionalist in its orientation. It was non-communist, but not too keen on political labels. The instincts of Cato and the SVLP were pro-western but nevertheless saw the future of the region through the prism of Caribbean eyes albeit hugely influenced by Anglo-Saxon politics and culture. In 1957-1958, the party which had a greater claim to being a party of "labour" was Joshua's PPP. Still, Cato's SVLP social democratic ethos was informed by the reforming praxis of the British Labour Party, adopted and adapted to the circumstances of St. Vincent and the Caribbean. Cato's SVLP was in the reforming tradition, too, of George Mc Intosh. Objectively, the SVLP and Joshua's PPP though joined in competitive political battle in colonial St. Vincent, and demonstrating somewhat different approaches and emphases, were both in the social democratic tradition with impulses to advance the cause of the working people and St. Vincent as a whole.

The immediate post-1957 election fissures continued to attend the PPP in 1958 and 1959. As was noted earlier, Young and Latham left the PPP for the SVLP within months of the elections. At the same time, one of the two 1957 independent election victors, Slater, joined the PPP. The warm-up to the 1958 West Indies federal elections to elect two representatives from St. Vincent to the Federal House of Representatives, occasioned intra-PPP travails; Maurice Browne and George King who had been PPP's defeated candidates in the 1957 elections in North Leeward and South Leeward, respectively, resigned from the PPP; Browne and King expected to be the PPP's candidates in the federal elections. Joshua, however, wanted neither; he advanced the names of Alphaeus Allen and Leroy Adams, both of whom were eventually chosen as the PPP's candidates for the federal elections. In the event Adams won one of the two seats in the federal elections and Milton Cato, the other, for the SVLP.

In early 1959, the Secretary-General of FIAWU, Leroy Commissiong, accused his uncle, Ebenezer Joshua, of dictatorial attitudes in the union. Stinson Campbell, a promising legislator from the 1957 elections and the Minister of Communications and Works, Federal Parliamentarian Leroy Adams, and other former members of their Youth Movement including Anderson and Davidson of the Kingstown Town Board, supported Commissiong and left the PPP. Simultaneously, Commissiong resigned from the FIAWU.

Commissiong's charge was the culmination of a series of accusations directed a Joshua. His opponents had long claimed that his financial dealings with the union were suspect, but Joshua's frugal lifestyle was not one which was consistent with allegations of financial improprieties. More telling was the criticism that he had caused the PPP to join the conservative regional Democratic Labour Party (DLP) for the federal venture instead of the far more progressive West Indian Federal Labour Party (WIFLP) in which the leading lights were Norman Manley of Jamaica, Grantley Adams of Barbados, Eric Williams of Trinidad and Tobago, Robert Bradshaw of St. Kitts and Nevis, and Vere Cornwall Bird of Antigua and Barbuda. The anti-Joshua critics also pointed to his undemocratic, one-man governance of both the PPP and FIAWU; this contention had much merit since both organisations were creations of Joshua to whom his supporters gave personal allegiance.

Before the actual open dissension and break-away had occurred in the FI-AWU, there was evidence of internal factionalism. Both the secretary-general and the President-General Ivy Joshua (who had succeeded Rennie Small in 1959) had offices at different places and each behaved as the chief executive of the union. The Joshua-dominated union executive accused Commissiong of attempting to divide the union. The internal divisiveness clearly prompted Samuel Slater to remark at the 1959 May Day Rally that: "Disunity and rivalry in unions in any country cannot win the necessary rewards for the people."

For his part, Joshua vehemently denounced his detractors as self-serving and their high-minded comments as hypocritically pious moralising. He levelled the improbable charge that they had planned to overthrow him in both the party and the union, and that it was his discovery of their plot which irked them.

Shortly following the spate of resignations from the PPP-FIAWU, Commissiong, Adams and Campbell set about forming their own organisations. Interestingly, they did not seek the political cover of the SVLP; they branched out on their own. On June 4, 1959, the National Workers Union (NWU) was launched with Leroy Adams as president-general and Commissiong as general secretary. This union was to form the base of support for their proposed National Democratic Party (NDP). Both these organisations were short-lived. Within days of the formation of NWU, police raided its premises. Whether this raid was directed by Joshua or the Administrator Alexander F. Giles was uncertain but under the circumstances a reasonable suspicion arose that Joshua had a hand in it. It was ironic that the police harassment of the NWU was at least mildly reminiscent of a similar kind of police activity against Joshua between 1952 and 1957. One week after the registration of the NWU, the FIAWU protested in a letter to the Registrar of Trade Unions that because NWU officials had "stolen" certain FIAWU books, the NWU registration was, in effect, the legalisation of a crime.

Though still commanding mass majority support especially in the rural areas in North Windward, Central Windward, St. George, and North Leeward, Joshua's strength was challenged in the urban areas by the SVLP and the NWU. The NWU had organised the workers at the cotton ginnery but that venture collapsed in the flames of a mysterious fire which destroyed the ginnery. The NWU was also organising workers at the arrowroot association and the Kingstown Banana Depot in an attempt to dislodge the FIAWU. At the banana depot, there was a collective bargaining agreement with the FIAWU, so the management there stalled the efforts of the NWU. At the arrowroot association where the FIAWU also had a collective bargaining agreement, it was getting the worse of an arbitration award which arose from an earlier industrial relations dispute. Justice J.W.B. Henry had been appointed as the sole arbitrator in a dispute between the arrowroot association and the FIAWU. On June 14, 1959, the Chenery award was handed down. Chenery rejected two of FIAWU's claims that: 1) The monthly paid employees were represented by the FIAWU's under the terms of the collective bargaining agreement; and 2) the benefits negotiated by the union be available only to union members. Chenery also recommended a 12 percent wage increase but without the retro-activity which the union had demanded.

In the Legislative Council Joshua and his PPP were in some difficulty. Shortly after the 1957 general elections, Joshua's government was secure with a six-to-two majority: Ebenezer and Ivy Joshua, Stinson Campbell, Afflick Haynes, Levi Latham, and Clive Tannis for the PPP and two legislators in the opposition, Herman Young (PLM) and Samuel Slater (Independent). By 1958, Young had joined the SVLP, and Latham had followed suit, having decamped from the PPP; Tannis deserted the PPP a little later; Campbell resigned from the PPP in 1959 and sat as an Independent. The legislative scorecard was thus: PPP 4, SVLP 3, and one Independent. The nominated members now held the balance of legislative authority; they were from the planter-merchant class who historically opposed Joshua. Division again plagued the people's representatives and caused the people's agenda to be compromised. Recognising his precarious position, Joshua attempted to woo Young who had shifted political allegiances several times in eight years and was thus a candidate to hop and skip again, politically; the offer of a ministerial post to Young was tempting but he stayed put on this occasion.

The question of which faction should take control of the elected government arose as an urgent matter in light of the fact that a new constitution was due to come into force from January 1960, with the appointment for the first time of a chief minister and correspondingly greater devolved authority to the elected representatives in the executive council. Tannis, Campbell and even the mercurial Young saw themselves as possible candidates. In the end, Tannis blinked and re-joined the PPP. Thus, was Joshua appointed chief minister.

The workers and their trade unions — the labour movement generally — had a vested interest in the outcome of the political manoeuvring and factionalism. It is self-evident that in a small economy like St. Vincent, with relatively high unemployment and a highly influential state sector, directly or indirectly, working people and their unions invest significantly in competitive political outcomes. Quite sensibly, working people who support a political party in or out of government have historically, been disapproving of those who create disunity and factionalism. They know, historically, the benefits of having their party in government. Indeed, one of the organisational weaknesses of political unionism is precisely the dependence on the party-in-government to cocoon the affiliated union. Rather than build a resilient trade union of committed members, organisationally independent of partisan politics, some trade unions have preferred short-cuts by taking refuge in politics. Even so, the political influence, and more, were so pervasive that they were impactful.

Since the alleged Commissiong plot to take over the FIAWU, Joshua once more assumed formal control of the leadership of the union. Never again was Joshua to experiment with an arrangement of leading the union from behind; henceforth, he would trust no one else with the presidency of the FIAWU. Evidently, he had concluded that not even careful constitutional checks and balances in the union could safeguard sufficiently his over-riding interests from possible political assault by other persons with leadership ambitions in what he considered to be his trade union.

The year 1960 marked both Joshua's accession to the office of chief minister and a prelude to a two-party tussle for leadership of the mass movement which the forthcoming elections in 1961 would confirm. The SVLP was quite active up and down the country seeking to build its base nationwide. It was getting quite favourable responses in North Leeward, South Leeward, Kingstown, South Windward, and St. George, and substantial pockets of support in every other constituency. The SVLP was building slowly its constituency branches and had established a formidable women's league, the women's arm of the party. The SVLP, without a traditional trade union base, was infiltrating, mobilising, and organising public support through community-based organisations, civil society groups, business entities, churches, sporting and cultural organisations. It had developed solid influence in two white collar trade unions: The Teachers' Union, which was registered as a trade union in 1952; and the civil service association, in existence since 1942, but which was registered as a trade union in 1954. Although both of them were restrained in their union activism, the Teachers' Union carried out an effective strike in 1961. The civil service association became restive, too, and threatened supportive strike action.

The SVLP was drawing support from working people, the peasants, especially the small farmers in the emerging banana industry, the professionals, teachers, public servants, and business people who yearned for a less confrontational, more disciplined, sophisticated and modern politics grounded in social democracy, nationalism, and regionalism. The SVLP received support from the planter-merchant elite but perhaps moreso because of their historical antagonisms with Joshua rather than an account of any particular enthusiasm for the SVLP; in other words for the planters, it was a matter of any credible alternative in preference to Joshua's PPP.

The SVLP critiqued Joshua on his old-fashioned style of populist politics, the PPP's alleged lack of credible programmes, and on what it considered to be the PPP's inadequacy in government. The SVLP mocked Joshua and the PPP on their rhetoric of being a working class party but without results to match their utterances. Joshua countered about his party's successes in government especially regarding jobs, wages and working conditions, housing, education, health, and roads.

The economic situation was challenging for the PPP within the colonial regime. The arrowroot industry was suffering from marketing problems; the sugar industry was on the decline; and the cotton ginnery was still in ruins. In the vital agricultural sector, only the banana industry was buoyant. Unemployment was moderately high at an estimated 15.5 percent out of a labour force of 24,856 persons; significant under-employment, due to much part-time work only, was on the rise; and wages and salaries were among the lowest in the Eastern Caribbean.

But the economic problems were not the result of Joshua's government. The dominant agricultural sector was uncompetitive; both the arrowroot and sugar industries were riddled with inefficiencies and were planter-dominated. The international market was unforgiving of prolonged insufficiency of production and lack of competitiveness, even though there was a limited preference for sugar in the United Kingdom market. Bananas which were introduced as a possible growth industry in the mid-1950s had become the major industry in concert with the declining sugar and arrowroot commodities. In time, the banana industry was to become dominant; by 1992, the industry's highest point, nearly 80,000 tons of bananas, with a value of over EC $100 million, were exported to a highly protected and preferential market in the United Kingdom.

For nearly 50 years from the mid-1950s onwards, bananas were the country's principal commodity export; this development paralleled the collapse of the sugar industry and the decline of arrowroot, both with plantation dominance. The socio-economic and political impact of bananas cannot be overstated.

The growth of, and alterations within global capitalism, including enhanced competitiveness in international trade combined with a host of inter-related factors in the political economy of St. Vincent, precipitated the death knell of plantation agriculture, one of the central domestic pillars of colonial over-rule. These inter-connected factors in the national political economy included centrally: The rise of political democracy and constitutional decolonisation; the emergence and consolidation of trade unions and popular political parties; the gradual increase in secondary and post-secondary education among the young population; the decline of plantation crops, mainly sugar cane and arrowroot, and which required, too, planter-owned factories — in the case of sugar cane as a plantation crop, an actual demise came in 1962; the growth of services, including tourism as a major economic pillar; and the introduction and expansion of the banana industry between 1955 and 1992.

The banana industry in St. Vincent, and the other Windward Islands, did not require plantation agriculture in order to meet the requisites of the preferential market in the United Kingdom. Small farmers all over mainland St. Vincent were able to grow a crop, economically on small parcels of land, including lands in the valleys and on elevations not suitable for sugar cane cultivation. The variety of bananas, the "lacatan" was suitable on several grounds: The reaping of a plant crop — the first bunch of fruits — from one cluster of plants and ratoon crops, from the same cluster, at short intervals thereafter, made it a crop with a relatively quick turnaround time; a crop not as labour intensive as sugar cane and arrowroot; and the required labour was not as onerous as for many other traditional crops; the applied technology for growing, harvesting, and preparation for the market was easily learnt and within the farming traditions; the organisation of the industry nationally was sound with participation by the farmers and the State, but run mainly by the farmers; the joinder of internal local and external marketing arrangements on a weekly basis worked efficiently; the shipping, on a weekly basis, was regular and properly-organised; and the external marketing arrangements were profitable.

Bananas, therefore, constituted a significant development of the productive forces (land, labour, plant variety, technology) in a special way; and the relations of production were altered because of the pre-dominance of small farming production. Bananas, as a weekly cash crop, freed the small farmers, and their workers, from waiting for an annual cash crop such as arrowroot and sugar cane. This was a freedom from the estate-owners, who owned the arrowroot and sugar factories, who capriciously regulated the price for the purchase of the sugarcane or arrowroot from the farmers; there was freedom, too, from the larger rural shopkeepers who no longer had to provide credit for groceries and other necessities until the next annual crop came around. Thus social relations within the communities were altered significantly, including the growth of a sturdy individualism within the whole of the community.

Bananas proved to be more lucrative than any other major crop. The quality of housing, personal transportation, living and lifestyle improved markedly. So, too, the outlook of the people in social and political terms. Many of these material changes assisted the SVLP politically. The PPP was still solidly based among the working people on plantations.

By the early 1970s, most plantations were being sub-divided for sale; this process began in the late 1960s. In some cases, the plantation owners did the sub-divisions themselves; in other cases the State purchased the estates and carried out land reform in which small farmers and former estate workers were beneficiaries. The last group of estates to hold out were those belonging to the "Orange Hill" group; these estates (3,400 acres) were first sold to a Danish non-governmental organisation in 1984, but which were compulsorily acquired shortly thereafter by the State and sub-divided to small farmers and workers. By 1961, an aggregate of 15,954 acres of land were held by small farmers in plots of land under 10 acres per farmer. After 1961, holdings by small farmers grew in numbers on account of enhanced land distribution.

The full effect of the demise of plantation agriculture and the boost to small-farming was, like most alterations within a mode of production and its material consequences, took time to be realised. But as these material alterations were occurring and the relations of production were changing, changes in forms of struggle, institutions, ideas, beliefs, political affiliations, and more, were being experienced, gradually at first but more fully later on.

All of these changes and alterations were acting on the nature and extent of the political competition between the PPP and SVLP as they prepared for the campaign for the imminent elections in 1961.

A mix of political issues was seized upon by the SVLP opposition against the PPP government. These included: Excessive overseas travel by Joshua and his ministers without much to show from these trips; the tax concessions granted to the legislators, including Joshua and his wife; the closeness between Joshua and some merchants in Kingstown who were seen as rapacious; the unnecessary conflicts between the PPP, on the one hand, and the public servants and teachers on the other; the failure by the PPP legislators to pass one single piece of ameliorative labour and social legislation, despite their boast of being the party of, and for, the working class; and the PPP government's failure or refusal to initiate any practical steps towards land reform.

Still, the bulk of the working people considered Joshua and his PPP more grounded and connected to them. Moreover, all things considered, the PPP government had performed commendably. Thus, when the general elections were held on April 21, 1961, under altered constituency boundaries and an additional seat, bringing to nine the number of constituencies at stake, the PPP won six seats to the SVLP, three seats. The margin of popular votes was close: the PPP received a total of 11,500 votes or 49.5 percent of the valid votes cast; the SVLP garnered 11,075 votes or 47.67 percent of the valid votes cast. Two independent candidates, one in the Grenadines and another in South Leeward obtained in the aggregate 654 votes or 2.8 percent of the valid votes cast overall.

The victorious PPP candidates were: Ivy Joshua (North Windward); Ebenezer Joshua (Central Windward); Afflick Haynes (West St. George); Alphaeus Allen (Kingston); Samuel Slater (North Leeward); and Clive Tannis (Grenadines).

Milton Cato returned from the Federal Parliament to lead his SVLP in the 1961 general elections. The three victors for SVLP were: Levi Latham (Marriaqua); Milton Cato (East St. George); and Herman Young (South Leeward).

Ivy Joshua again topped the polls in percentage terms with 83.2 percent of the vote in North Windward. Ebenezer Joshua defeated George Charles again in Central Windward by a margin of 69.1 percent to 30.7 percent. Herman Young topped the polls for the SVLP with 73.3 percent of the valid votes cast in South Leeward; Levi Latham was returned in South Windward with 69.3 percent of the votes; and Milton Cato became an elected representative for the first time with 65.6 percent of the votes in the newly-created constituency of East St. George.

Seven of the eight incumbents from the 1957 elections were returned to the legislature. The eighth, Stinson Campbell, did not contest the 1961 general elections. Two new faces entered the Legislative Council: Alphaeus Allen in Kingstown; and Milton Cato in the newly-created East St. George. Two old political warriors from the Eighth Army in 1951, namely, George Charles and Julian Baynes had their outings at the polls end in defeat. A new star for the SVLP emerged in Kingstown in the person of a young lawyer, Hudson Tannis, who lost to Allen in Kingstown; he performed commendably on his first electoral foray securing 1,576 votes or 48.5 percent of the votes cast. The general elections generated much enthusiasm with a voter turnout of 75 percent of the registered vote.

The PPP performed marginally better in percentage terms in the 1961 general elections compared to those of 1957; 49.5 percent of the votes in 1961 compared to 48.9 percent in 1957. In 1961, the PPP received 11,500 votes or 1,664 votes more than the number obtained in 1957. So, the PPP more than held its own with a marginal increase in voter support, but since 1954, the SVLP had come closer to it than any other political party. In 1961, the SVLP lost the popular vote by a mere 425 votes, and had improved its performance markedly since 1957 when it secured 3,912 votes or 19.4 percent of the votes cast. It thus increased its popular vote within four years (1957-1961) by 7,163; and its percentage share of the popular vote jumped from just under 20 percent in 1957 to 47.67 percent in 1961. Additionally, the SVLP's leader had secured a seat in the Legislative Council for the first time. Further, the results showed that the SVLP were challenging strongly in Kingstown, North Leeward, and the Grenadines, despite their losses in those seats. In all, the SVLP had performed impressively, even though it had lost the elections. A two-party system appeared to have been validated by the electorate. Joshua and the PPP, despite their victory, had serious political challenges ahead. The social democratic forces and the labour movement were divided into two political phalanxes; the unity of the people was divided into opposing political camps even though the *objective* differences between these two political entities were more imagined than real, save and except at the margin.

Given the advances made by the SVLP and the historic tendency for floor-crossing and political gymnastics by elected representatives, Joshua was unlikely to take political chances, despite his party's victory at the polls. His party's electoral performance in 1961 was commendable but not dominant. How would he now lead, taking account of a rising, genuinely competitive political party at his metaphoric heels? Would he lead in a more consensual and less personalised way? Was he sufficiently prescient to notice the alterations in the political economy, including an increasing shift from plantation agriculture to small-farmer banana cultivation, and make strategic or tactical shifts? Or would he continue to lead in the "old way" oblivious of altered and changing circumstances?

There was an early answer to these queries, at least on the trade union front, when the Annual Conference of Delegates of the FIAWU gathered on October 29, 1961 to consider the fall-out from the failed attempt of Leroy Commissiong to challenge him in the 1958-1959 period. Joshua opted for enhanced control by him. Accordingly, he strengthened immensely his position as president-general of the union. This was achieved partly by an amendment passed to the union's constitution in the following terms:

(i) That as a founder of the union he shall not be removed from the Presidency unless two-thirds of the financial members present and voting signifies the desire and by an absolute majority of the delegates present at an annual conference; (ii) he shall preside over any meeting of a branch once he is present and wishes to do so and only by his consent could the Chairman exercise such functions; (iii) that the President-General shall be obliged to accept the majority decision in all general policy matters of the union except where the union is in jeopardy of being undermined, subjugated or betrayed; (iv) that the President-General shall have the power to suspend the Executive Committee but shall forthwith call a Special Conference of delegates.

This amendment in effect made Joshua the president-general for as long as he desired to remain as such. The amendment merely formalised what the union had long been — the personal political and trade union machine of Joshua. This amendment was the handiwork of a leader who was brooking no challenge in *his* union.

One month after the general elections in 1961, the Teachers' Union went on strike for higher wages. It was only after parental protests and government intervention that the teachers returned to work. In September of that year the SVLP started their second attempt to combat the union nexus of the PPP by appointing Herman Young as party secretary, especially charged with the responsibility of reorganising party groups and reviving the defunct St. Vincent Workers' Union (SVWU) of which he was president. This trade union was registered on August 16, 1958, with Levi Latham as trustee, and R. Milton Cato as its solicitor. The SVWU never got off the ground, even in its second coming. In an interview with the author in August 27, 1970, Young claimed that it was not really a bona fide attempt at trade unionism but more like a façade or an illusion to impress the working class that the SVLP was truly a "labour" party. Young himself had no experience in trade unionism and admitted to the author that the job was not within his capacity. This latter fact was substantiated by Hudson Tannis, a lawyer, and a prominent leader in the SVLP, who confirmed to the author in an interview on September 8, 1970, that the SVLP placed little organisational importance to the SVWU. In any event, Tannis expressed the view that only the party leader, Milton Cato, and himself had the organisational competence to handle the trade union, but that they were too busy with their law practice and the party to attend to such matters. Important as trade unions were, the leaders of the SVLP considered that other political and organisational avenues provided greater opportunities for meaningful advance for the party. In that sense, they ceded the trade union front to Joshua. But the SVLP was strong in civil society, in the public service and teaching profession, among the small farmers and traders; and they had a coherent social democratic, nationalist, and modernising message which they delivered well on the platforms.

It is not to be assumed that because Joshua headed the elected government as chief minister that the Colonial Administrator A.F. Giles, supported him. The Administrator represented colonial and planter-merchant class interests which were not the primary, or any concern of Joshua. From the outset of the PPP government, Giles and Joshua were embroiled in continual conflict relating not only to different class interests, but also to the extent of their shared governmental authority; further, they appeared to dislike each other personally. As was to be expected, the planters' press, the planter-merchant class, the Civil Service Association, and the SVLP supported the Administrator either because of their shared interests or on tactical/opportunistic political grounds. Thus, when in December 1961, Joshua led a group of his supporters in a public protest to demand the removal of Giles, the various anti-Joshua forces coalesced against him. *The Vincentian* newspaper of December 16, 1961, labelled Joshua's demonstration, "a fiasco". But Joshua would not relent. In the PPP Bulletin, *The Voice* of January 30th, 1962, and March 21, 1962, Joshua demanded that Giles be recalled on the grounds that he had used the power of his office to bring the PPP government into disrepute. At the same time, Joshua urged that the nominated members in the Legislative Council, especially Cyril Barnard be removed; Barnard, the owner of 3,400 acres of land — the "Orange Hill" Estates — was labelled by Joshua as an "enemy of working-class people". Again, as in 1956, the popular working-class leader was coming to a head-on clash with the colonial administration and the planter-merchant class. This time, though, he was the chief minister and head of the elected government.

In 1962, the confrontation, as in 1956, took place between the FIAWU and the Mt. Bentinck Estates Company Limited. Though it had the form of an industrial relations dispute, both the union and the company represented forces and interests which, for a long time, had been in contentious battle for a decade in the political arena.

The success of the PPP at the polls in 1961 did not offer any political respite for Joshua; he was facing many difficulties both inside and outside his party. Within the party, the well-liked Afflick Haynes, the elected representative for West St. George, a two-term legislator who had won his seat recently on a PPP ticket with a hefty 63.5 percent of the votes, resigned from the party and also as Minister of Trade and Production in November 1961, and joined the SVLP; in December 1961, the Speaker of the Legislative Council, Newton Nanton, also resigned. His publicly-stated reason was that he was "morally and economically unable to understand the remission of taxation on one hand [for ministers of government] and the increase on the other." The teachers had gone on strike within one month of the elections; Joshua and the Administrator were at daggers drawn; *The Vincentian* on November 18, 1961 warned Joshua that the press cannot be muzzled despite his threats to that effect. In the North Windward area, the SVLP was agitating that Joshua had lost his militancy in defence of workers; the SVLP contended that Joshua had sold out to the management of Mt. Bentinck Estates and would never call a strike there so long as he was Chief Minister. The SVLP pointed out factually that there had not been a strike at Mt. Bentinck since Joshua's PPP was elected to government in 1957. What the SVLP did not say was that the pre-1957 difficulties in industrial relations were now better channelled and resolved largely because the management recognised the FIAWU in 1958. The SVLP's taunt that Joshua was compromising away the workers' rights must have irritated him, at the very least. In any event, matters were shortly to get out-of-hand for reasons touching and concerning industrial relations at Mt. Bentinck Estates, but involving much more.

A straight-forward holidays-with-pay issue became a cause célébre which occasioned, but not caused, events to get out of control. The FIAWU had on December 29, 1960, submitted a memorandum to Mt. Bentinck Estates as the basis for negotiations in 1961 for a collective bargaining agreement. Among other things, the memorandum contained the union's proposals on a range of matters, including holidays-with-pay for both factory workers and field workers. Regulations existed on holidays-with-pay for both categories of workers with a graduated number of holidays-with-pay depending on the number of days worked annually from a minimum of 100 days to 201 days and over, organised in particular bands of days worked annually.

It is evident that the FIAWU sought to include in the negotiated package a provision for workers who worked between fifty days and under 100 days. In the process, it rearranged the legally-regulated bands of days worked and in its proposals disadvantaged those who worked over 150 days annually. It was sloppy preparation by the union of which the management took advantage to save money on the holidays-with-pay particularly in respect of the better-paid factory workers who worked more than 150 days per year.

There was a dispute as to whether or not there was actually an agreement; the management insisted that there was; the union demurred, and claimed that the workers did not receive their due or any holidays-with-pay for the 1960-1961 sugar-cane crop.

What brought this holidays-with-pay issue to a head was the discovery by the factory workers that, in accordance with the Industrial Workers Order No. 34 of 1960, they were short-changed by the company; these were mainly workers who worked in excess of 150 days annually. One of the workers of the sugar factory posted the Regulation on the factory walls by way of information for his co-workers. Joshua thus found himself in the embarrassing situation of having made a proposal below the minimum required by the law for certain categories of workers. The management was, of course, duty bound to pay these factory workers their holidays-with-pay in accordance with the law; but it had already committed itself to making holiday payments for those who worked below the statutory minimum 100 days per year. Foolishly, the management stood firm on a purported agreement with the union in respect of certain workers for whom it paid below the statutory minimum. In this profound respect, Mt. Bentinck Estates did not have a legal leg on which to stand. Joshua now falsely asserted that all along he had submitted to the company the requisite fourteen days holidays-with-pay for the factory workers who worked more than 201 days annually; the management still illegally, wanted to pay eight days as per a purported agreement. For reasons grounded in considerations outside the parameters of the dispute itself, the management refused to budge and comply with the law. It was clear: A company can pay outside of the statutory minimum if it is favourable to the worker; but it cannot pay outside of the statutory minimum if it is disadvantageous to the worker.

In response to the management's recalcitrance, the union did not seek arbitration as required by the collective agreement; instead it mounted a picket line headed by Mrs. Ivy Joshua at the gate of the sugar factory in late February 1962.

The refusal of Mt. Bentinck Estates to back down on an issue on which it had no legal basis, and the determination of Joshua to flex his political muscles, moved the strike from the realm of industrial relations to a political confrontation between two historically antagonistic groups. In the midst of all this, Ebenezer Joshua raised the political stakes of repeating his call for the resignation of Cyril Barnard, a planter, from his position of a nominated member of the Legislative Council. Meanwhile, the FIAWU picket continued; it grew in size and militancy.

So, on March 1st and March 2nd, 1962, the company officials of Mt. Bentinck Estates called on the police, who were under the jurisdiction of the Colonial Administrator A.F. Giles, ostensibly to maintain peace and order but in effect to break the picket line. Duff James, then an FIAWU organiser at Mt. Bentinck, claimed in an interview with the author on July 30, 1970, that Ian "Sonny" Child, a sugar-producing estate-owner at nearby Grand Sable, had preceded the police with "a complement of his slaves" — James' description of Child's employees — in an attempt to smash the picket line. The intervention by Ian Child and the police precipitated much violence and several persons were seriously injured, including Child himself.

With the factory workers on strike, contingents of the agricultural workers at Mt. Bentinck Estates and those nearby were called out by the union in solidarity. Joshua, who at the end of February 1962 was in Barbados on government business, hurried home with Osmond Dyce, Secretary of the Barbados-based Caribbean Congress of Labour (CCL) to assist the union in resolving the matter. By the time Joshua had returned, some factory workers who were not staunch Joshua supporters, had trekked back to work. Meanwhile, the agricultural workers, especially the cane-cutters, now took the lead in keeping the holidays-with-pay alive; they also renewed the long-standing, but dormant, demand for an immediate "closed shop" system at Mt. Bentinck Estates. The company responded by bringing cane-cutters from outlying districts at great expense. With the strike nearly two weeks old, and with management effectively breaking the work stoppage, both the union and the company's General Manager, Mc Lagan, arranged a settlement on the substantive issues.

This settlement involved the company's acceptance of the "closed shop" system, a promise that the strikers would not be victimised, and an agreement that the holidays-with-pay issue be considered later. Shortly thereafter, however, the Managing Director of the company E.A.C Hughes repudiated the Mc Lagan-union agreement on the ground that the company's directives and position were not sought. The workers, having returned to work from the moment of the Mc Lagan-union agreement, were not inclined to resume strike action after the Hughes' repudiation. In the absence of a strike fund in the union and a lack of clarity in the definition of the issues in dispute by the union, the workers' reluctance to resume industrial action was understandable. One week later on March 16, 1962, the company decided to terminate factory operations giving its reasons as 1) increased labour costs, 2) diminishing supplies of sugar cane, and 3) deteriorating labour relations. This decision had adverse and severe repercussions on the country's economy. Workers and peasants especially the North Windward and Central Windward areas were most immediately affected. Jobs were lost by workers and peasant farmers had to look to another crop to occupy the farm lands to be vacated by sugar-cane. The country's balance of payments problems was to become seriously aggravated because of the necessity to import sugar and molasses. Large sums for imports of sugar and molasses were leaving St. Vincent: BWI$72,765 for part of 1962; and $563,364 in 1963.

The alternative — government control of the sugar industry — was dismissed by Joshua on the grounds that his government believed "in fostering private enterprise" and "socialism could never properly work in our present democracy." This shallow and misguided ideological stance was in stark contrast to his articulated philosophical position in the legislature in 1956 that: *"I am a leader of labour and hope to be a leader of socialism"*. It is plausible to argue that Joshua's refusal to countenance state ownership of the sugar factory at that time and his ideological back-sliding probably contributed to the weakening of the working people's confidence in support of his party and government.

The 1962 confrontation in the sugar belt demonstrated as much as the 1956 one did, that despite the weakness of the estates' case and their unreasonable actions, the planters were not challenged by the Labour Commissioner, the Attorney General, and the Administrator; rather, these high-ranking colonial officials connived with, and gave succour and comfort to, the plantocracy. Further, the police and the planters' press, *The Vincentian*, were put into service against the workers, as they did in 1956. The haughtiness and arrogance of the plantocracy, was manifested, in part, in an hysterical telegram of the management of Mt. Bentinck Estates to the Secretary of State for the Colonies in early March 1962, that "if police protection [is] unavailable, [the] only alternative will be to counter violence with violence." Amazingly, *The Vincentian* of March 3, 1962, reported on this telegram without one iota of critical commentary. In retrospect, this outburst was a symbolic last gasp of a dying plantation order which, within fifteen or so years, would wither away without even as much as a ceremonial farewell or decent burial.

Given the historical performance of the company's factory operations, it is difficult to accept the reasons offered by the company for its closure. The claim that increased labour costs were partly responsible for the cessation of the factory's operations had to be seen in the light of the fact that St. Vincent sugar workers were the most lowly paid in the West Indies. Cane-cutters in St. Vincent were paid BWI 66 cents per ton of sugar cane reaped and labourers, males and females, were paid 98 cents and 75 cents respectively per eight-hour day in 1956. The next lowest wage paid in the region in 1956 was in St. Lucia where 77 cents per ton of cane reaped in 1956 was paid; and $1.44 and 92 cents respectively were paid to male and female labourers per eight-hour day. The highest rate per ton reaped was $1.19 in Antigua; and the highest daily wages were $2.16 and $1.52 for men and women labourers respectively for an eight-hour day in Barbados. By 1962, the daily paid wages for labourers had increased to $1.40 for men and $1.12 for women in St. Vincent; but by 1962 also, the other sugar-producing colonies in the West Indies had wage increases much more significantly than these numbers.

At the same time the 1955 Jolly Report into the sugar industry of St. Vincent showed that its yield of sugar cane per acre was more than in many other countries in the West Indies. The 1952-1953 figures showed the yield per acre in tons, for example, in Antigua was 24.5; Grenada 30.0; Barbados 32.6; and St. Vincent 32.0. Further, the sugar industry was receiving major concessions from the government. For the 1946-1954 period, Jolly estimated, at a minimum, that the company received $210,000 of government assistance either through subsidies or controlled prices.

This State assistance did not end with the advent of ministerial government: In 1960-61, Joshua's government raised the price of local sugar to accommodate the company. This increase brought the company an additional $80,000 as was revealed in a letter by Joshua to E.A.C Hughes on March 16, 1962. Besides this, the company was allowed to import all its new machinery free of customs duties. When one notes the low wages paid, the major concessions allowed by government, and the reasonable comparable yields, it is hardly surprising that in the period 1949-1954, the net profit of the company as a percentage of the share capital fluctuated between 17 percent and 27 percent and dividends declared between 6-8 percent. It was Jolly's view that a declaration of higher dividends would have risked a possible withdrawal of government's subsidies and supports.

While all this was in the shareholders' favour, both the workers and the peasant sugar-cane cultivators suffered as a result of inadequate wages and low sugar-cane prices respectively. Neither high wages nor poor industrial relations in fact caused the closure of the factory. During the years 1957-1961 when the first period of sustained industrial relations calm had come to Mt. Bentinck, the company declared its smallest dividends: Jolly reported that for the 1958-1961 period the declared dividends were no more than 4 percent; in 1960-1961, no dividends were declared. On the other hand, the years of greatest industrial unrest were coincidentally the years of greatest prosperity for the company — the period 1951 to 1956. As a matter of fact the two-week strike of 1962 could in no way be compared to the two-month strike in 1956 in any of the respects of duration, property damaged, economic loss, or the extent of the acts of violence perpetrated.

While there was some validity in the management's contention that there were diminishing supplies of sugar-cane, the force of this circumstance had to be qualified. To begin with, the company, the *Vincentian* newspaper, and the opposition SVLP made it appear that the government was at fault in not providing necessary incentives to farmers to produce sugar-cane and that it was not implementing any initiatives to improve the yield per acre. But these views ignored several things. First, the introduction and expansion of bananas, a crop which involved less capital outlay than sugar-cane. Banana cultivation, reaping and transportation to market was less costly than sugar cane and it provided quicker and better financial returns. Overall, bananas were more economically attractive and more socially beneficial to the families of the peasant farmers. The peasant farmers supplied one-third of the sugar-cane; Mt. Bentinck Estates supplied another one-third; and the other estates, one-third also. Some of these estates were already by 1956 substituting sugar-cane cultivation with bananas. Secondly, as Jolly had noted in his report the company, by virtue of its monopolistic position in the production of sugar and molasses at the sole factory, ignored several of its responsibilities which involved:

> *(i) the investigation and distribution of more varied and more suitable varieties; (ii) the testing of cane and the improvement of the organisation of deliveries; and (iii) the rearrangement of the grinding season.*

Implementation of these recommendations by the company would have meant, in the final analysis, increased revenue and greater profitability for the company itself. Thirdly, the Cane Farmers' Association, established under the Colonial Development and Welfare Scheme to assist farmers with some of the very suggestions and recommendations which Jolly had made, did not function as expected. Ian Child, an estate-owner and an opponent of Joshua, became chairman of the association, which gradually took on irrelevant and counter-productive political agendas, and an anti-Joshua political outlook. In any case, it was repeatedly shown to be inefficient and deficient.

However, even if we were to make a concession that there were diminishing supplies of sugar-cane, it is instructive nevertheless to note that in its last three years of operation the tonnage of sugar produced was 4,119, 3,619, and 3,241 respectively for the 1958-1961 years. When one compares those totals with some earlier years, it would seem that tonnage of sugar produced was not the major question of and by itself; the issue for Mt. Bentinck concerned "financial returns to the shareholders' capital." For example, in 1949-1950 and 1950-1951, the sugar tonnage produced was 2,758 and 2,792 respectively, and the net profit of the company as a percentage of the share capital was 21 percent and 17 percent, and the declared dividend was 6 percent. Despite the fact that there were improvements to the factory, they were not of any magnitude to raise the spectre of idle machinery as a result of diminishing supplies to close the factory in 1962 when it did not do so in 1951.

Thus, there was another bundle of factors which really accounted for the closure but which the management did not disclose. These facts were that the management of sugar-cane cultivation and production by the company was highly inefficient; that Mt. Bentinck Estates and the other estate-producers of sugar-cane had failed or refused to modernise as modern capitalist enterprises; and that the "plantocratic" mode of functioning — the *ancien regime* — was out of step with the times. As such it was proving difficult for Mt. Bentinck Estates to provide adequate financial returns for the shareholders. So, the query which surely they must have posed to themselves was: Why take all this hassle and possible personal injuries from Joshua's PPP-FIAWU for meagre financial returns? But it was the wrong question since a sensible accommodation to social change and modernisation would have solved or at least ameliorated their problems. They were unable to break out of the "plantocratic" mode so as to reform and modernise; they were imprisoned by the strictures of their own class, its ethos, ideology, and social organisation. If living organisms and organisations do not adapt and change, they become dinosaurs.

The Jolly Report was scathing in its criticism of the Mt. Bentinck Estates company and its management. Jolly was persuaded "that the company has evidently been incapable of propelling the whole body forward at any time faster than a limp." There were comparatively low labour costs and relatively high yields but the company's total manufacturing cost was one of the highest in the West Indies. A ton of sugar in 1956 had a cost of $62.63 to be manufactured in St. Vincent while, on an average, in Barbados the cost was $32.02; the single highest comparative cost manufacturer in Barbados was $41.43 per ton of sugar. Further, the recovery rate of sugar in St. Vincent was 11.6 tons of sugar-cane to one ton of sugar while in Barbados, on an average, it took 9.21 tons of sugar-cane to produce one ton of sugar.

Given this constellation of debilitating factors, it was almost inevitable that, in an increasingly competitive global market for sugar, the company stared closure in its face. This bundle of factors, not the spurious ones offered by the management, made closure the realistic option. Government subsidies and concessions, fixed controlled prices at enhanced levels, low wages to workers, low price of sugar-cane to peasant cultivators, and good soil with a competitive yield were unable to keep the company afloat.

Thus, although the question of deteriorating industrial relations was stressed not only by the company but also by the opposition SVLP as a major reason for the termination of the sugar industry, it had very little role in the closure. The fact that a simple, straight-forward industrial relations issue was given such prominence reflected the extent to which the interplay of the under-developed economy, colonial over-rule, competitive politics, "plantocratic" hubris, historical antagonisms, and small size shaped the representation, and even public perception, of the reasons for the closure of the sugar industry. In a short step the pithy, but entirely false, summation was: Joshua killed sugar! That is what we now call in the contemporary period, "fake news".

It is one of history's ironies that of the participants in this confrontation at Mt. Bentinck in 1962, Joshua and his followers in the PPP-FIAWU were put on the defensive and suffered setbacks and losses, material and political, even though they had a just cause. The propaganda campaign launched against Joshua by the planters' press, *The Vincentian*, the planter-merchant elite, the colonial officials and administrators, and the opposition SVLP, painted Joshua as solely responsible for the death of the sugar industry. His government's failure to take over the factory operations and save the industry at that time was an error. For his part, he was unable to mount a campaign which equalled that of his opponents. Thus, more sinned against than sinning in this debacle in 1962, Joshua was not easily absolved in the public's mind; even many historians damn him on this matter without any careful study by them of the complexities of the situation.

Popular culture in the form of a famous song, "Joshua Gone Barbados." unfairly pinned the blame on him for the outcome of the 1962 strike.

The American writer, singer, musician, and artist, Eric Von Schmidt, had vacationed in St. Vincent in 1962 at the time of the strike, the details of which were partially misrepresented to him. The song has become a minor classic, including performances of it not only by Schmidt himself but also by Tom Rush, and two greats, Johnny Cash and Bob Dylan. The lyrics by Schmidt are as follows:

> Cane standing in the fields getting old and red
> Lot of misery in Georgetown, three men lying dead

And Joshua, head of the government, he say strike
  for better pay
Cane cutters are striking, Joshua gone away.

Chorus:
Joshua gone Barbados, staying in a big hotel
People on St. Vincent they got many sad tales to tell

Sugar mill owner told the strikers, I don't need you
  to cut my cane
Bring in another bunch of fellows, strike be all in vain.
Get a bunch of tough fellows, bring 'em from Zion Hill
Bring 'em in a bus to Georgetown, know
  somebody get killed.
And Sonny Child the overseer, I swear
  he's an ignorant man
Walking through the cane field, pistol in his hand

Chorus:
But Joshua gone Barbados, just like he don't know
People on the Island, they got no place to go.

Police giving protection, new fellows cutting the cane
Strikers can't do nothing, strike be all in vain
And Sonny Child, he curse the strikers,
  wave his pistol 'round
They're beating Sonny with a cutlass,
  beat him to the ground.

Chorus:
There's a lot of misery in Georgetown, you can hear the wom-
en bawl, Joshua gone Barbados, he don't care at all.

Cane standing in the fields getting old and red
Sonny Child in the hospital, pistol on his bed
I wish I could go to England, Trinidad or Curaçao
People on the Island they got no place to go.

Chorus:
Joshua gone Barbados, staying in a big hotel
People on St. Vincent got many sad tales to tell.

Certainly, Joshua did not run away; he did not desert his supporters or the strikers; he did not go to Barbados because of the strike; he was in Barbados for two days on normal scheduled governmental business unconnected to the strike. And he returned to St. Vincent promptly therefrom with the Secretary General of the Caribbean Congress of Labour (CCL), Osmond Dyce, in an effort to settle the strike.

CHAPTER V

POLITICAL UNIONISM, 1963-1969 CHALLENGES AND CONSOLIDATION

THE CHALLENGES TO THE PPP-FIAWU NEXUS: 1963-1966

A few months after the Mt. Bentinck strike, Joshua was to face potentially challenging opposition in trade unionism and labour matters generally; this time it was initiated by Duff James who had been General Secretary of the FIAWU for the previous two years. James, by his own admission, had long thought of Joshua as a "liberator of the masses" and shortly after leaving school joined Joshua's organisations. He had played an agitational role in the 1962 strike and faced several police charges for his militant role, but they went nowhere. Through the instrumentality of Osmond Dyce, Secretary-General of the CCL, James received a three-month trade union scholarship in June 1962 to attend the American Institute of Free Labour Development (AIFLD) in Washington. Dyce was reportedly impressed with James' organisational and leadership qualities during the 1962 strike. Rather than going through the FIAWU and Joshua to make the scholarship offer to James, Dyce dealt directly with the latter. This raised Joshua's suspicions about Dyce's intentions in this matter; it irked him; he had seen James as a political son and viewed James' secret manoeuvre as an act of ingratitude and a potential threat to his trade union leadership. While James was in the USA, Joshua dismissed him from the FIAWU.

On James' return to St. Vincent in September 1962, he stressed that the old concept of political trade unionism was passing. In a feature story about James in *The Vincentian* on September 29, 1962, he emphasised that a trade union movement, free and democratic, with no political control, was an essential constituent of a free society. Immediately, this was interpreted as a challenge to Joshua's PPP-FIAWU combination. This was metaphoric "music to the ears" of *The Vincentian* which had conjoined its historic planter-merchant bias to its new-found role as cheerleader of the opposition SVLP with its modernising approach and philosophy of moderate social democracy. Oft-times, *The Vincentian* had real difficulty reconciling its traditional planter-merchant outlook with Cato's more enlightened posture on several socio-political issues, including the necessity and desirability for strong trade unions.

James was soon to launch his trade union activities with the workers in the Kingstown area, which had important work-sites of the electricity company, sanitation and public health, the port, the major hospital, and the Department of Public Works. There was a strong anti-PPP base in Kingstown; it had won the Kingstown constituency against a SVLP candidate by only 88 votes in the April 1961 general elections; but on December 12, 1962, the PPP lost all three popularly-elected Kingstown Board seats to the SVLP.

As James began to build a base for his trade union activity which threatened FIAWU support and membership, Joshua wrote Osmond Dyce of CCL on November 6, 1962, on the matter. He alleged that James had been publishing material derogatory of his union and the labour movement, and warned that "the people of North Windward whom James had lured into much trouble, would fix him easily"; the "trouble" to which Joshua was referring was the 1962 strike and certain violent events therein. Joshua bemoaned the fact that James was receiving money from the International Confederation of Free Trade Unions (ICFTU) through the CCL while attacking the FIAWU, an affiliate of both the ICFTU and CCL. In the early 1950s, the FIAWU had been affiliated to the World Federation of Trade Unions (WFTU), the workers' international body which was created and supported by the socialist countries headed by the Soviet Union. After Joshua came to government in 1957, he cut his union's ties with the WFTU and went into the embrace of the American-dominated ICFTU, which was decidedly anti-socialist and pro-capitalist. International trade union entities were all utilised and manipulated by various adversaries in the raging Cold War, until the collapse of the Soviet Union in the early 1990s. All around, Joshua had been making his compromises strategically with international capitalism, but true to form, imperialism had no loyalties but to its self-interests. So, ditching Joshua was no problem for the ICFTU in preference for a more reliable moderniser in Duff James, as recommended by CCL.

Still, three major difficulties faced James in his attempt to organise his trade union. First and foremost, he had to combat a strong, though vulnerable, Joshua buttressed by governmental authority, a viable trade union and a political party. His profile as a fighter, historically for the working people, accorded him a lustre which not even his mis-steps and many unwise compromises were much able to tarnish. Secondly, most workers in the urban areas who had regular employment were either government employees or in private establishments which were unwilling for one reason or another to recognise a trade union that opposed Joshua's union and government. Thirdly, trade unionism in St. Vincent shortly after the closure of the Mt. Bentinck sugar industry, mistakenly took on the connotations of irresponsibility and lawlessness; thus, a significant body of workers, management, and the general public were somewhat sceptical of, or opposed to, trade unions.

In countering these challenges, James had three possibilities upon which to rely: 1) Regional and international support through the CCL; 2) the objective need in important clusters of workers to organise properly in a trade union; 3) and the growing sentiment that both the PPP government and the FIAWU had been unable to deliver a sufficiency of the promised benefits for the working people. In order to take advantage of these possibilities, James would need to display sound judgement and leadership skills, articulate a coherent message of trade unionism, and build a resilient trade union organisation. In starting up, James had to choose carefully which set of employees to organise initially.

In an interview with the author on July 30, 1970, James gave three main reasons for concentrating first on the electricity workers employed with the St. Vincent Electricity Services, owned by the Commonwealth Development Corporation (CDC): 1) The workers were mainly skilled with at least an average intelligence to be able to understand the issues involved; 2) electricity was a vital service for an "independent" or insurgent unionism, so as to exercise or exert leverage in other areas of employment; and 3) the CDC's Charter stipulated its desire to bargain with recognised trade unions, thus making it less difficult, at least theoretically, to gain recognition so long as the union obtained the majority support of the workers.

The response from the electricity workers was encouraging to James' initiative. So, on December 11, 1962, a steering committee was formed; it decided to recommend to the workers the establishment of the Commercial Technical and Allied Workers' Union (CTAWU). On December 30, 1962, a meeting of all the electricians and other workers of the company was held.

The next step was that of registering the trade union. Under normal circumstances, registration of a union is simple and straightforward. But in a small society with an undeveloped democratic ethos and political intrigues at all levels, "normal" conditions are not usually what they would be in a mature, liberal democracy. The battle for registration of the CTAWU inevitably involved political considerations and manoeuvrings. James, in his interview with the author, described the then Registrar of Trade Unions, Herbert Squires, as a "close friend and ally of Mr. Joshua". After a series of delaying tactics, Squires on May 6, 1963, gave three ostensible, legal grounds for refusing registration. CTAWU appealed against his decision to the High Court of Justice which, in Civil Suit No. 92 of 1963 in the St. Vincent circuit, granted provisional registration to the CTAWU for six months on June 22, 1963. It later received full registration.

Meanwhile, Joshua continued his denunciations of James and his union. James, who in a political address at Rose Place on July 19, 1963, repeated his desire for a separation of trade unionism and politics, was being drawn, inexorably, into the political fray by having to respond to Joshua's political attacks. Whether or not James originally held this view of a separation of trade unionism and politics merely to gain support for his union is difficult to ascertain. Undoubtedly his training at AIFLD would have conditioned him to espouse such a stance, but the extant circumstances on the ground in St. Vincent pulled him towards political unionism, if only in a more diluted and less extreme form to that built by Joshua.

As an experienced working class and political leader, Joshua recognised that a mere condemnation of James and the CTAWU was insufficient to stall their advance; so, Joshua sought to seize the initiative. His party's bulletin, *The Voice of St. Vincent* of July 6, 1963, reported on a series of new developments in the FIAWU. This union was about to submit a new claim to the management of Geest Industries (W.I.) Limited, on behalf of its banana workers. The water-front workers of the union were also attempting to establish what the FIAWU called "a powerful branch". Besides, there were glowing reports concerning the working and living conditions of labourers whom his government had recruited to work in Antigua. Joshua himself had gone to Antigua to show his interest in them and to investigate adverse reports on their conditions, which had been reported in *The Vincentian* of February 23, 1963.

Joshua's determination to block CTAWU's recognition at the CDC's Electricity Company was underscored in his counter to CTAWU's representational claim to the effect that the FIAWU had majority support of the workers. Joshua sought to tie James and his CTAWU to the SVLP so as to combat James' claim of building an independent, non-political unionism. Thus *The Voice* of July 6, 1963, admonished workers not to allow "opposition politics to disorganise you and ruin you of chances of honest representation." The battle for union recognition by the management of the electricity company was now between two competing unions. In the final outcome, CTAWU received recognition on November 1963, nine months after its initial demand. Joshua's method of winning back or gaining fresh union members was to rely largely on his political influence. James, on the other hand, with no such comparable political influence, paid far more attention to organisational details. Among other things, James had each worker individually write to the management affirming his or her membership of the CTAWU.

Having won representational rights at the electricity company, James and the CTAWU made attempts to organise workers directly employed by the government. According to James in his 1970 interview with the author, their first task was "to establish the right of government employees to belong to a trade union of their choice." Although both the constitution of the colony and the International Labour Organisation (ILO) conventions had already established that principle, the CTAWU was of the view that, in practice Joshua's government had subverted it. At its first Conference of Delegates on November 29th to December 1, 1963, CTAWU was pre-occupied with this question. The conference saw the first union-wide adoption of its aims and objects.

In an organisational sense, the CTAWU's aim was to represent workers in the fields of commercial, clerical, technical and allied crafts, skills and trades. It thus had a narrower organisational scope than the traditional "blanket" unions established by Mc Intosh and Joshua, the latter being far more successful. Despite the CTAWU's affirmation of its independence of political parties, it nevertheless adopted at its 1963 Conference a broad political aim "to fight whether by political or economic action or by social, welfare or community activity for the eradication of poverty, ignorance, and disease." At this first Conference, Leopold Martin, a former PPP supporter and FIAWU functionary, was elected president of the CTAWU; Martin had much earlier contested the 1954 general elections in the Central Windward constituency as an independent candidate; he had secured a respectable 13 percent of the vote in a five-way contest won by George Charles with 44 percent of the vote; subsequently Martin became a PPP-FIAWU activist but later switched his support to the SVLP. The 1963 CTAWU Conference elected Duff James, unopposed, as its General Secretary, the chief executive officer of the union.

At this time, problems confronted Joshua not only in union matters but also in the political arena itself. In September 1963, the long-anticipated *Report of the Commission of Enquiry into the Public Works Department* was published. A scandal of maladministration and possible financial impropriety shook the government to its very foundation. The Commissioners found that Mrs. Joshua, a holder of ministerial office in the government and wife of the chief minister had improperly interfered with the Public Works Department's affairs as regards employment of road gangs, their supervision, the keeping of records, and method of payment. Besides, they found that:

> *The interference had a profound effect upon the morale*
> *and efficiency of the civil servants...and had created an*
> *atmosphere of fear and diminished responsibility with a*
> *corresponding tolerance towards irregularities and the*
> *waste or misuse of public funds.*

In February 1964, the opposition in the Legislative Council called for the institution of criminal proceedings against Mrs. Joshua. The attorney general denied the request. The secretary of state in turn asked for Mrs. Joshua's resignation. She refused, and as Joshua would not advise her dismissal, the British suspended the much needed grant-in-aid. By the end of February 1964, the opposition to the government was beginning to have its effect, and Mrs. Joshua resigned her ministerial post.

Predictably, the SVLP did not leave matters there. In March, 1964, SVLP's leader and deputy leader, Cato and Young respectively, travelled to USA, Britain and Canada to seek "further reprisals" against the government for the irregularities. However, the momentum of SVLP's opposition to Joshua was soon to be checked, temporarily. In October 1964, without any forewarning, but in keeping with the fickle conventions of local politics, Young, deputy leader of the SVLP, switched to Joshua's PPP, and became a member of the government.

James and CTAWU continued their trade union activism in the midst of all the political controversies in and out of the legislature. In July 1964, the CTAWU began to organise the government's sanitation workers. In doing this James came under heavy attack from Joshua, verbally and in political-trade union activism. Although James claimed that he had the support of 51 percent of the workers, he did not want to push the recognition issue too prematurely; in all probability James was uncertain as to whether CTAWU's majority support was sufficiently solid to withstand the barrage from Joshua. Clearly, James' strategy was to consolidate CTAWU's support and secure a greater strength before confronting the powerful Joshua and his FIAWU. On December 10, 1964 — International Human Rights Day — Joshua remarked at a public meeting that if the sanitation workers wanted to strike, he would show them that "I am the God of strike; I will sweep with the broom in one hand and a gun in the other." This incendiary rhetoric of Joshua was indicative of the political temper of the country at the time. Several personal appearances by Joshua at the Sanitation Department to woo the workers to the side of FIAWU contributed to the delay of CTAWU's recognition at that workplace for over a year. Recognition of the CTAWU as the bargaining agent for the sanitation workers came on July 6, 1965.

The recognition by the government of CTAWU has been one of the most significant trade union victories in the history of St. Vincent; it was the first time that any government had recognised a union to which it, and its own affiliate union had been opposed. It is worthwhile to document some of the salient factors, and events, leading up to this recognition.

To begin with, the workers themselves played the greatest role and demonstrated in no uncertain terms the strength and power of an organised people. Even before the union was recognised, the CTAWU members at the Sanitation Department were settling disputes among themselves with the assistance of the union leadership. So impressed were the supervisors and foremen with the improved standard of work and discipline on the job that they themselves joined the union.

It was with this conscientious, committed worker support coupled with able leadership that the recognition breakthrough was possible. James, recognising fully that St. Vincent was still a colony over which the British government had jurisdiction, brought the matter in respect of the alleged violation of freedom of association to the International Labour Organisation (ILO), whose international labour conventions the British government had ratified. Specifically, the British government had ratified the following international conventions and declared their provisions applicable, without modification, to St. Vincent: The Right of Association (agriculture) Convention, 1921 (No. 11); the Right of Association (non-metropolitan territories) Convention, 1947 (No. 84); and the Right to Organise and Collective Bargaining Convention, 1949 (No. 98). It had also ratified the Freedom of Association and Protection of the Right to Organise Convention, 1948 (No. 87), and had declared it applicable with modifications to St. Vincent; these modifications related to the composition of the committee of management of a trade union, the taking of secret ballot in certain cases and the uses to which trade union funds may be put. Through an international affiliate, the International Federation of Commercial, Clerical and Technical Employees, the CTAWU submitted requisite detailed communications to the ILO in respect of complaints, touching and concerning the applicable international labour conventions, against the government of St. Vincent on November 24th and December 15th, 1964. The details on the matter are contained in *Case No. 415, 163rd Session (Geneva 1965, ILO): the 85th Report of the Committee on Freedom of Association.*

Because of the ILO's concerns, the British government decided to take action. The Colonial Administrator in St. Vincent, under the Public Utility Undertakings and Public Health Arbitration Ordinance, No. 4 of 1962, and its amendment, No. 15 of 1956, established a tribunal consisting of representatives of both employers and employees to adjudicate CTAWU's allegations. CTAWU suggested the names of three representatives — John Derek Knight, Vice President of the Grenada Trade Union Council and CTAWU's lawyer; Curtis B. Stewart, General Secretary of the Grenada Technical and Allied Workers' Union; and Osmond Dyce of CCL. Joshua, in full battle mode, would have none of it. He caused the government to ban Knight, Stewart, and Dyce from entering the country. A revealing memorandum submitted by Joshua to the country's Executive Council on June 25, 1965, charged that:

> *Duff James, Secretary of CTAWU has been preaching*
> *subversion of the St. Vincent government and he used*
> *the trade union movement in the West Indies run by one*
> *Osmond Dyce and foreign support to accomplish this end.*
> *By the aid of Dyce, Secretary-Treasurer of the CCL,*
> *Derek Knight and Curtis Stewart, well-known harassers*
> *of the essential services of government in the Caribbean,*
> *[CTAWU intended to effect their plan].*

The banning of the CTAWU's representatives had temporarily stalled James. Then the government, according to James in his July 1970 interview with the author, in an attempt to sabotage CTAWU's efforts, appointed as chairman of the tribunal, C.D. Archer — "an old reactionary about whose knowledge we had doubts in relation to the issue." It is at this point that James acted astutely. Instead of submitting a whole package of issues involving wages, conditions of work, alleged victimisation of workers and so forth, he merely requested the tribunal to determine whether CTAWU represented the majority of the workers in the Sanitation Department and if it did, whether it should be recognised. This tactical move short-circuited the purpose of the tribunal; one does not set up such a body to adjudicate on a principle long established and on an issue for which adequate recognition machinery existed. As a result, the British secretary of state ordered the dissolution of the tribunal. The Labour Department, the proper institution for determining recognition, then called for a poll of the sanitation workers, but the CTAWU refused on the ground that this was wholly unnecessary and thus demanded recognition through an ascertainment of majority worker support from the union's membership register. The Labour Department obliged; it carried out its check and found that CTAWU in fact represented a majority of sanitation workers.

James was greatly assisted in his mobilisation and organisation of the sanitation workers by a driver of one of the sanitation trucks, Cyril Roberts, who was to become an important leader in the CTAWU. A young man, Burns Bonadie of the St. Vincent Banana Growers' Association and a future distinguished trade union leader in CTAWU, St. Vincent and the Grenadines, and the Caribbean, also provided useful support.

Almost immediately after the government's recognition of the CTAWU in July, 1965 as the bargaining agent for the sanitation workers, Joshua unilaterally provided a 20 percent increase for these workers in a not-so-subtle attempt to marginalise the CTAWU. This was to lead to a further dispute which we shall discuss shortly.

While the sanitation workers' historic dispute over recognition dominated the trade union scene in 1964 and 1965, events of a lesser order are worth noting. Almost simultaneously with the sanitation workers' issue, the CTAWU was making attempts to organise the other government workers at the Mental Health Centre, the Kingstown General Hospital, and the Lewis Punnett Home for the indigent elderly. The CTAWU was strong among the mental health workers and eventually gained recognition at the Centre. But Joshua's personal appearance, conjoined with his political influence, at the Hospital and the Lewis Punnett Home, stalled a CTAWU victory among the workers at those two institutions.

Throughout 1964 and 1965, CTAWU conducted an ongoing public educational campaign on trade unionism. The first broadcast over the state-owned radio station in June 1964, delivered by Edmond M. Israel, treasurer of the CTAWU, evinced the union's interest in organising agricultural workers. However, the difficulties which had faced Mc Intosh, Charles, and Joshua again reappeared to render the CTAWU's efforts ineffective in this sector. The obstacles of seasonal employment, unemployment, the lack of a sustained trade union tradition and industrial discipline, and an undeveloped trade union consciousness among workers, again defeated unionism in the agricultural sector. Further, the union leadership, somewhat out of touch with the rural agricultural problems, was unable to make a significant appeal there. Moreover, Joshua's personal political strength in many of these rural areas, as a result of his more than a decade-long fight among these workers, negated the half-hearted CTAWU effort. After the first CTAWU broadcast, Joshua brought governmental pressure to bear on the radio station which refused subsequent CTAWU's broadcasts. From then on, dissemination of the information continued for a few more months through public meetings and the anti-Joshua newspaper, *The Vincentian*.

The CTAWU also attempted, unsuccessfully, to organise the store clerks in the business houses. Traditionally, these workers, though usually lowly-paid, did not have a history of trade union activism and a sense of working class consciousness. Further, they were scattered across a number of small enterprises which made them very difficult to organise. Moreover, the employers were invariably hostile to trade unionism in an area of work where workers' employment tenure was precarious and oft-times short-term.

By Joshua's own admission, the year 1964 found the FIAWU with increased challenges. In his Presidential address to the FIAWU's Annual Conference of Delegates on June 28, 1964, he highlighted three difficulties. First, in addition to the reduction in employment resulting from the loss of the sugar industry, the Geest Industries (W.I.) Limited had retrenched a significant number of its labour force by the introduction of conveyor belts to take the bananas from the Kingstown Banana Depot to the docked ship, instead of manually. Joshua complained that this was done without adequate consultation or compensation for the retrenched workers. A second FIAWU problem resulted from the reduced demand in the USA for agricultural workers, who were usually recommended through the FIAWU-PPP governmental connections. Thirdly, Joshua lamented that the union was in financial difficulties on account of the non-payment of union dues by the many union members especially those not in a bargaining unit with a "check-off" system. Still, despite these challenges and the CTAWU's competition, membership in the FIAWU rose to 1,792 in 1963, an increase of 258 members over the 1962 figure, largely on account of the formation of the seamen and waterfront branch of the union and the reorganisation of the "Geest" banana workers.

Both the CTAWU and the SVLP criticised Joshua for the state of dissatisfaction among workers generally, and especially from the employment practices at the newly-built, state-owned, deep-water harbour at Kingstown. They alleged that Joshua, as chief minister and FIAWU's leader, gave instructions to employ only financial members of his union; *The Vincentian* of January 16, 1965, reported prominently this allegation. The unfairness of this employment method appeared to have offended even some of the union's own members; accordingly, one Cecil Rose, a leader in the seamen's branch of the union, resigned.

Meanwhile, CTAWU was attempting to break FIAWU's stranglehold on the "Geest" workers. The reply of Geest Industries Limited to CTAWU's recognition request was that it had a two-year collective agreement with another union. One level of response by Joshua was to repeat the allegation that CTAWU's efforts were linked to, and directed by, the SVLP. In a letter to "Geest" on March 3, 1965, FIAWU claimed that "it is most unfortunate that active politicians should work alongside workers to incite them". The FIAWU singled out an alleged SVLP political activist "Jerry, who advertises meetings for SVLP and weekly ridicules the St. Vincent government" as an "agent provocateur". On March 17, 1965, Geest Industries allayed Joshua's anxieties by sending a circular to its employees pointing out that the company had a collective agreement with FIAWU of which its president was also the country's chief minister. The company's statement further stressed that:

> The company wishes all its employees to take full cogni-
> zance of these facts and to avoid all occasion for undue
> criticism or abuse of the government or union or their
> offices. Our company will not tolerate any such behaviour
> on its premises or in the course of its employment.

Predictably, CTAWU and SVLP resented this circular. The SVLP held a number of public meetings on the issue. CTAWU sent a telegram to the regional headquarters of Geest Industries demanding a withdrawal "of your most disgraceful notice" within forty-eight hours or "face a complaint of violation and infringement of Human Rights before the ILO and the United Nations."

By October 1965, Duff James, CTAWU, and the sanitation workers were to provide Joshua with further political anguish. James had referred to the 20 percent wage increase which the Joshua government had accorded these workers as a "union busting tactic in lieu of collective bargaining". CTAWU argued that it was an insufficient increase given "the nature of the work and the increased cost of living." James summoned his union's members at the Sanitation Department to a "go slow" with the possibility of strike action; he also threatened to call out the electricity workers in sympathy if his demands for wage increases and better working conditions were not met. The union and the government officials met for twenty-four different sessions before they arrived at a partial agreement. The major areas of the dispute were to be resolved by arbitration. In June 1966, the sole arbitrator, F.E. Glasgow, made an award on the eleven points of dispute, all items relating to wages, working conditions, holidays-with-pay, injuries on the job, overtime, sick leave, clothing allowance, vacation leave, termination of employment, and time-off for trade union business. The union's major demand, that of a claim for increase in minimum wages to $3.60 per day, an increase of almost 44 percent, was rejected.

CTAWU's threat of strike in both the sanitation and electricity services prompted the government to pass the Essential Services Ordinance, Number 10 of 1965, which repealed the Public Utility Undertakings and Public Health Ordinance; the object of the ordinance of 1965 was to prohibit strikes in essential services (electricity, water, health, hospital and sanitation) except after the expiration of a specified notice period or a failure to resolve the dispute at arbitration, within a stated period. The *Vincentian* newspaper, which had earlier questioned the necessity of James' strike threat, complimented its traditional nemesis, Joshua's government, on the introduction of this legislative measure.

Meanwhile, CTAWU continued to organise and mobilise workers especially in Kingstown. Three sets of employees were in its immediate focus in its quest for union recognition: Those at the Public Works Department; Geest Industries; and the Banana Growers' Association, mainly the office staff. The first two employment units had collective agreements with the FIAWU, due substantially to the influence of its political arm, the PPP, which was in government; indeed, it was not until the PPP was defeated at the polls that the CTAWU was able to win recognition in those two areas of employment. At the Banana Association, the CTAWU requested recognition. Assisting James at the Banana Association was a dynamic young employee, the nephew of Milton Cato of SVLP, Burns Bonadie, who later became a distinguished leader of CTAWU and a highly-respected regional trade unionist rising to the level of Secretary-General of the CCL. In a short time, the Banana Association recognised the CTAWU as the bargaining agent for its workers.

Between the first Conference of Delegates of the CTAWU in December 1963, and the second in 1965, the union took the lead in seeking to form a St. Vincent Federation of Labour. On February 3, 1964, James wrote to the Civil Service Association (CSA) and the Teachers' Union of the importance of such an umbrella union body. A steering committee of the proposed Federation of Labour was set up but the idea was soon abandoned when the Teachers' Union withdrew. Interestingly, no invitation to join the federation was sent to the FIAWU; clearly, James' antagonism to Joshua, and vice versa, made such an invitation a non-starter. The second CTAWU Conference of Delegates recorded its support for the idea of a Federation of Labour. At that Conference of Delegates, the constitution of CTAWU was amended to change the name of the union to that of the St. Vincent Workers' Union in a quest to broaden its scope as a "blanket union" to embrace all workers. In the upshot, the Registrar of Trade Unions refused to allow the change of name on the ground that it too closely resembled that of the St. Vincent United Workers' Union, a defunct but not legally non-existent entity.

From January 1966, competitive party politics assumed an ascendancy in anticipation of general elections later that year. At stake, too, was the prospect of leading St. Vincent under an advanced constitution of internal self-government in association with Britain — Associate Statehood — in which constitutional arrangement Britain would retain responsibility only for defence and external affairs. Under such an arrangement the chief minister's role and status would be upgraded to that of "Premier".

The country was divided politically between the PPP and SVLP, each with almost equal support to the other. The campaign for the general elections of August 22, 1966, was arguably the most intense and divisive ever in the country's history. The small size of the country and political competition for scarce material resources heightened political competition and tensions. The divisiveness was manifest even in commerce and retail trade. From the political platforms each party advised its respective supporters to boycott the businesses of those who supported the opposing political party; this heightened "political tribalism" was new to the politics of St. Vincent. The voter turnout was the highest — 84 percent of the registered vote — since the introduction of universal adult suffrage in 1951; 27,385 persons voted, an increase of 4,156 voters over the 1961 elections.

In the 1966 general elections, the PPP won five seats to the SVLP's four seats but the SVLP won the majority of the popular vote by 503 votes: 50.86 percent of the valid votes cast for the SVLP; 49.03 percent for the PPP. In these elections, five candidates from the 1951 Eighth Army of Liberation, were on the ballot, four of whom were incumbents, namely, Ebenezer Joshua in Central Windward, Clive Tannis in the Grenadines, Samuel Slater in North Leeward, and Herman Young in South Leeward; Rudolph Baynes, the fifth of these former Eighth Army candidates, had returned to the electoral fray on the SVLP ticket after skipping the 1961 contest, to be defeated in Central Windward by Ebenezer Joshua. Young, who had earlier switched from SVLP to PPP, was defeated as a PPP candidate by Joseph Lambert Eustace of the SVLP, who later became Speaker of the House of Assembly, and a Governor-General after independence. Neither Young nor Baynes ever appeared again on a ballot.

The PPP incumbents who won their seats in the 1967 elections were: Ebenezer Joshua, and Ivy Joshua overwhelmingly, and Samuel Slater, won his seat by a mere four votes; the winning incumbents for SVLP were: Milton Cato and Levi Latham. The victorious newcomers for the PPP were: Emmanuel Adams (Kingstown) and Roderick Marksman (West St. George). The successful newcomers at the polls for SVLP were: Joseph Eustace and James

Mitchell; Mitchell won the Grenadines seat in his first electoral outing with 57.1 percent of the valid votes cast. Mitchell, an agronomist, who had earlier returned from the United Kingdom was to play a leading role in the politics of St. Vincent and the Grenadines as Premier (1972-1974) and Prime Minister (1984 – 2000).

The results of the 1966 elections showed a modest swing in the popular votes to the SVLP, but after ten years in government the PPP was still a major political force, albeit in slight decline. Joshua's union, though challenged by the CTAWU, still held sway as the single largest trade union; it even enjoyed a small increase in its membership in 1966 over 1965: 5,214 members compared to 5,001; its financial membership was: 4,363 in 1966; and 4,006 in 1965. Undoubtedly, the PPP's hold on governmental authority greatly assisted the FIAWU.

Duff James, though not an electoral candidate, was involved in the 1966 elections. As a resident in the constituency of South Leeward, he was very concerned about representation in this area. Young, who had won the South Leeward constituency as a candidate of the SVLP in the 1961 elections with 73.3 percent of the popular votes, had switched to the PPP in 1964. James saw that Young was in decline, after his shift of political allegiance, and became interested in being a candidate. After all, James had done commendably well as the founder and leader of the CTAWU; he was possessed of presence and influence. In an interview with the author in July 1970, James claimed that he was offered the candidacy for South Leeward in 1966 by the SVLP on condition that he joined the party. He contended that he refused to join the SVLP but sought their support as an Independent Labour candidate, which, not surprisingly, they did not entertain. Thus, instead, J.L. Eustace was chosen. However, Hudson Tannis, deputy leader of the SVLP, disputed James' contention in an interview the author on September 8, 1970. Tannis insisted that on no occasion was James offered the candidacy. In any event, James campaigned against Young and for the SVLP's Eustace.

James' political activities engendered opposition to him in certain sections of the union. PPP supporters in his union did not like his pro-SVLP stance; and many SVLP supporters in the union did not trust him for one reason or the other. These circumstances combined to provide James' aspiring rivals in the union with an opportunity to challenge his leadership within a year.

THE DECLINE OF THE PPP, THE CONSOLIDATION OF SVLP, CONFLICTS IN CTAWU: 1966-1969

In the immediate period after the 1966 general elections, James began to critique the SVLP. He was evidently piqued at the lack of support by the SVLP for his possible candidacy in South Leeward, and he sensed that many SVLP supporters in the CTAWU, including influential members, were suspicious of his ambitions and dissatisfied with his leadership tendency to run the union by himself. James accused the SVLP of wanting to promote middle-class leadership in the country; he saw J.L. Eustace's selection as SVLP's candidate in that light; he felt challenged, too, by Burns Bonadie's influence in the union.

Efforts by him to counter the growing opposition to him in the union were cut short when he became ill in late 1966 and had to go to the United States of America for medical treatment. With James in an American hospital, Edmond Israel, the Assistant General Secretary of the CTAWU summoned a meeting of the union's executive to deal with what he alleged to have been James' mismanagement of the union. His critics within the union claimed that he had subverted the principle of independent unionism because of his active political participation; they further charged that he had grossly mismanaged the union's finances. As a result, Burns Bonadie, an influential member of the union, wrote CTAWU's international affiliate, ICFTU, about the state of the union's affairs. A representative of the ICFTU was promptly sent to St. Vincent not only to liquidate the union's debts but also to advise on what to do. A special meeting of the General Council was thus called and James was dismissed. Bonadie became Administrative Assistant and Israel remained as Assistant General Secretary. There was no election for the post of General Secretary. A year or so later, at the third Conference of Delegates on December 21, 1967, Bonadie was elected General Secretary and Richard "Dick" Neverson, an employee of Cable and Wireless was elected President. Cyril Roberts, a truck driver with the Sanitation Department, was elected as Vice President.

James claimed that his removal was engineered by a "conspiracy of the middle class and social elites" who, while being pleased at his opposition to Joshua, preferred the union to be managed by someone from their own class. This, he averred, intensified when he began to oppose SVLP. He asserted, too, in an interview with the author in 1970, that his followers, principally the sanitation and electricity workers were too apathetic to rally to his support as "they were basking in the sunshine of their achievements" secured under his leadership.

This "conspiracy thesis" of James was debunked by Bonadie and others who assumed leadership of the union after James' tenure. They insisted that James' management of the union and his one-man style of leadership precipitated his downfall. It was true that though the democratic structures of the union were formally in place, participation and decision-making by the rank and file were limited in practice. Had James paid more attention to the membership base of the CTAWU and less to party politics, his supporters might have rallied to his side.

Nevertheless, once the momentum started to oust James from the leadership of the CTAWU it was inevitable that political cross-currents would come into play. Caspar London, a highly committed working-class fighter for justice and socialism, who at the time was an organiser with the CTAWU, subscribed to the "conspiracy thesis" of middle-class usurpers against James. Still, James had himself to blame for his cavalier management of the union's affairs, his one-man style, and his growing disconnect from the members of the union. Lessons abound here.

In the political arena, events were unfolding which would have an effect not only on the immediate political future but also on the labour movement, including trade unionism. Shortly after the 1966 elections, the SVLP filed two election petitions through which they intended to upset the PPP election victory. PPP also countered with two such petitions. Amidst this state of electoral uncertainty the British government postponed to June 1967 the date when St. Vincent was to move in Associated Statehood with Britain. In March 1967, a dramatic resignation from the PPP government by Samuel Slater, and his joining the SVLP, precipitated a political and constitutional crisis. In the general elections of August 1966, Slater had won the North Leeward seat on a PPP ticket by only four votes over SVLP's James Ferdinand. Slater's crossing of the legislative floor from PPP to SVLP immediately reversed the five-to-four majority of elected members in the Legislative Council. The loss by Joshua's PPP of its elected majority prompted the British Secretary of State to dissolve both the Legislative and Elective Councils, and announce new general elections for May 20, 1967. This fascinating period of the political history of St. Vincent is well-captured in an informative essay by a political scientist, Dr. Kenneth John, in a local journal, *Flambeau* (March 1967).

In the May 1967 general elections, the SVLP won by a margin of six seats to the PPP's three. The SVLP garnered 14,501 votes or 53.8 percent of the popular votes to the PPP's 12,465 votes or 46.2 percent. Within nine months of the August 1966 general elections, the SVLP increased its popular vote by

571 votes, and the PPP's popular vote declined by 962 votes in elections in which 419 fewer persons voted overall. In short, the PPP was in decline; it was never again, by itself, to win any general elections; the SVLP was in the ascendancy. Between 1967 and 1984, the SVLP was to lead the government for fifteen of those seventeen years.

In the general elections of 1967, three seats for the PPP were won by Ebenezer Joshua (Central Windward), Ivy Joshua (North Windward) and Roderick Marksman (West St. George). The SVLP victors were: Milton Cato (East St. George), Levi Latham (South Windward), Hudson Tannis (Kingstown), Joseph L. Eustace (South Leeward), Samuel Slater (North Leeward), and James Mitchell (Grenadines). Of the victorious candidates, only two were from the original Eighth Army list in 1951: Ebenezer Joshua and Sam Slater; indeed they were the only two who contested in the elections in 1967. All the incumbents, save and except for Emmanuel F. Adams (Kingstown), from the 1966 elections were returned; in Kingstown, the promising, impressive, young lawyer Hudson Tannis of the SVLP, won for the first time.

As a consequence of SVLP's electoral victory in 1967, Milton Cato became the Chief Minister. On October 27, 1969 he was appointed as Premier under the Associated Statehood constitution. Other British colonies in the Eastern Caribbean except Montserrat had moved earlier to "Associate Statehood"; St. Vincent's more advanced constitution was delayed because of its internal political crisis. Barbados had, of course, attained its independence in November 1966, following Guyana earlier that same year, and Trinidad and Tobago on August 31, 1962; Jamaica, in the northern Caribbean, had become independent on August 6, 1962, following its referendum result in 1961 to pull out of the West Indian Federation, which collapsed shortly thereafter.

Joshua's FIAWU was to decline sharply after his party went into opposition subsequent to the general elections of May 19, 1967. In a small economy like St. Vincent, in which the government, historically, was, and is, a major employer of labour and a grantor of concessions or patronage to private sector employers, its support for this or that union is influential at more than the margin. When Joshua's PPP was in government, his FIAWU succeeded in concluding collective agreements on behalf of workers at the Public Works Department, the Kingstown Port, the main Kingstown General Hospital, Geest Industries, and even at Mt. Bentinck Estates, among other work places. In the absence of governmental authority, consequent upon the PPP's loss at the polls, the companion FIAWU soon found that its hold on most of these bargaining units started to unravel. Swiftly, the CTAWU filled the breach, in a more supportive political environment in which the SVLP was in government; it must have helped, too, that the Premier, Milton Cato, was the uncle of CTAWU's General Secretary, Burns Bonadie.

To be sure, the network of governmental control of state employment or patronage for the private sector is not impervious to successful challenge by a trade union not politically-connected to the government-of-the-day. After all, the CTAWU had broken the stranglehold of the PPP-FIAWU governmental alliance at the Sanitation Department in 1965 in its securing of collective bargaining rights. But to have broken this stranglehold required sound union organisation, committed workers, astute union leadership, and the incapacity of the FIAWU-PPP nexus to satisfy adequately or at all the workers' material demands. Increasingly after 1957, when the PPP assumed governmental authority, Joshua's FIAWU came to rely more on its political connections with a friendly government than on a thorough-going trade union organisation to maintain or enhance its membership. Thus, the FIAWU found that the PPP's loss of governmental authority affected it adversely; the personal political influence of Joshua without the support from government was insufficient to keep the FIAWU in play.

In June 1967, a few weeks after the SVLP's general elections victory, the abandoned idea of a St. Vincent Federation of Labour was revived, this time under the name of the St. Vincent Trade Union Congress (SVTUC); indeed weeks prior to the elections, the idea was mooted. Three of the four functioning trade unions, namely, the CTAWU, the Civil Service Association (CSA), and the Teachers' Union became members. The fourth, Joshua's FIAWU, refused the invitation to participate. In a letter to the CCL on June 4, 1967, Joshua thundered that:

> *The staff and officers of the TUC are sworn enemies and oppressors of the working-class movement and this stunt of trying to include us under their umbrella is merely to fool the world and the international bodies that this ruse is workable in St. Vincent...where the class warfare permits the gentry as the civil servant to look down with scorn at the leaders of the real working-class movement.*

Joshua had earlier, on May 20, 1967, the day after his party's defeat at the polls, informed the ICFTU, by letter on behalf of the FIAWU, that "the CSA and local capitalists" had plotted successfully in overthrowing the people's government in St. Vincent and claimed that "now they were ganging up to form the TUC." Clearly, Joshua saw the hand of the SVLP too, in this alleged conspiracy against him and his PPP-FIAWU combination.

Opposition to the revival of the TUC also came from Duff James. He contended, inaccurately, that the CTAWU had rejected the idea of the "federation of trade unions" at its 1965 Conference of Delegates and that the idea had not been re-examined by the union delegates as a whole. He further argued, along the line similar to Joshua, that the TUC was another middle class set-up designed to use the labour movement to support the status quo.

He also saw a naked "middle class" interest at stake in that the umbrella TUC was the vehicle by which the "middle class" to the detriment of ordinary workers, would hog the opportunities for trade union scholarships overseas offered by international trade union affiliates.

Strangely, the first President of the TUC was Frank Williams, the General Manager of the St. Vincent Banana Association, which in 1965 had originally refused to recognise the CTAWU as the bargaining agent for its office workers. Williams, a distinguished professional in his own right, also sat as the industrial employers' representative on the Wages Council. One year he was President of the TUC, the next he was the representative of employers! Burns Bonadie was to succeed Williams one year later as the TUC's President.

The Labour Commissioner, Ernest La Borde, also questioned at the time, the legal status of the TUC. In an interview with the author on September 9, 1970, La Borde explained that from the beginning he never dealt with the TUC officially. He cited the ILO Report on the question of trade unions to substantiate his view. The Report — *ILO (Geneva): Requests made by the Committee of Experts on the Applications of Conventions in March 1968 for Reply by October, 1968, Convention No. 87: Freedom of Association and Protection of the Right to Organise (1948)* — stated that "no measures have as yet been taken to incorporate provisions relating to the functioning of federations or confederations of labour in Ordinance No. 3 of 1950." La Borde further contended that because trade unions are prohibited from carrying on trade union business unless registered, the TUC could not operate because it had not been registered.

In the event, the TUC was barely functional in practice. Its activity centred mainly on issuing statements on this or that public policy issue, such as on the proposed Associate Statehood Constitution for 1969 and the Caribbean Free Trade Area (CARIFTA) and its impact on workers. It was also a central focal point for its members' collective interface with international affiliates, but even here its work was marginal. The TUC withered away.

Meanwhile the CTAWU membership continued to grow. Within three years of the SVLP's electoral victory in May 1967, the CTAWU membership increased from about 700 to 2,600. The increase in membership was attributable to CTAWU's organisation of workers, with breakthrough collective bargaining agreements at the Public Works Department, Geest Industries, Public Health, the Kingstown Port, and a few other smaller employment units in government and the private sector. The take-off of the industrial estate at Campden Park assisted trade union membership.

At most workplaces, CTAWU's support from the SVLP Government facilitated union recognition. There was, however, a modest battle for recognition at Geest Industries Limited. CTAWU applied for recognition as the workers' bargaining agent at Geest Industries on January 12, 1968, but the management reminded them that it had an existing agreement with FIAWU. However, the Geest management stated that it was prepared to bargain with any union which had the majority of its company's employees as members. CTAWU informed the company that it indeed had such a majority, which was subsequently verified by a membership check and poll conducted by the Labour Commissioner.

The CTAWU had at first refused to participate in a poll, then later acceded to it. In the interest of industrial peace, the management of the company had requested the Labour Commissioner to convene a meeting between CTAWU and FIAWU, but CTAWU refused to dialogue with the FIAWU. CTAWU raised the stakes by demanding recognition immediately; in default thereof, it threatened industrial action in two weeks, by September 11, 1969. This was averted when CTAWU convincingly won the poll and was officially recognised; on January 29, 1970, it signed a collective agreement with the company. This agreement, with enhanced workers' wages and benefits, replaced the FIAWU agreement of October 7, 1964.

It is true that CTAWU had to fight for recognition at Geest Industries, but its task was made much easier by an accommodating management in a political environment favourable to the CTAWU. In 1965, the management's attitude was not an encouraging one to the CTAWU when it had originally submitted a claim for recognition. Then, the PPP-FIAWU alliance ruled the political roost.

Towards the end of 1969, the SVLP's political ascendency was confirmed. Between its election victory in May 1967 and the commencement on October 27, 1969 of the country's ten-year apprenticeship in internal self-government under an Associate Statehood system with Britain, the SVLP was consolidating its political strength, though still challenged by the mass base of Joshua's PPP.

The SVLP had sufficiently managed the political process and the state administration to secure the advanced constitutional arrangement of internal self-government. Its leader Milton Cato assumed the honour of becoming the first Premier of St. Vincent on October 27, 1969. The SVLP had built itself into an impregnable position in one-half of the constituencies and was competitive in the others, save and except in the two where Joshua, and his wife Ivy were dominant. It had established close relations with the major religious denominations and sporting bodies, and three well-supported trade unions (CTAWU, CSA, and the Teachers' Union). In the domestic economy, strenuous efforts were being made in the area of economic diversification; and the Campden Park Industrial Estate was being slowly established. The SVLP government was also pushing education, health, social security, and the physical infrastructure as important priority areas for government action. Regionally, Cato and his SVLP were gaining respect; they were embracing CARIFTA and the newly-formed Caribbean Development Bank. It was instrumental in the founding of the West Indies States in Association (WISA), the precursor to the Organisation of Eastern Caribbean States (OECS).

Thus, by the attainment of internal self-government in October 1969, Cato and the SVLP could have felt reasonably satisfied that their two-and-one-half years in government were not without substantial achievements. Still, there were significant political and economic challenges at hand.

CHAPTER VI

THE ROAD TO INDEPENDENCE: 1969-1979

POLITICAL DEFIANCE TO SVLP DOMINANCE

In the ten years between internal self-government in 1969 and the attainment of formal constitutional independence on October 27, 1979, there were immense challenges to the people's quest for change, adjustments, and reformation in the political economy, which manifested themselves in the political process, the labour movement and trade unionism.

Within that period there were three general elections: In 1972, 1974, and 1979. In the 1972 general elections there was a contest for thirteen electoral seats. There was a tied result between the major parties: SVLP 6 seats, PPP 6 seats; the sole Independent Candidate, James Mitchell, became the Premier in a coalition government with Joshua's PPP. This coalition proved unstable and fell apart in two-and-one-half years. Fresh elections were thus held in December 1974 in which the old rivals SVLP and PPP worked out an electoral pact to trounce a Mitchell-led electoral combination: SVLP won eleven seats, and PPP, two seats; a SVLP-dominated government was formed but with Ebenezer Joshua holding, for an abbreviated period, a ministerial portfolio, while his wife, Ivy, remained in opposition. In 1979, the general elections were won by the SVLP with eleven seats; the two other seats were won by the Mitchell-led New Democratic Party (NDP) but without Mitchell in the winners' row; he had left his safe Grenadines constituency and contested the one in South Central Windward. In the 1979 general elections, the advanced social democratic United People's Movement (UPM), an alliance between the socialist-oriented Youlou United Liberation Movement (YULIMO), the social democratic Democratic Freedom Movement (DFM), and socialist-oriented — an inchoate "new left" — ARWEE (All of Us), contested, without gaining a seat, but performed creditably in winning almost 14 percent of the popular vote. On the UPM ticket were four individuals (Mike Browne, Parnel Campbell, Ralph Gonsalves, and Renwick Rose) who were to play important roles in the political life of the country, inclusive of that of the working people. Ralph Gonsalves was later to hold the Office of Prime Minister unbroken from March 29, 2001 for eighteen years unbroken, thus far; Parnel Campbell was later to become Attorney General under successive NDP administrations of James Mitchell. Mike Browne, between 2001 and 2010, was to hold the ministerial portfolios, first of Education and then of Foreign Affairs; and Renwick Rose became an important leader in the national and regional farmers' movement focussing on "fair trade" and addressing the trading and development issues in the Caribbean's interface with the European Union.

Between 1969 and 1979, the FIAWU was to decline to the point of extinction; the CTAWU came under severe challenge; and the CSA and the Teachers' Union were engaged in the process of transformation from being "service" organisations to active trade unions. Challenges to the CTAWU dominance were mixed: the St. Vincent Workers' Union (SVWU), emerged and fell apart; the National Union of Progressive Workers (NUPW), focussing largely on the plantations at Orange Hill, made little headway; and the National Workers' Movement (NWM), formed in 1977 and registered in 1979, progressed, but subordinate to the CTAWU in reach and membership.

In the post-1969 period, the anti-imperialist and nationalist struggles in the developing countries in Africa, Asia, and Latin America, and the fight for racial equality and human rights in the USA, Canada and Europe, impacted hugely the politics and working people's struggles in St. Vincent and the wider Caribbean. Young professionals, university graduates and progressive young persons generally were demanding reforms in the country's economy, society and politics beyond the offerings of a decaying colonialism, Joshua's PPP, or Cato's SVLP. Some of what they questioned appeared superficial, but reflected a nationalist and cultural awakening, for example, in the modes of dress, hairstyles and the like, incorporating or reflecting African and Caribbean sensibilities and discarding Anglo-Saxon mimicry. Ideas and possible solutions grounded in socialist orientation, the traditional communal solidarities of Africa and the Caribbean, an emancipation from mental slavery, the affirmation of Black Power, the value of "blackness" and "Caribbeanness", and more meaningful regional integration, flourished the study of Vincentian, Caribbean, African, Latin American, and Asian history as gateways to a deeper understanding of life, living and production, were being emphasised. The contemporary experiences of Fidel Castro's Cuba and Julius Nyerere's Tanzania were held up as possible alternative models, not for adoption, but for inspiration and some guidance. Caribbean thinkers and writers of the creative imagination were referenced as worthy of serious study and reflection: social scientists and historians of the "New World School" (Lloyd Best, James Milette, George Beckford, Norman Girvan, C.Y. Thomas, Woodville Marshall); novelists and poets (George Lamming, Derek Walcott, VS Naipaul, Edward "Kamau" Brathwaite); acclaimed scholars of an earlier generation such as C.L.R James and Arthur Lewis; and emerging Marxists like Walter Rodney, Trevor Munroe and Rupert Lewis.

In practical terms, on the ground, the young professionals and advanced contingents of the youths, working people and the peasantry demanded a quickening of colonialism's departure, genuine independence, deeper democratic governance, the end of the plantocracy, State participation in the ownership of banking and insurance, an education revolution, greater equality, an anti-poverty crusade, and an end to racism and petty racial-class prejudices.

In the upshot of all this, the Democratic Freedom Movement (DFM), the Young Socialist Group (YSG), Black Liberation Action Committee (BLAC), Organisation for Black Cultural Awareness (OBCA), ARWEE, Youlou United Liberation Movement (YULIMO) were formed, each with its own emphasis, but reflective of the quest for a better way, convinced that real alternatives were possible. The DFM, for example, had personalities drawn from the Kingstown Study Group, which had been publishing the influential journal Flambeau, and from the Education Forum of the People. Among the DFM's leading lights were Parnel Campbell, Kenneth John, Kerwyn Morris, and Eddie Griffith; they were in a reformist, social democratic tradition. ARWEE emphasised rural development and "socialist" solidarity; its leadership core were Oscar Allen, Simeon Greene, Earlene Horne, and Solomon Butler centred in the rural community of Diamond Village; OBCA and BLAC focussed on black culture and an inchoate socialist-oriented politics, out of which emerged young leaders such as Renwick Rose, Jim Maloney, and Junior "Spirit" Cottle. The YSG, as the name suggests, was more avowedly socialist — but still not fully formed in its ideas — than the other groupings, with personalities like Caspar London and Hugh Ragguette at the helm. YULIMO, founded in 1974, embraced the cultural nationalist and socialist currents of other groups; it took ideological guidance from Marxism-Leninism, Caribbean Marxists and revolutionaries like C.L.R James, George Padmore, Fidel Castro, Che Guevera and Walter Rodney; YULIMO was decidedly socialist and anti-imperialist; its weekly newspaper, *Freedom*, edited by Renwick Rose, YULIMO's General Secretary, was quite influential. Caspar London provided a working-class anchor for YULIMO. Several university students joined YULIMO, including Adrian Saunders (who in time – 2018 – became President of the Caribbean Court of Justice) and Glenroy Browne; so, too, did secondary school students like Jomo Thomas who, in time also – December 2015 – was installed as Speaker of the House of Assembly. So, too, did Ralph Gonsalves in 1975 join YULIMO while being a university lecturer at the Mona (Jamaica) campus of the University of the West Indies; from 1968, Gonsalves was engaged in radical student activism and left-wing politics in Jamaica where he had studied at university, and subsequently at Manchester University (United Kingdom), and Makerere University in Uganda.

In this period, 1969-1979, the entire region was in political ferment. In Guyana, the People's National Congress (PNC) government of Forbes Burnham was implementing "cooperative socialism". In Jamaica, Michael Manley's People's National Party (PNP) was pursuing a path of "democratic socialism". In Trinidad and Tobago, Eric Williams' People's National Movement (PNM), which had been in office since 1956 in the closing years of formal colonial over-rule, had opted for a brand of reformed state capitalism. In Barbados, Errol Barrow's Democratic Labour Party (DLP), between 1961 and 1976, had been crafting a "social democratic" way. All four leaders were nationalist and anti-imperialist. In 1973, their four countries, in defiance of American imperialism, established diplomatic relations with socialist Cuba; and Guyana, with the support of the other three countries, permitted the refuelling of Cuban military aircraft on their way to assist in the defence of Angola's independence.

All across the Caribbean were political parties and groups to "the left" of these governments. For example, in Guyana, Cheddi Jagan's People's Progressive Party (PPP) was a Marxist party and the principal opposition to Burnham's PNC; but there was also the Working People's Alliance (WPA) headed by Walter Rodney and Eusi Kwayana. In Jamaica, there was the Marxist-Leninist Workers' Liberation League which evolved into the Workers' Party of Jamaica (WPJ), headed by Dr. Trevor Munroe; the WPJ was numerically quite small with only pockets of popular support, but as a thorough-going Marxist-Leninist party it exercised great influence across the region. Indeed, in every country, there were, like YULIMO in St. Vincent and the Grenadines, radical nationalist, revolutionary democratic and Marxist groups or entities with Marxist leaderships.

Similarly, the trade union movement across the region was advancing progressive and even radical agendas. Trade unions which were large, and active in these respects, were the Oilfield Workers' Trade Union in Trinidad;

the Guyana Agricultural Workers' Union (GAWU); and the National Workers' Union of Jamaica.

On March 13, 1979, the revolutionary democratic New Jewel Movement (NJM) in Grenada, headed by the revolutionary democratic Maurice Bishop and the Marxist–Leninist Bernard Coard, took power by non-consensual means — by force — without any deaths, and established the Grenada Revolution which lasted until October 1983, when a political meltdown in the leadership killed the Revolution, which was swiftly buried by an American military invasion.

In the midst of all the questioning of the old order, the ancien regime, the multiple tussles and struggles within and between countries, the class and ethnic antagonisms, the alterations in the productive forces and production relations, the modes or forms of actions in the politics and trade unionism, played themselves out.

In St. Vincent and the Grenadines, the capitalist mode of production was maturing and under the overall systemic sway of monopoly capitalism globally. As the plantation system of old was disintegrating, more small farmers obtained more lands for cultivation, especially with bananas; as the economy diversified more workers became engaged in manufacturing, tourism, and allied services (electricity, telecommunications, water, financial services, shipping, and public administration). At the same time the SVLP government was pursuing state ownership in this or that sector of the economy.

Despite the CTAWU's successes in ramping up its membership and collective bargaining agreements, it was nevertheless beset by operational challenges. Its formal democratic framework did not mesh with its rule by a few; popular participation within it was limited; and its flow of communication between its leadership and membership left much to be desired. Critics within the union complained that the collective agreements were concluded without full disclosure to, and broad-based acceptance by, the union members in the relevant employment units; further, the close political affinity between the CTAWU and the SVLP rankled many union members and some of its secondary leaders. As a result of all this, dissent and dissatisfaction arose.

These very factors prompted one of CTAWU's rank-and-file organisers, Caspar London, to resign therefrom in August 1970, and with Duff James' support, organised and caused to be registered a new trade union, the St. Vincent Workers' Union (SVWU), a "blanket" union, on September 9, 1970. The SVWU, from the start, criticised the CTAWU's "veritable alliance" with the ruling SVLP. The SVWU questioned what it saw as a lack of internal democracy in the CTAWU, its vacillating leadership and "a lack of commitment to working class principles." Accordingly, SVWU denounced what it called "sell out" agreements, especially one with Geest Industries; it labelled it the "infamous Geest agreement". In an interview with the author in September 1970, Caspar London predicted, wrongly as it turned out, the demise of the CTAWU; he emphasised that trade unions required a radical, pro-working-class leadership which he claimed existed in the SVWU.

Six days after SVWU's registration, it won a poll against the CTAWU among the stevedores employed by the four Shipping Agents. Ralph Gonsalves, in St. Vincent conducting research on the labour movement, actively assisted Duff James and Caspar London in the union, including activist work at Port Kingstown among the stevedores and the employees of Geest Industries. There were 270 stevedores allegedly on the shipping agents' roster; the SVWU challenged the size of the voters' list but participated nevertheless in the poll upon one day's notice. In the event, 140 stevedores voted with the SVWU winning with eighty-nine votes to CTAWU's forty-eight votes, and three spoilt ballots. Despite this victory, the St. Vincent Employers' Federation, bargaining on behalf of the Shipping Agents, refused to recognise the SVWU. However, in May 1977, at the St. Vincent Electricity Services, the SVWU successfully challenged the CTAWU and became the workers' bargaining agent; the CTAWU lost the electricity workers after seven years of representation; the SVWU's efforts at Sanitation did not bring about the dislodging of CTAWU there, although it had made inroads.

The CTAWU bristled at the taunts that it was, in effect, the trade union arm of the SVLP. It insisted that it was independent of party politics and that the blood relation between SVLP's Milton Cato and CTAWU's General Secretary Burns Bonadie was purely coincidental, nothing more.

Unfortunately for the CTAWU, some in the SVLP's leadership were not so careful in making the distinction. For example, at a public meeting on September 10, 1970, the Minister of Communications, Works, and Labour Levi Latham, in attacking Caspar London's break from CTAWU, referred to the latter as the Labour Party union. Contrastingly, around the same time, on September 8, 1970, in an interview with the author, SVLP's Deputy Leader, Hudson Tannis, was adamant — and correctly so — that his party had no institutional or operational connections with the CTAWU. Informally, though, the SVLP appeared to exercise political influence on the CTAWU on account of the closeness of relations between the leaders of both party and union. It is likely, too, that the CTAWU's informal links with the SVLP assisted in keeping that party and government within the social democratic tradition, inclusive of the pursuit of policies favourable to the working people.

Still, despite the CTAWU's perceived closeness to the SVLP, the union was occasionally strident against the SVLP government or personalities within it. For example, the CTAWU led its members who worked at the Public Works' Department on a strike for higher wages in 1969. Again, in November 1970, the union threatened to call out on strike its 700 members working in the central government if Minister Levi Latham was not dismissed from his post. Latham was being blamed by the CTAWU for his general anti-union intransigence and his reluctance to cause the reclassification of certain posts in the Surveyors' Section of the Public Works Department — a relatively minor issue that the union sought to magnify. The CTAWU raised the surveyors' case and its call for Latham's dismissal through its regional affiliate, the CCL.

In the post-1967 period, with Joshua's PPP in opposition, the FIAWU found it quite challenging to retain its collective bargaining status and its membership in government departments or state enterprises. But, interestingly, the FIAWU was the convenient vehicle which Ebenezer Joshua was using to make political statements against the SVLP government. It was evident that within the PPP, Joshua was not able to perform his one-man leadership role as hitherto; but in the FIAWU, there were no such organisational constraints on him. In the PPP, persons such as Roderick Marksman (who had won the West St. George constituency in the 1967 general elections), and Othneil Sylvester, Alphonso Dennie, Emmanuel F. Adams, and Edgerton Richards, who had lost their constituency contests in 1967, were seeking to put the PPP on a more modern, organisational footing with internal democratic accountability. The real problem, though, for those who sought to promote internal party democracy and place constraints on Joshua in his capacity of Political Leader of the PPP, was the public perception that Joshua *was* the PPP; so, when he made political statements through the FIAWU, the public did not separate those from the PPP.

Thus, for example, the FIAWU passed a resolution on February 9, 1968, against the alleged SVLP government's policy of discrimination and victimisation directed at persons who supported the PPP; similarly, the FIAWU persisted in its protests against what it termed the "illegal ousting" of the Chairman of the Bequia Village Council while the PPP remained silent; so, too, the FIAWU's frequent public critiques against the government and the "Associate Statehood" constitution.

It is not that in the immediate post-1967 period the PPP was inactive, but it had a more collegiate look at the leadership level, in some respects emulating the SVLP. The PPP continued to hold frequent public meetings and was organising itself better at the grass-roots level for the 1972 general elections.

The SVLP's victory at the polls in May 1967, was greeted with enthusiasm by the Civil Service Association (CSA). Between 1957 and May 1967, the CSA and the public servants generally were in repeated conflicts with Joshua and his PPP government. Upon the SVLP's electoral victory, the CSA offered support to the new government. In its 1968 CSA Report, its President, a well-known SVLP supporter, Stanley Branch, reported that the CSA's relationship with the SVLP government had been "a good one".

However, governmental support was not a substitute for effective and proper organisation in the CSA. In 1967, the CSA's membership was 406 out of some 900 civil servants; of the members, 116 were in arrears of their dues. There was, across the public service, general dissatisfaction in the CSA's Executive. It had not succeeded in putting its house in order as suggested by the 1965 Gardner Browne Report on Salaries' Revision.

It was hardly surprising, therefore, that in 1969, when a group of young civil servants spearheaded by two university graduates, John Cato and Arnhim Eustace, challenged the existing CSA executive, it crumbled easily. Both Cato and Eustace had become "radicalised" as university students in Canada; they had seen racism first-hand and capitalist exploitation of the working people; they had lived through the anti-racism protests at the Sir George Williams University in February 1969, and the upsurge in North America of the demand for "Black Power". After returning to St. Vincent, both Cato and Eustace received employment in the public service on a temporary basis. Quickly, they realised that changes were required in the public service; they saw the CSA as a possible mechanism to effect some meaningful change for the better, for public servants, the public service and the people.

In September 1969, Eustace and Cato, began to organise mainly the younger civil servants to call for a vote of "No Confidence" in the Executive at a special meeting of the Association. The Eustace-Cato faction presented a slate of candidates which was comfortably elected. Eustace was elected President, and Cato, First Assistant Secretary. Of the seven who were elected to executive posts, five had the benefit of university education either at the degree or diploma level. They were all progressive, anti-colonial, social democratic modernisers of a younger generation.

The foundations of the new Executive's policy consisted of an attempt to make the Association more meaningful in the country's affairs; to change from the CSA's virtual alliance with the SVLP to an independent political line; and to revive the membership drive at the branch level. In a profound sense, these policy plans were a faithful manifestation, in a new period, of three of the CSA's core objects, as outlined in the 1961 edition of the *Constitution and Rules of the Civil Service Association:* 1) To strive for the general improvement of the public service and to protect the interest and welfare of its members; 2) to promote goodwill and understanding between government and its officers; and 3) to foster good relations with the general public. There were, too, a number of grievances for the new CSA Executive, including the anomalies, arising from the 1965 Gardner Browne Report, to be settled. It was Eustace's view, as expressed in an interview with the author on September 19, 1970, that many of these grievances, though simple to resolve, were not addressed by the former executive members because their closeness to the SVLP restrained them from acting in the interest of the CSA's members.

However, important as statements of policy and the settlement of minor grievances were, they were not by themselves sufficient to revive a barely functional organisation. Fortunately for the CSA's Executive, the SVLP Government provided the union with a mobilising issue, that of the arbitrary dismissal of John Cato from the public service. The public service broadly and a section of the informed public were uneasy about the Government's action in this regard. Because Cato and Eustace and a number of other young university graduates, including Kerwyn Morris and Parnel Campbell held membership in a recently-formed organisation, the Education Forum of the People (EFP), which opposed the programme and direction of the SVLP Government, the dismissal took on a decidedly political flavour. Shortly thereafter, Morris and Campbell were suspended from their teaching posts. The EFP espoused a brand of "Black Power" philosophy and it advanced reform options not on offer by either the SVLP or the PPP. The SVLP leadership viewed the EFP's reform proposals as inchoate and largely impractical.

The allegations against John Cato were that he had been discourteous to white Americans at the two departments where he had worked and that he had wrongly interfered in matters which were properly outside the scope of his authority. The CSA refuted these charges and called on the Public Service Commission (PSC) to substantiate them. The CSA's journal, *Touli* insisted that although the charges were not substantiated, Cato's appeal was dismissed; *Touli* (Volume 8, No. 4, March 1970) contended that the PSC had effected the dismissal "for reasons it is not prepared to state."

Whatever the rights or wrongs of the charges against Cato and his failed appeal, undoubtedly John Cato's anti-SVLP pronouncements in the public had at least irritated the government. The leadership of the SVLP government suspected, too, that Cato was the author of a highly critical article of the recently-proposed National Provident Fund (NPF) under a pseudonym, Lumumba Warjabi, in the second issue of *Touli*. Objectively, this critique of the NPF was anti-worker and cheap, opportunistic politics without ideological clarity; in a telling way, it pointed to ideational confusion among elements of the anti-SVLP activists in the CSA and EFP. By any objective standard, the NPF was good public policy for the working people; its later evolution into a National Insurance Service (NIS) received the support of the SVLP, and the New Democratic Party (NDP) of James Mitchell; the NIS was further consolidated under the Unity Labour Party Government. The asset base of the NIS at the end of 2017 was in excess of EC $500 million. It delivers a core of benefits for workers, including pensions and sickness benefits.

The John Cato dismissal provided the impetus and sparked a commitment on the part of the CSA to reorganise its many branches, even as older pro-SVLP public servants recoiled at the approaches of the EFP-inspired leadership in the CSA. This reorganisation ignited enthusiasm from CSA members, too, because of the imminence of another salaries revision. The CSA under Eustace's presidency prepared well for this revision exercise: branch memoranda and an overall memorandum were submitted; participatory meetings were held at all levels; and basic analyses were done internally by the CSA of the salary-structure, allowances and the like. An emphasis was placed on minor salaried personnel to receive the largest proportionate salary increase, but Pusinelli reported that the CSA's motives in this regard were "altruistic and not based on economic facts". The CSA Executive rejected the Pusinelli Report; it was only after the government agreed to enhance increases at the lower levels of the salary scales that the CSA relented.

The interest which the CSA had demonstrated on behalf of the lower paid public servants prompted an increased membership; it was reported that out of a total of 900 civil servants, the membership rose to over 500. The growing anti-SVLP sentiment among sections of the civil service, however, did not translate into political support for the EFP of which Arnhim Eustace and John Cato were members; the unintended beneficiary was Joshua's PPP, as evidenced later in the 1972 general elections.

The increased anti-government activism of the CSA and other public employees, such as some teachers, provoked the SVLP Government into responding with an unnecessary restraint on the political speech and actions of public servants in the form of the Public Officers (Conditions of Employment) Act which was enacted into law on October 12, 1971. The provisions of this Act went beyond the boundaries of the Civil Service Regulations in that it criminalised aspects of a civil servant's speech in public. The Act irked public servants and intensified the animus of many of them against the SVLP government. One of the first legislative acts of another Labour Government, that of the Unity Labour Party (ULP) in 2001, was to repeal this overly broad restraint on public servants' exercise of their fundamental rights and freedoms.

No parallel activism to that of the CSA in the early 1970s was occurring in the Teachers' Union based in the primary schools, or in the Secondary School Teachers' Association (SSTA) which had become registered as a trade union in 1957. It is true that the Teachers' Union had engaged in strike action against the colonial government in 1956 and the PPP government in 1961, but since then its leadership hardly stirred its members beyond "social club" activities; perhaps the teachers were not inclined to push the SVLP government which most of them supported politically. At the same time, in a general way, the members of the Teachers' Union and the SSTA benefited from the spill-off activism of the more vibrant CSA Executive. The "radicalisation" of the Teachers' Union was to await the arrival of socialist-oriented leadership in 1975.

In trade unions, as in other organisations, leadership is vital, but at the same time sustained organisational work is required to maintain the day-to-day requisites of the trade union. The CSA's burst of activism was not sustained. John Cato was soon off to the new Law Faculty at the University of the West Indies in Barbados as part of the first intake of law students. After the 1972 general elections, Arnhim Eustace was promoted to the senior ranks of the civil service under the coalition government of James Mitchell and Joshua's PPP. Similarly, the outstanding leader in the EFP, Parnel Campbell, joined Cato as a law student. To be sure, the EFP still had Kerwyn Morris and Eddie Griffith, but whatever their individual attributes the leadership skills of Campbell were missed; Dr. Kenneth John's return to St. Vincent and the Grenadines from the United Kingdom in late 1971 after completing his doctoral studies in Government and his professional qualification in the Law, strengthened the EFP's ranks; but he, too, did not possess the leadership magnetism or political energy of Campbell.

In April 1972, general elections were held. It was a two-party contest between the SVLP and the PPP, save and except in the Grenadines where the incumbent James Mitchell was offering himself to the electorate as an Independent candidate. After the 1967 general elections, Mitchell had served as the Minister of Agriculture and Trade in the SVLP government headed by Milton Cato; Mitchell was generally recognised as one of the better performers in that government and he had endeared himself to significant sections of the populace as a possible future leader. His youthfulness, his physical presence — tall and bearded — and his analytic mind impressed people; critics of the SVLP, including the EFP and the PPP, sought to distinguish him as being more "progressive", at least superficially so, from the rest of the SVLP. Shortly before the 1972 general elections, Mitchell and Milton Cato fell out, though not on any substantial policy question; so, he left the SVLP but there was not sufficient time for him to gather a party around him — he had failed in this regard in 1965 on his return from his overseas sojourn. Thus, he contested in the Grenadines as an Independent in 1972.

The general elections of April 1972 produced a tie between two parties: SVLP, six seats; the PPP, six seats. Mitchell, however, was re-elected in the Grenadines. In the upshot, after much political bargaining, Joshua conceded the Premiership to James Mitchell in a shaky coalition between a party and one man in which the one man, Mitchell, was the Premier, Joshua was Minister of Finance, and the other five elected members of the PPP were ministers of this or that portfolio.

The SVLP won 50.43 percent of the valid votes cast; PPP garnered 45.41 percent; and the Independent candidate, 4.16 percent. The winning SVLP candidates were: Milton Cato (East St. George), St. Clair Dacon (South Windward), Levi Latham (Marriaqua), Randolph Russell (East Kingstown), Hudson Tannis (West Kingstown), and Arthur Woods (Central Leeward). The PPP victors were: Ebenezer Joshua (South Central Windward), Ivy Joshua (North Windward), Victor Cuffy (North Central Windward), Clive Tannis (West St. George), Othneil Sylvester (South Leeward) and Alphonso Dennie (North Leeward). For the SVLP, the newcomers to the legislature were Dacon, Russell, and Woods, two of whom — Dacon and Woods — had a social democratic outlook; Russell was an enterprising businessman. For the PPP, the first-time elected members were Cuffy, Sylvester, and Dennie, of whom only Cuffy had socialist-oriented instincts.

In the 1972 elections, the number of constituencies were increased from nine to thirteen. Although the PPP won six seats, an improvement over the three seats in the previous elections in 1967 under a nine-constituency electoral configuration, its percentage vote fell from 46.2 percent to 45.41 percent; further in four of the seats, it was uncompetitive with scores in each of below

700 votes. The PPP was evidencing electoral decline: Its popular vote in 1972 was its lowest score in this regard since 1954 when it obtained 40 percent of the popular vote; since then its share of the popular vote was 48.9 percent in 1957; 49.5 percent in 1961; 49.03 percent in 1966; and 47.2 percent in 1967.

It is true that the SVLP's share of the popular vote fell to 50.43 percent from its 1967 number of 53.8 percent but that is because it lost the candidacy of James Mitchell in the Grenadines. In fact, on mainland St. Vincent itself, the SVLP increased marginally its popular vote and was uncompetitive in only two seats, those won by the Joshuas. On balance the PPP was declining and the SVLP was consolidating its base and expanding it, if only marginally. The acceptance by Joshua of a subordinate position in the government to that of James Mitchell signalled, too, his waning political stocks which admittedly were still significant. As plantation agriculture disintegrated and the economy became more diversified and modern, Joshua's appeal appeared to diminish; his plantation worker-base was frayed; so too, his traditional urban support.

The uneasy coalition of Mitchell and Joshua's PPP collapsed in September 1974; it lasted for almost two and one-half years. The coalition government, labelled derisively by Joshua as the "Mitchell Junta" after its collapse, was unable to withstand multiple pressures: the deteriorating economic situation consequent upon the global oil crisis of 1973, and continuing; the relentless opposition, up and down St. Vincent, by the SVLP; the constant internal bickering in the coalition government; the permanent dissatisfaction of Joshua and his wife Ivy with Mitchell as Premier — their settled grievance was that Joshua was robbed of his chance of being Premier by a political upstart, Mitchell; and the growing impossibility of three PPP ministers (Othneil Sylvester, Alphonso Dennie, and Victor Cuffy) in maintaining a cordial political relationship with Joshua — the other, minister, Clive Tannis kept his mature, long standing relations with Joshua. The coalition government was a complete mess, politically.

Still, there were a few noteworthy initiatives: In agriculture, Mitchell launched a grow-your-own food campaign and the government introduced a few new crops, including carrots; a land reform initiative was undertaken at Lauders, though in a rushed and disorganised way; a half-hearted attempt was made to prod the Public Service Commission to promote public servants based on merit; and regionally, it participated in the approaching final stages of the establishment of the Caribbean Community (CARICOM) on July 4, 1973 — an upgrade from CARIFTA's free trade arrangements to that of a customs union and functional cooperation in a wide range of subject areas.

The collapse of the Mitchell-Joshua coalition government plunged the country into intense political jostling, and even confusion. Mitchell, unwisely, after the dissolution of Parliament, dragged the holding of elections over a 90-day period of political frenzy. The government barely functioned; civil servants and other public employees became open political activists, mainly for the opposition SVLP. Mitchell, in a move laced with naked political self-interest, announced a salary and wage hike for civil servants, effective January 1, 1975, after the December 1975 elections. In an ex-post facto comment, Mitchell, in referring to the increase in emoluments, commented with sardonic wit: "Ah leave a hook in dey gill", meaning that he had burdened the incoming SVLP government with additional expenditure to be paid from a parlous Treasury!

SVLP RETURNS ASCENDANT AMIDST POLITICAL AND TRADE UNION CHALLENGES

In December, 1974, general elections were held. The old political foes, Joshua and Cato came to an electoral arrangement. The PPP contested the North Windward and South Central Windward seats (Ivy Joshua and Ebenezer Joshua respectively) with the support of the SVLP; and the SVLP contested, with the PPP, support in all the remaining constituencies with the exception of West St. George in which both SVLP and PPP were rivals. In West St. George, Joshua was unable to get Clive Tannis to stand down in favour of the SVLP's Arthur Williams who eventually won the seat. James Mitchell and Othniel Sylvester led the amalgam of the Mitchell-Sylvester Party, known popularly as "the Junta". The SVLP-PPP electoral arrangement won twelve of the thirteen seats (SVLP, ten; PPP, two); Mitchell was the only winner in the Grenadines from his team. The "Junta" was trounced decisively.

Indeed, the Mitchell-Sylvester Party (MSP), the "Junta." won only 4,497 votes in the eleven constituencies which it contested or 15.85 percent of the total votes validly cast of 28,360. It was a dismal showing for a political grouping which had held political power for over 30 months immediately prior to the elections. Six of the MSP eleven candidates lost their deposits, having secured less than 15 percent of the votes cast. Only three of its candidates scored over 30 percent of the votes cast in their respective constituencies: Sylvester, 32.2 percent in South Leeward; Alphonso Dennie, 40.5 percent in North Leeward; and Mitchell, 62.3 percent in the Grenadines. Three of the MSP's Ministers lost their seats: Cuffy, Dennie, and Sylvester.

Of course, the 1974 elections were unusual in that the two major parties, the SVLP and the PPP, ganged up politically against Mitchell's outfit. Still, never in the country's political history had the electorate turned so overwhelming against a political entity led by the outgoing head of Government. The people blamed the Mitchell-Sylvester team for the political mess which was created.

The two PPP candidates who had no SVLP opposition candidate against them — Mrs. Joshua in North Windward and her husband in South Windward — easily won their seats; PPP's Clive Tannis in West St. George was defeated by SVLP's Arthur Williams in a seat which the SVLP insisted on contesting, even though two years earlier in the 1972 election, the same Clive Tannis had defeated Arthur Williams by a margin of 56.2 percent of the vote to 43.8 percent. Evidently, Cato's SVLP felt it had the political whip-hand over Joshua's PPP in the entire country to insist on its candidate in West St. George. It was reflective, too, of Joshua's personal political bile against the Mitchell-Sylvester Party that he was prepared to throw his old political companion, Clive Tannis, under the proverbial bus.

Seven of the nine SVLP candidates who were not opposed by the PPP won their seats by huge, unnatural majorities. Scores between the 80s and 90s percentage range were recorded by the SVLP candidates in North Central Windward (Vincent Beache), South Windward (St. Clair Dacon), Marriaqua (Levi Latham), East St. George (Milton Cato), East Kingstown (Randolph Russell), West Kingstown (Hudson Tannis), and Central Leeward (Arthur Woods). In the other two of these nine seats, the SVLP candidates won against the MSP candidates as follows: Grafton Isaacs (67.8 percent) defeated the incumbent Othneil Sylvester (32.2 percent); and John Thompson (59.5 percent) was victorious against Alphonso Dennie (40.5 percent). In the tenth seat won by the SVLP, Arthur Williams (60.4 percent of the vote) defeated the PPP's Clive Tannis (38.5 percent) in a three-way fight in West St. George.

The aggregate results for the four parties which contested the 1974 elections were: SVLP, 19,003 votes or 67.0 percent of the total votes validly cast; PPP, 4,744 or 16.72 percent; MSP, 4,497 votes or 15.85 percent; the Democratic Freedom Movement (DFM), 217 votes or 0.8 percent; and the West Indian National Party (WINP) led by George Charles, which contested four seats, obtained 116 votes or 0.4 percent of the valid votes cast. This was the last time that George Charles, the populist labour leader of 1951, had his name on the ballot. The DFM, which evolved out of the EFP, ran two candidates who both lost their deposits: Kenneth John in West Kingstown (141 votes or 6 percent); and Edward Griffith in East Kingstown (76 votes or 3.2 percent); their "third party" candidacies made little political impact despite the fact they were, on paper, two good quality candidates with a progressive programme.

Among the elected intake of the legislature arising from the 1974 elections were newcomers: Beache, Isaacs, Williams, and Thompson; they all possessed a broad social democratic outlook in line with that of the SVLP as a whole.

A strange governance arrangement emerged from the 1974 general elections: Milton Cato, as expected, became the Premier; but Ebenezer Joshua became a Minister while his wife, Ivy, was named as Leader of the Opposition by way of a constitutional amendment. Political reality on the ground and the practice of the Westminster parliamentary model ought to have ensured the post of Leader of the Opposition for James Mitchell. After all, he was the principal figure in the elections campaign opposed to the SVLP-PPP electoral pact. The pettiness of small island politics, however, dictated otherwise; the antipathy of the SVLP and Cato to Mitchell was evidently made manifest on this matter. With Ivy Joshua and Mitchell on the opposition benches but none supporting the other, the legislature amended the Constitution to provide a result based on the length of tenure in parliament and the number of votes cast in the respective constituencies in the general elections for the respective claimants to the Office of the Leader of the Opposition. On these criteria, Ivy Joshua was duly appointed as such by the Governor-General. Thus, the bizarre situation arose in which Mrs. Joshua posed parliamentary questions for ministerial answers by a government of which her husband, Ebenezer Joshua, was a minister. It was widely felt, and publicly articulated, without demurrer from any of the Joshuas, that the husband actually prepared the parliamentary questions for the wife to ask of the government in which the husband held ministerial office. Within two years, this farce was resolved when Ebenezer Joshua resigned as a minister, and with the support of Ivy Joshua, he became the Leader of the Opposition.

In 1975, James Mitchell formed and launched his New Democratic Party (NDP) which, within nine years, in July 1984, became the governing party; the NDP was to remain in government until March 28, 2001.

The period 1972 to 1974 was pre-occupied with intensely partisan politics. Trade unions quietly went about representing workers at their workplaces at which collective bargaining units existed. The CTAWU was dominant among the non-pensionable employees in the central government and at a few other entities in the private sector, particularly in the manufacturing sector and telecommunications, and public sector enterprises — state companies and statutory bodies. The FIAWU had by this time lost collective bargaining status at all workplaces where it had hitherto been in command. The FIAWU's opposition political status, its disorganisation, and Joshua's increasing loss of political energy, and support, handicapped it. The two public sector unions, the CSA and the Teachers' Union were mainly inactive; and the CSA's energetic burst under the Arnhim Eustace-John Cato leadership lost momentum after the Pusinelli salary increases. In the political configurations opposed to the SVLP, a leadership vacuum existed: Joshua's stocks were falling rapidly; Mitchell's position was yet to be assured nationally; and no new political figure commanding broad acceptance was at hand. The SVLP's political ascendancy and its occupation of governmental office were to be affirmed in December 1974. In the ensuing months some members of the SVLP government became decidedly cocky; they even declared their government to be "the strongest in the world!" But real challenges beckoned.

In November, 1975, the industrial relations calm in the teaching service erupted into open protests by the teachers. Michael "Mike" Browne had recently become the leader of the Teachers' Union in tandem with Yvonne Francis. Browne, a professional educator, had returned from Canada with a post-graduate university degree, and was employed at the St. Vincent Teachers' College as a lecturer. His socialist-oriented politics, cultural nationalism, and general radicalism had drawn him into the membership of YULIMO. Yvonne Francis was an experienced primary school teacher and principal; she was affiliated to the EFP which had metamorphosed into the DFM; she was an accomplished primary-school teacher, well-respected in the Teachers' Union and in the community.

The Teachers' Union, led by its President Mike Browne, made a series of demands focussing on union recognition and collective bargaining, salary increases, working conditions, back-pay, educational reforms, and the repeal of the highly restrictive Public Servants (Conditions of Employment) Act. The SVLP-led government paid scant regard to the teachers' demands. Thus, the union launched a well-supported three-week strike in November 1975. But as the strike ended its second week, large sections of the teachers, who traditionally supported the SVLP, began to waver. The Teachers' Union was not organised to wage such a long strike; and the CSA and the CTAWU, for different reasons, did not come to the support of the teachers in solidarity. In that context the striking teachers returned to work without anything tangible to show for it.

The government's response to the strike was uncompromising. Simply put, the government was not too concerned about the teachers being on strike so long as the governmental machinery functioned; it was prepared to sit tight until the strike crumbled.

When on November 14, 1975, the teachers, some supportive parents and students marched in a huge protest in Kingstown, the police answered with batons and tear gas. The Teachers' Union President Mike Browne, its Vice President Yvonne Francis and eight other teachers were arrested, charged and detained. The Government claimed subsequently that the police acted on its own without political instruction; the Commissioner of Police, Robert O'Garro, years later publicly asserted this to be true and confirmed that he acted because the Teachers' Union had broken the law in that it marched without the police's permission. But the enthusiasm of Attorney General Arthur Williams, in legally pursuing the leaders of the march, prompted a settled public perception that the Government had directed the police to break up forcibly an illegal protest. The strike collapsed shortly after the police's intervention. The official response to the protest was clumsily, and oppressively handled by the SVLP; they were not even able to put the proverbial silk glove on the police's iron fist. Only much later did the SVLP government seek to mend fences with its core support among teachers. The memory of the teachers' strike, the protest march and the suppression of it, the arrest of the leaders of the Teaches' Union and their prosecution still rankles today. Annually, there is a "Remember November" march and rally by the Teachers' Union, which events have recently been poorly attended.

Numerous teachers suffered, in one form or another, for their role in the strike. On the day before the protest march on November 14, 1975, thirty-one teachers were arrested for unlawful assembly during a sit-in at the Ministry of Education. On the day of the march, among the teachers who were arrested, charged and detained in the holding cells were, in addition to the two aforementioned union leaders, the following: George Bailey, Simeon Greene, Ferdinand Toney, Cecil "Pa" Jack, Timothy Ottley, and Samuel "Kala" Gordon. The Magistrate's Court freed them. Other teachers were dismissed or transferred unreasonably. A few others resigned in frustration. Many of the affected teachers migrated overseas.

A roll call of the teachers who were personally penalised or who suffered individually on account of the teachers' strike, reveals overwhelmingly the names of persons who went on to pursue distinguished careers in teaching or in other professions or callings. One of those who suffered, Cecil "Blazer" Williams, became, in time, the long-serving Chairman of the Public Service Commission (April 2001 continuously to the present time – 2019). Among those who firmly held the metaphoric fort of struggle during the strike were female teachers in addition to Yvonne Francis, including Ann Williams (later Daniel), Yvadney Tyrell, and Angela Brooker. Both male and female teachers were united in a worthy struggle on behalf of the working people and trade unionism. In the process, the Teachers' Union was reshaped from "social club" to bona fide trade union. At the same time, an unwarranted overreach by Government was shown to be futile and counter-productive for all concerned. Always in these matters, mature conversations are undoubtedly preferable, particularly in a small society like St. Vincent and the Grenadines.

The immediate short-term defeat of the Teachers' Union highlighted, among other things, the question of trade union disunity. Mike Browne, at the urging of YULIMO, had been taking the lead to from a Trade Union Congress (TUC), a federation or confederation of trade unions, which had earlier in 1967 had an inauspicious false start, following upon the 1962-1963 failed effort at a federation of labour. In 1976, the active trade unions had set up a Joint Education Workers' Committee in an attempt to coordinate trade union education so as to break away from the externally-directed educational programmes; the unions also had taken since 1976, too, the efforts to hold a joint May-day — workers' day — rally annually, but even these efforts were patchily pursued and eventually petered out in the early years of the twenty-first century.

The teachers' strike, though a failure in itself to gain immediate material benefits, had marked a new phase of militancy in the Teaches' Union, and indeed, emboldened other workers to withdraw their labour, if only for short periods of time over the next three years,, in quest of increased wages. These workers were those at the main hospital, sanitation services, Public Works Department, the state-owned marketing corporation, the public utilities, and a few commercial enterprises.

In 1977 and 1978, the issue of trade union recognition was important for two young trade unions — the National Union Progressive Workers' (NUPW) led by Caspar London which was registered in 1975, and the Farmers and National Workers' Union (FNWU), registered in 1978, and led by an ex-CTAWU organiser, Brinsley Nickie. The NUPW had been organising the workers on the old FIAWU-PPP base at Orange Hill Estates. NUPW insisted that it had majority support on these Estates on its membership register; the management disputed this claim and the issue simply withered away. It was extremely difficult to organise agricultural workers and the NUPW simply did not have the resources, including manpower, to be effective. Similarly, the FNWU's effort in a state-owned enterprise failed. Not much was heard of the FNWU thereafter.

It is noteworthy that the trade unions which were formed and registered in the period 1970 to 1979 aimed, by and large, to shake the CTAWU's hold on the union membership, met with little success. The first of these unions, the SVWU was founded in 1970 by ex-CTAWU leaders, Duff James and Caspar London. The SVWU made a solid advance at the St. Vincent Electricity Services, but very little progress elsewhere. The second, the FNWU, whose leader, Brinsley Nickie also came out of the CTAWU stable, failed. The third, the NUPW of Caspar London, another former CTAWU organiser, did yeoman work but hardly progressed. London was opposed to poaching another union's members; he opted to focus on the unorganised agricultural workers, but he met with little success despite his extraordinary personal sacrifices and commitment to this cause.

As discussion on St. Vincent's move to constitutional independence gathered pace in 1978, the political parties, political organisations, trade unions, and civil society became engrossed in the conversations. The political parties and groups which supported the march to independence were the SVLP, YULIMO, the DFM, and ARWEE. Mitchell's NDP and Joshua's PPP opposed the move to independence. The trade unions which gave their active support to the independence drive were the CTAWU, the Teachers' Union, the SVWU, and the NUPW. The CTAWU basically followed the line of the SVLP; the leaderships of the Teachers' Union and NUPW were influenced mainly by YULIMO. The SVWU, with Duff James, equivocated at first, but eventually stood firm with the SVLP position.

The stance of the SVLP was simple and straightforward: Independence in the shortest possible time; independence, but within the frame of regional economic integration and functional cooperation; retaining the liberal democratic provisions of the Associate Statehood Constitution of 1969, plus the enlargement of constitutional authority to St. Vincent for defence and foreign affairs, and a few minor alterations; and incorporating the Grenadines in the name of the independent state, thus changing the name from St. Vincent to St. Vincent and the Grenadines.

YULIMO sought a root-and-branch overhaul of the extant constitution so as, among other things, to advance the social democratic revolution; deepen accountability, and strengthen democratic participation; upgrade the Magistracy with a security of tenure for the Magistrates; strengthen the independence and quality of the judiciary; reduce the powers of the Prime Minister; bolster parliamentary democracy; set up an independent Elections Commission to replace the Office of the Supervisor of Elections; broaden and fortify the extent, and protection, of fundamental rights and freedoms, including workers' rights; replace the Governor-General with a home-grown non-Executive President; and remove the requirement of appeals to the Privy Council, and replace it by a regional final appellate court. YULIMO published a monograph on its position explaining the meaning of genuine independence and advancing its constitutional proposals in a comprehensive document entitled, *Independence: The Beginning, Not the End*. No other political party published as extensive a document on this matter as did YULIMO. The principal authors of YULIMO's document were Ralph Gonsalves, Renwick Rose, and Caspar London.

The DFM called for some inconsequential reforms but its leading members were in the forefront of calling for more time for the public to discuss the draft constitution. Civil society, including trade unions, formed a National Independence Committee (NIC) under the leadership of a distinguished lawyer and former high-level public servant Henry Williams, to engage the government in a meaningful dialogue on the draft constitution, and the process towards the attainment of independence. Unfortunately, the SVLP government was dismissive of the NIC and did not treat it as a potentially valuable partner.

Joshua's PPP called not only for a delay of independence but demanded general elections before independence. It said not merely "NO" to independence under Milton Cato's SVLP, but adopted the backward posture that St. Vincent was not fit and ready for independence. The independence debate marked the sad decline of Joshua; this once proud, anti-colonial fighter had, over time, metamorphosed into a caricature, a defender of continued colonial rule. It is a matter of profound regret that he placed his own personal, political pique at, and animosity to, Milton Cato over a cause which he had spent much of his earlier political life espousing. Joshua had become irrelevant to a serious matter of great public importance.

If Joshua's PPP had little more than a nuisance value in the 1978-1979 conversations on independence, James Mitchell's NDP was backward to the core. Mitchell actually opposed independence for St. Vincent. He had earlier written that under Associate Statehood, St. Vincent was "as safe as sardines". It was a curious metaphor; the only "safe" sardines are dead ones in the tins. Mitchell's diversionary talk about pursuing independence with other Eastern Caribbean states in one united nation-state was, in the political context, nothing but a cloak under which to oppose independence for St. Vincent and the Grenadines; after all, Grenada, Dominica, and St. Lucia had already moved to independence separately. In 1979, James Mitchell preferred continued colonial over-rule, though with continued internal self-government, to an independent St. Vincent and the Grenadines!

St. Vincent as a metaphoric live sardine — not a dead one — in the hostile, choppy waters of the global political environment needed, more than ever, the instruments of independence and sovereignty to come to terms more efficaciously with, and to address more capably, the difficult external political economy and its challenges. An independent St. Vincent undoubtedly had the possibility of enlarging its political and economic space in its own interest, rather than being tied dutifully to Britain's external interests. Moreover, a free people had the inalienable right to govern themselves, not to be ruled under colonialism or neo-colonialism!

While unseemly bickering between, and among some political forces in St. Vincent over the necessity and desirability of independence, the three other Windward Islands had already proceeded to independence: Grenada in February 1974; Dominica in November, 1978; and St. Lucia in February, 1979. Political unrest in Dominica in 1978-1979 and the Grenada Revolution on March 13, 1979, prompted anti-independence hysteria from Joshua's PPP and Mitchell's NDP. But Jamaica and Trinidad and Tobago had both acceded to independence in 1962 and this accession caused no subversion of political democracy; so, too, the attainment of independence in 1966 by both Guyana and Barbados did not undermine democratic governance.

In April 1979, as the discussion on the issue of independence intensified, the La Soufriere volcano erupted. Some 20,000 persons had to be evacuated and housed temporarily in schools and other shelters outside of the evacuated areas in the north-eastern and north-western parts of St. Vincent. Although there were no casualties due to advanced warnings, the disruptions and economic loss were severe. Indeed, on Independence Day, October 27, 1979, thousands of persons were still living in temporary shelters.

Both Mitchell and Joshua refused to attend the independence constitutional talks in London. Mitchell, with Othneil Sylvester as his lawyer, filed a lawsuit to stop the march to independence but was unsuccessful. The SVLP government's invitation to the NIC arrived too late for that organisation to attend the talks in London. Thus, the SVLP government of St. Vincent and the government of the United Kingdom concluded their discussions and negotiations on the Constitution for an Independent St. Vincent and the Grenadines without any direct input from the parliamentary opposition or organised civil society, although one or two members of the government averred that they read the publications of the NIC and YULIMO. On July 26, 1979, at the Court of St. James, Her

Majesty Queen Elizabeth the Second, by and with the advice of Her Majesty's Privy Council ordered under the St. Vincent and the Grenadines Constitution Order that the scheduled Constitution of St. Vincent and the Grenadines will come into operation on October 27, 1979 — Independence Day!

Cato's SVLP, YULIMO and all other progressive pro-independence forces have been proven correct by history for their stances to proceed to independence, despite the presence of persons in shelters. Unfortunately, the SVLP government did not listen sufficiently to allied progressive forces on this matter. History rightly damns Joshua, Mitchell and others who doubted our people's fitness and capacity for independence!

In August 1979, three progressive political entities had coalesced to form the United People's Movement (UPM) in anticipation of general elections before the end of 1979. The constituent parts of the UPM were YULIMO, a socialist movement; the moderate social-democratic, People's Democratic Movement (PDM) — which itself was a merger between the DFM and Carlyle Dougan's tiny People's United Congress; and ARWEE, a rural, left-leaning, socialist-oriented group. From YULIMO the leading lights were Renwick Rose and Ralph Gonsalves; from the DFM, Parnel Campbell and Dr. Kenneth John; and from ARWEE, Simeon Greene and Oscar Allen. Campbell, Rose and Gonsalves constituted the collective leadership core of the UPM: Campbell (Finance), Rose (Organisation), Gonsalves (Electoral). This tri-partite compromise was fashioned because no pre-election agreement was concluded, despite efforts to do so, for the UPM to have a single leader. The PDM was opposed strongly to Gonsalves; YULIMO and Arwee supported Gonsalves but were strongly opposed to Campbell. So, the PDM suggested Rose to lead, to which suggestion both YULIMO and Arwee acquiesced. Within twenty-four hours, supporters of all three entities felt that despite Rose's solid credentials for leadership, he did not possess the mass appeal for political leadership at that time. So, the compromise was a troika of leaders with different functions. It was an unsatisfactory fall-back position. Certainly, at least at the margin, the failure to agree on one leader hampered the UPM.

Still, the UPM made an immediate impact on the young people, the progressive forces and sections of the working people; its leaders' relative youthfulness, academic and professional training and experience, their message of hope derived from socialist-oriented perspectives and their impressive policies and programmatic ideas for an independent St. Vincent and the Grenadines created a buzz of political excitement across the country.

In December 1979, general elections were held, the first in independent St. Vincent and the Grenadines. The SVLP won eleven of the thirteen elected seats with 54.4 percent of the 32,955 persons who voted validly; the NDP secured two seats with 27.4 percent of the votes; the UPM obtained 13.6 percent of the votes but won no seats of the twelve which it contested — it offered no candidate in the Grenadines; the PPP recorded 4.5 percent of the votes but failed to win a seat; and the lone Independent candidate lost in North Windward.

The highlights of the results of the 1979 elections were: 1) both Ivy Joshua and Ebenezer Joshua lost their seats in their former bastions of North Windward and Central Windward, garnering respectively 18.0 percent and 9.9 percent of the votes cast; Ebenezer Joshua actually lost his deposit and came last in a four-person contest; 2) James Mitchell, who left his safe Grenadines seat for Cosmos Cozier, lost the South Central Windward seat to SVLP's Offord Morris, a political neophyte, shop-keeper/farmer and community personality; Mitchell won 28.9 percent of the vote; 3) of the eleven seats contested by the PPP, nine of its candidates lost their deposits (below 15 percent of vote); only Mrs. Joshua, and Clive Tanis in West St. George secured their deposits; 4) five of the twelve candidates offered by the UPM won in excess of 15 percent of the vote in their respective constituencies (Parnel Campbell, Mike Browne, Simeon Greene, Kenneth John, and Ralph Gonsalves), three of whom (Campbell, Browne, Gonsalves) were to play important roles in the future competitive, electoral politics of St. Vincent and the Grenadines; and 5) SVLP candidates for the first time won the North Windward and South Central Windward constituencies, albeit with a minority share of the vote in many-sided contests.

This was the last occasion on which the name of Ebenezer Joshua was to be seen on a ballot in any popular elections in St. Vincent and the Grenadines. For twenty-eight years continuously since 1951, Joshua had been a significant force in Vincentian politics and trade unionism. His personal majorities in constituencies which he contested ranged from impressive to huge. As a percentage of the votes cast, Joshua's personal electoral numbers, from 1951 up to, and including, 1974, were: in North Windward in 1951, 63.4 percent; in North Windward in 1954, 79 percent; in Central Windward in 1957, 60.7 percent; in Central Windward in 1961, 69.1 percent; in Central Windward in 1966, 67.9 percent; in Central Windward in 1967, 66.7 percent; in South Central Windward in 1972, 86.7 percent; in South Central Windward in 1974, 91.1 percent. From these dizzying heights he fell, in South Central Windward, to 9.9 percent in 1979. The truth is that his national political stocks were beginning to slide by 1972, although he was still impregnable in two or three particular political fortresses in the north-east of St. Vincent and in West St. George. However, his joinder with the SVLP in 1974 signalled his acknowledgement that a national decline had set in; his subsequent break from the opportunistic coalition with the SVLP sullied him; his unprincipled manoeuvrings against independence in the period 1978-1979 occasioned his further political descent, culminating in his ignominious defeat in South Central Windward in 1979 and his PPP's humiliation at the polls in the general elections of that year. In 1984 he was used as a veritable political mascot by the NDP; and in 1987, he was the object of ridicule when he sought to revive the PPP in a by-election in Kingstown; his candidate received the derisive score of six votes! Never again, too, after 1979 was Ivy Joshua's name to be on an election ballot; she had served for 22 consecutive years in the North Windward constituency, from 1957 onwards.

Although the UPM did not win any seats in the 1979 elections, the performances of Campbell, Browne and Gonsalves marked them out as leaders for the future. All three were in their 30s at the time of the 1979 general elections: Campbell, the oldest, Browne, the youngest. Browne had won his political spurs in the 1975 teachers' strike and subsequently in the Teachers' Union and YULIMO. Campbell, erudite, a formidable intellect, and a prodigious worker, had displayed leadership qualities from 1969 after his return from his university studies in Canada. The SVLP government had called on his organisational skills to assist with the "statehood" celebrations in October 1969. He was a dedicated political activist in the EFP and DFM. In 1970, he entered the Law Faculty at the University of the West Indies (UWI) as a student. He excelled at his legal studies and was awarded a post-graduate scholarship to pursue his doctoral studies in law at Cambridge University in the United Kingdom. He successfully pursued his professional exams in England and was called to the Bar at Gray's Inn in November 1978. While working on his Ph.D he faced a choice: complete his Ph.D or return home to join the UPM in its build-up to the general elections. He chose the latter course and returned to St. Vincent in early September 1979. Gonsalves, from sturdy peasant stock with a rebel seed, had cut his political eye-teeth in the momentous "Rodney Affair" — a massive protest against the banning of Walter Rodney in Jamaica on October 16, 1968 — and in his leadership role as President of the Guild of Undergraduates, at UWI, Mona, Jamaica He was at the time pursuing his degree in the Social Sciences Faculty. He completed his first degree and his M.Sc degree at UWI, at which he won several academic and non-academic accolades. He was awarded a scholarship to pursue his doctoral studies in government at Manchester University in the United Kingdom (UK) at which he was awarded his Ph.D in July 1974. In the UK he also studied law. In September 1974, he began his career as a Lecturer at the University of the West Indies, first at Mona, Jamaica and then at Cave Hill, Barbados between 1976 and 1979. He obtained a one-year sabbatical and returned to St. Vincent in July 1979 to participate in the political work of YULIMO of which he was a member since 1975. He was one of the leading figures in pushing for the formation of the UPM in August 1979, thus uniting the nationalist, anti-imperialist, and social democratic/socialist-oriented forces under one political umbrella.

A fourth outstanding personality for the UPM was Renwick Rose who obtained 14.7 percent of the vote in a four-way contest in West St. George which was won by SVLP's Arthur Williams. Rose finished in third place behind Williams and Clive Tannis of the PPP, but ahead of the NDP's George Phillips. Rose was a brilliant student at the St. Vincent Grammar School who went into the employment of the State as a public servant and teacher. He was the organisational backbone of YULIMO and the UPM and the editor of their respective newspapers.

The SVLP, NDP and PPP attacked the UPM as a communist organisation which intended to establish a one-party state in St. Vincent. The UPM was attacked as godless, anti-Christian and a tool of Cuba and the Soviet Union. The raging Cold War unleashed vicious propaganda against the UPM and its leaders as being anti-American, supportive of Black Power and bent on bringing Cuban and Grenadian-style revolution to St. Vincent and the Grenadines. The anti-communist hysteria against the UPM was phenomenal. Political inexperience of the UPM leaders and activists and a relative disconnectedness from the working people themselves hampered the UPM in its political campaign. Still, it made a huge impact and dented the support of the SVLP, and temporarily stalled the emergence of an organised right-of-centre political umbrella, the NDP.

In the December 1979 general elections, the SVLP had a 54.5 percent share of the popular vote, much below the 67 percent in the 1974 elections which were admittedly unique because of the SVLP-PPP electoral pact of that year. The performance, however, was much better than its 50.4 percent of 1972; the SVLP's proportionate share of the vote in 1979 was the highest for that party for the preceding general elections of 1957, 1961, 1966, 1967, and 1972.

Undoubtedly, the SVLP's handling of the relief and recovery after the volcanic eruptions and the move towards independence, commended it and its political leader Milton Cato to the majority of the people. The SVLP government from 1967 to 1972 and 1974 to 1979 also performed creditably with important initiatives in the economy, education, health, social security, housing, and physical infrastructure. The SVLP, however, was unable to connect adequately with the yearnings of young people, and the political and cultural changes which were emerging across the region and the world. The SVLP had a moderate, social democratic frame for its economic and political policies, but it was socially and culturally conservative; it was slow to adapt to changes; its political approach was too gradualist; and though nationalist and regionalist, it was too wedded to a North Atlantic ethos. Further, the SVLP's governance was insufficiently open, transparent and participatory; and some of its ministers were too heavy-handed in coping with critics.

It is true that there were substantial areas on which legitimate criticisms were justified; still, though, the bulk of the people were satisfied with SVLP's performance in government. The people were unwilling to risk government in the hands of the young rookies of the UPM. The PPP had become, more or less, a political joke; and the people yet remembered the awful mess that the Mitchell "Junta" had made of governance in 1972 to 1974 and were unprepared to reward him. Mitchell, with his right-of-centre ideology and programme, had to wait his turn for another five years in more propitious circumstances. By and large, the bulk of the trade union members supported the SVLP in the 1979 elections, though substantial sections of the younger teachers and public servants gravitated towards the UPM. The CTAWU leadership was solidly behind the SVLP.

The configuration of the House of Assembly provided a challenge for Mitchell's NDP. For the first time since 1966, James Mitchell was out of the legislature. Two candidates for the NDP were successful in the 1979 elections: Calder Williams in North Windward, who won with 46.8 percent of the vote in a four-way contest; and Cosmos Cozier, by a landslide won 82.8 percent of the vote in a three-cornered fight in the Grenadines. Calder Williams, a former policeman, was a young inexperienced politician, who a few months earlier was not even a member of the NDP, became leader of the Opposition. Williams, though, was well-grounded among the poor, the working people and small farmers in North Leeward; his instincts were socialist-oriented and populist; he was tough, fearless and ambitious. Sooner or later he was bound to clash with James Mitchell, ideologically and politically.

The SVLP had three interesting newcomers to its cadre of elected members emerging from the 1979 elections: 1) Peter Ballantyne, a community-based activist and local preacher had defeated David Jack (an experienced administrator in the arrowroot industry and subsequently a Governor-General), Ivy Joshua and Caspar London; Ballantyne won 35.7 percent of the vote; 2) Offord

Morris, to whom an earlier reference was made, defeated Ebenezer Joshua in South Central Windward; and 3) Ken Browne, a young university graduate, had taken over the seat in Marriaqua from Levi Latham who supported him.

On the face of it, the SVLP was well-poised for a long-run in government. Still, some 45 percent of the popular vote had opted for other political preferences, mainly the NDP and the UPM. But these two parties were divided on substantial matters, ideologically and programmatically. One question unanswered by the 1979 general elections was this: which of the NDP or UPM will become the major opposition to the SVLP in the intervening five years before the next general elections? They represented two options: a right-of-centre NDP with its free enterprise and slavish pro-Western outlook, though under a populist masquerade; and UPM, a social-democratic/socialist-oriented alliance.

As Independence Day 1979 arrived, the CTAWU remained dominant in the trade union movement. Its long standing General Secretary Burns Bonadie had been recruited by the CCL as its Secretary-General based in Barbados, and Cyril Roberts, the President, ran the union in Bonadie's absence, but still under his guidance. A reliable female trade unionist, Alice Mandeville from the Cable and Wireless workforce, and a confidante of Bonadie, assisted Roberts. The NWM held on to its base among the electricity workers and at a few other employment units; it sought to pursue a deliberate line of independent trade unionism aligned to no political party in St. Vincent and the Grenadines and to none of the two large international trade union blocs dominant in the Cold War rivalries. The CSA and the Teachers' Union held their own in their respective spaces. The UPM attracted much support from the younger members of the CSA and Teachers' Union. Mitchell's NDP showed absolutely no interest in the labour movement or organised trade unions.

Within days of the December 1979 elections, an uprising on Union Island led by Lennox "Bumba" Charles occurred. On December 8, 1979, a number of residents on Union Island, mainly young men, led a protest against the socio-economic conditions on this island in the Southern Grenadines. They complained about the neglect of the island by the SVLP government. The results in the just concluded general elections showed that both the SVLP and the PPP had lost support of the earlier years in the Grenadines. Cosmos Cozier of the NDP won overwhelmingly the vote in each of the Grenadines islands: Bequia, Mustique, Canouan, Mayreau, and Union Island. Cozier obtained 82.8 percent of the popular vote on the NDP ticket; the SVLP candidate won 12.5 percent of the vote; and the PPP candidate, 4.7 percent.

The spontaneous uprising moved swiftly from protest to insurrection: the police station was over-taken, the police surrendered, other government officials left their posts, and for two days or so the leaders of the uprising were in tenuous control of parts of the island. The members of the SVLP government alternatively blamed the NDP and the UPM for masterminding the uprising. Both of these parties denied any involvement. The Royal St. Vincent and the Grenadines Police Force was mobilised and quickly took control of the situation. A state of emergency was declared. The Government, hastily and unnecessarily in a case of post-Grenada Revolution jitters and Cold War fright, invited soldiers from Barbados to assist in restoring law and order. Dozens of persons were arrested and detained at Fort Charlotte under the emergency regulations. Lennox Charles escaped by boat to Grenada where he was detained by the People's Revolutionary Government which, in due course, extradited him to St. Vincent and the Grenadines on non-capital offences. Subsequently, Charles was tried and sentenced to eight years imprisonment for his role in the uprising. He was freed before completing his sentence by the NDP government after Mitchell led his party to victory in the general elections of July 1984. Most of the detainees were released without charge. The bulk of them had nothing to do with the uprising. By Christmas 1979, Union Island had returned to calm.

In the aftermath of the Union Island uprising, the Barbados government, headed by J.M. "Tom" Adams, revoked the work permit of Ralph Gonsalves who was on sabbatical leave in St. Vincent and the Grenadines from his university lectureship in Barbados. The Adams' government falsely alleged that Gonsalves was a "security risk" and "an agent of Cuban and Soviet Communism". At one stroke, Gonsalves, with wife and young son, was wrongly and unfairly denied his right to work at a regional university of which St. Vincent and the Grenadines was a contributing member. The decision of the Barbados government was criticised across the region, including by *The Nation* newspaper of Barbados and by the distinguished political leader, Errol W. Barrow, who at the time was Leader of the Opposition in Barbados. In time, when Barrow's DLP was returned to office in 1986, Barrow removed from the official record the slurs and falsehoods against Gonsalves.

CHAPTER VII

A POST-INDEPENDENCE REVIEW OF THE POLITICAL ECONOMY OF THE LABOUR MOVEMENT 1980-2018

THE EXHAUSTION, DECLINE AND DEFEAT OF THE LABOUR GOVERNMENT, 1980-1984

As the year 1980 opened, the residue of the Union Island uprising of December 1979 was still being played out. Legal processes consequent upon the uprising were unfolding and the law and order situation in Union Island was being consolidated.

Early in 1980, Cosmos Cozier resigned his Grenadines seat without actually sitting in Parliament beyond the day on which he formally took the Oath of Allegiance. A by-election followed shortly thereafter in the Grenadines between two candidates: James Mitchell of the NDP and Earl Hazell of the SVLP. Predictably, Mitchell won the seat with 74.9 percent of the votes cast; Hazell obtained 25.1 percent of the vote. The by-election represented a substantial slippage by the NDP from 82.8 percent of the vote to 74.9 percent. The SVLP's Hazell doubled his December 1979 vote from 12.5 percent to 25.1 percent in 1980. In the 1979 general elections there was a third candidate, the PPP's Peter Alexander, who garnered 106 votes. In the 1980 by-election it was a straight NDP-SVLP contest. The voter turn-out in 1980 was slightly higher: 2,342, an increase of 87 votes over the votes cast in December 1979. Cozier out-performed Mitchell throughout the constituency; and Hazell's vote was much better in Union Island in the 1980 by-election than in the general elections in December 1979. Conceivably, Cozier was more likeable as a person than Mitchell in Bequia: he received 1,293 votes in Bequia to Mitchell's 1,241; and Hazell scored 292 votes in Bequia against Mitchell, 103 votes more than in the contest against Cozier. But in Union Island, the improvement in Hazell's vote in the by-election must have been connected to many voters' disgust at the uprising and Mitchell's failure to denounce it in unequivocal terms. In fact, Hazell won more votes than Mitchell in the by-election in Union Island: 252 votes to 245. In the December 1979 general elections, Cozier trounced Hazell in Union Island by 319 votes to 65; in 1979, the PPP candidate received 85 votes in Union Island. Mitchell actually fared badly in the polling station in Clifton Union. Although most residents in Union Island found the island's neglect by the SVLP government unacceptable, significant sections thereof considered the resort to violence and disorder was unnecessary, and wrong in the circumstances. Still, the detention of some innocent, hard-working and responsible members of the community, whose apparent cause for official suspicion of them as insurrectionists was their anti-SVLP political activism, rankled very much.

Between Mitchell's return to the House of Assembly and general elections in June 1984, there were numerous twists and turns in the parliamentary opposition, much of it a game of musical chairs with little or no impact on the country's politics. Calder Williams was reluctant to divest himself of the position of the Leader of the Opposition in the House and thus unwilling to give way to Mitchell. Williams' contention was that his position was protected by the Constitution of St. Vincent and the Grenadines which states in section 59(2) thereof:

> *Whenever there is occasion for the appointment of a Leader of the Opposition, the Governor General shall appoint the Representative who appears to him most likely to command the support of a majority of the Representatives who do not support the Government....*"

Williams was already the Leader of the Opposition, so no occasion existed to appoint another person as Leader of the Opposition, even though Mitchell had seniority of service as Representative and had secured more votes than Williams in his seat — the relevant considerations contained in the proviso to section 59 of the Constitution, for appointment to the Office of Leader of the Opposition in circumstances where neither member in the opposition supported the other.

Over the next five years or so (December 1979 – July 1984), there were three Leaders of the Opposition: Williams (from December 1979 to May 1981); Randolph Russell (from July 1981 to August 1982) after he had fallen out with Cato's SVLP and left the government as Minister of Health; James

Mitchell (from November 1982 to December 1983); then Russell again from early 1984 until the general elections of July 1984. Under the Constitution of St. Vincent and the Grenadines a Leader of the Opposition is required to advise the Governor General on the appointment of two Senators to complete the composition of parliament. So, as Leaders of the Opposition changed, there were new Senators. Thus, there were eleven opposition senators appointed between December 1979 and early July 1984: Emery Robertson, Jerry Scott, Victor Cuffy, Brinsley Nickie, Carlisle Ashton, Dennie Wilson, George Thomas, Bertram Young, Verold Haddaway, St. Clair Robinson, and Julian "Bucky" Boyea. It was veritable political comedy to a bemused public. Mitchell garnered political sympathy from this farce; the general public recognised him as the genuine leader of the parliamentary opposition.

Meanwhile, dissension arose, too, in the UPM. In February 1980, the constituent parts of the UPM, namely, YULIMO, DFM, and ARWEE were unable to agree on a philosophical and organisational way forward on a merger. YULIMO presented a paper with a clearly-defined anti-imperialist and socialist-oriented path, philosophically. ARWEE agreed, but the DFM found the YULIMO's anti-imperialism too strident and impractical and its socialist orientation, too radical and inappropriate for St. Vincent and the Grenadines. The DFM opted for a more accommodating posture towards imperialism and was wedded to a moderate, more reformist, social democracy. The organisational model for YULIMO was that of "democratic centralism." a direction in which the New Jewel Movement (NJM) of revolutionary Grenada, was moving. ARWEE was supportive, though not fully on this issue; but the DFM was opposed and called for a more flexible, open approach unencumbered by any bundle of stringent, selective criteria for party membership and organisational form. So, the DFM went its own way; thus, YULIMO and ARWEE merged to form the UPM as a single unified political party.

The truth is that YULIMO and ARWEE did not trust the DFM, and the DFM had a high level of distrust of YULIMO. Had the personalities involved in all three constituent entities exercised greater political maturity, it is likely that a three-in-one merger would have occurred. There was a sense that the jostling for leadership between the factions behind Gonsalves and Campbell lurked in the background, making it difficult for the merger to be consummated between YULIMO and DFM.

Shortly after the YULIMO-ARWEE merger into the UPM, the Central Committee and Political Bureau of the party consented for Ralph Gonsalves to take up a Visiting Professorship for six months at Queen's College, City

University of New York, and to proceed thereafter, from September 1980, to complete the 10-month course for his Bar Finals at Grays' Inn London as the necessary prerequisite to be called to the Bar in England and Wales and to be admitted to practice as a Barrister and Solicitor in St. Vincent and the Grenadines.

The confusion and dissension in the NDP, the refusal of the DFM to enter the merger of the YULIMO-ARWEE into a unified UPM, and the political quietism of the trade union movement, left the SVLP in a politically strong position. After all, it had secured a solid electoral triumph in December 1979; less than two months earlier it had led the country to independence; and it was pursuing its agenda with some vigour. In agriculture, the re-introduction of the sugar industry was ramping up; the Campden Park Industrial Estate was expanding; and its social programmes, including social protection, education and health, were accorded focussed attention. The socio-economic situation was yet quite challenging and the recovery from the volcanic eruption in April 1979 was still a work in progress.

In 1970, the SVLP government had established the National Provident Fund (NPF); in early 1980, it announced its intention to transform this basic social security safety net into a fully-fledged National Insurance Scheme (NIS) and had commenced preliminary work in this regard. In July 1980, the SVLP government enacted a path-breaking piece of labour legislation called the Protection of Employment Act. This statute law for the first time in St. Vincent and the Grenadines established the worker right against "unlawful dismissal" and the statutory remedies of severance payment or re-instatement. The common law had long recognised the right against "wrongful dismissal" for which the remedy was "damages", but the remedy was limited and the procedure for enforcement of the remedy lengthy, expensive and difficult. Severance payment under the Protection of Employment Act offered a simpler, swifter, less expensive, and more rewarding procedure. This is a law which the trade unions had been demanding for years. This was the sound, reforming, progressive side of the SVLP. Unfortunately, the SVLP government tripped itself up with some wrong-headed proposals, particularly in the area of law, order and security.

Life, living and production relations do produce complications and contradictions. When the challenges arise and events not of your own making emerge, you address them sensibly in accord with your principles, values and practical circumstances. A government, especially, must always be cognisant of all this and be guided accordingly. What occurred in the first half of 1981 was not the Milton Cato government's finest hour. In hindsight, the events of early 1981 in all likelihood contributed significantly to its loss of the 1984 general elections.

The immediate backdrop to the SVLP government's legislative folly of April/May 1981 demands a brief sketching.

Trade union activism and opposition political agitation prompted an unnecessary, ill-advised and wrong response from the SVLP government. The NWM was demanding union recognition at the state-run St. Vincent Electricity Services; the small and geographically-centred Workers' and Peasants' Union in North Leeward was clamouring for increased wages, better working conditions and trade union recognition at the State-owned Richmond Vale estate; the CTAWU, at the private sector owned Bottlers Limited, the maker of non-alcoholic drinks, and at the state-owned Central Water and Sewerage Authority, was demanding improved material conditions of work, and went on strike in April 1981; so, too, the teachers employed in the State-owned schools were demanding better wages and working conditions.

In the mix were the on-going and sharpened criticisms of the Government mainly by the UPM, on the ground nationally, and by its activists in one or more of these workplaces. Protests were taking place. But neither the trade union activities in themselves nor the political agitation, in all their import singly and in their combinations, ought to have unnerved a government which was re-elected comfortably a mere eighteen months earlier.

To be sure, there was a political restiveness among sections of the population, and regionally, the Grenada Revolution was inspiring working people. At the same time, though, bourgeois and monopoly capitalist reaction had set in globally and in the region. Edward Seaga's Jamaica Labour Party had dislodged Michael Manley's democratic socialist government from power in Jamaica; Tom Adams' centre-right government had been in power in Barbados for five years, having defeated in 1976 the more nationalist and pro-worker government of Errol Barrow's Democratic Labour Party; and so forth. Globally, Reaganism and Thatcherism were in the ascendancy, despite the apparent solidity of the Soviet Union and socialist countries.

In the widest, and narrowest, of political senses, the SVLP government ought to have felt safe and, objectively, unthreatened. For all the political influence of the UPM and its committed and hard working General Secretary Renwick Rose, and the activism of others like Caspar London and Mike Brown, the UPM's political base was narrower than in 1979 when the DFM was in an electoral compact with YULIMO and ARWEE. The leading lights in the DFM, with the exception of Parnel Campbell, were relatively inactive, and their political base was even narrower than that of the UPM. James Mitchell's NDP, always pro-business, pro-imperialist and suspicious of trade unions and street protests, was on the side-lines though it was to become the principal political beneficiary of the anti-SVLP activism. Neither Renwick Rose's UPM, nor Cyril Roberts' CTAWU, nor the Teachers' Union, nor the NWM, nor Calder Williams' WAPU benefited politically. This, too, is part of the contradictory mix arising from the practical evolution and political manifestation of production relations, and social interplay, and insurgent, and mainstream, politics.

The activists of 1981 did what they had to do because they considered it the right thing to do in defence of the people's rights. They won an important victory in having "the Dread Bills" — two pieces of "public order" legislation — withdrawn. These two Bills, the Public Safety and Public Order Bill and the Essential Services (Amendment) Bill were introduced by the SVLP Government, respectively, to contain public protests and tighten further the restrictions on strike action in essential services. It was a popular victory for democracy, not for politics. But Mitchell reaped a political harvest therefrom although he and his NDP were essentially by-standers to the popular protests. Clearly, the population-at-large were observing and making judgements about the Government's actions, the protestors' responses and Mitchell's stance from a distance.

These two pieces of "public order" legislation, which touched and concerned individual rights, workers' freedoms, and "public order" galvanised the population in a national protest against their passage. The trade unions (CTAWU, NWM, CSA, Teachers' Union), opposition parties (UPM, PDM), national personalities, civil society, and some churches raged against the proposed statutes, which sought to limit free expression, legitimate protests and freedom of association. Much of the proposed legislative provisions of the Public Safety and Public Order Bill were a codification of existing law, but particular clauses of the Bill touching and concerning basic rights and freedoms were rightly considered by the critics to be an unwarranted over-reach and a subversion of long-held constitutional rights. The trade unions contended that the proposed statutes, singly and jointly, if passed by the House of Assembly and enacted, had the potential to damage the trade unions' ability to function effectively in a stable system of industrial relations and an alive democracy. As was to be expected, the trade unions threw into the mix their dissatisfaction with their members' material concerns.

In May 1981, a broad-based National Committee in Defence of Democracy (NCDD) was formed to organise and mobilise the people against "the Dread Bills". An estimated 10,000 Vincentians took to the streets in a protest march demanding the withdrawal of the Bills. At first the Attorney General wanted to hang tough. In the end the SVLP government withdrew its proposed legislative measures from parliamentary consideration; they did not return to the Order Paper of the House of Assembly after the House's prorogation. The Government caved in to popular pressure.

The public had won a major victory, and it was a victory secured without the help of James Mitchell or his NDP. Yet he and his NDP benefited most at the expense of the SVLP. Objectively, the NDP had the largest support of any opposition party: the PPP was moribund; the PDM was lacklustre; and the UPM, a focal point for popular grievances and agitation against "the Dread Bills" was not seen as an alternative government. Of the principal opposition personalities, James Mitchell, though still not yet an acclaimed leader of the anti-SVLP national movement, commanded most support. Calder Williams was limited to his geographical base in North Leeward and even there his stature was in decline. And no dissident from the SVLP ranks was an alternative, as Randolph Russell found out when he resigned from the SVLP to pursue his own path in the period from July 1981 to July 1984, in his ill-fated People's Democratic Party (PDP).

In 1981, subsequent to the mass anti-government protests, the CSA registered a name change to that of the St. Vincent and the Grenadines Public Service Union (SVG PSU).

In July 1981, Ralph Gonsalves returned home from overseas; he was called to the Bar to practice law in St. Vincent and the Grenadines in September of the same year. He swiftly resumed his political activism in and through the UPM. In October 1981, at the UPM's Congress, he was elected unopposed as that party's Political Leader. Within one year, Ralph Gonsalves was to resign from the UPM (from the Political Bureau in August 1982 and the party itself in mid-October 1982) on account of its decision at both the level of the Political Bureau and an unrepresentative Congress to transform itself from a socialist-oriented or revolutionary democratic party into a Leninist party. Caspar London, a leading member of the Bureau, and some other UPM members also left the party. Again, a lack of political experience and maturity on "the left" of the political spectrum stymied its efforts and thus held back the advance of the working people's movement. Undoubtedly, the influence of Trevor Munroe of the Workers' Party of Jamaica and Bernard Coard of Grenada's NJM contributed to the political mistake of pushing to establish Marxist-Leninist parties in the extant condition of a political economy not conducive to the building of such parties. Munroe and Coard were to find out much later the consequences of their monumental error in this regard. Over 60 years ago, the distinguished Marxist intellectual and activist, C.L.R. James of Trinidad had so concluded on the wrong-headedness of building a Leninist party in the objective conditions of the Anglo-Caribbean. The further splintering of the UPM, following upon the 1980 departure of the PDM from the UPM electoral alliance of 1979, adversely affected the progressive, revolutionary democratic and anti-imperialist movement in St. Vincent and the Grenadines. It contributed to enhanced political space for Mitchell's NDP, with its right-of-centre outlook cloaked in populist garb.

On October 31, 1982, the Movement for National Unity (MNU) was formed with Ralph Gonsalves as its Political Leader and Cecil "Blazer" Williams, economist and cultural icon, as its Deputy Political Leader. Caspar London was elected to the MNU's Central Executive. Across the country, several UPM members pledged their support and a cadre of progressive persons, hitherto not aligned to the UPM, joined the MNU. This split in the UPM had occurred at about the same time that the NJM and the Grenada Revolution were unravelling. The UPM's leadership knew about internal difficulties in the NJM, but they were unaware of the full extent of its dissension until matters came to a head in October 1983 with the murder of the revolutionary leader, Maurice Bishop and several of his colleagues by a faction of the NJM supportive of Bernard Coard.

In St. Vincent and the Grenadines, the testing of the political temperature occurred in a by-election on September 12, 1983, to contest the Central Leeward by-election occasioned by the death of the incumbent representative Arthur Woods. In the 1979 elections, Woods had won the seat for the SVLP with 61.1 percent of the vote in a four-way contest; P.R. Campbell of the UPM had placed second with 24.8 percent of the vote; Owen Walker of the NDP had obtained 13.1 percent; and the PPP's Clive Raimie mustered one percent. In the 1983 by-election, the SVLP's Valcina Ash barely defeated the NDP's Herbert Young by 65 votes. Ash won 50.5 percent of the popular vote; Young obtained 48.3 percent; and Edgerton Richards of the St. Vincent National Movement (SVNM) got 1.1 percent of the vote. This latter party, which was founded a year or so earlier by a medical practitioner, Dr. Gideon Cordice withered away after its comprehensive rejection by the voters in the Central Leeward by-election.

Unity, the newspaper of the MNU, correctly headlined the by-election result as: "Ash wins, Labour loses". The NDP candidate, Herbert Young, obtained 1,334 votes or 1,043 more votes than that party's candidate, Owen Walker, in the 1979 general elections. Meanwhile, the SVLP's score actually increased by 54 votes, from Woods' 1,360 votes in 1979 to Ash's score of 1,414 in 1983. The political problem for the SVLP was this: in the by-election, of the 2,962 registered voters, a whopping 2,773 or 93.6 percent of the registered voters cast their ballots (nine ballots were rejected). In the 1979 general elections, the actual voter turn-out in that constituency was 2,243 or 63.9 percent of the registered voters which totalled 3,160 (of the 2,226 who voted, 17 ballots were rejected). Thus, 736 more voters voted in 1983 compared to 1979, although the electoral list had 198 votes fewer in Central Leeward. The results meant, therefore, that the NDP not only garnered the UPM votes of 1979, but also won, by far, most of the additional voters who turned out in 1983. The SVLP kept its base but, with the general elections for 1984 roughly one year away, once the NDP kept its 1979 voters, brought on board the bulk of the UPM voters and garnered most of the additional voters, (those who never voted or the new voters), it had a good chance of toppling the SVLP in 1984. Of vital importance, 18-year-olds would be voting for the first time in 1984; hitherto, the voting age was 21 years and over. Critically, too, the Representation of the People Act was passed in 1982 and operational from December 1982; it allowed for continuous registration and a picture-identification system. That was an operational tool with which to register and mobilise young, first-time voters.

In the by-election campaign, the UPM supported the NDP's candidate, although the UPM's candidate Parnel Campbell had received nearly twice the votes of the NDP's Owen Walker in the 1979 general elections. Mitchell had led them to believe that an ongoing pact between them was possible and desirable; Mitchell himself articulated that position publicly in the by-election campaign; he praised and thanked the UPM for their canvassing and independent campaign activities in support of Herbert Young.

There was neither an objective nor subjective basis for a Marxist or socialist party like the post-1982 UPM to provide any tactical or strategic support for the NDP, a centre-right political party led by a man, James Mitchell, who opposed ideologically everything the UPM stood for. For all its faults, limitations and weaknesses, the ruling SVLP was not a "fascist" entity that required a "popular front" against it; the SVLP led a moderate social democratic government that had economic and social policies with which the UPM could have provided at least critical support. The SVLP's cultural conservatism and political insensitivities, even heavy-handedness on occasion were irksome, but they ought never to have driven the UPM towards enabling, partially, the strengthening of Mitchell's NDP. The UPM's support of the NDP in the Central Leeward by-election was opportunistic and unwise; it was functionally, not ideologically, conceived; it was, at best, a species of antagonistic complicity that did not look beyond its immature antipathy to the SVLP. Interestingly, in the by-election campaign, the SVLP republished a YULIMO publication authored by Ralph Gonsalves in 1978 entitled: *Who is 'Son' Mitchell and Why He is Not the Answer"*.

Shortly after the by-election in Central Leeward, James Mitchell and a NDP delegation met with the UPM at the home of former President of the Teachers' Union Yvonne Francis-Gibson, to discuss further political cooperation. In his autobiography, *Beyond the Islands*, Mitchell recounts, summarily, this meeting thus:

> *I met the leftists to plan strategies for the next election.*
> *They were anxious to secure the majority of seats [for*
> *their party] even though they had not yet made it to*
> *Parliament. At the close of the meeting I called for a*
> *discussion on communism and Grenada. My line was*
> *simple: Grenada had cost me an election and I would*
> *not let it happen again. My party opposed military rule*
> *and seizure of property. We would not let the image*
> *of Grenada affect our chances in St. Vincent. They bi-*
> *zarrely insisted the early Caribs were communists and*
> *St. Vincent should 'return to the fold'.*

This is surely a caricature recollection by Mitchell to justify the NDP's "delinking" from the idea of any possible future election pact with the UPM of Renwick Rose and Oscar Allen. He had opportunistically used the UPM during the by-election, but now he wanted to dump them because of the deteriorating situation in Grenada, which was to spin out of control in mid-October 1983 with deadly consequences a week or so later. The UPM had actually helped, not hindered, the NDP's cause in the by-election, so any claim that Grenada lost the by-election is implausible; if the contention is about the December 1979 general elections, it is laughable. Moreover, it was never the UPM's policy to return St. Vincent to primitive communalism. History ought never to be so cavalierly and self-servingly rewritten as Mitchell has done in his autobiography.

In late October 1983, the killing of Maurice Bishop in Grenada permanently cooled Mitchell towards the UPM. The headline in the UPM's newspaper, *Justice*, at the time of the brutal murder of Bishop and his colleagues, was "Bloodshed Regrettable". Clearly, this was an unwise and understated — even callous — summation of the senseless killings. The chilling murders and the UPM's wrong-headed response were the real immediate inducements for Mitchell's flight from a NDP-UPM electoral pact, but Mitchell was never pre-disposed to link up with the UPM in an electoral alliance. They were philosophically, programmatically and organisationally too far apart. Notwithstanding the UPM's temporary illusions, the NDP-UPM pact was never really on the cards. Mitchell's embellishments in his autobiography are not necessary; they are part of Mitchell's stylistic proclivity to ridicule others so as to cover for his real reasons for acting one way or another.

The razor-thin victory of Ash in the by-election must have stunned the SVLP. Burns Bonadie of the CTAWU and regional CCL had earlier returned to St. Vincent and the Grenadines from Barbados in the first half of 1983. He was made a Senator and Parliamentary Secretary in the Ministry of Trade and Agriculture. He was an experienced political and trade union personality. He was grounded in the community. He was well-liked and he had a commanding platform presence. Still, he was unable to assist in pulling the undecided and progressive sections of the population to the SVLP. The youthful Ken Browne was unable to do so, too. The extraordinary organisational efforts of Duff James on behalf of Ash in a constituency in which he resided could not buck the trend against the SVLP. Public controversies around Arthur Williams and Grafton Isaacs, two of the SVLP Government's more outspoken Ministers, did not help the SVLP's cause; and Milton Cato and his deputy, Hudson Tannis appeared tired and unable to discipline those Ministers whom the public perceived to have been more errant than others.

More importantly, despite several sound programmatic initiatives in the socio-economic sphere, including the proposed National Insurance Scheme, the National Commercial Bank, the Marketing Corporation, Diamond Dairy, the reintroduction of the sugar industry, health and education, and many pieces of social reform legislation, the SVLP was not able to articulate a compelling developmental narrative for the country. Further, it appeared culturally conservative and thus uncool to the young people. Since 1979, the UPM and later the MNU were able to convince the bulk of the younger voters that the SVLP government was less than satisfactory in its efforts to improve people's lives now and in the foreseeable future. Moreover, its governance appeared somewhat heavy-handed and insufficiently open and flexible.

In July 1984, general elections were held. The NDP won nine of the thirteen seats with 51.41 percent of the 42,208 votes cast; the SVLP won four seats with 41.4 percent of the popular vote; the UPM led by Oscar Allen contested eight seats and won none — its share of the vote was 3.2 percent; the MNU contested four seats and won none — its share of the vote was 2.02 percent; and the PDP led by Randolph Russell contested four seats and won none — its share of the vote was 1.9 percent. Accordingly, the NDP's Political Leader, James Mitchell, was sworn in as the country's second Prime Minister.

Five years earlier, in the general elections of December 1979, the NDP had won 9,022 votes or 27.37 percent of the 32,955 votes cast. The continuous registration process under the Representation of the People Act, 1982, with identification cards for voters, including new voters 18 years and over, enlarged the voters' list. In 1984, the overall votes cast increased by 9,253 or 28.07 percent over the 1979 figure. The actual votes for the NDP candidates increased by 12,678 or 140.5 percent over the 1979 figure. The UPM vote in 1979 amounted to 4,467; in 1984, the UPM vote declined to 1,350 or 3,177 votes less than 1979. Basically, as in the Central Leeward by-election in 1983, the NDP in 1984 retained its base support, got most of the UPM votes of 1979, and secured the bulk of the additional votes. The SVLP's actual vote in 1984 was 17,493 or a mere 383 votes less than 1979; so, it held its base but it was unable to attract additional votes. Indeed in a few seats, third party candidates poached from the SVLP. For example, in 1984, Ralph Gonsalves gained 283 votes more than in 1979 (820 compared to 582), mostly at the expense of SVLP's Vincent Beache, who won in North Central Windward in a four-way contest with 47 percent of votes cast; similarly, in East Kingstown, Randolph Russell's 106 votes more than likely came from the SVLP and adversely affected Burns Bonadie, although even those votes would not have ensured an avoidance of his defeat.

Of all the third-party candidates, Ralph Gonsalves fared the best with 23.5 percent of the vote in North Central Windward. Next in line was Calder Williams' 21.1 percent share of the vote in North Leeward on the PDP ticket. The third parties did not do well. Of the sixteen candidates fielded by the UPM, MNU, and PDP, only Gonsalves and Williams scored in excess of 15 percent of the votes to save their deposits.

Both the UPM and the MNU fielded candidates of real merit. In some cases their candidates were of a high quality, assessed by any reasonable, objective standard. For example, the UPM offered meritorious persons: Oscar Allen, Victor Cuffy, Cecil Ryan, Adrian Saunders, Michael Browne, Glenroy Browne,

Nelcia Robinson, and Albert Maloney; the MNU presented to the electorate: Gonsalves, Blazer Williams, Caspar London, and Clive Bishop — all candidates of merit. But they did not commend themselves to the people at that time, in those circumstances, and as third-party candidates.

The NDP ticket of 1984, had all the makings of a pick-up side under a leader, James Mitchell, who was the sole author of the NDP's Manifesto, the sole organiser of campaign financing, and the only person with any national political heft or presence. Moreover, as the Founder-Leader of the NDP, Mitchell, had in common with most, if not all founder-leaders of political parties in the Caribbean, a sense of proprietorial ownership of his party; their conception has been that their respective parties belong to them; they own them as if they are their personal property, albeit without the requisite title deeds. Our region's history is replete with them: Alexander Bustamante and his Jamaica Labour Party; Dr. Eric Williams and his People's National Movement; Forbes Burnham and Dr. Cheddi Jagan respectively of their People's Progressive Party in Guyana; Errol Barrow and his Democratic Labour Party in Barbados; Eric Gairy and his Grenada United Labour Party; John Compton and his United Workers Party in St. Lucia; Ebenezer Joshua and his People's Political Party in St. Vincent and the Grenadines; Robert Bradshaw and his St. Kitts-Nevis Labour Party; and Vere Cornwall Bird and his Antigua-Barbuda Labour Party.

The NDP's electoral slate of 1984 reflected no coherent programme save and except their opposition to the Cato government; coherence in policy and programme belonged only to James Mitchell and this was a programme based on a centre right ideology, regional integration, and pro-imperialist rhetoric. He authored and owned the details. Those who signed up as candidates for the NDP in 1984, endorsed the Mitchell policies and programme. Above all the NDP campaign emphasised that Cato's SVLP had to go and the NDP was the only alternative at hand.

Of the thirteen candidates whom the NDP offered in the 1979 general elections, only three appeared on the 1984 ticket: James Mitchell, David Jack, and Jeremiah Scott. Herbert Young was held over from the 1983 by-election in Central Leeward. Four came from the PDM stable: John Horne, Allan Cruickshank, Edward Griffith, and the latter's brother-in-law, Marcus De Freitas. Three others had flirted in or on the edges of progressive politics: Louis Jones (with UPM and MNU); Julian Boyea (with MNU); and Burton Williams. One candidate, Olin Dennie, a lawyer, was the favoured son of an old Mitchell stalwart, Alphonso Dennie; and another candidate, Oswald George had affiliated himself with Mitchell after the 1979 general elections. Much of the NDP team had an unmistakable lightness of heft; but the ticket had Mitchell at its head. However, the likeability factor of the NDP candidates was, by and large, high.

The victorious NDP candidates in the 1984 general elections were: Mitchell in the Grenadines (81.8 percent of the votes); David Jack in North Windward (57.2 percent); Allan Cruickshank in South Central Windward (56.9 percent); Burton Williams in South Windward (49.8 percent); Marcus De Freitas in West St. George (62.6 percent); Edward Griffith in East Kingstown (58.4 percent); John Horne in West Kingstown (58.4 percent); Jeremiah Scott in South Leeward (52.2 percent); and Herbert Young in Central Leeward (52.1 percent). The NDP's losing candidates were Julian Boyea in North Central Windward; Oswald George in Marriaqua; Louis Jones in East St. George; and Olin Dennie in North Leeward.

Although the NDP won a comfortable margin of nine seats to four, its share of the popular vote was a less-than-comfortable 51.41 percent, slightly more than one-half. But the by-election of 1983 in Central Leeward and the general elections of 1984 indicated that the SVLP was only able to hold its political base; its inability to attract additional voters, including first-time voters, in sufficient numbers pointed to its awesome challenges in winning majorities again, unless it was reformed from within and/or from without.

It is noteworthy that several SVLP candidates in the 1984 elections fell below 40 percent in constituencies in which they fared comparatively much better in 1979: Grafton Isaacs in South Leeward, 36.0 percent in 1984 compared to 64 percent in 1979; Burns Bonadie in East Kingstown, 32.6 percent in 1984 compared to Russell's 57.1 percent in 1979; Arthur Williams in West St. George, 34.8 percent compared to 56.2 percent in 1979; Offord Morris in South Central Windward, 31 percent in 1984 compared to 44.3 percent in 1979.

Indeed, in three of the four seats which the SVLP won in 1984, its candidates' share of the vote fell: Milton Cato in East St. George, 55.2 percent in 1984 compared to 74.6 percent in 1979; Ken Browne in Marriaqua, 59.4 percent in 1984 compared to 82.8 percent in 1979; Vincent Beache in North Central Windward, 47.2 percent in 1984 compared to 56.5 percent in 1979. In the fourth victorious seat for the SVLP, John Thompson in North Leeward bucked the trend in a three-way fight with 45.9 percent of the vote in 1984 compared to 44.7 percent in 1979. One losing SVLP candidate, Peter Ballantyne in North Windward, did better in 1984 than in 1979: 42.5 percent compared to 35.7 percent. In terms of the trend, Ballantyne was SVLP's best performer in 1984!

The SVLP appeared not to have learnt the right lessons from these numbers. Confirmation of the SVLP's ongoing electoral challenges came in February 1985 in the East St. George by-election consequent upon the resignation, in December 1984 of its leader, R. Milton Cato, who had led the SVLP outstandingly for 29 years since the party's founding in 1955. In the by-election, Louis Jones of the NDP defeated Donald Browne of the SVLP, 59.5 percent of the votes to 40.5 percent. In just over five years (December 1979 to February 1984), the SVLP's vote in East St. George had slumped from 74.6 percent to 40.5 percent. This was an electoral meltdown that demanded significant strategic changes, as a matter of urgency, to arrest the SVLP's further political slide.

Unfortunately, the SVLP ducked the bold decisions regarding message, programme, personnel, organisation, and leadership. Instead it became bogged down in a divided leadership with attendant tensions. Vincent Beache became the Leader of the Opposition in the Parliament but Hudson Tannis succeeded Milton Cato as Political Leader of the Party. This was never the best model. Sadly, Hudson Tannis died shortly thereafter in an aircraft disaster. Instead of confirming Beache unopposed as Political Leader and uniting around him, the SVLP wasted precious time and focus on intra-party wrangling over leadership in which Stanley "Stalky" John, a lawyer, was Beache's principal antagonist. The SVLP did not sufficiently grasp the qualities and political strengths of Vincent Beache nor the extent of its electoral predicament.

NDP ASCENDANT, ITS COUNTER-REVOLUTION UNFOLDS, "LABOUR" FORCES REGROUP: JULY 1984 – FEBRUARY 1994

After its 1984 electoral defeat, the SVLP failed to attract new blood; it marked time organisationally; and it was unable to craft a compelling message. It appeared disunited. Meanwhile, James Mitchell's NDP government was unfolding a series of initiatives, a few of them touching people's lives favourably (land reform at Orange Hill, hard courts in villages), and organising itself politically. Even though the NDP was in the process of reversing many social democratic gains and state-involvement in the economy, Mitchell's counter-revolution — wrapped in populist clothing and delivered in style at least — had some coherence that for the moment was not yet opposed by the working people who adopted a wait-and-see attitude in a context where they did not see a more credible alternative. Moreover, the NDP was united with one leader. Mitchell was also recruiting quality political personnel. Stewart Nanton, a highly intelligent organiser, was put in the party's engine-room and made a Senator. In November 1985, Mitchell lured P.R. Campbell into the party and the Senate. He, too, was a top-notch strategic thinker and party organiser.

Another opportunity arose for the SVLP to test itself against the NDP in the 1987 by-election in East Kingstown, occasioned by the shocked death of Edward "Eddie" Griffith, Minister of Health, and a solid ministerial performer. In a six-way race, P.R. Campbell romped home as victor, overwhelmingly. Campbell won 60.3 percent of the vote; his nearest rival was SVLP's Burns Bonadie with 27.2 percent of the vote; in third place, Mike Browne of the UPM got 7.5 percent; Cyp Neehall of the MNU, Emery Robertson an Independent candidate, and the PPP's Percival Stapleton all trailed badly. Campbell performed better than Griffith who had secured 58.4 percent of the vote in the 1984 general elections.

SVLP's candidate, Burns Bonadie, performed worse than he did in the general elections of 1984 in which he had scored 32.6 percent of the vote. The 1987 by-election performance of Bonadie was the worst result ever for the SVLP in any Kingstown constituency. Since the SVLP's formation in 1955, it had fielded thirteen candidates in Kingstown seats (Kingstown, West Kingstown, East Kingstown) in nine elections in some thirty years up to 1984; the lowest score before that year was in 1957 when Rudolph Baynes received 37.7 percent of the vote in the Kingstown seat.

The by-election in Central Leeward in 1983, the general elections of 1984, the by-election in East St. George in 1985, and the by-election in East Kingstown in 1987 all pointed to substantial electoral challenges and a significant loss of support for the SVLP. The weaknesses revealed were not merely specific to particular constituencies or candidates; the problems were structural and strategic in nature; an over-haul or remake was required, but it was not happening at all or fast enough or in a sustained manner.

On the organised labour front, several trade unions were registered in 1987 and 1988: The LIAT Workers' Union was formed in 1987 to ensure that the local and regional management of the airline, LIAT, accorded a sufficiency of respect to the workers by addressing their long-standing concerns, particularly regarding working conditions and wages. The LIAT employees in St. Vincent and the Grenadines were of the view that better treatment was meted out to those who were employed in Antigua, Barbados and St. Lucia; they resented it. This was a small union but its leadership was militant and very keen on trade union solidarity. Their sense of grievance and frustration led them in 1988 to a successful sick-out which caused the removal of the local manager. The union was recognised as the bargaining agent for the workers in 1988.

A similar work-place specific union, the VINLEC Supervisory Workers' Union, founded to represent the supervisors at the St. Vincent Electricity

Services Limited, was also registered in 1988. In that same year, too, a professional body, the St. Vincent Medical Association, established since 1951, was registered as a trade union to represent the professional and workplace interest of medical doctors, dentists, veterinarians, radiographers, and an assorted group of professionals in the medical field.

Overall, the trade union movement continued its process of slow growth, consolidation and maturation. The NWM sought, without much success, to organise the workers at retail establishments; both the workers and the management at most of these employment locales found trade unions problematic. Occasionally, the NWM would publicly air its frustration at its lack of success in securing recognition as a bargaining agent at retail stores. Similarly, the agricultural workers scattered across small farms would prove difficult to be unionised, although in 1984 the small farmers themselves formed the National Farmers' Union (NFU) and registered it as a trade union; this though was not a workers' union but a small producers' union.

Despite the fact the NDP government closed down the sugar industry, closed the state-owned stone-crushers, ran-down the State-owned Marketing Corporation and its supermarket, scaled down operations of the largely State-owned Diamond Dairy, and brought low the Housing and Land Development Corporation, the trade unions barely protested to protect the jobs of the hundreds of workers who were laid off as a result of the slimming down of the state economic sector. The Mitchell-led NDP government was unashamedly private-sector oriented, and adopted the ideological stance of the International Monetary Fund (IMF) and the World Bank, which were busily promoting "the Washington Consensus" of reducing public spending, enhancing private investments, cutting out regulations of business operations, elevating the private interests over the public good, freeing up exchange controls, promoting free trade not necessarily fair trade, putting a tight lid on increases in salaries and wages, touting the idea of labour market flexibility, paying scant regard to trade unionism, and not-too-focussed on poverty reduction or social programmes designed to promote equity. This "Consensus" coincided with the rise and consolidation of Thatcherism and Reaganism respectively in the United Kingdom and the USA. All this was happening as the centrally-planned regimes in the Soviet Union and Eastern Europe were beginning to unravel. The acceleration and further entrenchment of the globalisation of monopoly capitalism held sway. Neo-liberalism was on the rise.

The collapse of the Grenada Revolution in 1983, the retreat of "socialism" in Jamaica and Guyana, the pull-back of Caribbean nationalism, and the slow-pace of regional integration, save and except in the Organisation of Eastern Caribbean States (OECS), which was established in 1981, emboldened, by and large, foreign and private capital and their representatives in our Caribbean. A veritable counter-revolution to social democracy, Keynesianism, socialism, and progressive nationalism was being enthroned. The labour movement itself was on the retreat and its political expression more muted, divided, and weakened.

In St. Vincent and the Grenadines, and elsewhere in the region, James Mitchell's push in May 1987 (at an OECS gathering in Tortola) for deeper regional integration in the form of a political union of the Windward and Leeward Islands divided the labour movement and placed the progressive forces in a predicament. The SVLP, the St. Lucia Labour Party, the Dominica Labour Party, and the St. Kitts-Nevis Labour Party all saw this post-1987 proposal for a political union of the independent countries of the OECS as a "made-in-Washington" idea designed to strengthen the over-rule of the governing regimes that were all decidedly pro-western. The "made-in-Washington" jibe clearly excluded the People's Action Movement government in St. Kitts-Nevis and the Lester Bird's Antigua-Barbuda Labour Party government in that country, which were both solidly pro-western, but which opposed the Mitchell proposal.

On the social democratic, socialist-oriented "left" there was also a division: Tim Hector of Antigua-Caribbean Liberation Movement (ACLM), though an avowed regionalist, considered the Mitchell proposal to be "made-in-Washington" and antithetical to a genuinely independent political union of the OECS region. George Odlum, the Political Leader of the Progressive Labour Party of St. Lucia, welcomed whole-heartedly the Mitchell idea that was supported, too, by Odlum's long-standing political nemesis, John Compton of the ruling United Workers' Party in St. Lucia. In St. Vincent and the Grenadines, Ralph Gonsalves of the MNU gave critical support to the idea of a political union, but distanced himself from Mitchell's "unitary" state as impractical in the circumstances and opted for a strong centre, in a federal arrangement more suited to our region's condition At the same time Gonsalves saw the dangers of a deepening imperial design and ensured that the MNU participated in the Standing Conference of Opposition Parties of the Eastern Caribbean (SCOPE), led by Julian Hunte of the St. Lucia Labour Party, which was created to address the Mitchell initiative. The MNU also took part in the deliberations of the Regional Constituent Assembly established to pursue the political union proposal.

In St. Vincent and the Grenadines, Burns Bonadie, a long-standing regional integrationist, broke with his SVLP because of its lukewarm stance on the political union proposal. This issue accelerated Bonadie's sense of disillusion-ment with the SVLP and his gravitation towards Mitchell's government, which culminated, in the post-1989 general election period, in his representing the OECS Farm Workers' Programme and St. Vincent and the Grenadines in a consular capacity in Toronto, Canada. Thereafter, Bonadie became a Senator and Minister in the NDP government and NDP candidate in Central Kings-town in the 2001 general elections. Bonadie's shift to the NDP did not herald a CTAWU closeness to that party as was the case between that union and the SVLP in the Milton Cato era. In any event, James Mitchell had no interest in trade unionism nor their activities, and he looked askance on any demand by trade unions for increased wages. His cynical posture always was that the union members had jobs and were thus fortunate. In his universe, capital was the undisputed ruler.

The general elections of May 1989, represented the highest point, po-litically, of the NDP; the lowest point for the SVLP since the 1957 general elections when it was in its infancy; the demise of the UPM; and the possibility of an enhanced political role for Ralph Gonsalves and the MNU. The NDP scored the most extraordinary electoral victory ever in the history of popular elections since universal adult suffrage in 1951; its wholly impressive feat has not been repeated by any party since 1989 in St. Vincent and the Grenadines. The NDP won all fifteen seats (the electoral constituencies were increased by two seats in 1989), with a 66.3 percentage share of the votes cast. The SVLP won none of the fifteen constituencies in which it offered candidates but obtained 30.3 percent of the votes cast; the MNU and the UPM ran two candidates each but none won; the MNU's percentage share of the popular vote was 2.34 percent; the UPM's 1.06 percent. Both UPM candidates — Oscar Allen in South Central Windward and Nelcia Robinson in South Leeward lost their deposits. One of MNU's two candidates, Cecil "Blazer" Williams, lost his deposit in East Kingstown; and the two SVLP candidates in the Northern and Southern Grenadines also lost their deposits.

The scale of the NDP's victory can be gauged from the following facts: In twelve of the fifteen constituencies, the NDP candidates won between 63.7 percent and 92.6 percent of the votes cast; in two other constituencies, the NDP victors scored 54.7 percent (South Windward), and 56.5 percent (Marriaqua); and only one NDP candidate Jonathan Peters, in North Central Windward, scored below 40 percent of the votes cast in a three-way contest with two strong political personalities, Vincent Beache of SVLP and Ralph Gonsalves of the MNU; in North Central Windward, Peters won 38.7 percent of the vote, Vincent Beache got 36 percent, and Ralph Gonsalves scored 25.3 percent of the votes cast, an increase over his 1984 tally and the best performance of any third-party candidate.

Several of the NDP's policies attracted public support: The land reform programme at Orange Hill Estates; the "basic needs" infrastructure programme, including footpaths in villages across St. Vincent and the Grenadines; the construction of multi-purpose hard courts in the communities; the thrust into tourism, especially in the Grenadines; the improved access, albeit modest, to water and electricity services by poorer folks; and the pushing for deeper regional integration. The leadership style of James Mitchell was engaging and relaxed; this drew him to people. Further, the NDP had recruited some likeable candidates from 1984 onwards who had not yet gone stale or disappointing to people in failing to deliver on promises. The more esteemed candidates included: Parnel Campbell, John Horne, Bernard Wyllie, Jeremiah Scott, Alpian Allen, Herbert Young, and Louis Jones. Still, the central thrust of the NDP's policies was driven by Mitchell himself; and the core of its policies and programmes was grounded in neo-liberalism, "free enterprise", rolling back the State sector, and "the Washington Consensus".

Since the 1983 election in Central Leeward, the writing was on the wall of the SVLP's unmistakable decline. The election of 1989 brought it to a crisis point but neither this fact nor its political implication, was yet to be appreciated by the SVLP leadership as a whole. A crisis is a condition in which the principals are innocent of the full extent of that condition and have no clear idea as to the way out of that condition. A crisis represented a moment of, and, for, change. But a dominant, and, incorrect perspective, in the SVLP's leadership was that the natural ebb and flow of competitive electoral politics would return the party to power. This fallacy was premised on the certainty that the NDP would fail in government. In other words, do nothing differently: Simply sit tight and wait until the metaphoric turn of the political wheel returns the SVLP to its natural place of governance. It is this kind of comforting complacency, and folly, that prompted some leaders in the SVLP to aver, in the wake of the narrow popular vote margin of the NDP in 1984, that the people had voted for a strong opposition but ended up, mistakenly, with a NDP government.

Still, the realistic wing of the SVLP led by Vincent Beache insisted that a thorough-going overhaul of the SVLP was required in terms of organisation, an intake of new blood, and a better message, more appropriate to the times in the changing global, regional, and national circumstances. Beache saw great value in the "Labour" brand and the accomplishment of the SVLP for the people, but he recognised that repeated losses of a major political party would render it politically toxic to significant sections of the electorate if urgent correctives were not taken. For him, this was not a matter simply of a change of a leadership face; a face-lift which still sought to keep the party rooted in past modes and glories would not succeed. Beache insisted that the SVLP must be more responsive and responsible to the people. He correctly analysed that the vast majority of the people who voted "Labour" — the working people, farmers, small business people, and professionals — were being held back by the anti-reform instincts of too many of its leadership, which were not shared by the people themselves. He considered that the people wanted the SVLP to embrace an unashamedly people-centred approach and fresh policy initiatives, not stale leftovers. He also proposed the heretic view, disdained by the "Labour Aloners." to reach out to Ralph Gonsalves, the MNU, and the UPM, even though he always felt that Oscar Allen was quaintly impractical. He cautioned the "Labour Aloners" that their insistence that the MNU and UPM leaders apply for membership in the SVLP was a non-starter. He was truly concerned that Mitchell's NDP, with its determination to roll back the State, enthrone the private sector, accord "open-sesame" treatment to dubious foreign investors, and practise "trickle-down" economics, will bring grief to the working people and the nation.

A group of "Young Turks" in the SVLP supported Vincent Beache's line; so, too, the bulk of the activist rank-and-file members. But there were others who hankered for the nostalgic, halcyon days of Milton Cato and Hudson Tannis; predictably, they ended with a caricature. Vincent Beache and the "Young Turks" were not concerned about the anti-communist and anti-socialist diatribe thrown at the leading lights in the MNU and UPM. Beache warned them that the day would come when political necessity would demand a unity between the SVLP and the progressive anti-Mitchell forces outside of the SVLP; so, it was better to do it orderly and unrushed, and to proceed immediately.

Independent of Vincent Beache, Ralph Gonsalves was thinking similarly, though from the perspective of the MNU. On the very night of the 1989 general elections, at a particular venue in Georgetown, Ralph Gonsalves calmly laid out the strategic thrust for the anti-Mitchell political forces to come together, to two of his closest confidantes, one of them being Julian Francis. He advised, however, that the "unity" idea would not come to practical fruition by way of a rational abstract conversation, but only by determined, focussed work of the MNU. He contended that the UPM was finished as an organised entity but it contained many good comrades with whom to work in structured ways; that the SVLP would consume itself with recriminations, bickering, and internal leadership squabbles for at least three years; that the NDP, devoid of a truly national party machinery and people-centred message, would over-reach and offend in a relatively short period of time; and that the global and regional political economy would provide spaces for progressive action. Accordingly, Gonsalves told his two close comrades that the MNU would take one-month's rest from political activism and then proceed to work non-stop in a focussed and unrelenting way to win the people to a well-articulated developmental agenda. He said that this was likely to be a fifteen-year project without a "unity" with the SVLP, but shorter, perhaps ten years, with them. He correctly advised that Vincent Beache and his wing of the SVLP would be critical in persuading the "Labour Aloners" to come to terms; but he insisted that the MNU had to engage assiduously, and relentlessly, with the people as a whole, in order to create the propitious conditions for a "unity" with the SVLP if possible, though separately if necessary.

Between the general elections of May 1989 and those of February 1994, several important happenings in the political economy occurred, including: The withering away of the Mitchell initiative of a political union of the Windward and Leeward Islands; the holding of a by-election in 1991 in the Southern Grenadines consequent upon the death of the incumbent Mary Hutchinson; the start-up of the tourism investment in Canouan; the controversial shipyard project at Ottley Hall between the State and an Italian investor; the beginnings of the devastating roll-back of the market preferences in the United Kingdom for Windward Islands' bananas on account of the United Kingdom's entry into the European Single Market from January 1993; and the electoral pact between the SVLP and the MNU in January 1994, leading in October 1994 to a merger between them as the Unity Labour Party (ULP).

As was expected, the NDP won convincingly the by-election in the Southern Grenadines in 1991. Two or so years earlier in the 1989 general elections, Mary Hutchinson of the NDP won 92.6 percent of the votes cast; the SVLP candidate, Sardine Hutchinson obtained 7.4 percent of the votes. The SVLP ducked the by-election; it refused to take part on the ground that the pending inquiry into an aspect of the alleged conduct of the Commissioner of Police, Randolph Toussaint, was the matter on which it was according political priority. It was not a convincing reason; it was more like an excuse. Were it not for the MNU, the NDP candidate, Stephanie Browne, in the by-election would have been unopposed. The results of the by-election were: Stephanie Browne, 84.99 percent of the votes cast; Olivia "Yvette" Bentick of the MNU, 14.27 percent. The MNU campaign was spirited; the campaign vehicle of the MNU was seriously vandalised and its campaign workers physically threatened. The

NDP took no chances: It devoted substantial material resources and time from the party leaders, including James Mitchell, to their campaign.

The MNU campaign undoubtedly raised its profile as a party which was not afraid to take the political fight into a fortress of the NDP. Since 1989, the MNU had been gathering momentum; quality personnel were joining, and the people were looking at it nationally as a growing political entity. Mike Browne, formerly of the UPM, resigned from the UPM shortly after the 1989 elections and joined the MNU. Every single week on Wednesdays, Fridays, Saturdays and Sundays, the MNU went on the road with community visits, internal party activities, and public meetings. It established the MNU Construction Brigade to assist poor persons on weekends with housing construction; a young builder, B.J. Lucas, who had attended the Communist Party School in Cuba as a member of the UPM, had joined the MNU and headed the Brigade. Weekly, the MNU published a newspaper, *Unity*. It published, too, *The Programmatic Platform of the MNU* and several monographs on important matters of public policy, history, and the political economy. The MNU was organising, doing active political work, advancing creative policies and programmes, and attracting quality people. It was developing as a modern, socialist-oriented political party in the Caribbean.

After the 1989 elections, Vincent Beache and Ralph Gonsalves often spoke informally about a possible nexus between the SVLP and the MNU. Gradually, the idea was gaining traction within both parties and the country. Still, there were reservations on both sides. Some in the MNU distrusted the SVLP and even bristled at the thought, given some SVLP stances in government and subsequently. Much of the SVLP, too, had misgivings. Confrontational, competitive political activism breeds mistrust and even malice; but astute leadership always demands a search for political space and cooperation in the interest of the people.

In mid-September 1993, Vincent Beache, the SVLP's immediate past Political Leader, and Terrance Parris, the SVLP's General Secretary, held a Saturday-morning meeting with Ralph Gonsalves at a hide-out at Rawacou. The subject was an electoral pact leading to a merger between the SVLP and MNU, including the possible division of seats and the actual names of possible candidates from both parties. Beache was to present the entire package of proposals from this meeting for, at least, approval in principle at a retreat of the SVLP's leadership on that very weekend at Randolph Russell's tourism facility at Wallilabou. On the Sunday night following, Beache informed Gonsalves that the proposals were rejected but advised that they keep the channels of communication open on the matter. This they did.

Meanwhile, after the decision at the SVLP's retreat in September 1993, the MNU was proceeding on the basis that it would contest the forthcoming general elections as a stand-alone party. It accordingly planned a march from Colonarie to Georgetown and a rally for jobs and improved living standards on Saturday, January 22, 1994. On January 21, 1994, Mitchell announced general elections for February 21, 1994.

On the very morning of the march and rally, Othniel Sylvester, distinguished lawyer and former candidate for the PPP and the MSP, telephoned Gonsalves with a proposal: That he and other nationals had formed a "Concerned Citizens' Group" and were inviting the SVLP and MNU the next day, Sunday, February 23, 1994, to a joint meeting at Marcole Plaza, Kingstown, to consider and hammer out, if possible, an electoral pact to oppose the NDP in the general elections of February 1994. Gonsalves agreed.

The MNU's march and rally was quite successful. A number of "the Concerned Citizens" attended the rally. The next day at Marcole Plaza, the leaders of both parties met with Sylvester in the Chair; other "Concerned Citizens" were present. The meeting began at 10:00 a.m. and went beyond midnight. At the end, there was an agreement on certain central points, among others, namely: (i) Vincent Beache will be the Political Leader of "the Labour-MNU Unity"; (ii) Stalky John and Ralph Gonsalves will remain leaders of the SVLP and MNU respectively; (iii) Of the 15 constituencies , the SVLP will run candidates in nine, and the MNU in six; (iv) A joint Election Manifesto will be prepared by a Committee co-chaired by Ralph Gonsalves and Stalky John, each of whom will prepare draft manifestos; (v) Each candidate will contribute $15,000 for his/her own campaign but general party campaign funds will be raised by the "Concerned Citizens" who will provide the monies to the central kitty through either Beache, John, or Gonsalves; and (vi) a campaign command structure was set up to work out campaign details.

The SVLP candidates were: Vincent Beache (South Windward); Stanley "Stalky" John (East St. George); Ken Browne (Marriaqua); Randolph Russell (Central Kingstown); Alwyn Westfield (South Leeward); Louis Straker (Central Leeward); John Thompson (North Leeward); Johnny Ollivierre (Northern Grenadines); and Henry St. Hillaire (South Central Windward).

The MNU candidates were: Ralph Gonsalves (North Central Windward); Venold Coombs (North Windward); Michael Browne (West St. George); Cecil

"Blazer" Williams (East Kingstown); Noel Jackson (West Kingstown); and Olivia Bentick (Southern Grenadines).

The "Labour-MNU" slate of candidates was of sound quality: Well-trained persons in various disciplines; self-made businessmen; experienced professionals; an active trade unionist; and community activists. All had given service to the people over a prolonged period. The "Unity" Manifesto was unmistakably social democratic and people-centred; it came from the bowels of the MNU with editorial amendments by the SVLP. In the run-up to the general elections of 1994, Ralph Gonsalves authored, and caused to be published, a book entitled *History and the Future: A Caribbean Perspective* which contained an analysis and programmatic details which fed into the "Unity" Manifesto.

Interestingly, the agreement, including the candidates and corresponding constituencies, was precisely what Vincent Beache and Ralph Gonsalves had agreed to at Rawacou in mid-September, 1993, but with one exception: In South Central Windward, Matthew Thomas of MNU was considered in preference to St. Hilaire. At the "Concerned Citizens" meeting, Thomas rejected the offer of candidacy; he was lukewarm to the "unity" but more particularly he insisted that if the Leader of "the Labour-MNU Unity" was not Ralph Gonsalves he was not contesting. Thomas, a sound professional pharmacist, a committed patriot and hard worker, was possessed of an inflexible mind which he brought to the world of politics; once he held an opinion, it was as though carved in stone for all time. Thomas had been doing a tremendous amount of political work in South Central Windward and had personally endeared himself to people. In less than a week his supporters bombarded him to change his mind; he reluctantly did so but it was too late to unravel the agreed "unity" package. Thomas, however, dutifully campaigned for St. Hilaire and the "Unity" ticket.

In the 1994 general elections, the NDP won twelve seats with 54.95 percent of the 46,934 votes cast; "Labour-MNU Unity" secured three seats with 43.96 percent of the votes; and three Independent candidates obtained, in the aggregate, 1.09 percent of the vote. Vincent Beache, Louis Straker, and Ralph Gonsalves won their respective seats on "the Unity" ticket. In South Windward, Beache obtained 55.2 percent of the vote; the NDP candidate Alfred Bynoe won 30.8 percent of the vote; and the incumbent, Burton Williams, who had earlier resigned from the NDP, ran as an Independent candidate, garnered 14.1 percent of the votes. In Central Leeward, Louis Straker, on his first electoral outing, defeated the incumbent, Herbert Young, by a margin of 51.3 percent to 48.7 percent of the votes cast. In North Central Windward, Ralph Gonsalves won 69.4 percent of the vote against the NDP's Vin Abbott who obtained 30.6 percent; Abbott replaced the incumbent Jonathan Peters who had returned to the USA in December 1993, to live. Gonsalves won the most votes absolutely of any candidate in the elections, 2,702, and secured the highest percentage of any constituency vote on mainland St. Vincent. Stanley John, the Political Leader of the SVLP, performed creditably, in a losing cause, in East St. George with 47.5 percent of the vote against Louis Jones of the NDP with 52.5 percent.

On the NDP side, their twelve winners in the 1994 elections were incumbents: James Mitchell, Monty Roberts, Allan Cruickshank, Bernard Wyllie, Louis Jones, Yvonne Francis-Gibson, Carlyle Dougan, Parnel Campbell, John Horne, Jeremiah Scott, Alpian Allen, and Stephanie Browne.

The only active trade union leader in the elections as a candidate was Noel Jackson, General Secretary of the NWM, who lost on the "Unity" ticket to the NDP's John Horne in West Kingstown. Noel Jackson had been a working people's fighter and trade unionist for over fifteen years. As leader of the NWM he had been militant in defence of the workers. In the eight or so years prior to the 1994 general elections, Jackson led NWM's strikes at several workplaces including: The Insect Vector Programme in September 1986; East Caribbean Metal Industries in September 1988; St. Vincent Electronics in June 1988; the French Restaurant in January 1990; SVG Port Authority in December 1990; and St. Vincent Brewery in 1990. Jackson was attracted to the policies and organisational work of the MNU to defend and promote the interests of the working people; and so, he joined the MNU in the early 1990s.

The former trade union leaders, Michael Browne and Yvonne Francis-Gibson, were in the elections as candidates in the same constituency for "Unity" (from the MNU stable) and NDP respectively. At the time of the momentous 1975 teachers' strike and protest, Browne was President of the Teachers' Union, and Francis-Gibson, the Vice President. Francis-Gibson defeated Browne in a close contest, 51.4 percent to 48 percent of the votes cast; a third candidate, Stanley Quammie formerly of the SVLP (he ran for the SVLP in 1979), an Independent candidate received 0.6 percent of the vote.

Vincent Beache became Leader of the Opposition consequent upon the 1994 elections; and an opposition was back in the House of Assembly after an absence of five years. The two "Unity" Senators appointed were Michael Browne and Michael Hamlett, a young banker by training who was to contest the East Kingstown constituency for the Unity Labour Party in 1998 and 2001; he sadly died within months of the 2001 elections, not yet 40 years old; he had great promise.

DECLINE OF NDP, POPULAR RESISTANCE, AND RESURGENT LABOUR: FEBRUARY 1994 TO 2000

The "Labour-MNU Unity" swiftly got to work, after the 1994 elections, to effect the merger between SVLP and the MNU. On October 16, 1994, the merged entity became a reality under the name, the Unity Labour Party (ULP). Vincent Beache and Ralph Gonsalves were elected unopposed as Political Leader and Deputy Political Leader respectively, at the inaugural convention of the party on October 16, 1994. Julian Francis, an accountant, banker and small businessman, the first cousin of Gonsalves, and formerly of the MNU, became the ULP's General Secretary. The party symbol was affirmed as "the Star." the symbol of the former SVLP, and the party organ was designated "Unity." the name of the newspaper of the former MNU.

Between 1994 and 1998, the ULP was very effective in the House of Assembly, in the communities, and on the political platforms. It established solid links with organised civil society and was relentless in its opposition to the anti-national, anti-working people, and anti-people policies of the NDP government. The ULP built itself as a modern, progressive party of advanced social democracy. It articulated with clarity its policies and programmes, and published them. The ULP, too, built excellent links in the region and internationally with like-minded nationalist, regionalist, internationalist, social democratic, socialist, and anti-imperialist parties and organisations.

Major policy failures of the NDP related to the Ottley Hall Project, the Winter Vegetables Initiative, the Offshore Finance Sector, Agriculture, generally Education, Health, the Physical Infrastructure, Housing, the Fight against Official Corruption, Poor Governance, Poverty Reduction, Trade Unions, and Foreign Policy. The NDP government had lost its way. Its counter-revolution against social democracy failed the people; its objective embrace of neo-liberalism, "the Washington Consensus." and imperialism's foreign policy agenda narrowed the developmental space for the people of St. Vincent and the Grenadines. The people realised that the NDP was leading them into a dead-end, a developmental cul-de-sac.

The labour movement was growing restive as evidenced by a number of workers' strikes and protests in the 1994 to 1998 period. These included: A "Sick-Out" staged by the PSU in 1995 at the ramshackle Public Library on account of its awful working conditions; in early 1996, the workers at Barclays Bank took industrial action — a one day sick-out — to force the management of the Bank, successfully, to recognise the CTAWU as their bargaining agent;

on October 29, 1996, the workers at Cable and Wireless went on strike for two working weeks to press for the reinstatement of an employee of 25 years, an Assistant Engineer, Dennis Gaymes; in November 1996, the Teachers' Union took industrial action (a sick-out) in protest against the government's failure to address certain aspects of the collective agreement, including the appointment of graduate teachers and other teachers; in January 1997, the Teachers' Union again embarked upon industrial action in the form of a successful two-day strike to address the intransigence of the government on the material issues of concern to teachers; in 1998, there were several work stoppages, at different places, including hotels, WIBDECO, and the Flour Mill, in an effort to pressure employers to treat properly with workers' grievances; and in 1998, the PSU led Nurses and Nursing Assistants in a picket of Parliament on the issue of pensions for Nursing Assistants.

The NDP's vaunted political machinery was failing it. For years, it relied on its governmental control of the state-owned radio station, National Broadcasting Corporation Radio 705, and a largely compliant, privately-owned SVG Television. The rise of "Talk Radio" on FM radio stations, particularly Glen Jackson on his WE-FM "Shake-Up" programme, meant that control of the media was now well-nigh impossible. Alternative voices of reason and substance were now being heard.

The NDP as an organisation was faltering badly. Stewart Nanton, the very able General Secretary, was in failing health. P.R. Campbell, the outstanding political organiser, strategist, and Attorney General, a person overall of immense intellectual gifts, was pressured by an opposition motion of no-confidence to resign in 1996 on account of allegedly impermissible personal loans from an offshore bank, the owner of which had close links with Prime Minister James Mitchell. In the parliamentary debate, Mitchell did not defend Campbell from the opposition critique; indeed, in crafty and cynical language, Mitchell threw Campbell under the proverbial bus. Campbell, the Deputy Prime Minister and the generally-accepted heir-apparent to Mitchell, was left by his colleagues to twist in the political wind. Perhaps, some of his colleagues felt, jealously, that he was too cocksure of his political strength and were not unhappy to see him go. The loss of Campbell to the NDP government was a major blow; and it reflected subsequently in its sloppy work, in and out of Parliament. The government had lost, too, a highly-skilled communicator in Campbell. More and more the government was looking ragged and ill-disciplined, reminiscent of the last two or so years of the SVLP government before its demise in 1984. Moreover, the people were experiencing the harsh lived consequences of Mitchell's anti-national, anti-worker, neo-liberal, and neo-colonial public policies. Even the IMF which was applauding the NDP government for its fiscal stance in 1989, was, by 1998, critiquing it on its less than satisfactory handling of the economy.

In June 1998, general elections were held. The NDP retained its parliamentary majority by winning eight of the fifteen seats, but with a minority of 45.3 percent of the 51,328 votes cast. The ULP won seven seats with 54.6 percent of the vote; and Burton Williams' Peoples' Working Party (PWP) just under 0.1 percent. The NDP lost four seats; and the ULP gained four. The vagaries of the first-past-the-post electoral system was at work to the huge disadvantage of the ULP. Again, for the second general elections in-a-row, Ralph Gonsalves secured the highest absolute number of votes in any constituency in the elections, 2,943, and the highest percentage of votes, 78.1 percent, in any constituency on the mainland, St. Vincent; James Mitchell garnered the highest percentage tally, 88.3 percent, in the Northern Grenadines.

The seven seats won by the ULP were by large majorities, ranging, at the lower end, from 56.3 percent in Central Kingstown (Ormiston Boyea) to 78.1 percent in North Central Windward (Ralph Gonsalves). In the eight seats won by the NDP, five of them were narrow victories ranging from a margin of 27 votes to 189 votes, in ascending order: East Kingstown, North Windward, South Leeward, South Central Windward, and West Kingstown. Less than three years later, the ULP was to win the latter four marginal seats, plus another.

The eight victorious NDP candidates in the 1998 elections were: Monty Roberts in North Windward (50.8 percent of the votes); Allan Cruickshank in South Central Windward (51.5 percent of the vote); Arnhim Eustace in East Kingstown (50.4 percent of the votes); John Horne in West Kingstown (53.0 percent); Alpian Allen in North Leeward (53.1 percent); Glenford Stewart in the Southern Grenadines (64.9 percent); and James Mitchell in the Northern Grenadines. Among the losing NDP candidates were holders of ministerial offices: Bernard Wylle, Louis Jones, and Carl Joseph. A former minister, Parnel Campbell, lost his Central Kingstown seat to a prominent businessman Ormiston Boyea; this defeat brought the curtains down on Campbell's career in competitive electoral politics.

The seven victorious ULP candidates in the 1998 general elections were: Ralph Gonsalves in North Central Windward; Vincent Beache in South Windward (67.3 percent of the vote); Girlyn Miguel in Marriaqua (63.3 percent); Stanley John in East St. George (62.3 percent); Michael Browne in West St. George (62.5 percent); Ormiston Boyea in Central Kingstown (56.3 percent);

and Louis Straker in Central Leeward (56.7 percent). The people had elected a formidable opposition; they actually voted for a government but got an opposition!

The ULP, through Vincent Beache and Ralph Gonsalves, made three prescient remarks about the 1998 results: First, they were unsustainable; secondly, one seat was not enough in a situation whereby the holder of the one seat had a substantial deficit in the popular vote; and thirdly, as soon as the government made an error of a sufficient magnitude to galvanise the country against it, it would be forced to call early elections. Accordingly, from the beginning the ULP demanded fresh elections to allow the electorate to deliver a proper mandate without the pain of a weak government amidst a hostile population. The NDP pledged to serve the full five years; it did not, to its subsequent detriment, listen to sane, mature voices.

Some elements in the ULP's leadership argued for a legal challenge to Eustace's marginal victory of 27 votes in East Kingstown. Vincent Beache and Ralph Gonsalves opposed this approach and persuaded the Party's Central Executive accordingly. Beache and Gonsalves contended that a legal challenge would, with inordinate delays, dampen popular enthusiasm, dissipate the party's resources and energies and divert its focus from the crucial organisational and political work which the times demanded. The ULP's Central Executive agreed: Put your faith in people, not in judges! The ULP thus embarked on a vigorous and focussed opposition in and out of the House of Assembly; it lifted its organisational capacity; mobilised resources, and built a close network among organised civil society to await the day and the hour for the inevitable, major political blunder by the NDP government. The mantra of the Beache-Gonsalves leadership at this time was: *Oppose* (the government); *Propose* (policies); *Expose* (reveal and critique government's wrongdoings); and *Depose* (constitutionally rid the country of the NDP government).

By October 1998, two ULP parliamentarians, Stanley John and Ormiston "Ken" Boyea, were openly questioning the ULP's strategy. They claimed, mistakenly, that it was not working; only four months had elapsed since the general elections and across the country pressure was mounting on the Government. In no important sector of the society and economy was the government supported; it was only a matter of time that they would do something really foolish and draw the people on the streets. John and Boyea were misreading entirely the political tea leaves. They mistook Mitchell's braggadocio and the bombast of the Minister of Finance Arnhim Eustace for political strength and sustainability. The government was on the political ropes. They knew it, the people knew it, and the ULP leadership, except John and Boyea, knew it.

Around the middle of October 1998, Stanley John made a move which would precipitate his personal political decline: At a meeting of the Central Executive of the ULP, John stated unequivocally that the real problem of the ULP during the 1998 elections and thereafter was one of Vincent Beache's leadership; he contended that Vincent Beache should resign sooner rather than later "for the good of the party". Gonsalves rebutted but Beache interrupted him and said in effect: "Stalky John is right; it is time for me to go; I will resign as Political Leader; I will explain to my constituents; let us prepare for a National Convention in December 1998 and choose a new Political Leader." Efforts by the Central Executive, in near unanimity, to persuade Beache to change his mind, was to no avail.

Subsequently, the date for the ULP National Convention was set for December 6, 1998. The only nomination for Deputy Leader was Boyea, so he was elected unopposed. John and Gonsalves were the two candidates for Political Leader. John was overwhelmingly defeated at the National Convention held at the St. Joseph's Convent, Marriaqua. Gonsalves received 78 percent of the delegates' vote and John, 22 percent. Both the defeat and the scale of it apparently took John by surprise. Somehow, he deceived himself into believing that something called "Old Labour" would defeat "Old MNU". He did not realise that the ULP was a thoroughly unified entity in which the artificial divisions, fuelled by the ghost of antagonistic political competition of yesteryear, held no political sway. Gonsalves stood on a progressive platform of social democracy; John's perspective mirrored the centre-right outlook that the bulk of the NDP had been espousing.

From December 6, 1998, until John and Boyea resigned from the ULP in early 2000, they sought to provide aid and comfort to the NDP Government in and out of Parliament. Clearly, they were not prepared to be led by Ralph Gonsalves in whom the working people and the nation as a whole had overwhelming confidence. John and Boyea even sought to fashion a political deal with James Mitchell. John actually entertained the thought that Mitchell would make way for him to head a John-Boyea-Mitchell government. It was all political fantasy. John and Boyea even tried to recruit two UPM parliamentarians — Louis Straker and Girlyn Miguel — to their cause, but they were completely rebuffed. The old days of political gymnastics and floor-crossing by political elites to undo the popular will, were not entertained by the comrades in the ULP.

Shortly after John and Boyea resigned from the ULP, they formed the People's Progressive Movement (PPM) with Boyea as Leader and John as his Deputy. They took with them marginal ULP personalities and supporters such as Ivan O'Neal, Amor Lashley, Frederick Ollivierre, and Relton John. They made little or no political impact. The people were determined to change the NDP government and they were unprepared to allow marginal breakaways and one or two individuals driven by personal ambition and personal animosity to Ralph Gonsalves to stand between them — the people — and the necessary and desirable change, in ridding the country of Mitchell and the NDP.

The electoral numbers on the political decline of the NDP told an interesting tale: never in the history of St. Vincent and the Grenadines, since universal adult suffrage in 1951, had there been a political party in office continuously, with such a huge slump in its popular vote. In the 1989 general elections, the NDP received 66.3 percent of the popular vote; in 1994, it obtained 54.5 percent; and in 1998, it got 45.3 percent. In other words, in a mere nine years the NDP's popular support fell by 21 percentage points, from 66.3 percent to 45.3 percent. It had become widely unpopular and it was unlikely to be rescued from electoral defeat next time.

Amidst all the political gymnastics of John and Boyea in the opposition, the working people looked to the ULP for support in their day-to-day struggles in life, living and production. The working people were not distracted by political antics designed to derail them. In 1999, several strikes, go-slows and work-stoppages occurred. In each case ULP activists assisted the workers' cause. In the public sector, the teachers in the primary and secondary schools went on strike twice in 1999 consequent upon a deadlock in the negotiations with the government over the teachers' demand for a salary increase. These strikes were overwhelmingly supported by the teachers. In each case, ULP activists, including teachers, gave solid support and meaningful encouragement. So, too, did the ULP leadership in the person of Ralph Gonsalves and others who marched on the streets of Kingstown with the Roman Catholic nuns, priests, parents, students, and the general public in their call for the government to pay the teachers employed in the secondary schools owned and operated by religious denominations (Roman Catholic, Anglican, and Seventh Day Adventists). The night before the march, the Minister of Finance, Arnhim Eustace denounced the nuns on television, labelling them "foreigners"; but these were selfless, Christian believers called to especial religious orders and service in St. Vincent and the Grenadines who happened to be from other Caribbean countries, mainly Dominica and Trinidad and Tobago.

In April 2000, the NDP government made the major mistake which Beache and Gonsalves had predicted would mobilise the people in an unprecedented manner. The trigger for a virtual closure of City Kingstown for two weeks (end of April into early May 2000) was a Bill presented to Parliament, the object and purpose of which was to enhance the pension and gratuity of Ministers and other parliamentarians, including nominated Senators. In the original Bill presented to the House of Assembly, a pension for Ministers' widows/widowers was also included. Arnhim Eustace, who introduced the Bill, had a few evenings earlier responded to the civil servants' demand for more than the government's offer of a twelve percent salary increase over three years, with a brusque: "Not one more cent for them". The civil servants, teachers and the general population were highly incensed.

Unmindful or dismissive of the people's anger on this matter, Eustace brought the Bill to the House of Assembly for debate. This was on the Wednesday of the Holy Week, 2000. On arrival at the gates of Parliament, the Prime Minister and Ministers of government were greeted by a well-populated picket line of comprised mainly of nurses dressed in their uniforms, teachers and civil servants. They demanded, among other things, the withdrawal of what they labelled "the Greedy Bill" and a salary increase in excess of the government's offer. The government sought to amend the Bill by cutting out the pension for Ministers' widows/widowers. The ULP opposition still objected to the Bill and demanded its permanent withdrawal.

During the proceedings in the House of Assembly, Prime Minister Mitchell left the Chamber and went to the Speaker's room to look down at the extent of the picket. Gonsalves, the Leader of the Opposition, followed him there. Gonsalves informally requested of Mitchell the Bill's withdrawal. Defiantly, Mitchell said in effect: "No'! Never mind this protest. Day-after-tomorrow is Good Friday, then Easter Sunday and Monday. After that things will be back to normal." Gonsalves advised him that "it is different this time", but Mitchell remained adamant that the Bill would be passed that very day. Indeed, the Bill was passed on account of the government's parliamentary majority, but which represented a minority of the people nationally. Three days later on Easter Saturday, a broad-based, non-partisan body was formed called the Organisation in Defence of Democracy (ODD), headed by Renwick Rose.

Over the Easter weekend, the ULP, the unions, organised civil society, and the ODD mobilised to close City Kingstown on the Tuesday after the Easter Monday. On Easter Monday, several NDP Ministers of Government were on radio apologising for the Bill, promising that it would not be assented to by the

Governor General, and pleading to give them time to return it to Parliament to be voted down. All this was to no avail. The public did not accept as genuine their contrived contrition. Indeed, the ULP, the trade unions, organised civil society, and the people as a whole argued that "trust", so fundamental to the relationship between a government and the people, had been broken and cannot now be so glibly repaired. The demand was now raised: fresh elections immediately! The teachers stayed away from school for two weeks. So did a large number of civil servants.

Over the next two weeks, the people, led by the ULP, blocked the roads into Kingstown on the days of their choosing. The NDP Government was powerless to stem the tide of public anger. Overwhelmingly, the members of the trade unions, especially the public sector unions, were fully engaged with the mass protests and the road blocks, although a few of the union leaders played vacillating and compromising roles. Broadly, civil society was fully supportive, save and except the sections of the leaderships of some civil society groups who had partisan political links with the NDP Government. Repeatedly, on numerous days over the two-week period huge crowds turned out in support, including on the occasion of public solidarity rallies. It is a beautiful thing to behold the bulk of the working people and their allies in solidarity for a just cause. Not even police intimidation on the protest days fazed the people or their leaders. It was a time of broad unity of the labour movement and supportive allies led sagely by the ULP. It was the mass confirmation on the streets of the popular support for the ULP in the 1998 general elections. The events of April-May 2000 reaffirmed that the political overrule by the NDP was in its terminal stages; its end was nigh. The validation of all this was to come in the general elections of March 2001.

CARICOM and the OECS sought to mediate. An OECS Heads of Government meeting was taking place in Grenada. The ULP, the ODD, trade unions and civil society representatives were invited to attend. After several hours of inconclusive discussions at the Grand Beach Hotel at Grand Anse, Grenada, James Mitchell suggested that he and Ralph Gonsalves go outside, with no one else, to seek an agreement. They went on the beach, argued and debated the matter for about an hour. They returned with an agreement. Central to it was the decision to hold general elections no later than March 31, 2001, or some two and one-half years earlier than the end of the five-year term. Between early May 2000, and when the elections were held on March 28, 2001, the NDP was in every sense a lame-duck government. James Mitchell resigned as Prime Minister on October 27, 2000, and Arnhim Eustace was selected as Prime Minister by the eight elected representatives of the NDP.

LABOUR RETURNS UNITED AS ULP GOVERNMENT: MARCH 2001-2018, THUS FAR

In the March 2001 general elections the ULP won twelve seats with 56.5 percent of the 58,284 votes cast; the NDP won three seats with 40.9 percent of the vote; the Boyea-led PPM received 2.6 percent of the national vote from the eleven constituencies which it contested. None of the PPM candidates won; indeed, they all lost their deposits. The political arm of the broad labour movement was elected to office overwhelmingly. The ULP, the party of the working people and nation as a whole, campaigned on a strong social democratic, nationalist, regionalist, and anti-imperialist platform, was now accorded the governmental responsibility to face the on-rushing challenges of the 21st century.

The ULP won a magnificent victory. Ralph Gonsalves won the highest number of votes and the highest percentage of votes in any constituency in the entire country. He was, too, the first candidate ever to score in excess of 3,000 votes. The actual numbers were 3,153 or 80.7 percent of the votes cast in the constituency of North Central Windward. He became Prime Minister at fifty-four years of age. Louis Straker was named Deputy Prime Minister and Vincent Beache, Minister of National Security. The other winning ULP candidates were: Montgomery Daniel, Selmon Walters, Girlyn Miguel, Clayton Burgin, Michael Browne, Conrad Sayers, René Baptiste, Dr. Douglas Slater, and Dr. Jerrol Thompson. Added to this elected parliamentary slate in the House of Assembly were four government Senators: Michael Hamlett who garnered 49.5 percent of the votes in East Kingstown against the NDP's Leader and out-going Prime Minister, Arnhim Eustace; Edwin Snagg who lost in the Southern Grenadines, but with a score of 44.1 percent of the votes — the best ever by a non-NDP candidate in that seat; Julian Francis (the ULP's General Secretary); and Juliette George (the ULP Women's Arm President). It was a talented team of great promise to execute a programme of advanced social democracy, meaningful regionalism, and internationalist solidarity. The ULP was well-prepared for the leadership tasks ahead. It saw itself, unapologetically, as a "Labour" government. And its record so indicates!

The ULP had several comprehensive documents before the electorate in which it articulated a compelling developmental narrative for the nation. Among these publications were the ULP's *Hundred Days Programme*, its *Election Manifesto*, and its *Youth Manifesto*. Additionally, Ralph Gonsalves caused to be published a collection of his essays, papers and speeches entitled *The Politics of our Caribbean Civilisation: Essays and Speeches*.

The twelve victorious candidates of the ULP in the 2001 general elections secured victories ranging from 49.7 percent of the votes in the case of Conrad Sayers in a three-way contest against Ormiston "Ken" Boyea and Joseph "Burns" Bonadie in Central Kingstown to 80.7 percent for Ralph Gonsalves in North Central Windward. Seven successful ULP candidates recorded scores in the range 50 percent-to-under 60 percent of the votes as follows: René Baptiste (50.1 percent in West Kingstown); Jerrol Thompson (52.3 percent in North Leeward); Montgomery Daniel (52.5 percent in North Windward); Douglas Slater (53.8 percent in South Leeward); Selmon Walters (56.2 percent South Central Windward; and Clayton Burgin (59.5 percent in East St. George). A further three successful ULP candidates secured results in the 60 percent-to-under 70 percent range: Michael Browne (62.3 percent in West St. George); Girlyn Miguel (66.6 percent in Marriaqua; and Vincent Beache (69.3 percent in South Windward).

The NDP emerged from the general elections at its lowest ebb since its victory in 1984. Its political leader Arnhim Eustace retained his seat by a mere 40 votes against his competitor, the young, gifted business executive, Michael Hamlett. The other two NDP victors were in the Northern Grenadines with Dr. Godwin Friday who had succeeded James Mitchell in that constituency; and Terrance Ollivierre, a teacher, in the Southern Grenadines. The NDP, between the 1989 and 2001 elections, a span of just under twelve years, had its popular vote slashed from 66.3 percent to 40.9 percent, over 25 percentage points.

More than likely, the bulk of the PPM votes came from former NDP supporters. The PPM died a natural death shortly after the general elections. Neither Stanley "Stalky" John nor Ormiston "Ken" Boyea ever returned to active electoral politics. Boyea lost his candidate's deposit by garnering less than 15 percent of the votes (his actual score was 11.0 percent) in Central Kingstown; and Stanley "Stalky" John also lost his deposit with 12.3 percent of the votes in East St. George.

Burns Bonadie, the veteran trade union leader, lost on the NDP-ticket in Central Kingstown; he was nominated as an opposition Senator but in September 2001 he resigned from that party and returned to the fold of "Labour" — the ULP. Since then he has continued his work in trade unionism, and as an adviser to the government on regional integration, worker education and industrial relations. He remains an activist for the ULP.

Since March 2001 the ULP has been in office continuously under the leadership of Ralph Gonsalves who has become the longest-serving Prime Minister in St. Vincent and the Grenadines. The ULP was re-elected in 2005,

2010, and 2015. It lost a referendum in quest of reforming, root-and-branch, the inherited Constitution of St. Vincent and the Grenadines which, despite its liberal democratic strengths, has many weaknesses and limitations.

In reviewing the 2001 to 2018 period, a synopsis of the politics of St. Vincent and the Grenadines will be presented; so, too, a summary of trade unions and a summation of the achievements of the most progressive social democratic, nationalist, regionalist, and anti-imperialist government in the history of St. Vincent and the Grenadines. The accomplishments directly beneficial to the working people will be highlighted. The ULP government has truly been a "Labour Government".

In the December 2005 general elections, the ULP was comfortably re-elected. It retained its twelve-to-three seats majority over the NDP with 55.4 percent of the 57,777 votes cast. In these elections there were some slight boundary changes consequent upon the 2001 Population Census and the appointment of a Constituency Boundaries Commission. The major change, unanimously agreed upon by the Commission, was to shift the communities of Caratal and Spring Village at the northern boundary of North Central Windward to the constituency of North Windward. The shift did not adversely affect Gonsalves, as the NDP predicted; he was still the best performer in the elections with the highest absolute number of votes and the highest percentage in a constituency: 2,887 votes or 81 percent. In North Windward, Montgomery Daniel also increased in absolute numbers, and proportionately, his tally of votes from 2,211 votes or 52.5 percent in 2001 to 2,405 votes or 54.3 percent. The ULP candidates were returned in their twelve seats of 2001. The only change in a ULP candidacy was in South Windward where Glen Beache replaced his father, Vincent Beache, who retired from competitive politics and thus declined to run in the 2005 elections. Beache had served "Labour" and his people in active, competitive politics since 1972, first in North Central Windward and then from 1994 in South Windward, where he actually lived. Vincent Beache had served with distinction.

The twelve successful ULP candidates in the 2005 general elections and their respective percentage share of the votes were as follows: Montgomery Daniel (54.3 percent in North Windward); Ralph Gonsalves (81.0 percent in North Central Windward); Selmon Walters (57.0 percent in South Central Windward); Girlyn Miguel (65.2 percent in Marriaqua); Glen Beache (67.6 percent in South Windward); Clayton Burgin (57.4 percent in East St. George); Michael Browne (59.0 percent West St. George); Conrad Sayers (50.2 percent) in Central Kingstown; René Baptiste (50.4 percent in West Kingstown);

Douglas Slater (51.3 percent in South Leeward); Louis Straker (56.9 percent in Central Leeward); and Jerrol Thompson (50.3 percent in North Leeward).

The three NDP candidates in the winner's row in the 2005 general elections were Arnhim Eustace (51.8 percent in East Kingstown — an increase of 1.3 percentage points over the 2001 elections); Godwin Friday (74.1 percent in the Northern Grenadines — a decrease of 2.4 percentage points of his 2001 figure); and Terrance Ollivierre (57.0 percent in the Southern Grenadines — a 2.1 percentage points increase over his score in the 2001 general elections).

The ULP's share of the vote in 2005 declined absolutely by 919 votes and by a 1.1 percentage point. Reduced majorities were evident in ten constituencies: South Windward, East St. George, West St. George, East Kingstown, Central Kingstown, West Kingstown, South Leeward, Central Leeward, North Leeward, and the Southern Grenadines. The NDP increased its popular vote from 23,844 votes or 40.91 percent to 25,734 votes or 44.5 percent; its absolute number of votes, thus increased by 1,890 votes. It was likely that the former Boyea-led PPM's 1,515 votes in 2001 went to the NDP in 2005, accounting for the bulk of their 2005 increase. In all this, it is to be noted that fewer persons, 507, voted in 2005 than in 2001.

Overall, the organised political expression of the labour movement, the ULP, performed commendably in the 2005 general elections.

In both the 2001 and 2005 general elections, the radio personality and political activist, Glen Jackson, played an important role in the ULP's victories. In April 2001, he was appointed as Press Secretary to Prime Minister Ralph Gonsalves. In that capacity he performed outstandingly. On March 6, 2006, he was murdered. The ULP lost a major communicator, activist and strategist in Glen Jackson; his death represented a huge blow to the ULP. The ULP Government, in his honour, has established "the Glen Jackson Scholarship" for training in media studies at the University of the West Indies.

In the 2005 elections, the Green Party, led by Ivan O'Neal, formerly of the PPM, fielded four candidates; they received, in the aggregate, 37 votes or 0.06 percent of the total votes cast. In the 2010 elections, the Green Party received 138 votes from the thirteen contested constituencies. In the 2015 elections, the Green Party obtained 77 votes from its seven contested constituencies. Both O'Neal and the Green Party have become the butt of proverbial political jokes. Of its twenty-four candidates offered over three elections, none ever came close to secure the return of his or her deposit of $500.00.

In the Constitutional Reform Referendum of November 25, 2009, the "Yes" campaign spearheaded by the ULP was defeated by the "No" campaign led by the NDP. The proposed Reform Constitution was rejected by a majority of 55 percent to 45 percent of the votes. The process began in October 2002, when both Prime Minister Gonsalves and Leader of the Opposition, Arnhim Eustace, jointly moved a parliamentary motion, which was unanimously passed by the House of Assembly, to proceed with constitutional reform. A Constitutional Reform Committee was established in February 2003 with the support and participation of the ULP and NDP. A Draft Constitution was prepared after extensive consultations in St. Vincent and the Grenadines and the Vincentian diaspora. Discussions on the draft were proceeding in a non-partisan manner; then, out of the blue, the opposition pulled out of the reform process in July 2007, citing spurious reasons. It had evidently taken a political decision based on absolutely no principle. The Draft Constitution was hailed by objective experts locally, regionally and internationally as a vast improvement on the existing Constitution, yet the NDP opposed it because it proved politically opportune to do so. The Draft Constitution proposed, among other things an enlargement of the individual's fundamental rights and freedoms; a reduction of the powers of the Prime Minister and an increase in those of the Leader of the Opposition (Minority Leader); a strengthened good governance in its requisites of openness, transparency, and accountability by empowering further the Office of the Director of Audit and the Public Accounts Committee chaired by the Leader of the Opposition, and the establishment of the Office of Ombudsman; the establishment of a Human Rights Commission; the bolstering of the independence and quality of the judiciary, including the Magistracy; making more democratic and representative the electoral system, with a mixture of first-past-the-post and proportional representation principles; setting up an independent Elections' Commission; replacing the Privy Council by the Caribbean Court of Justice as the final appellate jurisdiction; replacing the monarchical system with a republican one by removing the British sovereign as Head of State and putting in place a "home-grown" non-executive President elected by Parliament; and advancing a bundle of fundamental principles and values grounded in our Caribbean civilisation to guide the Constitution and its interpretation.

The opposition NDP, with support from moneyed British interests in Mustique and Bequia, the services of the "mind-benders" of the recently-discredited Strategic Communications Laboratories (SCL) of Britain, and further financial sustenance from international groups with an interest in the selling of our country's citizenship and passports, ran a shameful campaign of distortion, lies, backwardness, and political opportunism against the "Reform Constitution". The opposition NDP focussed on a few issues: the propagation of the false allegation that the Draft Constitution would take away a person's right to property; the absurdity that the removal of the Queen meant the enthroning of Ralph Gonsalves as a dictator; the unfounded propaganda that the removal of the Privy Council meant an end to impartial, independent justice; and the ridiculous falsehood, and non-issue, that God was not identified in the Preamble of the Draft Constitution as the source of the enumerated "inalienable rights".

The "No" platform unfortunately succeeded in conducting a scorched-earth political campaign which appealed to their political base, fortified in their certainty that the "Yes" campaign would not be able to obtain the requisite two-thirds majority to alter the fundamental, entrenched clauses of the Constitution. The government, with civil society support, ran a national campaign, not a politically partisan one. While the NDP paraded their party colours to attract their base, the Government could not use the ULP colours or slogans. In the end, the "No" campaign won with scaremongering and unprincipled electioneering. In the process, they achieved their political purpose in delivering a setback to the ULP and Ralph Gonsalves; but a metaphoric political "blackeye" does not an election campaign make, as the NDP found out in 2010.

In the general elections of December 2010, the ULP ran an astute campaign. Cognizant of the referendum setback, its messages to its core support, including those who did not vote in the referendum were simple: "Own the Party, Own the Campaign, Own the Government"; "Too Far to Turn Back Now"; "Defend Your Party, Defend Your Government, Defend Your Gains!" The base of the party rallied against the big-moneyed interests which were behind the NDP, the resources from the international sellers of citizenship and passports who wanted the NDP to do their bidding, and the slickness of the dishonest SCL. The ULP focussed on its achievements and its compelling developmental narrative as reflected in its many party publications including its *Election Manifesto* and its *Youth Manifesto* for 2010. Additionally, Ralph Gonsalves authored, and caused to be published two books: *The Making of the Comrade: The Political Journey of Ralph Gonsalves*, and *Diary of a Prime Minister: Ten Days Among the Benedictine Monks*.

The ULP Political Leader, Ralph Gonsalves, is on record as saying that it was his most challenging campaign since he became party leader in 1998, but it is the one which he enjoyed most because it tested his mettle and that of the ULP, especially its loyal base of working people. Unfortunately, he was without his principal lieutenant, Louis Straker, who had retired from elective politics. To be sure, the ULP had monumental achievements to its credit but the political winds were metaphorically at the NDP's sails since the Referendum of November, 2009.

In the upshot, 62,799 persons voted in the general elections of December 2010, or 5,022 more than 2005: The ULP won eight seats with 32,099 votes or 51.1 percent of the votes cast; the NDP, seven seats with 30,562 votes or 48.66 percent of the votes; the Green Party received 138 votes or 0.21 percent. The ULP retained the constituencies of North Windward (Montgomery Daniel with 52.5 percent of the vote); North Central Windward (Ralph Gonsalves with 79.8 percent); South Central Windward (new-comer Saboto Caesar with 56.4 percent); South Windward (new-comer Frederick Stephenson with 59.4 percent); Marriaqua (Girlyn Miguel with 56.2 percent); East St. George (Clayton Burgin with 52.6 percent); West St. George (new-comer Cecil Mc Kie with 54.7 percent), and Central Leeward (new-comer Maxwell Charles with 51.6 percent). In each constituency the ULP's vote fell, marginally in most cases, and more substantially in a few others. Ralph Gonsalves emerged yet again with the highest absolute number of votes, 3,044, in the entire country and the highest percentage of a constituency vote on mainland St. Vincent, but his percentage vote slipped slightly from 81 percent in 2005 to 79.8 percent in 2010. The ULP lost their seats in Central Kingstown with 45.6 percent of the vote; in West Kingstown with 44.1 percent; and in South Leeward with 48.0 percent, where there were new-comers as candidates; and the ULP incumbent, Jerrol Thompson lost in North Leeward with a score of 47.7 percent of the votes. On the other hand, the NDP advanced in each constituency, marginal to moderate; but the NDP's advance was contained.

On the NDP side, the four new elected Parliamentarians were: St. Clair Leacock (54.1 percent of the vote in Central Kingstown); Daniel Cummings (55.7 percent in West Kingstown); Nigel Stephenson (52.0 percent in South Leeward); and Roland Matthews (52.0 percent in North Leeward). Arnhim Eustace retained his East Kingstown seat with 54.9 percent of the vote. Both Godwin Friday and Terrance Ollivierre retained the NDP strongholds respectively in the Northern Grenadines (80.2 percent of the vote) and the Southern Grenadines (63.1 percent).

It was a remarkable political achievement by the ULP in all the circumstances: A third term victory in the midst of an unfolding and biting global economic depression, the worst since 1929, which was manifested in St. Vincent and the Grenadines with negative rates of economic growth in 2008, 2009,

2010; a natural disaster on October 31, 2010; the loss of the market preferences for bananas in the British market; and a rising fiscal deficit. All around the Caribbean, Latin America and Europe, governments were being washed away by electorates who were feeling the pain and suffering of the economic meltdown globally. The ULP with its pro-working people achievements and agenda weathered the storm. Still, there was much work to be done.

In the general elections of December 2015, the ULP won its fourth successive five-year term with a majority of the seats (eight), with an increased number of votes (34,246), an increased percentage of votes (52.3 percent), and a strengthening of its support in every constituency, save and except in South Windward and Central Kingstown where there was marginal slippage. It was an impressive performance: A fourth-term victory with an increase in the popular votes in a context of the continuing deleterious impact of the global economic downturn, multiple adverse weather events, a relentless anti-people campaign by the NDP and its social allies, "commess" and fabrications from the anti-ULP "internet crazies" on social media. Sound policies, good organisation, strong leadership, and a committed working people's base of the ULP kept the neo-liberals and backward politics at bay.

From the referendum of 2009 to the general elections of 2015 and continuing, the internet, social media, YouTube, Twitter, Instagram, and other applications and platforms of revolutionary information communications technology have grown in importance in transmitting facts, "fake news." and opinions about politics and governance in St. Vincent and the Grenadines, and elsewhere.

Political parties, their employees, advisers, consultants, and supporters utilise the modern information technologies to communicate to and with the general public and targeted audiences within it. During the referendum of 2009 and the general elections of 2010 and 2015, the Opposition NDP hired a British firm, Strategic Communications Laboratories (SCL) as its elections consultant. SCL advertises itself as a group of "mind benders" who draw inspiration, from among other sources, the techniques of Goebells, the propaganda master of the notorious Nazi, Adolph Hitler. SCL's off-shoot, Cambridge Analytica, came to prominence in the United States of America after Donald Trump was elected as President in 2016. Cambridge Analytica was hired by the Trump campaign and conducted allegedly nefarious work to assist in Trump's election. SCL, in its promotion, boasted, among other things, of its successes in the Caribbean, but it did not succeed in St. Vincent and the Grenadines in the 2010 and 2015 general elections. It has admitted publicly that it carried out a "targeted" campaign against Ralph Gonsalves on the internet by writing fake and scurrilous stories about him in such volumes that these stories would receive prominence on Google and other search engines on the first and second pages in relation to Ralph Gonsalves' profiles.

Generally, the "internet crazies" from St. Vincent and the Grenadines, most of whom live abroad in North America and Europe, post a series of lies, unsubstantiated scurrilities, innuendoes and "fake news" in relation to Ralph Gonsalves and the ULP in a determined, coordinated effort to tarnish the good name of the ULP and its leader. Invariably, these "internet crazies" are driven by personal animus, personal agendas and personal ambitions, with no fear of any legal penalty.

The political effect of internet disinformation and propaganda is still being hotly debated. Some research points to a negative impact of the "fake news"; other research insists otherwise. The net effect may well be inconclusive.

Still, as Professor Anya Schifrin, Director of Media and Communications at the Columbia University School of International and Public Affairs, points out in an article entitled "Disinformation and Democracy: The Internet Transformed Protest But Did Not Improve Democracy" (*Journal of International Affairs*, Fall/Winter 2017, Volume 71, No. 1).

> *The new conventional wisdom became that the Internet had dispersed the power of international organisations and governments and emerging communities online have undermined traditional state authority.... The recent scholarship makes it clear that the nature of activism and protest had changed and that the web was not just recreating earlier forms of protest.*

Professor Schifrin poses a vital question in this regard and answers as follows:

> *Is the Internet killing our democracy and paving the way for uninformed mob rule? Democracy rests upon the assumption of an educated populace; this is part of why public education is important. Understanding the important issues of the day, as well as government representatives' positions on these issues, is necessary for citizens to participate actively in a democracy. Without this knowledge, voting decisions may be arbitrary, and*

> *government can be based on capturing voters or pander-*
> *ing, and can cease to be a truly functioning democracy.'"*

The ULP incumbency in eight bastions was confirmed in the 2015 elections. Undoubtedly, Louis Straker's return form his voluntary five-year sabbatical to candidacy in Central Leeward was a boost for the ULP; in that constituency he lifted the ULP vote from 51.6 percent in 2010 to 53.3 percent in 2015. New candidates such as Camillo Gonsalves, Jomo Thomas, Carlos James, St. Clair "Jimmy" Prince, and Deborah Charles provided an additional impetus to the ULP campaign. Outstanding candidates like Saboto Caesar (who was the incumbent in South Central Windward), Frederick Stephenson (incumbent in South Windward), Cecil Mc Kie (the incumbent in West St. George), Ralph Gonsalves (incumbent in North Central Windward), and the wily veteran Montgomery Daniel, the incumbent in North Windward, completed the slate of candidates on mainland St. Vincent to complement Edwin Snagg and Herman Belmar, persons of real quality, in the Grenadines. The campaign manager, Julian Francis, the ULP's General Secretary, was excellent; his teamwork at the centre was special. The veteran Vincent Beache advised the campaign and participated actively. The younger men and women in the leadership of the ULP are steeped in progressive, social democratic and anti-imperialist values and ideas. The NDP, with all its foreign-sourced money and SCL advisers, was no match for the ULP in 2015.

The ULP in the 2015 general elections campaigned on its excellent record in government, its quality leadership, its quality candidates, its progressive bundle of social democratic, regionalist, pro-people, and anti-imperialist policies. Objective observes have commented favourably on the ULP's compelling developmental narrative and its firmness in the face of imperial machinations. As always, the ULP *Election Manifesto* and the *Youth Manifesto* for 2015 were superb. Also available for public reflections were publications of late 2014 authored by Ralph Gonsalves entitled: *Our Caribbean Civilisation and the Political Prospects; and The Case for Reparatory Justice for Native Genocide and African Slavery.*

In the December 2015 general elections the performances of the ULP candidates, compared to the results in the 2010 general elections in the thirteen constituencies in which there were improvements, were as follows: Montgomery Daniel (North Windward): 53.0 percent of the vote in 2015, 52.5 percent in 2010; Ralph Gonsalves (North Central Windward): 79.8 percent in 2015, 79.78 percent in 2010; Saboto Caesar (South Central Windward): 56.7 percent in 2015, 56.4 percent in 2010; St. Clair Prince (new candidate in Marriaqua): 58.3

percent in 2015, 56.2 percent in 2010 for Girlyn Miguel; Camillo Gonsalves (new candidate in East St. George): 54.9 percent in 2015, 52.6 percent in 2010 for Clayton Burgin; Cecil Mc Kie (West St. Georg): 55.5 percent in 2015, 54.7 percent in 2010; Robert Luke Browne (East Kingstown): 48.2 percent in 2015, 45.0 percent in 2010; Deborah Charles (new candidate in West Kingstown): 44.9 percent in 2015, 44.1 percent in 2010 for Michelle Fife); Jomo Thomas (new candidate in South Leeward): 48.7 percent in 2015, 48.0 percent in 2010 for David Browne; Louis Straker (returned as candidate in Central Leeward): 53.3 percent in 2015, 51.6 percent in 2010 for Maxwell Charles; Carlos James (new candidate in North Leeward): 49.9 percent in 2015, 47.7 percent in 2010 for Jerrol Thompson; Herman Belmar (Northern Grenadines): 23.8 percent in 2015, 19.5 percent in 2010; and Edwin Snagg (Southern Grenadines): 38.7 percent in 2015, 36.5 percent in 2010.

The two constituencies in 2015 in which the ULP's candidates recorded marginal decline were: Frederick Stephenson (South Windward): 58.6 percent in 2015, 59.4 percent in 2010; and Wordsworth Phillips (new candidate in Central Kingstown): 44.4 percent in 2015, 45.6 percent in 2010 for Elvis Charles.

In the 2015 general elections two of the ULP's five first-time candidates won their seats: St. Clair "Jimmy" Prince in Marriaqua and Camillo Gonsalves in East St. George; the latter victor actually scored the highest number of actual votes in the elections, 3,135. The three losing ULP candidates with the largest swing to them were Herman Belmar in the Northern Grenadines, Luke Browne in East Kingstown, and Carlos James in North Leeward. Again, Ralph Gonsalves, in North Central Windward returned the highest percentage score of votes in the country.

The solidity of the ULP's electoral triumph in 2015 can be gauged, in part, from the fact that its candidates secured proportionate increases at the expense of the opposition NDP in the ULP's two most marginal winning constituencies of North Windward and Central Leeward. In South Central Windward, which the NDP's advisers in SCL had assured it that it would win comfortably in 2010, it lost by 13.2 percentage points, (ULP's Saboto Caesar won 56.4 percent of the vote; the NDP's Addison Thomas garnered 43.2 percent). Since South Central Windward first came in the ULP's winning column in 2001, it has won that seat in each of the last four elections (2001, 2005, 2010, and 2015) with percentage scores of the votes respectively of 56.2 percent, 57.0 percent; 56.4 percent, and 56.6 percent. In other words, ULP has consolidated its support over four successive elections. In East St. George in 2015, the ULP's candidate, Camillo Gonsalves, increased his party's majority by 2.3 percentage points at the expense of a formidable and experienced candidate, Dr. Linton Lewis of the NDP. In the other four winning ULP seats in 2015, the victory margins over the NDP are as follows: North Central Windward, 79.8 percent to 19.7 percent (a margin of 60.1 percentage points); Marriaqua, 58.3 percent to 41.6 percent (a margin of 16.7 percentage points in South Windward, 58.6 percent to 40.8 percent (a margin of 17.8 percentage points); West St. George, 59.0 percent to 41.0 percent (a margin of 18 percentage points).

Let us look at the fragility, by comparison, of the three most marginal constituency successes of the NDP's seven victories in 2015: In North Leeward, the NDP candidate's margin was cut by a 0.9 percentage point between 2010 and 2015 resulting in an actual NDP majority of merely 12 votes, a reduction from a 182 vote-majority in 2010; in South Leeward, the NDP candidate's margin was cut by a 1.1 percentage point between 2010 and 2015, resulting in an actual NDP majority of 118 votes, a reduction from a 199 vote-majority in 2010; in East Kingstown, the NDP's Political Leader, Arnhim Eustace, had his margin reduced by 3.6 percentage points between 2010 and 2015, resulting in an actual NDP victory of 149 votes, a reduction from a 467 vote-majority in 2010.

To nail the point further about the solidity of the ULP's 2015 electoral triumph, the actual majorities of the two ULP most marginal winning constituencies are: North Windward, 323 votes in 2015 compared to a majority of 250 votes in 2010; and in Central Leeward, 313 votes majority in 2015 compared to 150 in 2010. In South Central Windward, the ULP's majority in votes over the NDP in 2015 was 588 votes compared to 568 votes in 2010; in East St. George, the ULP's majority in votes over the NDP in 2015 was 607 votes compared to 283 votes in 2010; in Marriaqua, the ULP's majority in votes over the NDP was 756 votes compared to 598 votes in 2010; in South Windward, the ULP's majority in votes over the NDP in 2015 was 759 votes compared to 786 votes (a decrease of 27 votes); in West St. George, the ULP's majority votes over the NDP in 2015 was 578 votes compared to 429 votes in 2010; and in North Central Windward, the ULP's majority in votes over the NDP in 2015 was 2,270 votes compared to 2,243 in 2010.

In the period 2001 to 2018, the four main trade unions (CTAWU, NWM, PSU, SVGTU), the working people, and the nation as a whole have found a "labour" Government which is strongly supportive of the labour movement and the working people. The working people know that the government has delivered for workers. Recently, though, a few individuals in the respective leaderships of two public sector unions, the SVGTU and the PSU are spoiling for a fight with the Government, driven not by their members' real agenda, but by their own personal grievances and anti-ULP political preferences. The overwhelming majority of their members see through their personal and partisan political stratagems. Meanwhile, the CTAWU and NWM are expanding their memberships, consolidating their day-to-day union work and securing additional gains for their members.

The membership of the unions over the 2000-2017 period has been as follows: CTAWU's membership has increased from 1,586 in 2000 to 3,800 in 2017, a rise of 140 percent; the National Workers' Movement (NWM) has had its membership grow from 637 in 2000 to 925 in 2017, an increase of 45 percent; the SVGTU's membership has decreased from 1,258 in 2000 to 1,100 in 2017, a decline of 13 percent; the PSU's membership has increased from 1,371 in 2000 to 1,420 in 2017, a rise of 4 percent.

The growth in trade union membership in the CTAWU and NWM has taken place in the state enterprises, the manufacturing sector, telecommunications, and the services sector, including banking and tourism. The decline in the membership of the Teachers' Union is attributable mainly to the fact that a number of primary school teachers have been shifted to the secondary schools and the Teachers' Union has not organised well among the secondary schools, The shift has occurred as a consequence of the introduction in 2005 of universal access to secondary education and thus the movement of the 11 plus to 15-year-old students from the primary school to the secondary schools. Some teachers had to be reallocated to the secondary schools accordingly. The numbers show that at the end of 2004, the Teachers' Union had 1,244 members but, year by year, since then, a slow continuous decline in membership has been noted.

In the case of the PSU, its current membership of 1,420 includes public servants in the central government and employees in several public enterprises outside of the civil service such as the National Broadcasting Corporation; National Sports' Council; St. Vincent and the Grenadines Postal Corporation; and the Building, Roads, and General Services Authority (BRAGSA);.but there are some 3,600 central government employees so, the PSU has a scope for enhanced membership. The PSU does not actually have the majority of the public service employees as its members.

Since 2001, the bulk of the trade unions' industrial actions have been instituted by the leaderships of the public sector unions, the PSU and SVGTU, and the other unions which represent unskilled public sector employees. The sequence of these actions has been, in summary, as follows: In 2002, the PSU picketed the SVG Port Authority in respect of a collective bargaining on behalf of a particular category of workers; in 2005 and 2007, the PSU picketed and instigated an ineffective work-to-rule regarding severed workers in an organisational restructuring by the government; in 2007, there was another misguided, ineffective and unsupported work-to-rule in the public service by the PSU; in 2007, another ineffective picket by the PSU and the SVGTU on the Reclassification Exercise which the government was actually carrying out for the material benefit of its employees; in November 2015, a few weeks before the general elections of early December 2015, the leadership of the PSU and SVGTU organised a wholly ineffective solidarity march for salary increases and for a go-slow and work-to-rule in the public service — the vast majority of the teachers and civil servants were dismayed at the attempted use of their unions in furtherance of a partisan political cause; a picket in 2015 by the PSU outside the office of the National Sports Council over a collective agreement which agreement was being concluded satisfactorily. In 2016 the management of the privately-operated St. Vincent Shipyard Limited halted operations temporarily after the workers properly demanded payments of outstanding salaries and wages, and in December 2016 workers at the Buccament Bay Resort protested for several days, for good cause, in respect of unpaid wages by an insolvent enterprise which operated in an unprofessional manner.

Meanwhile, the ULP continued to be responsive and sensitive, to the working people in its representation of their interests. A summary of the ULP's achievements, especially on behalf of the working people is now hereby reviewed.

SUMMARY REVIEW OF ACHIEVEMENTS OF LABOUR, 2001-2018

The ULP Government has advanced the cause of workers and their organisations in unprecedented ways and levels, truly reflective of a "Labour Government". The direct benefits relate to enhanced wages and salaries, in real terms, improvements in working conditions, retirement benefits, education and training, and workers' representations.

A summary itemised list includes the following:

(1)   The payment in 2001 of some $3 million in severance pay to over 1,000 former estate workers at former government estates at Orange Hill/Rabacca; Wallilabou, and Richmond Vale which had been owed to the workers for sixteen years;

(2) The payment of severance pay in 2001 and 2002 to hundreds of other workers who were due these payments for several years by the former NDP administration, including government sanitation workers who were transferred to the state-owned Central Water and Sewerage Authority; Banana Growers' Association workers; workers at the former state-owned Diamond Dairy; and workers at the state-owned Belle Vue Arrowroot Factory;

(3) Payment of severance payments promptly to workers who had been transferred or terminated due to a reorganisation of state enterprises or the central government departments' conversion into public enterprises; for example, former employees of St. Vincent Marketing Corporation, Public Works Department, and local Government workers; hitherto, there were no previous government paid severance payment in these circumstances;

(4) Payment on an on-going basis of a "compassionate gratuity" to non-pensionable workers in the Central Government who reached retirement age; the "compassionate gratuity" is calculated at the rate of two weeks pay for each year worked; these workers also, as per usual, receive their ongoing pensions under the National Insurance Services Act;

(5) Funding from January 2003 by the then wholly state-owned National Commercial Bank (now Bank of St. Vincent and the Grenadines) to its workers at the inauguration of their pension scheme up to fifteen years in arrears from 1978, at a cost of $2 million; thereafter, the pension scheme has been contributory between workers and the Bank; this pension arrangement was more favourable than the one proposed by CTAWU, the union representing the workers;

(6) Enacting a new Protection of Employment Act in 2004 which repealed and replaced a 1980 Act by the same name first passed by the SVLP; this 2004 Act has enhanced workers' benefits, including severance payment; in 2004, the NDP opposed the increase in these benefits on the ground that they are likely to make businesses uncompetitive and too expensive to operate;

(7) Payment of tax-free bonuses annually from December 2002, until the global economic crash of 2008, to all public sector employees;

(8) Raising statutory minimum wages for all categories of workers on four occasions in seventeen years; hitherto the NDP government increased minimum wages once in seventeen years;

(9) Increasing minimum pensions at the National Insurance Services (NIS) four times between 2002 and 2012, and another increase is in the offing; between 1987 and 2001, the former NDP administration increased the minimum pensions only once, in 1999; average pensions have increased from $44.27 weekly in 2000 to $149.79 in 2017, an increase of 238 percent;

(10) Widening the categories and increasing the extent of non-contributory pensions at the NIS for elderly working people (former workers and peasants); the number of non-contributory non-pensioners at the NIS amounted to almost 1,500 in 2017;

(11) Making contributory pension payments at the NIS to 7,109 pensioners, an increase of 4,229 pensions or 144 percent increase over the number of 2,940 contributory pensioners at the end of the year 2000; total pensions payments for the year 2000 amounted to $6.52 million, rising to $50.82 million in 2017, an increase of 679 percent, while contribution income in 2000 was $17.052 million, increasing to $61.669 million in 2017 — an increase of 261.6 percent.

(12) Average annual insurable wage of the NIS contributors in the year 2000 amounted to $12,058 but rose to $21,569 in 2017, an increase of 79 percent.

(13) Presiding over the creation of over 8,000 jobs between March 2001 and the onset of the global economic crisis of 2008, which impacted St. Vincent and the Grenadines negatively; in the immediate post-2008 years there were job losses and a temporary decline in job-creation. The 2012 Census showed that there was an increase in the employed population of some 6,000; the active number of registrants at the NIS mirrors this movement of gainfully employed persons. In 2000, the number of active NIS registrants was 30,373 (active employees and self-employeds), which rose to 38,952 in 2005, declined to 36,491 in 2015, but increased in 2018 to 40,728 active registrants, an increase of 10,355, a reflection of job increases.

(14) Providing increases in salaries/wages, and allowances in real terms to all categories of central government employees in excess of 40 percent on average for the years 2001 to 2017; the nominal increases amount to 75 percent, on an average. Real salary/wage increases outstripped increases in productivity measured by the level of increase in Gross Domestic Product;

(15) Implementing a Reclassification Exercise in the Central Government which resulted, among other things, in salary increases of over 60 percent on an average; over 60 percent of the employees were reclassified upwards; none was reclassified downwards;

(16) Maintaining the annual increment for Central Government employees of approximately two percent of salaries; all other governments in the OECS have removed this annual increment; this annual increment benefits in excess of 50 percent of the employees who are not yet at the top of their salary scales;

(17) Reduction of the extent of personal taxation on the working people by increasing from $12,000 in 2001 to $20,000 in 2018 annually (an increase

of over 66 percent) the threshold income upon which no taxes are to be paid; at the same time the top rate of income tax has been reduced from 40 percent to 30 percent;

(18) Making Nursing Assistants pensionable from October 27,2015;

(19) Instituting the Youth Empowerment Service (YES) programme for young persons between the ages of 16 years and 30 years, which provides one-year job placement and training opportunity for 500 out-of-school persons; monthly stipends are paid. This programme has been in operation continuously from October 2001 to today and has been assessed by the UNESCO as a "best practice" in Latin America and the Caribbean;

(20) Implementing in 2014, and continuing the Support for Employment and Training (SET) for 170 college and university graduates on an annual basis; a monthly stipend/wage is paid;

(21) Instituting a 100-percent mortgage programme (no down-payment) for housing construction for central government employees;

(22) Presiding over an increase in per capita Gross Domestic Product (GDP) from an average of under $10,000 in 2000 to over $20,000 in 2017.

(23) Removing, legislatively in 2001 certain unreasonable constraints on freedom of expression and association of Central Government employees by repealing the Public Officers (Conditions of Employment) Act which was on the statute books since 1970; both the SVGTU and the PSU had long complained about this fetter on freedom of expression and freedom of association.

(24) Facilitating deeper participation of the working people in national governance through representation on the boards of statutory enterprises, and other public enterprises, and generally through other institutional arrangements and consultations;

(25) Embarking on periodic special public works programmes at least thrice each year to facilitate targeted employment; each of this special works projects amounts to at least EC $2.5 million;

(26) Enacting the Occupational Safety and Health Bill to better protect workers at work places;

(27) Enhancing markedly the benefits for the working people and their children through a bundle of government programmes including those in education, health, social security, poverty reduction, housing, citizen security, disaster preparedness, physical infrastructure, social development (women, children, elders, youths), sports, culture, regional integration, and foreign policy.

Still, as the "Labour" government itself insists, there is much more work to be done.

The ULP's performance in respect of this latter bundle of its programmes which benefit the working people and the nation have been detailed elsewhere. Here a summary will suffice of important performance highlights.

First, there has been effected an extraordinary Education Revolution for living and production. The ULP government has transformed the delivery of education in terms of access, spread and quality in each of its sub-sectors: Early Childhood, primary, secondary, post-secondary, tertiary, technical and vocational, special needs, adult and continuing, teacher education, and nursing education.

In 2001, in early childhood education, there had been access for about twenty percent of children in the three-to-under five year age group; in 2018, access is in excess of ninety percent. This initiative has had the additional public policy benefit of freeing mothers for the job market. In primary education, the curriculum and teaching methods have been revamped. Trained teachers have jumped from about one-half in 2000, to in excess of ninety percent in 2018. University graduates, who numbered four in the primary schools in 2000, are now in excess of one-half of the primary school teachers in 2018. Student performance has jumped in respect of the then required-level measurement of the Common Entrance Examination for students in the eleven plus age group, from under forty percent to above eighty percent in the Caribbean Primary Exit Assessment, introduced in 2014 by the Caribbean Examination Council (CXC) for the same age cohort of students. In secondary education, under forty percent of the students of the eleven plus-to-twelve-year age cohort entered secondary school in 2000. Since September 2005, there has been universal access to secondary education — all students of the relevant age enter secondary school. More than seventy-five percent of the teachers are university graduates and almost all are teacher-trained. Student performance at the exit examination (CXC-"O" Level) after five years of secondary education has improved significantly. In post-secondary education at the four divisions of the Community College (Divisions of Arts and Sciences, Teacher Education, Nursing Education, and Technical and Vocational Education) enrolment has jumped from under 600 students in the year 2000 to in excess of 2000 full-time students in 2018 with offerings of Associate Degrees in a wide range of areas, and in selected areas of study for university degrees, which offerings did not exist in 2000; flexible post-secondary education, including distance learning, has been introduced for part-time students. Student performance has improved greatly, comparatively, over time in St. Vincent and the Grenadines and comparatively with other countries in CARICOM. University education has mushroomed magnificently from a restrictive number of students to hundreds annually at universities across the world, particularly in the Caribbean, to such an extent that the country is on target to achieve the goal, on average, of one university graduate per household by the year 2030. Employees in the central government are accorded generous study-leave with pay, to attend universities. Scholarships and financial assistance, including student loans for economically-disadvantaged students whose loans are guaranteed at the financial institutions by the government, are granted. Bbetween 2001 and 2017, the government guaranteed over $90 million in this loan programme for economically-disadvantaged students. Teaching and nursing education, adult and continuing education, technical education at the level of Technical Institutes, and special education have witnessed phenomenal advances in every material particular. The Government now trains more nurses than are needed in St. Vincent and the Grenadines; so, there is an "export of nurses". Student nurses receive a "free" or highly subsidised education at the professional and Bachelor's Degree level and are paid a monthly stipend to attend the School of Nursing.

The physical, educational, information technology, and other educational facilities have improved, and expanded, immeasurably. Several primary and secondary schools have been built; early childhood centres have been constructed; a School for Children with Special Needs has been built in Georgetown to complement those in Kingstown and Bequia. The SVG Community College has been physically expanded hugely in each of its Divisions. A modern Technical Centre has been built in Kingstown. A modern Public Library has been constructed. Fourteen Learning Resource Centres have been built across the country. A one lap-top-per-student was rolled out for children in primary, secondary and post-secondary education. A modern Archives and Documentation Centre has been constructed. The Government has collaborated with the University of the West Indies in the expansion of the physical facilities and academic offerings of the Open Campus in St. Vincent and the Grenadines, by guaranteeing a loan of US $6 million from the CDB; and four offshore medical schools have been set up, providing medical education for overseas students, but also facilitating the training of medical students from St. Vincent and the Grenadines at concessional fees.

Meanwhile, the Parliament has put on the statute books a modern Educational Act, the SVG Community College Act, the Further and Higher Education (Accreditation) Act, and the Sector Skills Development Agency Act. Incidentally, each of these commendable pieces of legislation came in for spurious criticisms from the opposition NDP. Each of these has advanced the cause of and for the working people.

Over the years 2001 to 2018, the ULP government has improved significantly the delivery of Health and Wellness Services. In this regard, the "Labour" Governments have done the following, among other things: repaired or renovated thirty-two clinics; built and equipped seven new, modern clinics; installed adequately-supplied pharmacies in all thirty-nine clinics; built a modern polyclinic at Stubbs and is in the process of equipping two new ones (at Mesopotamia and Buccament); restructured and renovated the Georgetown Hospital as a PAHO-designed Smart Hospital; built and equipped, with Cuba's assistance, a Modern Medical and Diagnostic Complex at Georgetown with a wide range of diagnostic, surgical, dialysis, and medical facilities — the most significant single health facility constructed since the 19ᵗʰ century in St. Vincent and the Grenadines; improved markedly the delivery of health care and hospital services at the main Milton Cato Memorial Hospital (MCMH), despite the awful legacy left there by the previous NDP administration; rebuilt major sections of the MCMH with the help of the European Union, including a top-of-the-line Paediatric Wing [in conjunction with the Mustique Charitable Trust and the World Paediatric Project (WPP)], which is recognised as the centre of critical paediatric care in the OECS; improved the delivery of pharmaceuticals through the state-operated pharmacies by filling ninety percent of the prescriptions, up from seventy percent; rebuilt and extended the Mental Health Centre; integrated multiple medical missions from overseas into the national health delivery system; tackled aggressively chronic non-communicable diseases such as hypertension and diabetes; lifted enormously the quality of elderly care; enhanced hugely the delivery of quality water; ensured that garbage is collected nation-wide and properly disposed of to an extent never imagined hitherto; lifted, to an extraordinary degree, the training of health personnel at all levels; staffed the hospital and clinics with a sufficiency of medical, nursing and health personnel, and in a wide range of specialities, as never before; reduced phenomenally under-nourishment to below five percent of the population from in excess of twenty percent in 2000. Moreover, all the health indices have shown improvements, in some cases, dramatic improvements.

Among the central policy planks of the ULP government has been the reduction of poverty. Undoubtedly, this "Labour" government has been the most successful in waging the war against poverty and under-nourishment. Indeed, the Food and Agricultural Organisation (FAO) of the United Nations has honoured St. Vincent and the Grenadines twice during the lifetime of the ULP administration for its extraordinary achievements in reducing both extreme poverty and indigence ("dirt poor" poverty) and under-nourishment to under five percent of the population.

In 1996-1997, the former NDP administration caused a poverty assessment of St. Vincent and the Grenadines to be conducted by Kairi Consultants of Trinidad and Tobago. The assessment revealed that poverty was experienced by 37.5 percent of the population; indigence was assessed at 25.7 percent of the population. In 2009, in the midst of the global economic recession and its deleterious impact on St. Vincent and the Grenadines, the ULP government engaged Kairi Consultants again to conduct another poverty assessment in light of the targeted-specific poverty reduction programmes and developmental economic strategy which the ULP administration had been pursuing since April 2001. The results of the poverty assessment in 2009 showed that the ULP government's war on poverty was working: Poverty had been reduced to 30.7 percent, a fall of almost one-fifth (18.13 percent decline); and indigence has dramatically decreased to 2.9 percent, a decline of 88.7 percent from the 1997 figure. Corresponding studies of under-nourishment by the FAO show that in 1995, under-nourishment was at 22 percent of the population; by 2012, under-nourishment had fallen to 3.9 percent.

The ULP government found this relatively small level of indigence to be intractable. In light of the government's adoption of the Sustainable Development Goals (SDGs) at the United Nations in September 2015, the ULP pledged in its Manifesto for the 2015 general elections to eliminate extreme poverty and to attain Zero Hunger by 2030. Accordingly, in the early months of 2016, the ULP government secured parliamentary approval of the Zero Hunger Trust Fund Bill and swiftly established a Zero Hunger Trust Fund to drive, in conjunction with the government's economic policy and targeted-specific anti-poverty interventions, the quest to bring about Zero Hunger and Zero Extreme Poverty. A whole raft of measures has been introduced to more perfect the school feeding programme, provide relevant training to unemployed youths in the more impoverished parts of the country, secure work attachments for youths; and strengthen the social safety net.

Through the Ministries of Health, Social Development, Education, and Housing there has been a bundle of programmes designed to assist the working people, poor and the indigent. For example: In the Ministry of Health, nutritional support for pregnant women, free or highly subsidised pharmaceutical products for the poor, and subsidised water delivery for the elderly poor. In the Ministry of Social Development, the following anti-poverty programmes of relevance are The Home-Help for the Elderly; Public Assistance to over 4,500 persons (mainly the elderly poor and children of the poor) amounting to $250.00 monthly for the poor over 60 years of age (up from $50 monthly in 2000 under the NDP government), and for those under 60 years of age,

$225 monthly; a Foster Care Programme; targeted programmes for abused women, and children; providing material and social interventions in the areas of housing, transportation for students, and bereaved persons. In the Ministry of Education, the school feeding programme for primary schools, despite its limitations, has been hailed as a "best practice" in the OECS; and there are multiple support services for students.

In Housing, in seventeen years the ULP has distributed over 5,000 building lots for poor and working people; built over 1,400 low-income houses; built or repaired nearly 1,000 houses for the poor and indigent; provided building materials for thousands of persons; and embarked on a special Lives-to-Live Housing Programme for the elderly and disabled persons. According to the Population and Housing Census of 2012, households (families with houses) increased by over 20 percent between 2001 and 2012. Interestingly, too, the average number of persons living in a household declined over the same period from 3.5 to 3 persons. These are major achievements in circumstances in which there has not been a decline in the population overall. The working people have undoubtedly benefited substantially from the ULP government's housing programme.

In terms of physical infrastructure, disaster preparedness, access to tele-communications, and access to electricity, there has been extraordinary progress under the ULP government; these have all touched the working people. The road network has been extended; more bridges have been built than in any other period in our nation's history, including the hitherto seemingly impossible bridge over the Rabacca Dry River, an expanse of three or so football fields; the construction of the Jet Airport at Canouan and the International Airport at Argyle. An international airport for over fifty years has been touted as an impossible dream, but the ULP government achieved it. The ULP government has developed, too, for the first time ever, a Comprehensive Disaster Management Strategy (CDMS); established the National Emergency Management Organisation (NEMO); enacted the first modern emergency management legislation to replace the out-moded colonial law of 1947; built significant coastal and river defences; legislated appropriate planning laws to strengthen resilience; and established disaster and resilience components to the Contingency Fund. In this age of climate change, St. Vincent and the Grenadines has had, between 2010 and 2015, damage and loss arising from natural disasters amounting to $700 million or some 35 percent of Gross Domestic Product. Natural disasters adversely affect the poor and working people disproportionately; sound disaster management programmes are programmes for the working people, and the nation, particularly since climate change has brought about natural disasters which are unfamiliar, unprecedented in their frequency and intensity, and thus urgent for action. Climate change is an issue of existential significance for St. Vincent and the Grenadines!

Under the ULP government, electricity access has been increased markedly, from connections to seventy percent of households to ninety-eight percent. Reliability and a sufficiency of supply are now taken for granted by the consumers. Renewable energy has been emphasised as is evidenced in the refurbishing of the three hydro-power plants, the push for solar energy, and the current unfolding of a US $100 million geothermal project scheduled to deliver 10 megawatts of electric power by 2021. By that time renewable energy is slated to provide 80 percent of the country's electricity needs. The revolution in information communications technology has prompted the phenomenal expansion of voice and data telecommunications services, including of the internet, although the service providers need to provide an even better service. Under the Telecommunications Act, a Universal Service Fund has been established; it is funded by a portion of the providers' revenues to build out telecommunications services in geographic areas where it would be otherwise uneconomical to do so. This USF helps the poor and the working people.

The "Labour" Government between 2001 and 2018 has done remarkable work in uplifting sports and culture, including the construction of vastly improved facilities, enhancing the training in the areas of sports and culture, and restructuring for the better the organisational systems to deliver the government's policies in sports and culture in concert with the relevant stakeholders.

St. Vincent and the Grenadines has developed, under the ULP administration, an enviable record for strengthening citizen security apparatuses, good governance, openness, transparency, and accountability. It has received high scores from international agencies, both governmental and non-governmental, for tackling official corruption, demonstrating good governance, providing transparent public administration, and delivering economic and political freedom. This was a far cry from the situation prior to 2001, under the NDP administration, when St. Vincent and the Grenadines was blacklisted for money-laundering, inadequately-regulated international financial services, and disregarding international regulators on fishing, and poor governance.

In summary, over the period in excess of seventeen years, thus far under the ULP government, St. Vincent and the Grenadines has created over 6,000 jobs, doubled its Gross Domestic Product (GDP), doubled its per capita GDP, reduced poverty and indigence significantly, enjoyed greater material equality (Gini Coefficient moved from 0.56 in 2000 to 0.41 in 2012), and made phenomenal strides in education, health, housing, physical infrastructure and disaster preparedness, electricity and telecommunications, sports and culture, good governance and the rule of law.

Yet during that very same time of the accomplishments, St. Vincent and the Grenadines has been severely buffeted and damaged by natural disasters; the diminution of the banana market preferences in Britain to the point of extinction; the global economic depression of huge magnitude, and continuing in its aftershocks; the loss of 17 percent of GDP through the insurance meltdown of CLICO and BAICO; and the slowdown in the regional economies. Despite all this, the "Labour" Government has made immense advances for the working people and the nation.

SUMMATION OF THE CONDITION OF PROGRESSIVE POLITICS AND THE LABOUR MOVEMENT IN THE POST-1979 PERIOD

In the almost forty years since independence in 1979, remarkable changes have occurred in the politics and labour movement in St. Vincent and the Grenadines. The anti-SVLP radicalism of the DFM/PDM, YULIMO, ARWEE, the UPM, and the MNU, initially benefited politically the James Mitchell-led NDP and contributed to undermining the SVLP in and out of government.

The brunt of the opposition of the new political formations was directed at the SVLP. When the hope and promise of a unified "left" movement splintered in February 1980 and shattered in October 1983, much of the leadership of the UPM of 1979 and most of its supporters rallied to the political cause of Mitchell's NDP in the 1984 general elections and shortly thereafter. The fractured remains of the UPM after October 1983 were unable to regroup and reset its philosophical frame and organisational functioning in order to be viable. Further, the collapse of the Grenada Revolution and its bloody internecine battles that precipitated the Revolution's demise, placed the remnants of the UPM in a political tailspin from which it was difficult to recover. Fortuitously, the Gonsalves-led MNU was able to escape the hubris of the destruction of the Grenada Revolution, and to chart a course which resonated better with the working people and nation; moreover, the MNU pursued its political work most determinedly after the NDP's ascent to political office in July 1984. The truth is that the MNU never saw the NDP, for all its modernising guises and its superficial national cultural posturings, as anything other than a vehicle for James Mitchell's ideological commitment to an imitative conservatism, bourgeois liberalism with colonial shackles, an undeveloped capitalism on the periphery linked to monopoly capitalism globally, neo-liberalism, neo-colonialism, admixed with a mish-mash of not-too-significant reforms of its DFM/PDM wing, which had reposed itself into the arms of the NDP; so too, in the latter respect, the displaced remnants of the PPP. Further, Mitchell's "one-manism" in style and content that drove the NDP's governance was anti-developmental.

It took the SVLP at least eleven years, from the Central Leeward by-election of 1983 to the impending 1994 general elections to recognise that simply living in the past of the SVLP glory years under Milton Cato, especially between 1966 and the early 1980s, would undo its possible return to political dominance. Its failure and/or refusal to refresh itself philosophically, organisationally, and in personnel, presaged its huge popular decline between the general elections of 1979 and 1989.

The eleven years between October 1983, when the MNU was formed, and January 1994, when the February general elections of that year were announced, the collective leadership, membership and supporters of the MNU were able to define a path of advanced social democracy/socialist orientation and link sufficiently with the people to show that a better and different way was possible in the country's governance than that which was on offer by the NDP government in the ten years, 1984–1994. The MNU had correctly analysed too, that at the core of the SVLP's praxis of building the economy, in conjunction with a viable private sector, was its thrust to establish a strong state economic sector as necessary, desirable and in the interest of the people. Thus, the MNU saw possibilities in this approach away from the NDP's slavish adherence to a "free enterprise" model that was unworkable in its pure form anywhere, and particularly so in St. Vincent and the Grenadines. The SVLP government had demonstrated that a strong state economic sector had a positive role to play in concert with the private sector and the cooperative sector, for example, the credit unions. Thus the SVLP Government caused the state to act in ownership or control of aspects of the economy such as the establishment of the state-owned National Commercial Bank; the ownership and operation of the monopoly entity in electricity services, the St. Vincent Electricity Services Limited; the setting up of the St. Vincent Marketing Corporation as a central marketing agency for the export of agricultural products and as an operator of a supermarket to compete in that area of business in which there was little or no competition to a single private sector company; the introduction of the sugar industry with state-ownership of the factory and the provision of lands for sugar farmers; the founding of the largely state-owned Diamond Dairy to produce mainly milk, but also fruit juices; and the ownership and operation of stone crushers to produce raw material for the construction industry in the State and private sectors. Interestingly, the NDP Government closed the operations of the sugar industry, Diamond Dairy and the stone-crushers, and slimmed down the Marketing Corporation. The NDP government announced too, its intention to privatise the electricity company and the commercial bank.

At the same time, the MNU recognised that the state economic sector was in need of reorganisation, streamlining, democratising, and greater accountability so as to avoid any tendency towards a kind of deformed state capitalism. But the SVLP government's approach possessed much merit in the context of an undeveloped national capitalist class, an insufficiency of production and a lack of a sufficiency of foreign direct investment.

The MNU also correctly analysed that the SVLP had a far better bundle of policies and programmes touching on education, health, housing and social security than the NDP. They possessed real possibilities for further advance. The SVLP's historic weaknesses were cultural conservatism; a lop-sided, reactive pro-Western foreign policy; and a heavy-handed, insufficiently democratic pattern of governance. The only area in which the NDP trumped the SVLP was in its cultural liberalism and a more relaxed style of leadership; but style, like fine silk sometimes hides eczema. On foreign policy, the NDP was far more instinctively pro-imperialist than the SVLP. For example, the Cato government was reluctant to approve of the invasion of Grenada by the USA, while James Mitchell of the NDP welcomed the invasion with enthusiasm. Cato wanted a regional solution. Mitchell opted for one directed by imperialism.

Further, by 1994 it was evident that a dominant section of the SVLP led by Vincent Beache was social democratic to the core, and was keen on charting a more nationalist foreign policy. All these factors, plus the electoral arithmetic, dictated first a "Labour-MNU Unity" electoral compact in the February 1994 elections and then a full-fledged merger of the SVLP and MNU as the Unity Labour Party (ULP) in October 1994.

The core leadership of the ULP (Vincent Beache, Ralph Gonsalves, Louis Straker, and Julian Francis) did yeoman service in the cause of uniting the labour movement politically in conjunction with a whole raft of the progressive generations, including those who had been in the UPM, but without the DFM/PDM faction which was within the NDP's bosom. Vincent Beache was able to lead very astutely the Labour-MNU Unity from three seats with 43.9 percent of the vote in 1994 to 54.6 percent of the vote and seven seats of a merged ULP in the 1998 elections. The bulk of the memberships and the top leaderships of the four principal unions — CTAWU, NWM, PSU, and SVGTU — supported the ULP in its quest for governmental authority. In this process, Vincent Beache led the ULP and the wider labour movement in slashing the NDP popular vote from 55 percent in 1994 to 45 percent in 1998, reflected in the NDP's fall from twelve seats to eight seats. During the internal challenges of the ULP in 1998 to 2000, Vincent Beache's role was pivotal in ensuring that the Stanley John-Ken Boyea axis did not triumph; he too was vital in the battles against the NDP government in 2000 and the general elections victory in 2001.

The NDP government left the country in 2001 in an awful mess. The ULP government had to clean up that terrible state of affairs and put the country on a solid developmental path. In summary, the mess which the NDP government left for the ULP administration included unemployment at 21 percent of the population; poverty at 37 percent; indigence at 26 percent; lowest economic growth in the OECS; poor educational and health systems; an illiteracy rate in excess of 20 percent of the population; highly-inadequate housing provisions for the poor and the working people; run-down physical infrastructure, including a cut-off of the north east of the country by the Rabacca Dry River with no bridge; a run-down condition of schools, clinics, police stations, and other public buildings; no international airport and no jet airport anywhere in St. Vincent and the Grenadines; highly inadequate sports and cultural facilities; only 70 percent or so of the households were connected to water and electricity; poor governance; several "black lists" against St. Vincent and the Grenadines by international agencies and countries; little or no respect for workers, trade unions and civil society; no effective machinery for disaster management; low regional and international prestige; bad management of the country's finances and the quest to solve this problem by selling St. Vincent and the Grenadines citizenship and passports; the virtual collapse of LIAT and regional air transport; limited garbage collection and disposal; large-scale illegal squatting; and abject neglect of agriculture and fisheries. All of these, and more, the ULP government has had to address between 2001 and currently. And it has been doing so successfully! At the same time, the ULP government has had to chart and implement a bundle of policies derived from a compelling developmental narrative. This it has been doing successfully too and the voters have so confirmed this in their repeated mandates to the ULP.

The criticism has been levelled by some that since the ULP formed the government in 2001, the trade unions, particularly the public sector unions have been relatively dormant and are not pressuring the employers, whether the State or the private sector, for enhanced benefits. None of this is true. However, the far more favourable political environment for trade unionism and the working people under the ULP has prompted the unions, especially their rank-and-file members, to act more maturely by and large, in relation to the government.

A few relevant factual considerations put this matter into context. First, there are more trade union members currently than in 2000. The two "blanket" unions have seen their membership increase significantly: In the CTAWU, union membership has jumped from 1,586 in the year 2000 to 3,800 in 2018, an increase of 140 percent. In the NWM, the increase in membership over the same period has been from 637 to 925 members or a rise of 45 percent; in the PSU membership has risen from 1,282 in 2001 to 1,420 currently or an increase of 11 percent; and the Teachers' Union's membership has fallen slightly from 1,239 in 2001 to 1,100 in 2017. In the public sector, there is no restraint, legal or otherwise, to organise fully the teachers and public servants in their respective unions. If the public sector unions make a greater organisational effort to recruit more members around a core of issues that touch and concern the respective workers, they would increase their memberships; provided they act reasonably, since the teachers and public servants are easily turned off by irrational posturing and political grandstanding by their union leaders. The workers are not supportive of any trade union leader who seeks though partisan politics or a jaundiced personal agenda to undermine the political efficacy of their "Labour Government" which they know to be acting in their interest.

In the private sector, the trade unions face the difficulties of organising very small numbers of workers in a multiplicity of small enterprises. The age of large-scale plantation agriculture is over. The small family farms are not easily susceptible to trade unionism. In the services' sector, the individual employment units are also small. Still there are workers in sufficiently large private sector entities which are available for enterprising trade unions such as CTAWU and NWM to be organising. The extent of trade union membership in 2018 in the aggregate in St. Vincent and the Grenadines was in excess of 7,300. This number is way below the 34,923 employees who are active registrants at the NIS, which number itself is estimated by the NIS to be no more than eighty percent of those who ought to be registered. Clearly, there is much work still to be done by the trade unions to organise a higher percentage of workers.

The ULP government has had, since its election to government in March 2001, the unequivocal policy of ensuring the recognition of any trade union as the workers' bargaining agent at any employment unit where the union has a simple majority of the workers at that entity on its membership register.

It is to be noted that over the past eighteen years, the issue of union recognition has not been contentious. Even if employers are reluctant to engage trade unions, the Labour Department and the Government as a whole, insist that such formal engagement be fully encouraged and supported. Thus, for example, the pre-2001 resistance among the employer class and officialdom to trade unionism and their official recognition, is not entertained by the ULP administration. It is after all, a "Labour" Government.

It is to be acknowledged that many workers stand askance against trade unions because they do not truly understand the value of trade unions to them, collectively and individually. It is to be recognised, too, that some workers are disillusioned by the performance and the industrial or anti-developmental political antics of some union leaders that prompt them to keep such unions and their leaders at bay. The substantial answer to all this is for the workers not to reject or be indifferent to trade unions, but to join them and insist on internal trade union democracy so that better worker representation would be ensured.

To be sure, there is a strong ideological current of global capitalism and neo-liberalism that discourages trade unions and other collective working people's organisations. Indeed, many of the Caribbean's professional and intellectual classes propagate this view as a shared mantra of "the Washington Consensus". In a speech entitled "Ensuring our Tomorrows" to the 56th Annual Conference of the National Union of Public Workers in Barbados on March 16, 2000, Ralph Gonsalves, then Leader of the Opposition in St. Vincent and the Grenadines addressed this very issue, thus:

> It is utterly amazing that today, many of the inheritors of the social democratic revolution — the children, grandchildren, and great grandchildren of the workers and peasants of the 1930s — are in the forefront of maligning the work and heroic efforts, historically and in the contemporary period, of the trade union and the political party. These ungrateful inheritors of the struggles and sacrifices of their forbears with the symbols of university education behind their names and their bank-owned Volvos, Pajeros, and BMWs on the streets, absurdly question the very necessity for trade unions and political parties. Their consciousness warped or made false by the neo-colonial and neo-liberal abstractions of the World Bank and the International Monetary Fund, they prattle loftily and stupidly about their quest for a

'no party democracy' and for 'a labour market flexibility without the external rigidities imposed by trade unions'.

In effect, such members of the 'new professional class', who I reiterate are among the principal beneficiaries of their grandparents' solidarity with one another in collective organisations, now eschew or condemn solidarity. Instead they extol 'individualism' as the path to self-emancipation without realising that in our history the embrace of that very notion has meant continued servitude for the oppressed, the dispossessed, and the down-trodden. This infantile 'individualism' will make us no more than individual atoms to be manipulated by the metaphoric physicist in his laboratory. In the society-at large, an organised economically-dominant class — and they are almost always united and coherent despite internal differences and contradictions among them — will manipulate us in their sophisticated social laboratory.

This summation on solidarity among and between the people of St. Vincent and the Grenadines and nations globally is at the core of the actualisation of the compelling developmental narrative advanced by the "Labour" Government continuously since March 29, 2001. The foundation principles which drive the ULP government are the following:

(1)   The affirmation that the nation of St. Vincent and the Grenadines is founded on the belief in the supremacy of God and the freedom and dignity of man and woman.

(2)   The people's desire that their society be so ordered as to express their recognition of the principles of democracy, free institutions, social justice, and equality before the law.

(3)   The people's realisation that the maintenance of human dignity presupposes safeguarding the right of privacy, of family life, of property, and the fostering of the pursuit of just economic rewards for labour.

(4)   These articulated freedoms, principles, and ideas are the central bases for the elaboration of a people-centred vision in which education, training, applied science and technology are vital for achievement.

(5)   The philosophical premises of governance and public policies are grounded in an advanced social democracy that is at once universal in its

understanding and particularistic in its application to the condition of St. Vincent and the Grenadines and our Caribbean civilisation.

(6)   The elaboration of a socio-cultural framework reflective of our Caribbean civilisation, including its Vincentian component, which is unique and possessed of a legitimacy, authenticity, nobility, and its own history of adoption, adaptation, home-grown creations. All this emerges from a population mix in a specific landscape and seascape, as a metaphoric symphony of coherence, though with occasional dissonance, with the result that: We are the songs of the indigenous people (the Callinago and the Garifuna); the melody of Europe; the rhythm of Africa; the chords of Asia; and the home-grown lyrics of the Caribbean itself. This Caribbean civilisation, including its Vincentian component, is endowed with its own trajectory for further ennoblement and development.

(7)   The fashioning of a modern, competitive, many-sided post-colonial economy, that is at once national, regional, and global, to underpin the material base for our Caribbean civilisation; the economic praxis accordingly embraces a tripartite economy of the private, cooperative, and State sectors, functioning as a harmonious whole in the people's interest focussed on job and wealth creation, poverty reduction, material upliftment, and equity. The result is complete restructuring of an historically mono-crop economy enmeshed in colonial trading and financial relations.

(8)   The delivery of a bundle of policies and practical programmes touching and concerning every facet of human endeavour in life, living, and production in an age of deleterious climate change, technological advances, and rampaging globalisation, acknowledging a "small State exceptionalism." always.

(9)   The strengthening of regional integration to the fullest extent possible.

(10) The pursuit of a foreign policy that affirms we in St. Vincent and the Grenadines are friends of all and subjected to none; and that a better world is possible. This foreign policy is to facilitate our nation in the enhancement of its capacity to address more efficaciously the challenges in our regional and global environment in the interest of our people's humanisation.

These foundation stones are the anchor for the "Labour" Governments' public policies and programmes which have been detailed in the Election Manifestos of the ULP in 2001, 2005, 2010, 2015; the writings and speeches of the ULP leaders; and in the ULP governments' myriad public policy documents, including its *National Economic and Social Development Plan, 2013-2025*. The summary of its achievements sketched earlier are reflective of the policies of the most progressive government in the Caribbean Community. They have been, and are, the accomplishments of the working people, the labour movement (including the ULP), and the nation as a whole.

Still, there is much work left to be done to implement the ULP Government's policies and programmes that connect intimately with the seventeen Sustainable Development Goals (SDGs) adapted at the United Nations in September 2015. The challenges, extant and prospective, are immense. In addressing this matter on the eve of the 2015 general elections Prime Minister Ralph E. Gonsalves stated, among other things:

> *There is a veritable development chasm or divide in St. Vincent and the Grenadines, made manifest as a consequence of our nation's limitation of material resources, our historical legacy of under-development, the contemporary challenges of modern globalisation and trade liberalisation, and our country's extraordinary vulnerability to natural disasters. This chasm or divide cannot be crossed by 'baby steps' or by persons possessed of a debilitating caution or 'learned helplessness'. 'Baby steps', and an accompanying pessimism, will condemn us to fall below the widening gorge. This chasm or divide can only be crossed by bold leaps of faith and reason, by applying one's heart to wisdom, by trusting in our people's goodness and capacity, by creative ideas fashioned into implementable practical programmes buttressed by an enduring love for the people of St. Vincent and the Grenadines. Leading this venture is not for the weak, the tired or faint-hearted. It is leadership tried and tested, proven in battle, and blessed by Almighty God for the tasks at hand and those ahead which will ensure the shaping of our future together, for the better.*

CHAPTER VIII

TWO FINAL NOTES
ON LEADERSHIP AND WOMEN

LEADERSHIP IN THE LABOUR MOVEMENT
AND THE NATION: 1935-2018

For the last seventy-five or so years, thus far five political leaders have emerged, each in different circumstances, to lead the national movement, not necessarily the labour movement, for change, ostensibly for the better: George Augustus Mc Intosh (1935-1951), Ebenezer Theodore Joshua (1951-1967); Robert Milton Cato (1967-1984); James Fitz-Allan Mitchell (1984-2000), and Ralph Everard Gonsalves (2001-2019), thus far. One may quibble about the starting and terminal points of each of these leaders' chronological span, but broadly they appear correct. Mc Intosh never held any executive political authority in the central government but his political activism in and out of the colonial legislature, marked him as the political leader of the national labour movement over the 1935-1951 period. Joshua's leadership role in the national labour movement, inclusive of his tenure in government as the premier elected representative in the 1957-1967 period, can hardly be questioned. Cato led his Labour Party in Government for 15 of the 17 years between 1967 and 1984. He was the Leader of the Opposition in the 1972-1974 period. The chronological periods roughly assigned to Mitchell and Gonsalves correspond to their respective Prime Ministerships, even though their activism pre-dated those years. Their dominance in the national mass movement in their Prime Ministerial years is an historical fact.

In a brilliant book, published in 1869 and entitled *The Eighteenth Brumaire of Louis Napoleon*, its author, Karl Marx stated:

> *Men make their own history, but they do not make it*
> *as they please; they do not make it under self-selected*
> *circumstances, but under circumstances existing already,*

> *given and transmitted from the past. The tradition of*
> *all dead generations weighs like a nightmare on the*
> *brains of the living.*

Leaders, great men, and women too, make history, but only to the extent that the circumstances of history permit them so to make. To be sure, there are some leaders, more than others, who push the boundaries of the possibilities, which the circumstances do provide, to the furthest or most extraordinary extent. C.L.R. James in his *Black Jacobins* made the same point, as indicated earlier, in utilising Marx's insights,in his study of the role played by Toussaint L'Ouverture in the making of the Haitian Revolution towards the end of the eighteenth century.

In assessing each of the five main leaders in St. Vincent and the Grenadines, we must place each of them in his specific historical context, objectively, including his socialisation, life's experiences, outlook, ideas, beliefs, disposition, political style, and actions. It is a many-sided assessment which is complex. A process of evaluation and re-valuation takes place. The very perspective of the assessor influences the analysis. Even dispassionate historians are loaded with biases, some more than others. Contemporary accounts are useful, but they too, like journalism, are but a rough first draft, often a partisan draft, of history. Autobiographies do help but such works are almost always self-serving, although insights do emerge, oft-times not as the author intended. Of the five long-serving leaders of St. Vincent and the Grenadines, two have written autobiographies: James Mitchell's *Beyond the Islands* written after he demitted office as Prime Minister and published in 2006; and Ralph Gonsalves' *The Making of the Comrade: The Political Journey of Ralph Gonsalves*,written while still in office and published in 2010 two or so months prior to the 2010 general elections. So, there is still much of his story left to be told by him. Mitchell, and especially Gonsalves, are the two leaders who have written extensively, far more than any of the others. Thus, much of their reflective work is available for critical scrutiny.

Assessments of leaders are, invariably, best done after the passage of a sufficiency of time to provide the requisite distance between the leaders' activism and the very assessment itself. Still, there are unvarnished facts to record, and measured commentary to make in the interim that may or may not be persuasive or conclusive.

Of the five leaders, four of them, in varying degrees, consciously set out to represent the working class. Only James Mitchell did not see himself as socialist, socialist-oriented or social democratic, which historically and universally, have been the philosophical wellsprings for proper representation of the working people. In his autobiography, Mitchell proclaimed himself a "centrist liberal". Mc Intosh and Gonsalves, throughout their political careers, have emphasised their "socialism" or advanced social democratic perspectives. Joshua, prior to his ascent to governmental office in 1957, saw himself as a "leader of labour" who hoped to be a "leader of socialism". Towards the end of his political career he had abandoned the working class militancy of his earlier years and metamorphosed into political opportunism and even backwardness, not only in his unequivocal embrace of monopoly capitalism but also in his stance against independence in the 1978-1979 period.

Mc Intosh and Joshua were active leaders of trade unions and the labour movement. Cato caused a short-lived trade union to be founded as an ally to his St. Vincent Labour Party, but he was himself personally unattached to trade unionism. After the founding of the CTAWU in 1963, Cato's SVLP sought to establish and maintain close relations with that union. His focus on the "labouring" people prompted the choice of the central word "Labour" in his party's name, even though his party's origins were "middle class" with a political philosophy of moderate social democracy. Mitchell's outlook was grounded in a quest to establish "a property-owning democracy" tied to monopoly capitalism, with no appetite for an independent St. Vincent and the Grenadines. He advocated instead for a possible independence in a regional grouping tied to Britain, Canada and the USA. Mitchell neither evinced any interest in trade unionism nor saw himself as a spokesman for the labour movement. Of all the leaders, Gonsalves has been the most ideological in terms of a philosophical frame grounded in socialism, socialist-orientation, and advanced social democracy applied to the circumstances of St. Vincent and the Grenadines and the Caribbean. A corollary to an inevitable feature of this bundle of political ideas was, and still is, his profound anti-imperialism. His membership of YULIMO, UPM, MNU, and the ULP attest to all this.

A reading of Gonsalves' autobiography would reveal, too, that he was an office-holder in the executive of the West Indies Group of University Teachers (WIGUT) at the University of the West Indies, Mona, Jamaica, where he was employed as a Lecturer (1974-1976). He was too, adviser and educator to the University and Allied Workers' Union and the Trade Union Congress in Jamaica; an educator to the Barbados Workers' Union Labour College in Barbados (1974-1976); and adviser to and sometimes activist for the SVWU and NUPW in St. Vincent and the Grenadines in the 1970s. Gonsalves has also written, in solidarity, on trade unions and the labour movements in St. Vincent and the Grenadines, the Caribbean and Africa (Uganda, mainly). His theses for his Masters' and Doctoral degrees are on the subjects of the labour movement in St. Vincent and the Grenadines and Uganda, respectively. Over the entire fifty years of his political activism, thus far, 1968-2019, he has been always a combatant in solidarity with and acting in the interest of the working people. He has been and is, a "Labour" man!

Mc Intosh's sixteen years (1935-1951) dominance as the undisputed leader of the labour movement nationally in St. Vincent, marked him out as an out-standing, even heroic, labour leader. His extraordinary efforts and achievements on behalf of the working people have been sketched earlier in this book. They are too, outlined in other publications, including the excellent volume *The 1935 Riots in St. Vincent: From Riots to Adult Suffrage*, authored by the eminent Vincentian historian, Dr. Adrian Fraser; and Ralph Gonsalves' book entitled *The Making of a National Hero: A Consideration of Mc Intosh, Joshua, Cato, and J.P. Eustace* (including *The Trial of George Mc Intosh and the 1935 Uprising*).

Mc Intosh rightly viewed himself as a "socialist" or "social democrat". Gordon Lewis labelled him, not inaccurately, but not fully, as a "Fabian social-ist". He was non-communist, but not anti-communist. He was "no Leninist insurrectionary" — to use Lewis' term — yet he was admiring of the contri-butions of V.I. Lenin, Joseph Stalin, and the Soviet Union to the world struggle against monopoly capitalism, imperialism, fascism, and colonialism. Of the five dominant political leaders since 1935, Mc Intosh is the only one who never held any executive authority in government due to the colonial constitutional limitations of his time, 1935-1951.

About Joshua, both Mitchell and Gonsalves have written, the former not sympathetically, the latter much more so, despite his telling critiques of Josh-ua's latter years. Mitchell, who worked with Joshua in the 1972-1974 coalition government, wrote, in his autobiography, of Joshua thus:

> *Joshua was to remain eternally in mental opposition,*
> *willing to side with any cause challenging authority.*

That was Mitchell's take on Joshua's instinctive support for the prison wardens on an issue in dispute at the prisons.

On the subject of Mitchell's negotiated purchase of Lauder's estate from the Hadley family, he reported in his autobiography that he had called on Joshua as Minister of Finance to pay up. Mitchell wrote on this matter as follows:

> *With some show of arrogance, Joshua declared that*
> *that was a problem for his colleague in Government, the*

> *Financial Secretary, whom he insisted to be his sworn*
> *enemy. (Joshua still used the term 'they'. I could not get*
> *him to accept the principle of 'we'.) It really was an*
> *unbridgeable divide between trade union rabble-rouser*
> *and Minister of Finance. On that, I am afraid, old*
> *Joshua never really crossed.*

The disdain of "rabble-rouser" and "old" Joshua in Mitchell's recounting is palpable. Joshua's record was not of a "rabble-rouser" whether in or out of Government; and in 1974, the year to which Mitchell referred concerning the transaction on Lauder's estate, Joshua was only 66 years old, certainly younger than when Mitchell retired as Prime Minister at the age of 70 years in October 2000! On the occasion of Joshua's death on March 14, 1991, Mitchell had spoken similarly in his "tribute" on radio that "Joshua was good at breaking down, not building-up."

After thirty years had elapsed since the 1974 collapse of the Mitchell-Joshua coalition government, Mitchell was to write damningly, with no conclusive evidence, in his 2006 autobiography of Joshua's role in the fall of the government:

> *In the end, Joshua accepted money to cross the floor,*
> *unlike [Alphonso] Dennie who had honourably rejected*
> *it. As political fortunes fluctuated over the years, with*
> *the merchants disillusioned with the taxation [Gross*
> *Turnover Tax] imposed on their gross earnings, and*
> *supporting my alternative policies, I got confirmation*
> *from the magnanimous contributor himself.*

Most reasonable persons are unlikely to accept Mitchell's slur against Joshua purely on the word of the alleged "contributor", twenty years after the event, when Mitchell had by then become Prime Minister. Was the "contributor" telling Mitchell something which he knew Mitchell wanted to hear as part of a confidence-building measure to secure patronage from the State under Mitchell's leadership? It is unlikely that Joshua needed "money to cross the floor"; the disgust he had developed for Mitchell and his colleagues was enough of a reason to bring down the coalition government!

Mitchell was not yet done with Joshua in his autobiography. In commenting on the post-1974 Milton Cato-Ebenezer Joshua electoral compact and subsequent government, Mitchell wrote:

[Milton] Cato had described his government as the strongest in the world but it soon began to flounder. Brushed aside in Cabinet as an irrelevance and ignored by his once worshipful supporters, Joshua and his wife abandoned the Government they had helped to build and joined the Opposition. I urged him to return to the marketplace and tell the people his side of the story. He had a wonderful reception to his speech, and he decided to repeat it the next week, only to find that the crowds the week before were satisfied with the upset and now were nowhere to be seen. He had fired his last cannon. The leader that had aroused the masses, challenged colonialism and fought the plantocracy, had abandoned his friends, and in the process outsmarted himself.

The bitterness within the Mitchell-Joshua coalition of 1972-1974 towards Joshua is loudly trumpeted in Mitchell's autobiography. Joshua died 17 years after the collapse of that coalition, but as reported by Mitchell: "[Alphonso] Dennie, [Othniel] Sylvester, and [Victor] Cuffy refused to attend Joshua's funeral." Gratuitously, Mitchell informs us:

I read a lesson [at the funeral service], both for Joshua, and later his wife, meeting their expenses with state funerals. I could not bear to see his living conditions in his last days. I changed his furniture. I gave him a police driver....I named our main airport in honour of Joshua before he passed on.

These material benefits, on Mitchell's testimony, accorded to Joshua, were not from Mitchell's pocket. They were from the Consolidated Fund of the government of St. Vincent and the Grenadines! Was it necessary to detail these? The telling surely rankles! Maybe Mitchell's naming of the Arnos Vale Airport as the "E.T. Joshua Airport" was pure political opportunism on Mitchell's part to reaffirm his supposed link to Joshua in the eyes of Joshua's former supporters.

One thing is certain: Mitchell was keen on benefiting politically from Joshua's defeat. Mitchell's decision to leave his safe constituency in the Grenadines and contest the South Central Windward seat in the 1979 general elections was pure political calculation. In his autobiography he stated:

If I were to lead the country, I thought it would be best
if I did so from the mainland. Moreover, if Joshua were
defeated, we would become the traditional party for the
disadvantaged poor.

Of course, with Mitchell's "centrist liberal" outlook it was not possible for his NDP, on a sustained as distinct from an episodic basis, to ever be the "party for the disadvantaged poor". In the 1984 general elections, Joshua, in an opportunistic return to an anti-Cato, anti-SVLP mode, was permitted by the NDP to mount its platform as an election mascot to accommodate nostalgia but not to be heard from. Joshua was to be seen but never permitted to speak. The NDP's hope was that his anti-SVLP lustre of yesteryear would rub off on Mitchell's NDP. The sad reality though, was that in Joshua's last political outing in South Central Windward in 1979, he had received less than 10 percent of the votes cast in that constituency. In the 1974 elections he had received 91.1 percent of the vote and in the 1972 election he had earlier obtained 86.7 percent of the votes in that very constituency. Long before the 1984 general elections, even before 1979, Joshua was a spent political force!

Undoubtedly, Joshua and his PPP were major political forces in the post-universal adult suffrage period up to 1972. But the PPP's strength must not be exaggerated. The PPP was founded in early 1952 and it contested general elections by itself in seven of the eight general elections between 1954 and 1972. In the 1974 general elections, the PPP contested three seats but in two of them it was part of an electoral compact with the SVLP. In none of these general elections did the PPP reach the 50 percent mark in popular votes! In 1954, it was the only party to contest the general elections. It contested in all eight seats for the legislature. The other nineteen candidates were all independents. The PPP won three seats and garnered 40 percent of the votes. Joachim was challenged in the Law Courts and there was a by-election that Samuel Slater won.

In the 1957 general elections, the PPP won 48.9 percent of the popular votes and won five seats to form the government. The People's Liberation Movement led by Herman Young won one seat; two Independent candidates won seats; and Milton Cato's SVLP did not win any seat but garnered 19.4 percent of the vote from the seven seats that it contested. In the 1961 general elections, the PPP was at its peak. It won six of the nine seats with 49.5 percent of the vote. The SVLP gained three seats with 47.8 percent of the vote. In the 1966 elections, the PPP won five of the nine seats with 49.03 percent of the vote. The SVLP secured four seats with a majority of the popular votes, 50.8

percent. In the 1967 general elections, the PPP's popular vote further declined to 46.2 percent from which it secured three of the nine seats. The SVLP obtained 53.8 percent of the vote and garnered six seats in the legislature, and thus formed the government for the first time after four general elections. In the 1972 elections, the PPP won six of the thirteen seats with yet another further decline in the popular vote to 45.4 percent. The SVLP won six seats also but with 50.4 percent of the votes. The lone Independent candidate, James Mitchell, won in the Grenadines. In the 1974 elections, the PPP and the SVLP had an electoral compact. The PPP won two of the thirteen seats with 13.4 percent of the vote. The SVLP won ten seats with 69.0 percent of the vote and the Mitchell-Sylvester Party won the Grenadines seat. In the 1979 general elections, the PPP contested eleven of the thirteen seats but won no seat. Its share of the popular vote had fallen abysmally to 4.5 percent. The SVLP won eleven of the thirteen seats with 54.4 percent of the vote. The NDP obtained 27.4 percent of the vote and two seats. The UPM received 13.6 percent of the votes and got no seat. The general elections prior to 1954 — in 1951 — the Eighth Army of Liberation had won all eight seats.

So, across eight general elections between 1954 and 1979, the PPP won three elections (1957, 1961, 1966), but never secured a majority of the popular votes. In that period, the SVLP contested seven elections (1957-1979) and won four but received a majority of the popular vote on five occasions, all under the leadership of Milton Cato. From these statistics the conclusion is clear: the SVLP, from 1957 to 1979, was a more significantly successful political party at the polls than the PPP. The SVLP's political base was broader and deeper than the PPP's.

Let us look at Ebenezer Joshua's personal performance in the three constituencies in which he contested between 1951 and 1979. In North Windward, Joshua's percentage vote was: 63.8 percent in 1951, 79 percent in 1954. In Central Windward Joshua's percentage vote was: 60.8 percent in 1957, 69.1 percent in 1961, 67.9 percent in 1966, and 66.7 percent in 1967. In South Central Windward Joshua's percentage share of the vote was: 86.7 percent in 1972, 91.1 percent in 1974 and 9.9 percent in 1979. He served as a member of the legislature unbroken for 28 years from 1951 to 1979. He won his seat on eight out of nine elections. It was a remarkable personal performance: Barring his ignominious defeat in 1979, he returned personal electoral triumphs in a range between 63.8 percent to 91.1 percent of the votes cast in the three constituencies which he contested.

In completing the SVLP's electoral performance post-1979 up to 1994, after which time it merged the MNU to form the ULP, its record is as follows: in the 1984 elections, the SVLP won 41.4 percent of the votes cast and obtained victories in four of the thirteen constituencies; the NDP won nine seats with 51.4 percent of the votes — it thus formed the government for the first time. In the 1989 elections, the results were as follows: NDP won 66.3 percent of the votes and all fifteen seats; the SVLP obtained 30.3 percent of the votes and no seat

In the 1994 elections the results were: the NDP retained twelve of the fifteen seats with 54.9 percent of the votes; the SVLP-MNU Unity ticket won three seats with 43.9 percent of the vote (SVLP, 26.5 percent; MNU, 17.4 percent). In the 1998 elections, the results were as follows: NDP won eight of the fifteen seats with a minority of the votes, 45.3 percent; the ULP obtained seven of the seats with a majority of the popular vote, 54.6 percent.

From 2001 to 2015 the era of ULP dominance was established under the leadership of Ralph Gonsalves. In the 2001 general elections, the ULP won twelve of the fifteen seats with 56.5 percent of the vote; the NDP won three seats with 40.9 percent of the vote. In 2005, the ULP retained government with twelve seats with 55.4 percent of the vote; the NDP got 44.5 percent of the vote with three seats.

In the 2010 elections, the ULP won eight seats with 51.1 percent of the vote; the NDP secured seven seats with 48.7 percent of the vote. In the 2015 general elections, the ULP won eight of the fifteen seats with 52.3 percent of the vote; the NDP got 47.4 percent of the vote and seven seats.

In the fifteen general elections between 1957 and 2015, "Labour" (SVLP-ULP) won a majority of seats seven times and an absolute majority of votes cast on ten occasions. The results for the principal parties opposed to "Labour" over this period are as follows: PPP (1957-1972) scored three victories by itself and once with Mitchell as an Independent. The NDP under the leadership of James Mitchell won four general elections over the period 1984 to 1998 (1984, 1989, 1994, 1998) but lost the popular vote in 1998 to the ULP. The PPP never won an absolute majority of popular votes in any general elections but it was the single largest popular party in the general elections of 1954, 1957, and 1961. In the latter two elections the PPP won the majority of seats too. In 1966, however, although it won the majority of seats, it lost the popular vote to the SVLP. "Labour" (SVLP/ULP) won an absolute majority of the popular votes in the following ten general elections (1966, 1967, 1972, 1974, 1979, 1998, 2001, 2005, 2010, 2015), compared to the six occasions combined for the PPP and the NDP (1957, 1961, 1966, 1984, 1989, 1994). "Labour" won the majority of seats on seven general elections (1967, 1974, 1979, 2001, 2005, 2010, 2015) more than any other single political party but the PPP, MSP, NDP together won the majority of seats eight times (1957, 1961, 1966, 1972, 1987, 1989, 1994, 1998).

These statistics lead inescapably to the conclusion that over the 58-year period (1957-2015), "Labour" (SVLP/ULP) has been the most popular vote winner; after a stable two-party system emerged in the 1961 general elections, it has endured since. "Labour" has won a majority of seats on more occasions than any other party singly. Since 1961 however, the electoral opponents of "Labour", namely PPP, MSP, and NDP, have together won the majority of seats on an equal number of occasions as "Labour". Since 1961 "Labour" has held governmental office for many years longer than its political opponents combined. The statistical evidence shows that "Labour" has been the natural party of governance! The data indicate too, that the constituency boundaries are demarcated to the disadvantage of "Labour" in terms of seats.

Milton Cato's individual constituency performances over the twenty-seven year period 1957 to 1984 were as follows: in 1957, in South Leeward, 29.6 percent; in seven elections in East St. George: 1961, 63.6 percent; 1966, 61.9 percent; 1967, 69.8 percent; 1972, 79.5 percent; 1974, 97.5 percent; 1979, 74.6 percent; and 1984, 55.2 percent.

These are impressive numbers and confirm Cato's constituency performances as outstanding: In the last seven out of eight general elections, Cato was victorious in his constituency with scores of between 55.2 percent and 97.5 percent.

Milton Cato's social democratic credentials are of a very high quality, impressive indeed, and reflective of his SVLP being faithful to the core ideals of the labour movement and the nation as a whole.

A summary of the governmental performance of Cato's SVLP supports this conclusion:

(1) The shaping of the liberal democratic Constitution of an independent St. Vincent and the Grenadines in conjunction with the British government. This Constitution, despite its many weaknesses and limitations, has been the fundamental base upon which St. Vincent and the Grenadines has built, over the past 38 years, a democratic society; representative government; the protection of inalienable individual rights and freedoms; an independent judiciary

of quality which has delivered justice for all; an impartial and neutral public service devoid of partisan politics; responsible and responsive good governance; the maintenance of law and order; and the upliftment, markedly, of the material conditions of life and living.

(2) The superintending of the expansion of secondary, post-secondary and tertiary education as follows: Built six secondary schools at North Union, Adelphi, Carapan, Barrouallie, Troumaca and Union Island; built the Teachers' College, the Technical College and established a modern Nurses' Training School; expanded access to tertiary education at University of the West Indies and elsewhere.

(3) The delivery of an extensive, low-income housing programme and the distribution of housing lots to low-income and lower middle-income persons. These several housing estates have evolved into well-built communities, including those at Campden Park, Sharpesdale, Peruvian Vale, and Fair Hall.

(4) The extension of the range and quality of medical and health services through, among other things, the significant expansion of the Kingstown General Hospital (now the Milton Cato Memorial Hospital); the building of the Georgetown Hospital; the construction of several clinics, nation-wide; the training and recruitment of a substantial number of health personnel; the rolling out of the first phase of the modernisation of the state's pharmaceutical services; and improvements in public health, and in the care of the elderly.

(5) The strengthening of the social safety net for the poor, the vulnerable and the working people through several measures, including the expansion of the many-sided public assistance programme (monthly assistance, help with building materials, school supplies and uniforms, etc.); the establishment of the National Provident Fund Scheme, the precursor to the National Insurance Services (NIS); and the presentation to Parliament of the NIS Bill for its first reading in July 1984 to set up the NIS (the Bill fell because Parliament was dissolved, but the incoming NDP government passed an almost identical Bill in 1987).

(6) The substantial diversification of the economy through, among other things, the following initiatives and measures: the establishment of a one-stop investment agency, the Development Corporation, to drive foreign and local investment; the founding of the Campden Park Industrial Estate with several manufacturing enterprises; the reintroduction of the sugar industry; the establishment of Diamond Dairy; the passage of the first Act of Parliament for the development of Mustique as an international tourism destination; the early steps toward the diversification into tourism; the enhanced diversification in agriculture; and the setting up of embryonic offshore and international shipping finance services.

(7)   The establishment of the state-owned National Commercial Bank and overseeing the expansion of the banking and insurance sectors.

(8)   The setting up of the National Lottery in 1984 to fund sports and culture in St. Vincent and the Grenadines.

(9)   The modernisation of the state administration and the delivery overall, of good governance, including according persons above eighteen years the vote and modernising the electoral system with the passage of the Representation of the People Act, 1982.

(10)   The implementation, in partnership with Cable and Wireless, of the first modern telephone system in St. Vincent and the Grenadines.

(11)   The enhancement of air and sea transportation access with the elemental improvements of the Arnos Vale Airport (renamed by the NDP government as E.T. Joshua Airport), including night landing facilities; and the expansion and modernisation of Port Kingstown.

(12)   The huge development of the city of Kingstown, including the Land Reclamation Project on the Bay Front.

(13)   The passage of path-breaking legislation, for the better, by successive Cato governments, including the following statutes: The Representation of the People Act, 1982; the Eastern Caribbean Supreme Court (SVG) Act, 1970, establishing the framework for our justice system; the Residence Act of 1975 and the SVG Citizenship Act of 1984 to govern the granting of residence and citizenship to non-Vincentians; the facilitation of economic development through the Caribbean Development Bank Act, 1970; the International Financial Organisation Act, 1970; the Regional Development Agency Act, 1968; the Caribbean Food Corporation Act, 1981; the SVG marketing Corporation Act, 1975; the Eastern Caribbean Central Bank Act, 1983; the Companies (Windward Islands Banana Growers' Association Registration) Act, 1982; the Development Corporation Act, 1970; the Housing and Lands Development Corporation Act, 1976; the Arrowroot Industry Act, 1976; the Public Telephone Act, 1969; the Hotels Aid Act, 1969; the protection of consumers through the Price and Distribution of Goods Act; the setting up of a modern regime of taxation through the Income Tax Act, 1979; the removal of bastardy from the statute books with the passage of the Status of Children Act, 1980; the Protection of Employment Act, 1900, which provided severance payment or reinstatement for the first time ever in the case of the new statutory wrong of unfair dismissal as a companion to the common law regarding wrongful dismissal; the strengthening markedly of the protection of women against violence though the Domestic Violence and Matrimonial Proceedings Act, 1984; the enhanced protection of our patrimony through, among other laws, the Beach Protection Act of 1981, the Continental Shelf Act of 1970, and the

Preservation of Historic Buildings and Antiques Act of 1976; the strengthening of the health sector through legislation such as the Immunisation of
Children Act, 1982, and the Nurses, Midwives and Nursing Assistants Act,
1978; very importantly, the bolstering of the right of the individual not to
be subjected to torture, cruel, inhumane and degrading punishment through
the passage of the United Nations Declaration on the Prevention of Crime
and the Treatment of Offenders Act in 1984; and the enactment of a raft of
measures to modernise and improve the efficiencies of the state administration.

(14) The participation in and advocacy of the West Indian Federation; the
"Little Eight" federal venture; the West Indies Associated States (WISA); the
Caribbean Free Trade Area (CARIFTA); the Organisation of Eastern Caribbean States (OECS); the Caribbean Community (CARICOM); the University
of the West Indies; and West Indies Cricket.

(15) The establishment of the basis of the foreign policy of St. Vincent
and the Grenadines in high principle and pragmatic self-interest for St. Vincent and the Grenadines. Though appreciative of traditional friends (United
Kingdom, Canada and the USA), Cato's foreign policy went beyond, however
tentatively, these traditional citadels.

James Mitchell's personal constituency performances in the nine elections between the 1966 and 1998 showed the following: five victories in the
Grenadines in 1966 (57.1 percent), 1967 (61.1 percent), 1972 (57.3 percent),
1974 (62.3 percent), and 1984 (81.8 percent); three victories in the Northern
Grenadines: 1989 (91.4 percent), 1994 (91 percent), 1998 (88.3 percent). The
lone defeat for Mitchell was in South Central Windward in 1979 when he lost
with 28.9 percent. Mitchell's performance has been extraordinary in his eight
constituency victories in general elections (plus a ninth in a by-election in the
Grenadines in 1980), with scores ranging from 57.1 percent to 91.4 percent.
Mitchell, too, has given the longest service of any successful candidate, serving
an aggregate of some 34 years (1966-2001) in Parliament, save for a short
break between his defeat in South Central Windward in December 1979 and
his return to Parliament in early 1980 through his victory in a by-election in
the Grenadines.

Ralph Gonsalves' personal constituency performance, all in North Central
Windward in his nine elections thus far between 1979 and 2015, have been as
follows: 1979 (19.1 percent), 1984 (23.5 percent), 1989 (25.3 percent), 1994
(69.4 percent), 1998 (78.1 percent), 2001 (81.0 percent), 2005 (81.0 percent),
2010 (79.8 percent), and 2015 (79.8 percent). His first three electoral outings
were in minority parties. Indeed, in two of these (1984 and 1989), he ran, for
all practical purposes, as an Independent. His six victories since 1994 have

ranged, impressively, from 69.4 percent to 81.0 percent. Gonsalves has served the longest period in active electoral politics — an aggregate of over 39 years from December 1979 to 2019 thus far, but as an elected parliamentarian for 25 years thus far: 1994 to the present. He is still, metaphorically at the political crease; a dispassionate assessment of him will be better done by someone else.

Two other exceptional leaders in "Labour" (SVLP – ULP) have been Vincent Beache and Louis Straker. Their exceptionalism has been marked on account of their leadership roles, their longevity of service, their success at the polls, and most importantly, their service on behalf of the people, in an out of Parliament. Vincent Beache first became a candidate for the SVLP in 1972 in North Central Windward. In the following four elections (1974, 1979, 1984, 1989) he remained as a candidate in that constituency. In 1994, he shifted to South Windward where he won thrice (1994, 1998, 2001). He won six of the eight elections which he contested: three in North Central Windward and three in South Central Windward, with majorities ranging from 47.2 percent in a three-way contest in 1984 to 96.0 percent in 1974. In all, he served the people, especially the working people, in electoral politics for thirty-three years (1972-2005), twenty-eight years of those as an elected Parliamentarian (1974-1989; 1994-2005). He served as Political Leader of the SVLP (1986-1992) and as the ULP's Political Leader (1994-1998); he had two stints as Leader of the Opposition (1984-1989, and 1994-1999). He was a Minister of Government both under SVLP and ULP. Arguably, he was the best Prime Minister St. Vincent and the Grenadines has never had.

Louis Straker, of Central Leeward, is one of the three "Labour" representatives (Beache and Gonsalves were the other two) who formed a formidable team when an opposition returned to the Parliament consequent upon the 1994 general elections. He is one of few representatives in the post-independence period who was never defeated at the polls. Straker's victories in Central Leeward spanned the period 1994 to 2015: he won in 1994, 1998, 2009, 2005, and 2015 — he did not contest in 2010, but came out of retirement to win again in 2015. Straker's share of the vote ranged from 51.3 percent in 1994 to 59.0 percent in 2001. He has served as Deputy Political Leader of the ULP and Deputy Prime Minister.

Other distinguished "Labour" representatives have been Montgomery Daniel in North Windward, Girlyn Miguel in Marriaqua, and Michael Browne in West St. George. Daniel first ran on a SVLP ticket in 1989, and skipped the 1994 elections and returned to contest in 1998 and in every general elections since then up to 2015, thus far. In the aggregate, Daniel has been in electoral politics for twenty-six years, contesting six elections and winning four consecutively since 2001 with victory scores ranging from 52.5 percent to 54.3 percent. Girlyn Miguel won all her four consecutive elections in Marriaqua (1998-2010) with majorities ranging from 56.2 percent to 66.6 percent of the vote in the constituency. Miguel served as Deputy Political Leader of the ULP and Deputy Prime Minister in the 2010 to 2015 period. She is the second most successful female candidate in our country's history. Michael Browne first contested elections in 1979 in East Kingstown for the UPM. He again did so in 1984 and in the by-election in 1987. In 1994 he returned to the polls as a candidate in West St. George as the MNU candidate on the "Labour-MNU Unity" ticket. He was victorious for the ULP in West St. George in 1998, 2001, and 2005. Thus, between 1979 and 2010, a period of thirty-one years, Browne has been active in electoral politics, in and out of Parliament. He and Clayton Burgin of East St. George (2001, 2005, 2010 victories) were the original architects of the ULP's Education Revolution.

In the post-independence era, two leading personalities from the NDP deserve separate commentary, too: Parnel R. Campbell and Arnhim Eustace because of their immense political contributions.

Parnel Campbell, a towering intellect, outstanding lawyer and a superb organizer, had his first outing at the polls in December 1979 on the ticket of the UPM in the Central Leeward constituency. He polled 24.8 percent of the vote in a four-way contest won by Arthur Woods of the SVLP who secured 61.1 percent of the vote. Campbell's performance was the best of the UPM's candidates. When the UPM coalition fell apart in February 1980, Campbell remained with the PDM. He sat out the 1984 general elections when many of his former DFM/PDM colleagues rushed onto the bandwagon of James Mitchell's NDP. Upon the death of his former DFM/PDM colleague, Edward Griffith, Campbell was selected as the NDP's candidate for the by-election in the East Kingstown constituency in 1987, which he won with 60.7 percent of the vote in a field of six candidates. Swiftly he became the Attorney-General in the NDP government in which capacity he served until his resignation therefrom in 1996. He contested and won the Central Kingstown constituency (this constituency was created and the boundaries reconfigured ahead of the 1989 general elections) in two successive elections: 1989 with 76.4 percent of the vote and 1994 with 63.1 percent of the vote. He lost his seat in the 1998 general elections with 43.7 percent of the vote.

Campbell was made the NDP government's Deputy Prime Minister immediately after the 1994 general elections. He was widely acknowledged, in and out of the NDP, as Mitchell's heir-apparent until his enforced resignation from the government in 1996. He nevertheless subsequently held the office of Chairman of the NDP up to and after Arnhim Eustace's elevation as President of the NDP in October 2000 and as a short-lived Prime Minister for five months until March 28, 2001.

Arnhim Eustace, an economist by training, had had a successful career as a national and regional public servant respectively in the government of St. Vincent and the Grenadines and the Caribbean Development Bank (CDB_). Upon his retirement, Eustace entered electoral politics. He was first elected as a parliamentary representative in East Kingstown on a NDP ticket in the June 1998 general elections with 50.4 percent of the vote. He was returned as the representative for East Kingstown in four successive elections: 2001 (50.5 percent of the vote), 2005 (51.8 percent of the vote), 2010 (54.9 percent of the vote), and 2015 (51.3 percent of the vote).

Eustace led his party to defeats in the four general elections under his leadership in 2001, 2005, 2010, and 2015. He, however, successfully led his party's "NO" campaign on the proposed "Reform Constitution" in a popular referendum in November 2009. Eustace resigned as President of the NDP and Leader of the Opposition in late 2016. He was succeeded by Lorraine Godwin Friday. He had earlier served as Minister of Finance in the NDP government between June 1998 and March 2001.

Over eighty years have elapsed since March 25, 1937, when the first "Labour" representative was elected to the legislature in St. Vincent and the Grenadines. George Augustus Mc Intosh, the leader of the SVWA and SVLP, on that day became the first elected representative with direct organisational links to a working people's organisation. The other victors for "Labour" in 1937 — N.S. Nanton, H.A. Davis, A.C, Allen, and O.D. Brisbane — had no real ties to the labour movement. Since then, until 2015, the following other eighteen persons with trade union connections have offered themselves as electoral candidates: St. Clair Bonadie, Ebenezer Duncan, George Charles, Ebenezer Joshua; Ivy Joshua; Herman Young; Charles Griffith (FIAWU-PPP); Leopold Martin (Independent candidate, but subsequently in FIAWU and CTAWU), Calder Williams, Michael Browne, Yvonne Francis-Gibson, Caspar London, Burns Bonadie, Cecil "Blazer" Williams, Noel Jackson, Conrad Sayers, Arnhim Eustace, and Ralph Gonsalves. Only six of this number have never won elections: Griffith, Martin, London, "Blazer" Williams, Burns Bonadie, and Jackson. The last two-named (Bonadie and Jackson) have been the most important union leaders in post-independence St. Vincent and the Grenadines.

In the sixteen years from the 1935 Uprising until the attainment of universal adult suffrage. George Mc Intosh was focussed on a social democratic, anti-colonial, and anti-fascist programme with the following main elements: attainment of universal adult suffrage and constitutional decolonisation; deepening democracy and freedom for working people through a legislative framework supportive of trade unions, freedom of religion (removing the legal restrictions for worship by the Spiritual Baptists), and freedom of association to build a political party and trade union; providing land to the landless through a state-sponsored Land Settlement Scheme; advocating the setting up of light manufacturing industries; pushing for much better education, housing, and health systems; improving people's wages, conditions of work, and level of material living; fighting for self-determination within the frame of "closer association" with other British colonies in the Caribbean; battling against fascism and Nazism during and after the Second World War; and organising on a firm footing the working people and nation.

The elements of Mc Intosh's programme, singly and as a whole, constituted the core of the stirrings and commencement of a social democratic revolution. There was nothing socialist about it. His socialism was aspirational. It was neither practical nor possible for there to be a more advanced programme in the conditions of the political economy, society and political geography of St. Vincent at the time.

Ebenezer Joshua's efforts were to build upon the social democratic achievements of the labour movement under Mc Intosh's leadership. The Eighth Army, Joshua's PPP and Cato's Labour Party all advanced the social democratic revolution in an evolving capitalist mode of production in the changing political circumstances of universal adult suffrage, embryonic ministerial government under devolved authority to elected representatives, further constitutional liberalisation, self-government, and independence. These alterations in the form and content of the political superstructure buttressed the evolving maturation of the working people and nation as they organised themselves into functioning political parties and trade unions. The changing of the central bases of the economy from sugar and arrowroot to banana and then to services, especially tourism, shaped the alteration of the level of development of the productive forces, the nature of production relations, and consequentially, the politics. The advances in technology, education and skills further developed the productive forces and aided their modernisation for the competitive market national, regionally and globally. In the process, the material conditions of life and living improved, and successive PPP and SVLP governments, to a greater or lesser measure, facilitated that improvement. Joshua's PPP and Cato's SVLP were in the social democratic frame initiated by Mc Intosh's SVWA – SVLP combination. Joshua's blast against the planter-merchant elite and colonialism represented, rhetorically, a more militant social democracy than that of Mc Intosh, and Cato. It was a kind of radical populism in the circumstances. Joshua was to drop his aspiration to "socialism" as the responsibilities of government and his narrow political and economic space dawned upon him. In time he was to become, sadly, a defender of the colonial status quo in his opposition to independence and an apologist for a modernising capitalism. It is evident too, that he was imprisoned by the limitations of his ideational framework, the low level of the political consciousness of his supporters, the comparatively low level of the development of the productive forces, the undeveloped role of the working people in the social organisation of labour, and the small size and limitations of the colonial economy.

The quest of Cato's SVLP to advance the people's social democratic condition and hasten the arrival of internal self-government and independence was an outgrowth of the earlier work of Mc Intosh and Joshua. Cato realised too, from practical experience, not from ideology, that the State was required to play a more activist role in the economy. Thus, the State assumed ownership of larger chunks of the economy than hitherto, for example, in commercial banking, marketing of agricultural produce, the supermarket business, the sugar industry, a dairy, agricultural lands, intra-island vessels, air transport, a national lottery, a philatelic bureau, and stone-crushers.

One of the ironies in the evolution of the political economy is that Cato's government presided over the dismantling of the plantocracy (1967-1972) and (1974-1984), but Joshua for all his militant critique of the plantocracy was not accorded the opportunity so to do. To be sure, Joshua's PPP-FIAWU shook the plantocracy with their activism but it did not fall. The fact remains that, other than Joshua's acquisition of the small estate in Fancy — challenging agricultural lands — Joshua did not purchase or acquire one square foot of a plantation between 1957-1966 when he held the reins of government, albeit in a colonial, political straitjacket. Indeed, colonialism, through pressure from Royal Commissions between 1897 and 1945, colonial experts, and later from George Mc Intosh, purchased plantations for distribution to small farmers and workers, and in some cases to manage them as going concerns; but Joshua did not, other than the small estate at Fancy. Cato's governments did so substantially, for example, at Mt. Bentinck, Langley Park, Gorse, Colonarie, and San Souci; and so did Mitchell's governments at Diamond, Lauders, Mt. Wynne-Peter's Hope, and Orange Hill. In fact, Mitchell documents Joshua's resistance to the purchase of Lauders estate during the Mitchell-Joshua coalition of 1972-1974. Land Settlement under colonialism was effected at Three Rivers, South Rivers and Park Hill prior to the rise of Mc Intosh's SVWA. In December 1945, the colonial government purchased estates in North Leeward and Central Leeward and placed them in two respective Land Settlements at Richmond Vale and Wallilabou. The Richmond Vale Settlement consisted of seven estates ranging from sixteen acres to 625 acres, admeasuring in total 2,653 acres. The Wallilabou Land Settlement comprised six estates ranging from five acres to 332 acres, admeasuring in the aggregate 1,351 acres. Both Land Settlements amounted to 4,004 acres. The small-scale ownership of the bulk of those lands today in North Leeward and Central Leeward are primarily due to the initial efforts of colonialism, and then of Cato's SVLP and the ULP.

Joshua's verbal attacks on the plantocracy and the organisation of the FIAWU on the estates did not cause, directly, the dismantling of plantation agriculture that occurred between 1970 and 1985. To be sure, workers' demands for higher wages and their greater insistence on their rights at the work place increased the estates' expenditure on wages and work conditions; but as has been shown earlier, in the examination of the reasons for the closure of the sugar industry in 1962, the real problems revolved around the inefficiencies of plantation agriculture, the failure and/or refusal to adapt to socio-political changes, and the growing competitiveness in the overseas' markets in respect of price, quality and sustainability of agricultural exports. Plantation agriculture had become an economic anachronism in St. Vincent. Modern capitalist modes, techniques and their requisites had not enveloped it. The highly subsidised British market for bananas between 1955 and 1993 propelled small farming agriculture and the popular demand for more land. At first, the Mt. Bentinck, Langley Park, Colonarie and Sans Souci estates devolved ownership to Basil Bascombe, not of Caucasian stock, but of a Callinago and Portuguese mixed heritage, to own and run these estates. Balcombe had distinguished himself as an enterprising planter at Fancy in the extreme north-east of St. Vincent. In time, Balcombe's estates were purchased by the Cato government in the 1974-1979 period. Other estates across St. Vincent and the Grenadines were either sub-divided by the owners themselves or purchased by the governments led by Cato and James Mitchell between 1967 and 1985, for distribution to small farmers and workers. The last of these big estates, Orange Hill Estates (3,500 acres) was acquired, for sub-division to small farmers, by Mitchell's NDP in 1985 from the Danish non-governmental organisation that had purchased these lands from the Barnard family.

Cato's cultural conservatism grounded in Anglo-Saxon values, his limitation in understanding the young intellectuals' attraction to "Black Power" and socialism, and his intolerance to political criticism outside of the parliamentary mechanisms, masked his strong nationalism, his profound Caribbeanness, his social democratic outlook, and practical programmes to uplift the working people and the nation. He was not timid in the use of the State to drive the economy in the extant circumstances of an undeveloped and risk-averse private sector. Undoubtedly, Cato's SVLP deepened social democracy and advanced the cause of the working people in significant material ways.

Despite the limitations of the outlooks of Mc Intosh, Joshua and Cato and the weaknesses in their political praxis, they gave outstanding service to St. Vincent and the Grenadines. They provided visionary and pioneering leadership. They secured extraordinary achievements and attained the highest levels of excellence in their respective eras that have benefited our country, and indeed they altered positively the course of the history of St. Vincent and the Grenadines. They were initiators and continuators in various ways of the national social democratic revolution that has not run, as yet, its full course in St. Vincent and the Grenadines.

The era of Mitchell's NDP (1984-2001) sought to roll back and dismantle the priorities of the people-centred focus of the social democratic revolution of Mc Intosh, Joshua, and Cato who, despite their disagreements and different emphases, constitute a continuum and a common trajectory of social democracy. In many fundamental respects, Mitchell led a counter-revolution, though skilfully masking it at first, with populist and libertarian impulses and actions. Mitchell succeeded in linking the former PPP political base, which tribally, was opposed to Cato's SVLP in electoral combat; the bulk of the younger intellectuals and professionals attached to the DFM who had borne the brunt of the Cato government's heavy-handedness in responding to their critiques; and a section of the business community, including small business operators. It was always an uneasy coalition of interests kept together by Mitchell's outstanding skills in manipulating political and business elites and aspiring seekers of political power, with an admixture of rewards and punishments.

The simple truth is that the NDP was, and still is, an electoral coalition of political office-seekers and business elites with a political brand evolved through governance, and resting on a diminishing old PPP base laced with an antipathy towards "Labour", not grounded in any coherent body of principles, philosophy or practice outside of a near-slavish embrace of "free enterprise" linked to monopoly capitalism, neo-liberalism and neo-colonialism. Certainly, the NDP has never possessed a core social democratic philosophy, although opportunistically for electoral purposes, it has raised this or that specific social democratic programme of a limited nature.

A starting point in assessing Mitchell is to recognise that he has been the most thoroughly Anglo-Saxon leader, in cultural terms, that the country has produced thus far. His informality of dress is but a peculiarity of his Bequia upbringing and his general unfussiness about the trappings of protocol. But his political praxis over the years revealed that his model of what is best in everything is British, European, American, and Canadian. His support for the British monarchy and the Privy Council is now legendary. He has been unable to bring himself to embrace the Caribbean Court of Justice as the final appellate jurisdiction in preference to the Privy Council, despite his undoubted commitment to regional integration. Mitchell has never exhibited any real confidence in our Caribbean civilisation to create anything of excellence. Indeed, the idea of a Caribbean civilisation has been alien to him. His cynicism about people and things Caribbean have been Naipaulian in scope and meaning.

Although Mc Intosh, Joshua, and Cato rightly saw the private sector as important to the mix of economic drivers, Mitchell has been the first leader to stakeout the ideological position of the Washington Consensus, following upon Ronald Reagan and Margaret Thatcher, to assert unequivocally that the private sector is the engine of economic growth; globalisation and neo-liberalism are deserving of support if only they could make some especial allowances for small island developing States; the State machinery should be reduced to the smallest extent possible to provide for basic functions, but not involving State ownership of any of the means of production or any robust regulation of business; trade unions are, increasingly, an anachronism in the modern capitalist enterprises and should be tolerated, not necessarily encouraged; the provision of housing should be left to the private market place and government has no business in building low income houses; public expenditure on education, health, social services, and non-contributory pensions should be restricted to basic provisions in these areas, and the market be encouraged to participate in them; the government must never run a fiscal deficit, and it must always strive to balance the its budget, even if it unbalances the country in the process; support be given for whatever fiscal or other concessions are required to satisfy foreign investors, even if they distort the economy or the community and undermine the overall public good; and the State ought to restrict to a minimum the extent of socially ameliorative legislation so as not to drive up business costs and thus reduce competitiveness.

All these approaches and programmatic details of Mitchell and his NDP were, and are, antithetical to the economic advance of social democracy. It is a dog-eat-dog philosophy unmoved from any doctrine of social solidarity. Indeed, the NDP government's closure of several worthy state economic enterprises and the slimming down of others are reflective of a doctrinaire "free enterprise" philosophy.

Mitchell's NDP was strong on one progressive public policy: Land Reform. Admittedly, though, the NDP's land reform was focussed mainly on land distribution, not a thorough-going land reform which included supports in training, credit, marketing, advice on best agricultural practices, and the provision of cultivation inputs. With this substantial caveat, his land reform programme at Orange Hill Estates and Lauders, for example, was, in principle, commendable. This was in keeping with his quest for a "property-owning democracy". Unfortunately, though, the slip-shod manner of the land reform left the potential beneficiaries without the actual "fee simple" ownership of the lands. Indeed, much land became owned by his party's supporters who were not the intended beneficiaries.

On the question of democratic, parliamentary governance, Mitchell's NDP mastered the art of having Parliament meet infrequently; of limiting the effectiveness of the Office of the Director of Audit and the Public Accounts Committee; of blocking other channels of openness, accountability and transparency; and curbing, in diverse ways, public criticisms of its policies, and actions. It remains a major stain on Mitchell's record that he opposed Constitutional reform in 2009, designed to deepen democracy and protect a widening of freedoms. He opposed the reforms in a most unbecoming, exaggerated, and scaremongering way in conjunction with the discredited Strategic Communications Laboratories (SCL) of Britain — an entity to which he was formally identified on its letterhead as an adviser/consultant.

The foreign policy of Mitchell's NDP was decidedly pro-western to an almost slavish degree, save and except in a limited way in relation to Cuba on which he distanced himself somewhat from position of the American Government. He opposed the Grenada Revolution and he welcomed the American invasion of that country in October 1983. As a clear marker of his external political allegiance and their knock-on effects nationally, Mitchell played a leading role in the Caribbean Democratic Union (CDU) and the International Democratic Union (IDU), both regional and international associations of conservative and right-wing parties. Currently, his NDP continues in this tradition.

The ULP, in contrast to Mitchell's NDP, has embraced a praxis of advanced social democracy in every area of the national political economy. It has been an inheritor of the values and practices of the best of the social democratic revolution of Mc Intosh, Joshua, and Cato and has extended and deepened this social democratic revolution in all areas, in the interest of the people. Regionally, the ULP government has been in the forefront of deepening the integration movement. In its foreign policy it has been firmly nationalist, anti-imperialist, non-aligned, grounded in the multilateralism and principles of the Charter of the United Nations. The ULP, as a party, has links with Socialist International, a grouping of social democratic/socialist parties globally. It too, has party-to-party links regionally and globally with like-minded political parties.

Importantly, the ULP has elaborated and celebrated the notion of "our Caribbean civilisation" and its magnificent Vincentian component. It repeatedly reaffirms that although our people are not better than anyone, no one is better than us. Education, science and technology are pushed by the ULP as crucial for our people's advance.

Although Mc Intosh, Joshua, and Cato came from the same social democratic stable, each has had his own emphases which were shaped by their own moulding and the times in which they functioned. Mc Intosh's profession as a druggist/pharmacist, Joshua's as a trade unionist and hitherto as a teacher, and Cato's as a lawyer, must have influenced the methods and approaches of their political praxis, at least at the margin. Each was undoubtedly shaped by his upbringing in a small, colonial society; so too, James Mitchell, although he was of a later generation. Mitchell, by profession, was an agronomist, which certainly influenced him, for example, in his attachment to land reform, albeit limited. Of the four leaders (Mc Intosh, Joshua, Cato, Mitchell) over the sixty-five years (1935-2000), Joshua was the only one who was not a trained professional.

To one degree or another, each of them was endowed with a measure of charisma or especial quality of a commanding presence that attracted them to their followers. But the concept of charisma must surely possess a remarkable elasticity to embrace four personalities so different in physical appearance, style, training, personal dispositions, and ability to communicate. Each was an excellent communicator in his political work but with different styles and voices. Joshua perhaps had the most commanding delivery style and greatest impact of oration, not necessarily content.

This matter of the personality, presence and actions of leaders have always fascinated political scientists. Nicola Machiavelli in the fifteenth century Italy,

Max Weber in early twentieth century Germany, and Richard Newstadt in the 1960s in the United States of America, among others, have all addressed these phenomena in developed countries, but which, with the necessary adaptation, may provide insights for us in developing countries, including the Caribbean. In 1963, an American political scientist, Edward Shils, in an interesting essay entitled "Demagogues and Cadres in the Political Development of New States" offered the concepts of "demagogy" and "rhetorical charisma" to aid the understanding of leadership in new or emerging countries. To him, "demagogy" involves:

> *An attempt by flamboyant oratory and the display of a radiating personality, to incorporate the masses of the population into a great national effort; it almost always arouses the more clamorous among them to demands and expectations which far exceed the possibility of fulfilment"*

The problem with analyses such as Shils' resides not in observable traits of "demagogy" itself, but in the almost inevitable dispute as to who is a demagogue. The real difficulty is that different classes or groups may see different leaders as demagogues. A demagogue to one class or group may be a statesman to another. The value orientations of the observer are critical in this regard. And since values derive from fundamental societal forces, the demagogue must be seen in relation to these forces. Shils side-steps this issue in his analysis. Leaders who are ascribed the label "demagogue" usually receive the ascription from persons whose prejudices, however sourced, are pre-disposed to such an assessment, which is then confirmed in the same circular way, grounded in biases. This surely is not a helpful way to assess leadership.

In the Caribbean, a Sri Lankan political scientist, Archibald Singham, who lectured at the University of the West Indies in Jamaica, developed, in his fascinating book published in 1967 and entitled *The Hero and the Crowd in a Colonial Polity*, the concept of "the hero" (derived from the sociologist Max Weber's notion of charisma) and applied it to Eric Matthew Gairy in the colonial polity of Grenada. Singham argued that in colonial politics "a potential hero must possess the quality of charisma of a special kind, capable of mobilising the crowd but not of developing a sustained following." The hero does not have a genuinely-organised mass party and his control of the mass is through the instrument of the crowd. This is achieved, according to Singham, by the hero mesmerising the crowd's emotions for short periods of time.

What Singham has written of Gairy in this regard possibly has applicability to other Caribbean leaders similarly located, including George Mc Intosh and Ebenezer Joshua.

Mc Intosh never experienced any sort of executive authority at the national level but Joshua did, albeit in an Executive Council still controlled or influenced significantly by the colonial Administrator-in-Council and other officials such as the Attorney General and Financial Secretary. Did Joshua ever become the full beneficiary of the "institutional charisma" of a chief executive in the government which, somehow boosted his political profile of personal charisma, heft, sustainability, and importance to the population? Did Cato and Mitchell derive authority form the "institutional charisma" of being Premier and Prime Minister? Does "institutional charisma" add to personal charisma? If so, in what way ways? Is personal charisma a valid category of explanatory power?

Singham's analysis has been subjected to a perceptive critique by Gordon Lewis in his 1968 classic, *The Growth of the Modern West Indies*, in the following terms:

> *It is doubtful if a schematic analysis that sees Gairy as the Weberian charismatic leader and the Grenada Government as the embodiment of rationalist bureaucracy does anything more than describe the institutional superstructure while ignoring, except for a brief description, the social class struggle out of which Gairyism emerged... For charisma is not a self-generating first cause; it grows out of deep social crisis.... It merely provided the crisis with its appropriate leadership. To be properly understood it must be seen in terms of (1) its socio-cultural environment and (2) the old-style Grenadian leadership that preceded it.*

Lewis' analysis is persuasive. It is self-evident that a leader's personal attributes had, and do have, an impact on followers, but these attributes must necessarily be sufficiently encompassing and connected to the major needs, interests and concerns of the followers. When the major needs, interests and concerns no longer find the hope of reasonable fulfilment or adequate address through a particular type of leader, they reject him or her. This is in fact what happened personally to Mc Intosh in 1951, to Joshua in 1979, to Cato's SVLP in 1984, and to Mitchell in 1998 and then his party in 2001. This reality exemplifies the fact that the followers of any leader are not merely metaphoric atoms to be manipulated by him or her in a social laboratory called politics. The followers are men and women of flesh and blood who are located somewhere in the political economy; and the relations between themselves and other classes or groups provide the basic clue to any understanding of their responses to political leaderships.

It is thus vital to our understanding of the leadership of Mc Intosh, Joshua, Cato, Mitchell, and Gonsalves, to appreciate that their political ideas and actions, central to their respective leaderships, cannot be grasped outside the contours of the mode of production, the society, cultural matrices, actual economic activities, and the polity of St. Vincent and the Grenadines. Political leadership is not an autonomous factor which transcends permanently, as distinct from episodically, the amalgam of the political economy, society and culture which determines ultimately the nature and character of the leadership itself. Political leadership is linked inextricably to the level of the development of the political forces, the nature of the production relations and the appended super-structural forms, ideas, beliefs, laws, religion, and the like. The leadership takes its ideology, ideas, policies, and programmes from the classes or groups, and inter-locking associations, which it objectively represents. The political style in which the leadership envelopes himself/herself is derived primarily from the selective use of beliefs, ideas, symbols, and culture of the society which have acceptability among the groups that largely comprise the followers. The leader's own personality make-up and skills are, of course, critical to the form and manifestation of the leadership itself.

It is apt to conclude this discourse on "leadership" with an incisive, compelling, and lengthy quotation, from Gordon Lewis' book, *Slavery, Imperialism and Freedom: Studies in English Radical Thought* (published by *Monthly Review Press* in 1978):

> *The impact of personality on historical development is, of course, undeniable; that both Henry and Elizabeth Tudor were strong-willed monarchs no doubt contributed to the final victory of sixteenth-century England against the Catholic reaction. But no less undeniable is the fact that such impact can only occur in certain given historical situations. It is the total parallelogram of socio-economic-cultural forces which at any given moment explains and conditions the influence any individual person exercises on the historical process. The character of an individual, however outstanding, is a*

factor in that process only to the degree that those forces permit it to be so. It is true that within the framework, that factor will have enormous influence.... Yet before such personal drives can in any measure influence the cause of events they must, first, be comfortable to the primary needs of the time, and secondly, fully deployable under the prevailing conditions of the times.... It is misleading...to see the outstanding individual as the prime shaper of events. He is, rather, the product and agent of impersonal forces. He may take the initiative in certain directions of action and policies; he may see further than others; he may dramatize in his person the requirements of a new class or a new nation. But all along, he is the instrument, albeit unconsciously, of the inherent logic of social and economic structures.

WOMEN IN POLITICS, TRADE UNIONISM AND THE POLITICAL ECONOMY: 1951-2018

The first woman to contest a seat in any general elections in St. Vincent and the Grenadines was, as noted hitherto herein, Floris Simmonds, who ran as an Independent candidate in the Grenadines in 1954. No woman had contested in 1951 at the time of the first elections under universal adult suffrage. She obtained 84 votes or 7.1 percent of the votes cast in a four-way electoral contest that included two other Independent candidates, Clive Tannis and Cyril Mitchell; and the PPP candidate, Gabriel Forde. Tannis won the seat with 42.3 percent of the vote. Mitchell was second with 40.3 percent of the vote. Forde received 10.4 percent. Floris Simmonds' name never appeared on another ballot as a candidate. Since then, too, no female candidate offered herself as an "Independent".

Over the next fifteen general elections and five by-elections from 1957 to 2015, a grand total of 31 female candidates contested in these elections; seven of them — all from the major parties — won seats; and none of the 18 candidates for any minor party ever won a seat.

The first victorious woman in elections was Ivy Inez Joshua, the Grenadian-born wife of Ebenezer Joshua, the Political Leader of the PPP. She won the constituency of North Windward in 1957 with 83.3 percent of the vote, against Egerton Richards of the PLM who received 16.7 percent of the votes. Ebenezer Joshua had won the North Windward seat in the two previous elections in 1951 and 1954 with respective shares of the vote of 63 percent and 79 percent. Ebenezer Joshua decided to leave this safe seat for Mrs. Joshua and offered his candidacy in Central Windward. Ivy Joshua contested, thereafter, in every general elections, in the North Windward constituency for six times up to 1979 when she lost her seat to the SVLP's Peter Ballantyne in a five-way contest. She obtained 18.0 percent of the vote in 1979 in a third-placed finish behind Ballantyne and the NDP's David Jack. On the six occasions that Ivy Joshua was successful in winning the seat, her share of the vote in North Windward ranged from a low of 71.1 percent in 1966 to a high of 84.1 percent in 1974. It is to be noted that in every constituency in 1979, the PPP vote collapsed humiliatingly.

The second most successful female candidate in the electoral history of St. Vincent and the Grenadines was Girlyn Miguel of the ULP in the constituency of Marriaqua. Girlyn Miguel won the four elections which she contested between 1998 and 2010. She thus served in Parliament for 17 years (1998 to 2015). Her winning share of the vote ranged from a low of 56.2 percent in 2010 to a high 66.6 percent in 2001.

Three other women (Yvonne Francis-Gibson in West St. George, Stephanie Browne in the Southern Grenadines — both from the NDP — and the ULP's René Baptiste in West Kingstown) won elections twice. In the case of Stephanie Browne, her first victory in 1991 was at a by-election, consequent upon the death of Mary Hutchinson who had won the seat in 1989 with 92.6 percent of the vote. The other victories of these three female candidates were in general elections. In the 1989 and 1994 elections, respectively, Yvonne Francis-Gibson obtained 66.1 percent and 51.4 percent of the votes cast. Stephanie Browne's percentage votes in her constituency were 85.6 percent in 1991 and 86.8 percent in 1994. Mrs. Browne defeated another woman, Olivia Bentick of the MNU in straight contests on both occasions. In the 2001 and 2005 general elections, René Baptiste won respectively, with 50.1 percent and 50.4 percent of the votes cast in West Kingstown. In 2001, she defeated John Horne who had held the seat hitherto for seventeen years.

The seventh woman ever to win a seat in the Parliament was the SVLP's Valcina Ash in the Central Leeward constituency. She won in a by-election in 1983 as a consequence of a vacancy arising from the death of SVLP's Arthur Woods who had last won the seat with 61.1 percent of the vote in a four-way fight in 1979. Mrs. Ash won the by-election by a slim margin in a three-way contest: 50.6 percent of the vote for Ash, 48.3 percent for NDP's Herbert Young and 1.1 percent for SVNM's Egerton Richards. In the 1984 general elections, Herbert Young defeated Mrs. Ash, 52.1 percent to 47.9 percent of the votes.

Thirteen of the thirty-two female candidates in the post-adult suffrage electoral history of St. Vincent and the Grenadines were from the major political parties: from "Labour" (SVLP/ULP) there were six; from NDP, six; PPP, one. The minority parties fielded eighteen female candidates between them: Green Party, ten; the PPM, three; Democratic Republican Party of Anesia Baptiste, two; the MSP (Mitchell-Sylvester Party), one; the UPM, one; and the MNU, one. The lone Independent female candidate ever was Floris Simmons in the 1954 general elections.

The seven female candidates for the major political parties who did not get elected in any general elections were for "Labour" (SVLP/ULP): Valcina Ash in 1984, although she won a by-election in 1983; Celithia Davy in 1989; Michelle Fife in 2010; and Deborah Charles in 2015; for the NDP: Ruth Woods in 2001; Advira Bennett in 2005; and Vynette Frederick in 2010.

No female who contested an election in a constituency either as an Independent candidate or as a candidate of a minor party has ever won. These 19 female candidates and their respective percentage votes since 1954 are as follows: Floris Simmonds (Independent in 1954, 7.1 percent of the vote), Pearlina John (MSP in 1974, 2.5 percent), Nelcia Robinson (UPM in 1984 and 1989, 11.8 percent and 3.8 percent respectively), Olivia Bentick (MNU in 1991 and 1994, 14.0 percent and 13.2 percent respectively), Nicola Daize (PPM in 2001; 1.6 percent), Laverne Grant (PPM in 2001; 1.3 percent), Amor Lashley (PPM in 2001; 2.2 percent), Ella Cain (GP in 2010; 0.4 percent), Carvenia Culzac (GP in 2010; 0.1 percent), Orit De Roche (GP in 2010; 0.4 percent), Sabrina Els (GP in 2010; 0.1 percent), Cedney John (GP in 2010; 0.3 percent), Yvonne Simon (GP in 2010; 0.2 percent), Alphine Simmons (GP in 2010; 0.1 percent), Natasha Black (GP in 2015; 0.3 percent), Marsha Caruth (GP in 2015; 0.2 percent), Adella Samuel (GP in 2015; 0.1 percent), Anesia Baptiste (DRP in 2015; 0.9 percent), and Karima Parris (DRP in 2015; 0.5 percent).

The women who achieved ministerial offices in government were Ivy Joshua, Stephanie Browne, Girlyn Miguel, and René Baptiste. Three others who contested elections were appointed to the post of Parliamentary Secretary: Valcina Ash, Mary Hutchinson and Deborah Charles (as Senator).

In the trade union movement, the following women achieved, at one time or another, leadership positions: Yvonne Francis-Gibson, Joy Browne and Wendy Bynoe (President of the Teachers' Union), Ivy Joshua (President of the FIAWU); and Alice Mandeville (President of the CTAWU). Women have been active in trade unions at lower levels to great effect.

As in several other Caribbean countries, women are woefully under-represented as electoral candidates, elected representatives or appointed senators. Several reasons have been proffered for this wholly unacceptable under-representation. They range from: a patriarchy, that has historically carved out particular roles for men and women, still persists in the allocation of leadership positions in politics and trade unionism largely to men; the nastiness of competitive politics that turns off women; the very matrifocal nature of the Caribbean family that has led women, moreso in our region than elsewhere such as North America and Europe, to commit predominantly to "family" and thus eschew leadership in politics and trade unionism; the political economy of monopoly capitalism which sustains the unequal division of labour in the higher echelons of politics and trade unionism, but which is not evident to the same extent or at all in areas such as the public service and teaching; and the deliberate choosing of other more valuable career options by educated women or those more compatible with their strong and abiding family commitments.

Fundamentally, the deeply-embedded historical structures of patriarchy and the nature of the contemporary political economy of monopoly capitalism define the contours of the male-female participation in the activism of politics and trade unions. To be sure, there have been women in leadership positions in the Caribbean, including St. Vincent and the Grenadines, but the record shows this is the exception rather than the rule. It is changing but not fast enough, particularly in the context that roughly one-half of the electorate and over forty percent of the labour force are women.

Heavily skewed enrolments at post-secondary educational institutions and at universities in favour of women are likely, in the foreseeable future, to see far more women in the leadership of political parties, parliament, government, and trade unions. Areas of work, including the professions of law, medicine and business, which not-too-long ago were the near-exclusive preserves of men, are now increasingly being populated by women.

The political parties, trade unions and the State are required pro-actively to seek the recruitment of quality women candidates for high offices in hold-out preserves of men. Both mainstream political parties in St. Vincent and the Grenadines search for women to become engaged in political activism at high levels, but the historical and contemporary forces of the societal arrangements and the political economy restrain advancement in this regard. In 2009, the ULP government pushed, as part of the proposed reform constitution that was rejected in the popular referendum, a guiding principle that political parties strive to recruit at least one-third of their candidates for parliamentary elections from each gender group of males and females.

Currently, in the Parliament of St. Vincent and the Grenadines there is no elected representative who is a woman. There are, however, two senators who are women in a unicameral legislature that consists of fifteen elected representatives, six senators, an Attorney General, and the Speaker. In the last general elections in 2015, the ruling ULP offered one female candidate to the electorate; the opposition NDP offered none.

Since the onset of the twenty-first century, there have been four general elections thus far. In these the ULP offered four female candidates. Girlyn Miguel in the elections of 2001, 2005, and 2010 was elected to Parliament on these three occasions. Another, René Baptiste contested, successfully, in two elections in 2001 and 2005. The third (Michelle Fife) and fourth (Deborah Charles) of the women offered were unsuccessful in 2010 and 2015 respectively. The NDP offered three unsuccessful candidates: one each in the elections of 2001 (Ruth Woods), 2005 (Advira Bennett), and 2010 (Vynnette Frederick); it offered none in 2015. The Attorney General during the 2001-2017 period, whom the ULP government chose as a public servant rather than a representative or senator, but who sat constitutionally in Parliament, was a woman, Mrs. Judith Jones-Morgan. She has been, thus far, the longest-serving Attorney-General in our country's history.

The policies of the labour movement (trade unions and "Labour" political entities) have contributed immensely to the overall empowerment and socio-economic improvements of women. Still, there are limitations to be satisfactorily addressed and weaknesses corrected. Both mainstream political parties (the ULP and NDP) have expressed their commitment to advancing further and faster the optimal advancement of women, the full achievement of their rights and genuine gender equality.

The St. Vincent and the Grenadines Population and Housing Census Report 2012, concludes its discussion on "Gender and Development Issues" thus:

> *In summary, males outnumbered females in the population and labour market; however, more females, than males, attained higher level education. The empirical analysis highlighted four major findings. First, women maintained higher enrolment; they predominated in school attendance at university level, and a larger*

proportion accomplished higher degrees. This outcome was the same regardless of employment status. Second, women made achievements in the labour force, through improved participation, although a larger proportion were managing households, without the support of a spouse or partner. Third, despite women's remarkable achievements in education and in the labour market, generally, there was an under-representation of women in most areas of paid employment. Finally, men remained the main participants in the labour force, particularly in paid employment.

The data in the Census support this summation in the following elements:

(1) "Female labour participation increased steadily from 41.2 percent in 1980, to 56.1 percent in 2012. The increase in female participation may be on account of improved education among females, as women who attain higher education tend to go to the labour market seeking economic autonomy. Although male participation [in the labour force] remained relatively high, it declined gradually from 84.1 percent in 1980 to 70.2 percent in 2012. These intercensal changes suggest that the gender gap in labour force participation is converging. Similar results were revealed among household heads."

(2) "The main participants [employees] in the private sector continued to be men in 2012. In every area of private work, men outnumbered women, except in the area of unpaid work, where women (56 percent) were the majority. Between 2001 and 2012 there was an increase in the number of public sector employees. There was also a shift from males, being the main participants, to females, in the public-sector work. Generally, the data show that women's participation increased in every area of paid employment."

(3) In 2001, the gender composition of paid employees in government was male (50.8 percent), female (49.2 percent). By 2012, this had increased for women thus: female (56 percent), male (44.0 percent). In the private sector in 2001, the numbers in paid employment were males (63.2 percent), women (37.8 percent). In 2012, the comparable numbers were males (61.4 percent), women (38.6 percent).

(4) Some striking data in favour of women show that in the period 2001-2012, there was a 55.8 percent increase in the number of professional women in the workplace and a 3.6 percent decline in the number of professional men. The actual numbers for professionals in 2001 were males (1,611), females (1,920); in 2012, the comparable numbers were males (1,553), females (2,991). Favourable data for women are evident in some other areas. In respect of "Technicians and

Associate Professionals" the numbers were: 2001, males (896), females (866); 2012: males (1,436) and females (1,470. In the category "Service and Sales Workers", the numbers were: 2001, males (2,621), females (2,581); 2012: males (4,442), females (6,188). Men, however, continue to outnumber women in the following occupational groups: managers,;skilled agricultural-forestry-fishery workers; craft and related trades workers; plant and machine operators and assemblers; and elementary occupations.

(5) Among the employed, more women reached university level and obtained higher degree qualifications. In 2012, of the 3,032 university graduates in employment, 1,729 were women and 1,303 were men. Of the 5,230 employees with a pre-university/post-secondary/college qualification, 2,897 were women and 2,333 were men. Male employees with primary and secondary education outnumbered women in the workplace.

(6) It is to be noted that unemployment among university graduates amounted to 1.5 percent of the labour force in 2012. Unemployment among persons with a pre-university/post secondary/college qualification amounted in 2012 to 10.3 percent of the labour force. Unemployment overall, in 2012, amounted to 21.5 percent of the labour force, more or less the same as in 2001, although more persons of working age (40,821) were employed in 2012 than in 2001 (35,548 persons). In 2012, more women in the labour force were unemployed (24.3 percent) than men (19.4 percent). Thus, a reverse of 2001 when there was more unemployment among males (22.5 percent) than females (18.3 percent). But in actual numbers more females were employed in 2012 (17,131) as compared to 2001 (13,745). The actual comparable employed males were: 2012 (23,690), 2001 (21,843).

On "Demographics, Health, and Gender Issues" the *SVG Population and Housing Census Report 2012* states as follows:

> *The data from the 2012 census indicated that, with the exception of the 0-4, 30-34 and 75+ age groups, males outnumbered females in all age cohorts. This resulted from higher sex ratios at birth and lower mortality among the female population. At the household level, males were predominantly heads of households, which is consistent with views held, by the population, regarding gender roles. These male household heads were more likely to be married or in a union than female household heads. Of the 25.6% of household heads who were "Married and Living with Spouse" the majority (86.9%) were male. Similarly, of the 14.9% of*

household heads who were in a "Common Law Union."
67.9% were male, indicating that more females than
males were lone household heads.

On "Health and Gender Issues" the 2012 Census Report concludes:

The data reflected that more females than males were
diagnosed with chronic illnesses such as Arthritis, Diabe-
tes, Asthma, Heart Disease, and Hypertension. Although
females have higher levels of morbidity, they have a
longer life span than males, as is evident in higher life
expectancy at birth. [Female life expectancy was 72.64
compared to male life expectancy which was 67.38 in
2012]. The census data do not provide sufficient infor-
mation to explain this phenomenon. However…census
statistics reveal that females are more likely to attend a
health care facility than their male counterparts, suggest-
ing that females are more attentive to their health status.

Higher incidence of chronic illnesses noted among fe-
males, in census statistics, may be as a result of males
under-reporting, or lacking knowledge of, the status of
their health. Under-reporting of illnesses by males is
common to Vincentian society. Further, as was revealed
in the "Survey of Living Conditions" (2008), men are
more likely to lose pay on account of illness; and, as a
consequence, they refrain from reporting on the status
of their health. On the other hand, females are more
open to the possibility of illness and seek prevention
and curable methods; and, as such, mortality rates, due
to chronic illnesses, for females under age 65, are lower
than that of males. In addition, of the minority of
persons who reported that they visited a family plan-
ning clinic in 2012, the majority were female. This may
suggest that issues relating to reproductive health have
been feminized.

A central "health and living" issue of great moment for women is that which concerns violence against women and the commission of sexual offences against them. This is a matter that the ULP government has been addressing aggressively in terms of public education, institutional supports for women, policing and prosecutions, strengthening of the legal system, and fortifying the laws in respect of the protection and defence of women and children. A bundle of relevant reforms in each of these areas, and more, has been instituted. Much more still remains to be done. It is a vital area on which thorough-going official reports and analyses have been done by regional scholars, sensible corrective recommendations have been made and are being pursued systematically by government, including path-breaking legislation on domestic violence.

At a glance, the actual progress of women, currently, can be further gauged in part too, by the following: Sixty-five (65) percent of the students at the Community College are women in a context where enrolment has more than tripled since 2001; 70 percent of Vincentian students at universities are women in a context too, where enrolment has nearly quadrupled; two of the four Cabinet Secretaries since 2001 have been women; the two Accountants-General, the three Directors of Audits, the two Clerks of the House of Assembly, and the two Deputy Governors-General have been women; the longest serving (2001 – 2017) Attorney General in the history of St. Vincent and the Grenadines has been a woman; the Director of Planning from 2001 to 2018, and the longest in the history of St. Vincent and the Grenadines, has been a woman; five of the nine Permanent Secretaries are women; the Labour Commissioner and Deputy Labour Commissioner are women; the Chief Education Officer is a woman; more than 60 percent of the Principals in primary and secondary schools are women; the Chief Medical Officer is a woman; the Permanent Representative and Ambassador of St. Vincent and the Grenadines to the United Nations is a woman; (two of three of St. Vincent and the Grenadines' Ambassadors to the UN since 2001 have been women; and currently three-quarters of the staff at this Overseas Mission are women); the Ambassador of St. Vincent and the Grenadines to the USA and the Organisation of American States is a woman (two of the three since 2001 have been women, including the youngest ever at 31 years); the Deputy High Commissioner to the United Kingdom and the Deputies at the SVG Embassies in Venezuela and Cuba are women; the President of the Family Court, the Chief Magistrate and the Acting Director of Public Prosecutions are all women; the Chief Justice of the Organisation of Eastern Caribbean (OECS) Supreme Court is a woman; two of the three resident High Court Judges in St. Vincent and the Grenadines are women; the Supervisor of Elections and the immediate past Supervisor of Elections are women; more than one-half of the Consultants and Senior Registrars in the health system are women; 150 police officers out of a total of 900 are women, up from a handful (women now routinely occupy senior ranks of the Police Force; the highest-rank held by a woman is that of Superintendent — one of eight — (she is the youngest Superintendent, in her thirties, in the whole of

CARICOM); the Speaker of the OECS Assembly is a woman, a Vincentian; and the Chairpersons of numerous public enterprises, including critical ones such as the St. Vincent Electricity Services, and the Central Water and Sewerage Authority, are women.

The ULP administration has had a deliberate policy of advancing qualified women into the highest ranks of the public service and state administration. Indeed, in many areas, women preponderate. There is no affirmative action in relation to women's employment and promotion. By dint of their quality they rise. The surest way for their advancement, and that of men, is for them to be properly educated and trained, then afford them every possible opportunity to advance without any gender discrimination whatsoever.

Historically, in St. Vincent and the Grenadines, in the Caribbean and in countries all over the world, philosophical or ideational perspectives reflecting the interests of classes or groups possessed of an identity of interest, have shaped the understanding of the actual realisation, or otherwise, of women's empowerment or the advancement of their practical concerns.

As long ago as the late nineteenth century, the German socialist Clara Zetkin emphasised in a speech in 1899 in Paris, France, on the occasion of the centennial of the French Revolution, that, "The emancipation of women, together with all of humanity, will take place only with the emancipation of labour from capital." She affirmed the urgent need of women to obtain paid work so as to enable them to achieve and maintain economic independence. In the process, Zetkin blasted the "bourgeois women's movement" as offering no solution to the "woman question". Indeed, she labelled this movement as a vain effort "built upon sand ---- with no basis in reality." Zetkin elaborated this stance a few years later, in 1907, in a speech at the First Congress of Socialist Women. "There cannot be a unified struggle for the entire female sex.... No, it must be a class struggle of all the exploited without differences of sex against all exploiters no matter what sex they belong to."

"Bourgeois Feminism", historically, has sought only to advance as its focus, women's juridical rights under the extant social order without any trajectory to alter the nature of the existing political economy, its capitalist relations of production, and its attendant cultural, ideational and institutional superstructure. Bourgeois feminism, in its contemporary settings, seeks to detach the question of women's rights from the basic social issues by making it a separate question. This bourgeois feminist approach, and content, are frequently promoted by opportunistic petit-bourgeois elements from the intellectual and professional class of women and men who often attach themselves to this or that like-minded political party or group.

In its more extreme form, bourgeois feminism is uninterested in national, racial or ethnic struggles in its purported quest for women's emancipation and empowerment. It is concerned almost exclusively with "women's lives". The bourgeois/petit-bourgeois feminists ignore the profound inter-connectedness between anti-colonial and anti-imperialist struggles, working people's struggles, black and indigenous people's struggles, and the struggles of women. They fail to grasp that historically, and in the contemporary political economy, monopoly capitalism maintains its overrule by subjugating and dividing countries, the working people, ethnic groups, and gender constellations. The programme to combat this subjugation and division necessarily emphasises a struggle for the enlargement of freedom and our people's material possibilities. The execution of such a programme demands an effective linkage between the oppressed nations and classes/groups within them and their multiple inter-connections globally, under leaderships wedded to genuine transformation, for the better, of the existing socio-economic order.

In an interesting essay entitled *"Rosa Luxemburg's Critique of Bourgeois Feminism as Early Social Reproduction Theory"* authored by Ankica Čakardić, Professor at the University of Zagreb (February 25, 2018), it is stated thus:

> *Bourgeois feminism plays an important part in the maintenance of capitalist class-structures.... The bourgeois class of women demands the political right...only for the ruling class of women, and from an individualist standpoint they hold no interest in tackling the issue of the position of women in general or class-related causes of the oppression of women.*

Čakardić insists that bourgeois women play an important role in perpetuating the established social relations. Indeed, as Roxa Luxemburg posited in a 1912 essay entitled "Women's Suffrage and Class Struggle":

> *Aside from the few who have jobs or professions, the women of the bourgeoisie do not take part in social production. They are nothing but co-consumers of the surplus value their men extort from the proletariat.*

Bourgeois feminism often becomes wrapped up with a divisive "biological feminism" that sees biological differences as involving and affording an unbridgeable gap to concerted activism, ideationally and practically, between males and females. This is self-evidently a species of sophistry which is dangerous because it undermines solidarity between men and women organised in classes or coherent groups acting for their joint upliftment. Bourgeois and petit-bourgeois feminists, including biological feminists, espouse a narrow perspective on patriarchy which abstracts it from the mode of production and the production relations within it, and treats it as an autonomous constant across societies and time in a mechanistic either-or-way.

In avoiding a narrow understanding of patriarchy in any social formation as simply, without more, the hierarchical ordering of society based on gender, it is necessary and desirable to go back to basics. No mature and realistic understanding of the evolution of human civilisation and history can hold that patriarchy is its determining driving force. The matter at hand is far more complex, many-sided and otherwise rooted.

Frederich Engels in the Preface of the first edition (1884) of his impressive volume, *The Origin of the Family, Private Property and the State* stated persuasively:

> *According to the materialistic conception, the determining factor in history is, in the last resort, the production and reproduction of immediate life. But this itself is of a twofold character. On the one hand, the production of the means of subsistence, of food, clothing and shelter and the tools requisite therefore; on the other, the production of human beings themselves, the propagation of the species. The social institutions under which men of a definite historical epoch and of a definite country live are conditioned by both kinds of production: by the stage of development of labour, on the one hand, and of the family, on the other.*

Patriarchy evolved historically. It arrived in pre-capitalist societies, and evolved in a particular condition, under the capitalist mode of production. A class-based society has utilised patriarchy to exercise order and control in the interest of the economically-dominant class. Under capitalism, this dominant class is the bourgeoisie. The quest of the capitalist class for hegemony through the appropriation of the workers' surplus value and its control of the state apparatus, has turned a pre-capitalist patriarchy into a fully-fledged "capitalist patriarchy" as one of the buttresses for capitalism's domination and continuance. In the Caribbean, the immediate pre-capitalist form was the slave mode of production that was imposed by an external mercantile capitalism in a colonial system, centuries after "classical" slavery in Europe and elsewhere had ended. Slavery in the Caribbean was that of the enslavement of African bodies by Europeans. Thus, colonialism, class, race/ethnicity, patriarchy, culture, religion, and particular legal forms, are all inextricably intertwined, but they rest on the material foundation of the mode of production (the productive forces and production relations, that is to say, class relations), and exchange relations between the metropole and the hinterland.

During slavery, there were, roughly, one female slave for every two male slaves. The natural increase of the slave population was low, and was unable by itself to replenish the population on account of three basic factors: extremely low fertility of the slaves, high mortality rates, and high sex ratios (far more males than females). After the slave trade was abolished in 1807, the planters paid somewhat more attention to the health of the slaves because the replacement of labour had to be effected by the children born of the slaves resident on their plantations.

Under slavery, women performed multiple roles. Labourer or skill worker in the fields, workshops, or in the planters' households; mother of children; partner to a male slave; domestic worker in the slaves' barracks (dwellings); provider of sex (forced or consensual) to a white male (planter, overseer, estate functionary, planter's son, colonial official) or occasionally to a white female; or more or less permanent mistress to a white man. In all these roles the woman in slavery was in subordinate power-relationship to white males and females, and black males.

Some earlier analyses of West Indian family structure and women in it that were sourced to the condition of slavery, have undergone reassessment from solid empirical studies. Important in this regard was Professor B.W. Higman's original research made available in an article entitled "Household Structure and Fertility on Jamaican Slave Plantations: A Nineteenth-Century Example" and published in the journal, *Population Studies* (Volume 27, Pt. 3, November, 1973). Higman authoritatively advises:

> *It is generally agreed that the marital instability and casual mating characteristic of West Indian family structure depress fertility. These conditions are traced to the mating organisation of the slaves. The stresses placed on the African family systems of the slaves are obvious: the continued importation of slaves, most of them young adult males; the ruthless separation of kin*

> *through sale or removal; the overwhelming authority*
> *of the master, reducing the dependence of children on*
> *their parents and the economic role of the male house-*
> *hold head.* Yet, in spite of these stresses, there is
> evidence of strong bonds of kinship and sense of
> family among slaves. *[My Emphasis]*.

Strong support for Higman's conclusion has come from Professor Michael Craton in an article entitled "Changing Patterns of Slave Families in the British West Indies", and published in the *Journal of Interdisciplinary History* (Volume X, No. 1, 1979). Craton's research in this regard was chiefly from the Bahamas, a non-sugar, largely non-plantation colony.

The upshot of all this for contemporary life, living, politics, and production is that women's centrality in the West Indian family and the positive impact of familial coherence are cornerstones for development and women's embrace of the growing opportunities for economic independence and advancement. In other words, there are no historic dysfunctionalities to constrain women *qua* women in themselves; the constraints are systemic in an evolved patriarchy and the capitalist mode of production. The struggle is on to unshackle these so as to accord a sustainable basis for women's development and empowerment.

In Africa, motherhood and child birth were celebrated in the family and the community. Under slavery in the West Indies, both were compromised and undermined unless the slave owner placed a value on the child as a potential replacement for a slave. He saw child bearing/child rearing in strictly economic terms. In Africa, women worked in the productive process in and out of the household, in *the interest* of her family and community. Under Caribbean slavery, the female slave had the surplus value of her work appropriated entirely by the plantation owner. Family life and sexual relations were generally without oppression in traditional Africa. In the Caribbean, under slavery, the female slave served production and sexual functions for those who controlled the slave mode of production and its exchange capitalist linkages. The very complex of functions that the female slave had to perform under slavery generated contradictions in and to the very system of slavery itself.

The official line of the planter-merchant elite and the Colonial Administrators during slavery painted the female slaves as troublemakers, deficient mothers, indolent workers, and veritable Jezebels, stuffed with immorality. In truth, the reverse was true: The female slaves were generally unwilling to make matters even more terrible or hazardous for themselves, their partners and their children. They were hard and skilled workers. They were good mothers who sought to marry African precepts and Christianity, and they inculcated much sound teaching to their offspring and their communities. It was the system of slavery and the enslavers at every turn that dehumanised them, including through rapes.

Writing on this very subject in the context of the southern United States of America — similar in this respect to the situation in St. Vincent and the Grenadines during slavery — Dr. Jennifer Hallam of the University of Pennsylvania, in an article entitled "The Slave Experience: Men, Women, and Gender" states as follows:

> *Whenever possible, black slave women manipulated their unique circumstances in the struggle for their personal dignity and that of their families. As often as black men, black women rebelled against the inhumanities of slave owners. Like their ancestors and counterparts in Africa, most slave women took their responsibility for their children before their own safety and freedom, provided for children not their own, and gave love even to those babies born from violence. For their experience and knowledge as caregivers, elderly women were among the most revered on plantations. For enslaved men, escape to freedom was the most promising avenue for preserving masculine identity and individual humanity. For the slave woman, faced with the double onus of being black and female and the added burden of dependent children, womanhood and personhood were easier gained within the slave community.*

The multiple skills acquired, developed, displayed, and transmitted to their offspring, especially the females, have kept Caribbean families and communities together up to the contemporary period. These skills have frequently not been rewarded by the market of the capitalist mode of production. These skills still await their full harnessing for national development. Rhoda Reddock in her book, published in 1994, and entitled *Women Labour and Politics in Trinidad and Tobago: A History* traces, excellently, this bundle of issues. Her summary advice is apt:

> *Today, more than ever, women are a political force which cannot be ignored. As always this movement is not monolithic — class and ethnic, as well as political divisions continue to be significant. The lesson to be learnt from*

our history is that it is not enough to fight for a more dominant role in this inequitable, patriarchal system. The challenge is to work towards transforming this system through the creation of new forms of human and social relations.

Angela Davis in an insightful article entitled "The Black Woman's Role in the Community of Slaves" (published in *The Black Scholar* magazine, December, 1971) makes a fascinating and relevant observation of enslaved women which has contemporary significance, thus:

"Traditionally the labour of females, domestic work is supposed to complement and confirm their inferiority.... But with the black slave women, there is a strange twist of affairs: in the infinite anguish of ministering to the needs of the men and children around her (who were not necessarily members of her immediate family), she was performing the only labour of love of the slave community which could not be directly and immediately claimed by the oppressor. There was no compensation for work in the fields, it served no useful purpose for the slaves. Domestic labour was the only meaningful labour for the slave community as a whole....

Precisely through performing the drudgery which has long been a central expression of the socially conditioned inferiority of women, the black woman in chains could help to lay the foundation for some degree of autonomy, both for herself and her men. Even as she was suffering from her unique oppression as female, she was thrust by the force of circumstances into the centre of the slave community. She was, therefore, essential to the survival of the community. Not all people have survived enslavement; hence her survival-oriented activities were themselves a form of resistance. Survival, moreover, was the prerequisite of all higher levels of struggle.

At the same time that the African female slave was daily engaging in practical acts of survival for her community, so too, was the Callinago and Garifuna woman during the Callinago-Garifuna nation's resistance against British colonialism, the British land grab and the genocide against the entire indigenous race. The Callinago, Garifuna and African women, in their survival and resistance, laid the basis for the strengthening of the family, community and nation after emancipation in 1838 and beyond. The women of the Madeiran and the Indian indentured servants subsequently did essentially the same for their ethnic group, their community and nation. All these women, oppressed in different forms and ways and at varying levels through class, ethnicity and gender were themselves the fulcrum around which the working class evolved and consolidated, and the society became increasingly creolised.

Biology aided these processes within first the slave mode of production and, after emancipation, the developing capitalist mode. In addition to her functions in the productive system, the female slave also performed a specific sexual role in the evolution of slave societies in the Caribbean, Brazil and the United States of America. In her path-breaking book, *Women in Class Society* (published by Monthly Review Press in 1978), Heleieth Saffioti wrote thus in the context of Brazil which applies aptly too, to St. Vincent and the Grenadines:

> *This sexual exploitation [of the female slave] augmented her reification, but at the same time helped to expose the true foundations of the caste society. She was a mere tool of her master's sexual pleasure and nothing indicated that this relation between slave and master ever went beyond 'the primitive and purely animal level of sexual contact'. Yet its issue, mulatto offspring, became a dynamic point of ferment for social and cultural tensions. By demanding the female slave administer to his sexual needs, the master was treating her at once as an object and as a human being. The sexual act became for her a process of reification, while her role as a thing (that is, an instrument of labour) assumed human aspects. The characteristic of sex, whose mode of operation is basically determined by the mode of production, came to have a weighty influence over the mode of production itself.*

Over time, procreation between males and females of different races/ethnicities contributed immensely to the solidity of the society and its creolisation within the capitalist mode of production, inclusive of its production relations upon, and within which the working class and the labour movement developed and consolidated. In the 2012 Population and Housing Census, 25,111 persons or 16.2 percent of the total population of St. Vincent and the Grenadines identified themselves, or were identified by the census-taker, as of "mixed" ethnicity, meaning an admixture of two or more of the following ethnicities:

Indigenous, African, White Caucasian, East Indian, Portuguese, or other ethnic group (Arab or Chinese).

Over time too, the development and consolidation of the capitalist mode of production with its external monopoly capitalist linkages, have shaped and ultimately determined the role and place of women in the working class, the labour movement and the society, enmeshed as they have been too, by the constellations of ethnicity and gender.

Historically, in the Caribbean and elsewhere, the women of the property-owning classes have always defended the exploitation of the working people, including working women. It is in the class interest of the women of property-owning families to do so even if the male head of the household is in patriarchal dominance over these women in the family. These two sets of women — bourgeois (property-owning) and working class women — have their gender in common but that commonality in no way masks or mutes the antagonism, objectively and subjectively, that exists between these two sets of women in the different and opposed classes.

Ankica Čakardić is persuasive when she writes as follows:

> *Socialist women's universal demands arose as an effect of social material motives and causes, ultimately finding more in common with men belonging to the same class than with the women of a higher class. This was in spite of the fact that, historically, the appearance of women in the labour market was frequently seen as an attempt to introduce cheaper competition for the male labour-force, which in turn influenced the decline in the price of labour. Considering the problem of the female labour force, socialist women point out that the workload of women is additionally aggravated by reproductive labour within the household sphere. One could almost speak of the 'first wave' of social-reproduction theory, when Zetkin states: 'Women are doubly oppressed, by capitalism and by their dependency in family life'.*

So, the apt questions are posed: How can a working woman attain her fullest freedom and optimal empowerment if the workingman is not freed of all his shackles? Can a working woman be truly free under monopoly capitalism? Of course not! To be sure, altered relations of production do not translate automatically to "gender" freedom in a social condition of patriarchy, ethnic and cultural restraints, the residue of the spirit of colonialism's gubernatorial governance and the baggage of neo-liberalism.

In the battle for women's full emancipation and empowerment, progressive women must establish the requisite alliances in the nation and abroad. Divisive and wrong-headed neo-liberal, bourgeois, petit-bourgeois, and biological feminism will not help the broad mass of women overburdened by monopoly capitalism, imperialism and their allies at home and abroad.

In St. Vincent and the Grenadines, the employment status of women, a central basis for the enlargement of their possibilities, needs exploration. The 2012 Census data tell us of the employment status of women as follows: Fifty-six (56) percent of the persons in paid employment in government are women; 36.4 percent in paid employment in statutory bodies are women; 38.6 percent in paid employment in private business are women; 30.9 percent in the self-employed category with paid employees are women; 32.1 percent in the self-employed category without paid employees are women; 29.7 percent in the apprenticeship group are women; and in unpaid family labour, 55.6 percent of the persons are women.

But this latter number of women in unpaid family labour receive no direct remuneration because, historically, this labour in the household is not recognised in the capitalist political economy as being worthy of remuneration. Rosa Luxemburg addressed precisely this issue in a 1904 article entitled *The Proletarian Woman* as follows:

> *This kind of work is not productive in the sense of the present capitalist economy no matter how enormous an achievement the sacrifices and energy spent, the thousand little efforts add up to. This is but the private affair of the worker, his happiness and blessing, and for this reason non-existent for our present society. As long as capitalism and the wage system rule, only that kind of work is considered productive which produces surplus value, which creates capitalist profit. From this point of view, the music-hall dancer whose legs sweep profit into her employer's pocket is a productive worker, whereas all the toil of the proletarian women and mothers in the four walls of their homes is considered unproductive. This sounds brutal and insane, but corresponds exactly to the brutality and insanity of our present capitalist economy.*

*And seeing this brutal reality clearly and sharply is the
proletarian woman's first task.*

It is also the proletarian man's first task! On the specific issue of "unpaid
family work" in St. Vincent and the Grenadines, 44.4 percent of the persons
who are engaged in it are males. The discourse here is not against unpaid family
labour, but the assessment or representation of it in societies as being without
productive value. Where there is productive value created through the wage
system the battle of working people (men and women) is for a better deal now,
be it through trade unionism or the government itself, directly or indirectly,
and a determined quest to transform the existing mode of production, inclusive
of its production relations, grounded in the principles of justice and equity in
the system of material reward for labour.

One category of wage labour in which women pre-dominate almost exclusively is that of the domestic or household worker. Due to their spatial distribution across a multiplicity of homes and the semi-private space in which they
work, it has not been practicable for them to be organised in trade unions; but
still there is no reason for them to be relegated to the margins of the labour
movement. Bourgeois feminism never brings them into their compass. Indeed,
many of these feminists personally treat these domestic or household workers
quite shabbily and with class disdain. Minimum wage laws exist for them, and
the ULP government has thrice increased these minimum wages since 2001,
but the monitoring of these laws needs to be drastically improved. Moreover,
the conditions of work of domestic/household employees demand far more
attention from the labour movement and the democratic state.

While it is true that the capitalist mode of production had not invented
women's oppression, it has made and shaped its own telling "woman question"
from the gender oppression of females inherited from a previous class-based
society. Still, socialist societies have been unable to address this matter as efficaciously as originally envisaged, suggesting therefore that gender inequality
possesses a "relative autonomy" that has to be addressed in a profoundly cultural way, but not disconnected at all from its material base. Thus, the reiteration
is required that the "woman question" can never be divorced from the nature
of the mode of production, especially its production relations.

Is this bundle of issues relating to women amenable to an equitable solution, given the fact that it has arisen and persisted, to one degree or another,
in different forms and content since the dawn of civilisation? In 1877, Lewis
H. Morgan attempted the frame of a possible answer in his impressive book,

Ancient Society, Researches in the Lines of Human Progress from Savagery through Barbarism to Civilisations (published in London), thus:

> Since the advent of civilisation, the outgrowth of property has been so immense; its forms so diversified, its uses so expanding and its management so intelligent in the interests of its owners that it has become, on the part of the people, an unmanageable power. The human mind stands bewildered in the presence of its own creation. The time will come, nevertheless, when human intelligence will rise to the mastery over property, and define the relations of the state to the property it protects, as well as the obligations and the limits of the rights of its owners. The interests of society are paramount to individual interests, and the two must be brought into just and harmonious relation. A mere property career is not the final destiny of mankind, if progress is to be the law of the future as it has been of the past. The time which has passed since civilisation began is but a fragment of the past duration of man's existence; and but a fragment of ages to come. The dissolution of society bids fair to become the termination of a career of which property is the end and aim, because such a career contains the elements of self-destruction. Democracy in government, brotherhood in society, equality in rights and privileges, and universal education, foreshadow the next higher plane of society to which experience, intelligence, and knowledge are steadily tending. It will be revival, in a higher form of liberty, equality and fraternity of the ancient gentes.

The fact that patriarchy has endured through slave, feudal, and capitalist modes of production does not elevate it above the material order as the ultimate determinant of human behaviour or gender relations, but signifies that it first arose in the class-based social formation of classical slavery, subsequently reinforced by succeeding modes of production. Modern patriarchy emerged and was buttressed in the Caribbean through slavery and the plantation system, initiated first by mercantile capitalism, then industrial capitalism, under the political instrument of European colonialism.

Comparative history teaches that as the productive forces, including labour, developed and private property and exchange arose through the creation of a surplus, class antagonisms emerged with a division of labour. Indeed Karl Marx and Frederich Engels held in *The German Ideology* that "the first division of labour is that between man and woman, for child breeding". Engels subsequently in 1884 insisted in *The Origin of the Family, Private Property and the State* that:

> *The first* class antagonism *which appears in history coincides with the development of the antagonism between man and woman in monogamian marriage, and the first class oppression with that of the female sex by the male. Monogamy was a great historical advance, but at the same time it inaugurated with slavery and private wealth, that epoch, lasting until today, in which each advance is likewise a relative regression.*

The earlier misery, or even the repression, in the dialectical advance of monogamy has, over-time, been muted or exacerbated by the cultural, ideational, legal and political apparatuses of the society underpinned by the evolving mode of production, especially the production relations within it. It follows that women's economic independence is vital in sustaining and strengthening the equality achieved in the cultural, juridical, ideational, and political spheres. The labour movement has been critical in the bolstering of women's economic independence. The "Labour" Administrations in St. Vincent and the Grenadines have facilitated all this through economic initiatives, the Education Revolution and social empowerment interventions of a strategic kind with and on behalf of women. But the work, the struggle, is far from complete.

Under conditions of "primitive" communalism in Europe and in pre-Columbian Caribbean societies there was in households a "mother right" condition and the affirmation of the dominant role of the women in such households. Slavery in the Caribbean led to the overthrow of "mother right" and was a historic defeat of the female sex. Yet, the matrifocal inheritance in households has persisted at the same time as the rise of a specific patriarchy and its subsequent sustenance by post- slavery capitalism. The plantation character of Caribbean capitalism, its integration with monopoly capitalist exchange relations globally, the cultural plural/social stratification structures fuelled by ethnicity and race, the propagation and acceptance of a substantially patriarchal religion, and colonial overrule, shaped the nature of the patriarchy that emerged.

Bourgeois feminism and its invariable companion, biological feminism, in the Caribbean and elsewhere, divide the working people and nation and thus limit their possibilities in the struggle against monopoly capitalism and neo-liberal hegemony. The labour movement and "Labour" governments must be guided accordingly in their policies and practical programmes for the further empowerment and liberation of women, and men. Ankica Čakardić puts it eloquently:

> As neo-liberalism successfully exploits gender for the purposes of its class-interests of capital, we are facing an important task of designing anti-capitalist strategies based on resistance to the market and its reproduction, thereupon focussing simultaneously on the domestic sphere and reproductive processes within the framework of the capitalist mode of production.

This line of argument was recently succinctly and impressively presented by Catherine Rottenberg, a Fellow in Sociology at Goldsmiths University (London), in an article entitled "Feminists Must Reject Neo-Liberalism If We Want to Sustain the Me Too Movement" and published in *The Independent* (May 29, 2018), a British newspaper.

Rottenberg advises thus:

> Over the past half decade, we have witnessed the rise of a peculiar variant of feminism, particularly in the US and the UK, a variant that has been unmoored from social ideals such as equality, rights and justice. I call this neoliberal feminism, *since it recognises gender inequality (differentiating itself from* post-feminism, *which focuses on individual women's "empowerment" and "choice." yet repudiates feminism) while simultaneously denying that socioeconomic and cultural structures shape our lives.*

> This is precisely the kind of feminism...in which women are construed as completely atomised, self-optimising, and entrepreneurial.

> Yes, neoliberal feminism might acknowledge the gender wage gap and sexual harassment as signs of continued

*inequality. But the solutions it posits elide the structural
and economic undergirding of these phenomena....*

*This feminism is also an unabashedly exclusionary one,
encompassing only so-called aspirational women in its
address...lending itself not only to neoliberal but also
neo-conservative agendas.*

Clearly, the complexities of and the limitations in effecting revolutionary change in a small, resource-challenged developing country like St. Vincent and the Grenadines, located within the orbit of the nearby-citadel of monopoly capitalism, demand both creative resistance and accommodation to neo-liberal globalisation. In a speech entitled "Ensuring our Tomorrows" and delivered to the 56th Annual Conference of the National Union of Public Workers of Barbados on March 16, 2000, Ralph Gonsalves (Political Leader of the ULP), stated in this regard as follows:

*In all the to and fro on globalisation, two opposed schools
of thought and action have emerged in the Caribbean
regarding our strategic and tactical approaches to this
phenomenon. One is of surrender, the other is of resistance, creative responses and the ennobling of our
Caribbean civilisation. Essentially, the advocates of the
surrender or 'roll-over-and-play-dead' option stress that
the region is incapable of resisting globalisation and
its effects, good and bad. Thus, they conclude that the
Caribbean civilisation should surrender its independence
(in fact, if not in name), its autonomy, its political and
cultural space, its right to self-determination and its
sovereignty, and allow the United States of America and
other advanced industrialised countries of the West to
remake us in their own image and likeness. This school
of thought and inaction has found support among rapacious, unpatriotic sections of the professional class and
the business community and those elements among the
youths who thrive on frivolities, hustling, and imitative
lumpen behaviour fashioned in the ghettos of North
America.*

*In countering the ravages occasioned by aspects of glo-
balisation from outside and the veritable domestic can-
cer bred by those who raise the flag of surrender from*

inside... the alternative path is one based on a culture of resistance and the creative building of our society, economy and civilisation.

This culture of resistance and creative construction of our socio-economic apparatus must be grounded in more than what the economic and political theorists and practitioners normally offer. We must go to the collective wisdom of the folk; the creative imagination of our people and their artists, poets and novelists; the tried and tested values which have come from the bowels of the people; and the abundant social capital which resides in our people.

Accordingly, a ten-point agenda was sketched for "our better tomorrows" touching and concerning education, new and more productive attitudes to work and production, economic development, reduction of socio-economic inequities and poverty alleviation, deepening political democracy, linking the Caribbean civilisation at home and that in the diaspora, building on the stock of social capital, a practical embrace of science and modern technology, resisting cultural imperialism, and regional integration. The ninth item on the agenda was stated thus: *"A pronounced emphasis on an enlarged and meaningful role for youth and women in the development process."* This agenda, marked out by the ULP leadership in opposition has been crafted into an even more compelling developmental narrative as the twenty-first century and its further challenges, including climate change, have unfolded.

In the labour movement's quest to build a feminism that goes beyond a simple identification or biological distinctions in order to facilitate change in the political economy and society, "Labour" must be mindful, in the words of Professor Catherine Rottenberg, that: *"The movement for gender equality is increasingly entangled with neoliberalism, which has mobilised feminism to advance political goals and enhance market value."* That kind of neo-liberal or bourgeois feminism does not threaten monopoly capitalism, its production relations, its cultural baggage, and the very patriarchy which it sustains. It is central to the labour movement's agenda to challenge monopoly capitalism and to ensure that a better way is possible for all humanity (men and women) and the diverse peoples within it.

Much progress has been made in the economic, social and political advances of women in St. Vincent and the Grenadines, regionally and globally, particularly since the initiation and unfolding of the United Nations Decade for

Women, 1976-1985. Still, a great deal remains to be done in this hugely uneven developmental process for all humanity, women and men. One central developmental issue for women, and men, remains to be resolved in the on-going global quest "to integrate women into development". Over twenty years ago, Geertie Lycklama à Nieholt addressed this matter wisely, and still relevantly, in an essay entitled "Women and Development: Some Theoretical and Practical Considerations" [published in a 1997 book, edited by Elsa Leo-Rhynie, Barbara Bailey, and Christine Barrow, *Gender – A Multi-Disciplinary Perspective*] by clarifying that the "integration of women" has mostly led to "integration into mainstream capitalist development". Persuasively, she argued that:

> *Not only are women thus institutionalised within a type of development which is capitalist in nature, but also this type of development is patriarchal in nature and biased against women. Feminists have criticised the strategy and pointed out that women are already fully integrated into development, since in fact, without all the work that women are doing, there would be no development. The problem is that women's work (domestic work, subsistence production, bringing up the next generation and caring for the sick and elderly) is not recognised as valuable work in comparison with wage work. Women are usually subsumed under family and therefore it is thought that they, like their children, are being provided for by the husband or father. This assumption is not true for millions of women. Such a strategy denies the conflicts of interest which often exist between women and men and the unequal distribution of power among them. The integration and institutionalism of women into mainstream development without transformation of that type of development will in many cases only lead to a further undermining of women's socio-economic position; we have witnessed this process often during the past few decades. Institutionalisation is not a neutral process. It is very important to critically assess into what one is being institutionalised, how and under what conditions. Women and development is a highly political phenomenon which needs to be recognised as such.*

That is a central enduring question yet to be fully resolved in the political economy. To be sure, while much theorising and analysis on "feminism" and the "women" question have enhanced our understanding and uplifting corrective actions, a central perplexing query still remains: *Why Are Women Oppressed.* That is actually the title of a fascinating book written by an Icelandic scholar, Anna G. Jonasdottier, and published in 1991 by Temple University Press in Philadelphia, USA. She posed the query thus:

> *Why, or how, do men's social and political power positions with respect to women persist even in contemporary Western societies where women and men are seen as formally/legally equal individuals, where almost all adult women are fully or partly employed, where there is a high proposition of well-educated women, and where state welfare arrangements, which absolutely benefit women, are relatively well-developed.*

This query has resonance, too, in our Caribbean. As Jonasdottier observes: *"Even though equality exists in the form of legal rights and formally equal opportunities, there must be some underlying mechanisms that curtail women's actual possibilities of realising their opportunities."* Upon a review of the literature of this fundamental and inter-connected issue, she acknowledges the powerful analytic salience of "the historical materialist" approach but offers an alternative mode of theorising about contemporary patriarchy which goes beyond "socialist feminism" to focus on "a specific socio-sexual struggle". In other words, she focusses on "sexuality and love" rather than the economy and work. Yet her focussed categories are profoundly connected to and grounded upon the economy and work of women and men. The debate continues.

While the ongoing debate on the theoretical questions (which contain profoundly practical implications) ensues, there are urgent tasks regarding the empowerment and development of women, and men that must continue to be addressed. Central to these ongoing endeavours is the requisite for *solidarity* among women and men, particularly those increasingly marginalised by monopoly capitalism and neo-liberalism, to improve and transform for the better, their lives, living and production. In this regard is the apt observation of the Caribbean scholar, Alicia Trotz, in a monograph *Gender, Generation and Memory: Remembering a Future Caribbean* [Working Paper No. 14, 2008, Centre for Gender and Development, University of the West Indies, Cave Hill].

> *In some ways the limited successes of feminism in crossing some institutional barriers has led to greater ideological conservatism among a younger generation of women who shy away from identifying themselves as*

feminist....Young women seem to draw on individualistic language of self-respect and do not make sustained links between their experiences and the wider landscape in which such inequalities are embedded....We might well ask whether neo-liberal emphases on the self are being manifested in the ways in which responses to discontent are increasingly individualised and privatised.

Those are the challenges that face activists today as we engage a new generation.

CHAPTER IX

SUMMATION AND CONCLUDING REFLECTIONS ON THE LABOUR MOVEMENT

Formal emancipation for those who laboured without pay came on August 1, 1838. The formal end of slavery did not bring about the material upliftment of the working people. The exploitation, in economic terms, was no longer of the entire value of the slaves' labour power. The period of the legal appropriation of the workers' surplus value under an evolving capitalist mode of production was instituted. Henceforth, what was paid to the workers was that portion of their created value which was deemed necessary for the basic necessities of life. For nearly 100 years after the abolition of the enslavement of African bodies in St. Vincent, the nominal value of the wages of workers remained the same.

Industrial capitalism and its representatives in Britain removed the shackles of slavery, but the plantation system, buttressed by European (specifically British) racism, remained intact nevertheless. It was not until the mid-1980s, some 140 years after slavery's abolition that the last vestiges of plantation system finally disintegrated, although its unravelling commenced a decade or so earlier. Racism, that malaise of the hearts and minds and an instrument of socio-political domination by the British, remained robust for 100 years after slavery's end. It then lingered on, became frayed, and finally through the fever of history, inclusive of intense social democratic struggles, the evolution of the political economy and the alteration of production relations, racism or ethnic prejudice or discrimination dissipated from institutional governance and social relations, save and except for insignificant, diffused, though troubling, residues. A debilitating patriarchy still endures, buttressed by monopoly capitalism and neo-liberalism, even though gender discrimination no longer exists legally, amidst many-sided advancement and empowerment of, by, and for women.

To be sure, slavery's end meant that, legally, the worker (the former slave) was able to sell his or her labour power to whichever employer he or she chose; or, indeed not to sell his or her labour power at all, or to become engaged in own-account economic activity. However, the notional freedom to do something and the possession of the actual capacity to do so are two different things, entirely. Thus, most workers remained tied through paid employment and residence on this or that plantation. Even 100 years after slavery's termination, slightly over 100 plantations still controlled over two-thirds of the arable land in St. Vincent, a predominantly agrarian economy.

Admittedly, many labourers having been formally freed from enslavement, left the plantations and built "free" villages, based substantially on own-account artisanal work or peasant farming on the fringes of Crown Land, or subsistence fishing. Over time, educators and entrepreneurs arose from among these sturdy rebels against the plantation life.

During slavery and, for over 100 years, thereafter, there was a concerted effort by colonial officialdom and the planter-merchant elites to corral the population into embracing the Anglican religion — the established religion in Britain since the Reformation and Henry VIII's break with Roman Catholicism in the first half of the sixteenth century. The Callinago, the Garifuna, and the African people who were forcibly ripped from their continent were actively encouraged into Anglicanism. Methodism was a tolerated alternative of the colonial regime, and much less so Roman Catholicism, until the Portuguese indentured labourers from Madeira arrived between 1845 and 1850 and stayed largely true to the Catholicism of their homeland.

Actively discouraged by colonial officialdom, the planter-merchant elite, the Anglicans, Methodists, and Roman Catholics, were forms of indigenous religious worship. The traditional spiritualism of the Callinago, and the infusion of African religious beliefs by the enforced arrivants from Africa and the Garifuna were denounced by the Euro-centrics in government, commerce and religion. Specifically disdained were "Shakerism" and its adherents — "Shakers" or "Spiritual Baptists". Indeed, in 1912, the colonial legislature passed the Shakerism (Prohibition) Ordinance which made illegal the practice of this branch of Christian pilgrim witness, infused with African religious forms. Between then and 1953, dozens of Spiritual Baptists were arrested, charged and imprisoned for practicing the religion of their choice. It was not until 1962 that the Prohibition Ordinance of 1912 was formally repealed. Mc Intosh, Joshua and Cato were in the forefront of demanding an end to the proscription against "Shakerism". Later, Parnel Campbell, a Spiritual Baptist leader and distinguished

Attorney General during the NDP governance, advanced mightily the cause of Spiritual Baptists who were accorded, even though grudgingly, widespread official acceptance. Ralph Gonsalves, although not a Spiritual Baptist, also helped in his own way: He was the Warden of the Spiritual Baptists' Friendly Society and the lawyer for the Spiritual Baptist Organisation for St. Vincent and the Grenadines for 20 years (1981-2001) prior to his assumption of the Office of the Prime Minister. He has remained close to the membership and leadership of the Spiritual Baptists.

According to the Population and Housing Census of 2012, the Spiritual Baptists account for approximately 10 percent of the population, slightly more than the Methodists, and almost four percentage points above the Roman Catholics. The Anglicans number 14 percent, a fall from 48 percent in 1980, and over 60 percent of the population two decades earlier. Constitutional de-colonisation and cultural-religious influences from North America ensure that Pentecostals and Evangelicals number in excess of 30 percent. The Seventh Day Adventist religion, a twentieth century entry into St. Vincent and the Grenadines, amounts to over 12 percent of the population. This religion has a strong base among persons of Indian origin, the descendants of the Indian indentured labourers who arrived between 1861 and 1881. In total, some 70 percent of the population are adherents of religions which believe in full immersion water baptism; about 30 percent (Anglicans, Methodists, Roman Catholics) practice their traditional baptism of the sprinkling of "holy water" on infants.

The shift in religious affiliations represents, in part, the population's casting off older forms and embracing newer ones. This change is reflective of a more libertarian questioning of traditional authority structures, yet committed to order, discipline, renewal, and redemption. It is a metaphor, too, for the social democratic alterations which have been taking place in St. Vincent and the Grenadines, particularly since the mid-1930s, save and except for the period (1984-2001) of the counter-revolution of James Mitchell's NDP against social democracy.

The demographics of labour are part of the foundation of the political economy. By the mid-1840s, the available labour force of former enslaved Africans was insufficient to meet the production requisites of the plantation economy. Madeira was a logical place from which to source labour. The island was tropical/sub-tropical. It had a history of sugar cane cultivation. The economy of that island was challenged and workers were looking for employment opportunities elsewhere. The island was part of Portugal, which had friendly treaty arrangements with Britain since the 14th century, and it was a port of call in the triangular trade between Europe, Africa and the Caribbean. So, some 2,000 Madeirans were recruited as indentured servants bound for St. Vincent between 1845 and 1850. Between 1861 until 1881, East Indians numbering some 2,500 were brought to St. Vincent similarly as indentured servants.

Between the early 1880s and the global capitalist economic depression of 1929-1931, the economy of St. Vincent was horribly gutted and was reduced to a near ruinous condition. "Free" trade arrangements and the competition from European beet sugar in the British market; natural disasters (the terrible hurricanes of 1898 and 1926; the massive volcanic eruption of 1902),;effective competition from elsewhere in respect of price, quality, and supply for St. Vincent's arrowroot starch and cotton; and plant diseases, especially in the case of cotton all conspired to undermine, in turn, the principal export commodities of cane sugar, arrowroot starch and raw cotton. In the 50 years between 1881 and 1931, the population barely grew because of mass migration of some 40,000 Vincentians to other countries (mainly the Eastern Caribbean islands of Trinidad and Barbados, British Guiana, Cuba, Venezuela, Central America, and the United States of America). Emigration was the option to escape poverty in an economy which was a veritable disaster, with little or no prospects for sustained amelioration.

Matters were soon to get worse. The world economic depression in capitalist North America and Europe further sent the economy of St. Vincent into a more pronounced tail spin: decline in export trade, huge increases in the price of imported commodities and an additional rise in unemployment. The colonial government had absolutely no clue as to a credible developmental path forward. The planter-merchant elite were also clueless. There was a profound economic and political crisis. The principals were innocent of the extent of the condition and they had no idea as to an alternative path. So, the people — the workers, peasants, and the small middle class — revolted. The anti-colonial uprising of October 1935, as did others in the British West Indies in the 1930s, ushered in the beginnings of the social democratic revolution, many tasks of which are yet to be completed.

The uprising of 1935 brought George Augustus Mc Intosh to the centre-stage of the leadership of the national, mass political movement. Out of this historical juncture arose an organised political party, and the for the time structured trade unions were made permissible by appropriate legislation in 1933 and its subsequent amendments in the late 1930s and early 1940s. Over a 16-year period (1936-1951) the Mc Intosh-led. SVWA, SVLP, SVWU, and

SVPCU were politically dominant among the people but were a powerless minority in a colonial legislature in which the majority of the members were colonial officials and personages from the planter-merchant elite, selected and appointed by the Colonial Governor in consultation with his locally-based Colonial Administrator.

The Mc Intosh-led national mass movement pushed colonialism to introduce ameliorative measures designed to improve, even if marginally, the people's welfare. An improved Trade Union Ordinance was passed into law in 1950. In 1951, universal adult suffrage with no literacy qualifications for electors and no property qualifications for electoral candidates was introduced. Mc Intosh was a strong proponent of both measures, which facilitated the further evolution of the social democratic political project.

A series of events and evolutions in the political economy world-wide and regionally, including in St. Vincent and the Grenadines, engendered in the post-1930s a greater militancy among working people and national movements globally. These included the Second World War (1939-1945), the rise in political consciousness among subject peoples under the grip of colonialism; the contradictions within global capitalism the conflicts and struggles world-wide between monopoly capitalism led by the United States of America and a maturing socialism led by the Soviet Union (which was established in 1917), and gradual constitutional decolonization in the colonies, including St. Vincent and the Grenadines.

In 1951, the Eighth Army of Liberation led by George Charles and Ebenezer Joshua emerged in St. Vincent to contest the general elections of that year under universal adult suffrage. Mc Intosh, the tribune of the people since 1935, and his political organisations were brushed aside electorally by the ostensibly more militant and impatient Eighth Army. The machinations of colonialism, the immaturity of the leaders of the Eight Army, their undeveloped political consciousness, and the organizational weaknesses of the national mass movement, caused a deep split in the national movement itself. Undoubtedly, the split held back the advance of the process of social democracy and presaged the divisions in mass movement which are still with us today, although in a different form.

By 1957, a two-party system was in the making with Joshua's PPP — founded in 1952 — as the single largest political force, but its main competitor yet to be fully shaped. By 1961, Robert Milton Cato's SVLP — which was established in 1955 — consolidated itself as the PPP's principal political rival in the competitive electoral arena.

The changing nature of the political economy affected profoundly the contours of the political support of the PPP and SVLP respectively, and determined considerably their future. Joshua's PPP was based largely among the workers on the agricultural estates, particularly in North Windward, North Central Windward, South Central Windward, West St. George, North Leeward, and casual and unskilled workers at mainly state-operated entities, in and out of the central government, especially in Kingstown. The problem for Joshua's PPP was that plantation agriculture was unravelling and by the mid-1970s was, substantially, in its terminal stages. Sugar cane and arrowroot production on plantations had run their course by the early 1960s.

Meanwhile, in 1956, banana production emerged as the single most important export commodity with trade preferences in the United Kingdom market. By the mid-1960s, bananas had become dominant in export earnings. Bananas were grown principally on small farmers' holdings which increased in numbers as the plantations were dismantled and sub-divided. These more entrepreneurial and individualist small farmers found the populist message of Joshua's PPP and its railings against the plantocracy insufficiently appealing, even irrelevant, to their condition. More and more, they gravitated to the SVLP which, under Cato's leadership fashioned a political coalition between them, the teachers and public servants and workers who were becoming increasingly engaged in the non-plantation economy. The seeming modernity of the leadership of SVLP further cemented their appeal.

Alterations in the mode of production (productive forces and production relations) do not deliver automatically, precisely, uniformly, or immediately, resultant changes in the form, nature, and extent of political support for this or that contending political entity. The matter is far more complex and fluid, awash with influences from personalities, accidents and a veritable parallelogram of forces. The application of an historical materialistic analysis is not mechanistic. It is not the simple resolution of an elementary mathematical problem. It is dialectical and thus immersed in contradictions to unravel and resolve in their changing dimensions.

But undoubtedly, the process of the disintegration of plantation agriculture and the ongoing constitutional decolonisation undermined the efficacy of Joshua's PPP, although it was established to bring about precisely the achievements of these two central goals. Joshua and his PPP were unable to reset their policies and programmatic platform beyond their early blasts against the plantocracy and colonialism. In the process, the PPP lost its popular appeal by 1974. Thereafter, he and his party became caricatures of their former selves, so much so that by 1979 backwardness, opportunism and his personal antipathy to Cato caused him to degenerate into actually opposing independence for St. Vincent and the Grenadines.

Milton Cato's SVLP was founded in 1955, the year before bananas became ascendant in the economy. In government between 1967 and 1984, save and except for a two-year (1972-1974) interposition of an opportunistic coalition between Joshua's PPP and a lone individual, James Mitchell of the Grenadines, Cato's SVLP altered the shape of the economy, oversaw the substantial dismantling of the plantation economy, achieved internal self-government and independence, modernised the State apparatus, established a state economic sector in conjunction with a modernising capitalism, consolidated good governance, and instituted a bundle of core social democratic initiatives in education, health, housing, and social security. Indeed, Cato's SVLP built upon and extended immensely the process of the social democratic revolution which was initiated and had its solid foundation laid under the successive leaderships of the national mass movement by Mc Intosh and Joshua.

The undoing of Cato and the SVLP was that they failed and/or refused to grasp the on-rushing changes of modern globalisation, the infrastructure requisites (including jet airport and international airport development) for tourism, and at the same time the intellectual challenges to globalisation, through "New World", "Black Power", "socialist", or "Marxist" critiques or an amalgam of them. In the upshot, Cato and the SVLP were unable to bridge what appeared to be a growing chasm between them, on the one hand, and the younger professionals, university graduates, secondary school students, and radicalized working people, on the other. The seeming unbridgeable gulf took on cultural, political and generational guises, but it was grounded in differing approaches or emphases towards modern capitalist globalisation. Cato's SVLP was more inclined to accommodate itself to the dictates of monopoly capitalism. The younger generation demanded resistance and creative responses where possible. Still, the younger intellectuals, professionals, university graduates, and radicalised working people lacked clarity, cohesion and political maturity. They were largely isolated from the mass of working people and their socio-cultural institutions, including religious constellations.

In the early mid-1970s, a plethora of nationalist, cultural, social democratic, socialist-oriented, and socialist organisations, mainly, BLAC, OBCA, YSG, YULIMO, ARWEE, DFM, PDM, and UPM were formed. Lurking outside of the many nationalist, progressive, anti-colonial, anti-imperialist political groups was James Mitchell and his NDP, founded in 1975 in the aftermath of the collapse of the PPP-Mitchell coalition government in September 1974 and the subsequent general elections of December 1974, in which the Mitchell-led MSP was decimated politically, save and except in the Grenadines where Mitchell won a comfortable, but not overwhelming victory.

In the watershed general elections of December 1979, the first after independence was attained, three main options faced the electorate: the SVLP in the apparently safe hands of Milton Cato; the NDP, a hastily put-together group of largely disparate individual office-seekers under the leadership of Mitchell whose recent stint in government (1972-1974) had ended with his image hugely diminished; and the UPM, a left-wing, anti-imperialist, socialist-oriented/social democratic coalition of three entities (YULIMO, ARWEE, PDM) under the untried leadership troika of Parnel Campbell, Ralph Gonsalves, and Renwick Rose. By then, Joshua's PPP had become a laughable non-entity.

In the event, the people chose Cato's SVLP with a solid plurality of votes and an eleven-to-two majority of seats, the two being NDP candidates, even though Mitchell was not one of them.

Mitchell was yet to hitch his ideological moorings fully to what later became to be his true self, an advocate of neo-liberalism to the right of centre. He called himself, quite generously, "a centrist liberal". There were more than glimpses of it while he was in the opposition, but he masked it with his easy-going leadership style, his evident love for reading that informed his articulation of issues, his unfussiness about matters of protocol, his commitment to regional integration in the Caribbean, his agronomist's quest for land reform, and his patriotism. Mitchell benefited in 1984 from the popular agitation of the political "left" and the labour movement in the 1975-1984 period without he and/or his NDP being at the centre of the anti-SVLP protests and agitation.

Mitchell never showed any consistent endorsement or propagation of social democratic ideas or implementation of an agenda to assist in the completion of the tasks of the social democratic revolution of Mc Intosh, Joshua and Cato. Mitchell's NDP was tied unequivocally to the Washington Consensus of the late 1980s and 1990s, to the British monarchical system, to the Privy Council in London as the final court for St. Vincent and the Grenadines, to the hegemony of American imperialism, to Euro-centric cultural values and institutions, and to modern capitalism, including his wholly uncritical embrace of dubious foreign investors, for example, at Ottley Hall and in offshore banking. The bundle of issues which focused on "the social", "the democratic", "the nationalist", "the anti-colonial" and "the anti-imperialist" concerned Mitchell very little. At the end of Mitchell's NDP governance of nearly 17 years, St.

Vincent and the Grenadines had fewer persons employed than a decade earlier: a poverty of 37.5 percent of the population; indigence ("dirt poor" conditions) of 25.7 percent; social inequality at a very high score of the Gini Coefficient at 0.54; the access of secondary school education to only 39 percent of the 12-year olds; the accessibility of potable water and electricity to less than 70 percent of households; no programme for low-income housing; and a run-down health sector. Worse was the dead end scenario and hopelessness of his approach to the further development of St. Vincent and the Grenadines and the cynical learned helplessness that his government engendered. For example, Mitchell mouthed the idea of tourism development as a viable option for the country's economic advance, but without an education revolution and the building of an international airport or jet airport, tourism development was not possible; yet Mitchell's NDP failed to address the matters of education and airport access. All these horrible outcomes, and more, occurred at a time (1984-2000) when favourable economic conditions globally were in evidence, when the preferential market in Britain for the bananas from the Windward Islands (including St. Vincent and the Grenadines) had yet to be practically abolished, when oil was priced on the international market at under US $20 per barrel, and when natural disasters were far less frequent, less intense and much less damaging to life, limb,and the economy than is the case today.

James Mitchell before his ascendancy to the Office of Prime Minister in July 1984, and occasionally thereafter, demonstrated the skill of "talking left" and "tacking right", of mouthing people-oriented ideas but governing to the contrary.

Mitchell's NDP in effect led a counter-revolution against the social democratic revolution of the people and their leaders in the 1935-to-1984 years of Mc Intosh, Joshua, and Cato. Together they formed a continuum of a quest for social democracy, but Mitchell undermined it with the mirage of a "property-owning democracy" that he failed to deliver, and his embrace of neo-liberalism, hook, line, and sinker. He was never attuned to social solidarity, always to a robust individualism and a veritable Darwinian survival of the fittest. The triumphal era of Margaret Thatcher and Ronald Reagan suited him well;. They were his philosophical soul-mates; but he never understood that in a small, resource-challenged country on the periphery of monopoly capitalism, though nevertheless enmeshed in it, this rugged individualism, heroic as it may seem, would never work in St. Vincent and the Grenadines, if indeed anywhere else. Solidarity in the moulding of the social individual is always preferable to the dog-eat-dog "free market" world of the atomised individual.

The progressive, socialist-oriented, nationalist and anti-imperialist forces that coalesced with immense promise for the general elections of December 1979, blew their chances of possible governance or parliamentary representation by themselves, owing to their political immaturity, ideational confusion, organisational weaknesses, and an insufficiency of links with the people. It is not so much that they won no seats in the general elections of 1979 that was their defining failure. Indeed they had performed creditably with almost 14 percent of the popular vote; but their collective folly in allowing their coalition to disintegrate, delivered the progressive movement in St. Vincent and the Grenadines a major setback, a near-paralysing blow from which it took nearly two decades to recover fully. That disintegration, plus the collapse of the Grenada Revolution in October 1993 due to internecine blood-letting, shackled the advance of the progressive "left".

One wing of the progressive movement resident in the DFM/PDM sold itself, body and soul to Mitchell's NDP without being able to influence the NDP government, save and except in marginal ways. Indeed, the NDP remade most of them from their condition of underdeveloped political consciousness into apologists for neo-liberalism, austerity, imperialism and anti-people policies. In fact, they do not now even mask their intent or window-dress their language. They are "right-wing" philosophically and intend to govern that way. They plan, if given a chance to govern, to subvert the impressive social democratic gains the ULP has chalked up for the people since March 29, 2001, uninterruptedly.

The other wing of the progressive movement — the UPM of Oscar Allen, Ralph Gonsalves, and Renwick Rose — was to splinter in August – October 1982 on ideological grounds. The UPM soldiered on politically on the fringes until it withered on the political vine. The MNU of Ralph Gonsalves, Caspar London, and Cecil Blazer Williams devised a clearer path through all the hubris and worked tirelessly among the people for twelve years (1982-1994) until its merger with the SVLP as the ULP. In the process the ULP emerged as a united, advanced social democratic, anti-imperialist, regionalist, and people-centred political party. It has been and is the natural inheritor of the best of the social democratic emphases of Mc Intosh, Joshua and Cato. It has been and is providing the leadership to consolidate, extend, and complete the central tasks of the social democratic revolution in a new period of immense complexities of monopoly capitalism, a neo-liberal disorder, trade liberalisation, the revolution in information technology, and debilitating climate change.

The ULP government has had to elaborate a people-centred vision: an economic strategy premised on the quest to build a modern, competitive, many-sided, post-colonial economy that is at once national, regional and global, driven by integrated tri-partite economic sectors (the State, private sector, and cooperative sectors); an overarching socio-cultural rubric of the further ennoblement and development of our Caribbean civilisation, including its Vincentian component; a broadening and deepening of political democracy and good governance; a bundle of regional integration policies to bolster the political and socio-economic development through the OECS, CARICOM, the Bolivarian Alternative for our America (ALBA), the Association of Caribbean States (ACS), and the Community of States of Latin America and the Caribbean (CELAC); a coherent, independent foreign policy attuned to the country's interests but within the context of the fundamental precepts of the Charter of the United Nations; and the fashioning of specific policies and detailed programmes for the social democratic agenda and the sustainable socio-economic development of St. Vincent and the Grenadines, within the framework of the 17 Sustainable Development Goals elaborated by the United Nations. In effect, the ULP has crafted a compelling developmental narrative to roll-back or reverse the Mitchell counter-revolution and restore the trajectory of social democracy in a more advanced form and content in a new, and even more challenging period.

In its interface with monopoly capitalism, neo-liberalism and imperialism, the ULP government has adopted a strategic posture of resistance and creative response *and* accommodation where necessary and desirable. It is a complex exercise demanding clarity of thought, focused organisation and astute leadership. The elaboration of the thesis of "Small State Exceptionalism" and the assiduous building of solidarity alliances in the regional and international arena are vital in the pursuance of the ULP's strategic approaches on behalf of the people.

Meanwhile, sections of the leadership of the trade unions, especially the public sector unions, are in danger of seeking selfishly to build or consolidate a "labour aristocracy" in opposition to the interests of other workers who are less well remunerated, protected or secured in their employment, and in conflict, objectively, with the poor, indigent and the struggling small farmers.

An important query arises from the evolution of the working class in St. Vincent and the Grenadines, thus: Has there really emerged as yet a "labour aristocracy" that undermines the solidarity of the labour movement and the further development of the social democratic revolution?

Neither the working class nor the membership of trade unions in St. Vincent and the Grenadines and elsewhere is homogenous. There are material and social differences or differentiations in their composition. As a consequence, the concept of a "labour aristocracy" was fashioned first in Britain in the late 19th century but since then its applicability has been extended to the condition of the working people in other developed capitalist countries and those of the developing world.

The British historian Eric J. Hobsbawm in an essay entitled "The Labour Aristocracy in Nineteenth-Century Britain", originally published in 1954 (republished in 1964 in a volume, *Labouring Men: Studies in History of Labour*) identified the following criteria of a "labour aristocracy":

> *First, the level and regularity of a worker's earnings; second, his prospects of social security; third, his conditions of work including the way he was treated by foremen and masters; fourth, his relations with the social strata above and below him; fifth, his general conditions of living; lastly his prospects of future advancement and those of his children.*

Hobsbawm contended that the starting-point for the modern debate on "labour aristocracy" crystallises around and identification of "a distinctive upper strata of the working class, better paid, better treated and generally regarded as more 'respectable' and politically moderate compared to the mass of the proletariat."

In an article published in *Monthly Review* (December 1, 2012) entitled "Lenin and the 'Aristocracy of Labour'." Eric Hobsbawm traces the concept "labour aristocracy" thus:

> *The term itself is almost certainly derived from a passage written by [Frederick] Engels in 1885 and reprinted in the introduction to the 1892 edition of* The Condition of the Working Class in England in 1844 *which speaks of the great English trade unions as forming 'an aristocracy among the working class'.*

> *The actual phrase may be attributable to Engels, but the concept was familiar in English politics-social debate, particularly in the 1880s. It was generally accepted that the working class in Britain at this period contained a favoured stratum — a minority but a numerically*

large one — which was not unusually identified with
the 'artisans' (that is, the skilled employed craftsman
and workers) and more especially with those organised
in trade unions or other working-class organisations.

V.I. Lenin, the leader of the Bolshevik Revolution in Russia, emphasised the presence of a "labour aristocracy' in Britain as outlined in his book, published in 1917, *Imperialism: The Highest Stage of Capitalism.* Lenin argued that British capitalism's "vast colonial possessions and a monopolist position in world markets" by the mid-19th century had created a small stratum of "labour aristocrats" within wider working class in Britain and an impoverished under-class of workers in the colonies. This "labour aristocracy" tended to be selfish, defended imperialism, was chauvinist, and divisive in the working class movement. By 1920, in his "Preliminary Draft Theses on the Agrarian Question for the Second Congress of the International." Lenin critiqued these workers who concerned themselves *"exclusively with their narrow craft, narrow trade interests, and smugly confine themselves to care and concern for improving their own, sometimes tolerable, petty bourgeois conditions".*

In the contemporary political economy, globally, the concept of "labour aristocracy" is not applicable only to skilled machinists, craftsmen and other industrial workers as in the late 19th century and early 20th century. Today, more highly paid workers in information technology, specialised services, and the better-paid employees in the public sector (especially those with tenured security), are identified as part of the "labour aristocracy" or one in the making.

The concept of a "labour aristocracy" in the modern period has been critiqued as limited as an explanatory tool on several grounds: 1) Race, gender, and social status criss-cross to provide complexities to the traditional concept; 2) the political behaviour of a "labour aristocracy" is not predicted, necessarily, on its income and role in the social organisation of labour; and 3) labour solidarity is a value which a "labour aristocracy" often shares with less well-off workers. Indeed, it has been suggested that lowly-paid workers are no more militant as a group in pursuance of their interests than better-paid workers.

While it is true that all working people have a particular relationship to the means of production which accordingly grounds their commonality, it is nevertheless true that there exists different strata among the working class in the public and private sectors, utilizing the criteria identified above by Hobsbawm. Let us look at the factual situation in St. Vincent and the Grenadines.

The Population and Housing Census Report, 2012, presents three bundles of data of relevance regarding employment by "status." by "occupation." and by "industry":

TABLE I

Employed Population by Status in Employment and Sex, 2012

Status in Employment	Sex				Total	%
	Male	%	Female	%		
Paid Employee, Government (Local and Central Government)	3,839	44.0	4,891	56.0	8,731	21.4
Paid Employee, State Owned Company/Statutory Board	1,069	63.6	612	36.4	1,681	4.1
Paid Employee, Private Business	10,684	61.4	6,712	38.6	17,396	42.6
Paid Employee, Private Home	736	37.3	1,238	62.7	1,973	4.8
Own Business with Paid Employees	873	69.1	390	30.9	1,263	3.1
Own Business without Paid Employees (Self-Employed)	5,327	67.9	2,523	32.1	7,850	19.2
Apprentice/Learners	45	70.3	19	29.7	64	0.2
Unpaid Family Worker/ Employee	198	44.4	248	55.6	445	1.1
Volunteer Worker	64	57.1	48	42.9	112	0.3
Other	271	70.4	114	29.6	384	0.9
Don't Know	58	81.7	13	18.3	70	0.2
Not Stated	527	61.9	324	38.1	851	2.1
Total	**23,690**	**58.0**	**17,131**	**42.0**	**40,821**	**100**

The data on *Employment by Status* (Table I) show that the private sector employs most persons but the single largest employer (25.5 percent) is the Government (Local and Central Government and State Enterprises).

TABLE II

Currently Employed Population by Occupational Group, 2012

Occupational Group	Count			%		
	Male	Female	Total	Male	Female	Total
Managers	968	661	**1,629**	4.1	3.9	**4.0**
Professionals	1,553	2,991	**4,544**	6.6	17.5	**11.1**
Technicians and associate professionals	1,436	1,470	**2,906**	6.1	8.6	**7.1**
Clerical support workers	606	1,905	**2,511**	2.6	11.1	**6.2**

Service and sales workers	4,442	6,188	10,630	18.8	36.1	**26.0**
Skilled agricultural, forestry and fishery workers	4,230	880	**5,110**	17.9	5.1	**12.5**
Craft and related trades workers	4,995	472	**5,467**	21.1	2.8	**13.4**
Plant and machine operators, and assemblers	1,928	110	**2,038**	8.1	0.6	**5.0**
Elementary occupations	3,246	2,220	**5,466**	13.7	13.0	**13.4**
Not Stated	286	234	**520**	1.2	1.4	**1.3**
Total	**23,690**	**17,131**	**40,821**	**100**	**100**	**100**

The data in Table II show that 22.2 percent of the employed population, *by occupation*, comprise managers, professionals, technicians, and associate professionals. By and large, these are among the better-paid workers in the country. Conversely, elementary occupations, service and sales workers, and clerical support workers are among the more lowly paid. These categories in the aggregate account for 45.6 percent of the employed population.

TABLE III

Currently Employed Population by Industry, 2012

Industry	Count			%		
	Male	Female	Total	Male	Female	Total
Agriculture, Forestry and Fishing	3,903	905	**4,808**	16.5	5.3	**11.8**
Mining and quarrying	34	7	**41**	0.1	0.0	**0.1**
Manufacturing	1,446	615	**2,061**	6.1	3.6	**5.1**
Electricity, gas, steam and air conditioning supply	276	60	**336**	1.2	0.4	**0.8**
Water supply; sewerage, waste management and remediation activities	270	54	**324**	1.1	0.3	**0.8**
Construction	4,433	317	**4,750**	18.7	1.9	**11.6**
Wholesale and retail trade; repair of motor vehicles and motorcycles	3,370	3,512	**6,882**	14.2	20.5	**16.9**
Transportation and storage	2,571	525	**3,096**	10.9	3.1	**7.6**
Accommodation and food service activities	1,234	1,788	**3,022**	5.2	10.4	**7.4**
Information and communication	304	228	**532**	1.3	1.3	**1.3**
Financial and insurance activities	240	552	**792**	1.0	3.2	**1.9**

Real estate activities	29	19	**48**	0.1	0.1	**0.1**
Professional, scientific and technical activities	221	375	**596**	0.9	2.2	**1.5**
Administrative and support service activities	765	416	**1,181**	3.2	2.4	**2.9**
Public administration and defence; compulsory social security	2,125	1,851	**3,976**	9.0	10.8	**9.7**
Education	840	2,328	**3,168**	3.6	13.6	**7.8**
Human health and social work activities	262	1,136	**1,398**	1.1	6.6	**3.4**
Arts, entertainment and recreation	150	208	**358**	0.6	1.2	**0.9**
Other service activities	433	449	**882**	1.8	2.6	**2.2**
Activities of households as employers	470	1,494	**1,964**	2.0	8.7	**4.8**
Activities of extra-territori al organizations & bodies	14	17	**31**	0.1	0.1	**0.1**
Not Stated	300	275	**575**	1.3	1.6	**1.4**
Female	**23,690**	**17,131**	**40,821**	**100**	**100**	**100**

The data on employment by industry (Table III) show that public administration, defence, social security, education, health, and social work, account for over one-fifth (20.9 percent) of the employed population by industry. Wholesale and retail trade employ 16.9 percent of the employed population. Agriculture, forestry and fishing employ 11.8 percent, and accommodation and food services employ 7.4 percent.

In the 2018 Budget (Estimates of Revenue and Expenditure) of the central government, compensation to employees and retirement benefits for employees amount to 60 percent of the recurrent budget, exclusive of amortization and the sinking fund contribution for the payment of the public debt. When the latter two debt-related items are included, the compensation and retirement benefits for employees amount to 47 percent of the overall recurrent budget. Thus, central government's employees' salaries, wages, allowances, retirement benefits (including the government's contribution to the National Insurance Services – NIS) take a disproportionate chunk of government's recurrent spending. Indeed, compensation and retirement benefits for central government employees amount to 59.2 percent of central government's current revenue (tax revenue and non-tax revenue).

It is to be noted that "retirement benefits" constitute the single largest growth item in the government's recurrent spending. Currently, central government's employees (civil servants, nurses, doctors, teachers, police officers) who have security of tenure — over 90 percent of the employees have secured tenure — receive two pensions: a non-contributory State pension which, at its highest, amounts to almost 67 percent of the retiree's salary (33 1/3 years multiplied by 2 percent annually); and a contributory pension from the NIS (the government as employer pays a monthly contribution of 5.5 percent of the employee's salary, the employee pays 4.5 percent) which at its maximum will provide a pension of 60 percent of the salary. In other words, as the NIS matures, the employee may receive up to 127 percent of his/her salary as the aggregate pension (non-contributory pension from the government and the contributory NIS pension). Clearly, this is unsustainable and requires reform! The rest of the working people and the peasantry will revolt against what would in effect be unsustainable pensions for a veritable "labour aristocracy." since such pension payments will come at the expense of other working people and producers who are not government employees.

Since 2001, the salaries of public servants have increased in *real terms* by over 40 percent (that is after a discount of the nominal increases for inflation), much above the real (not nominal) increase in national productivity measured in terms of the growth of the Gross Domestic Product. These salary increases have been occasioned by regular salary enhancements, increases in allowances, a reclassification exercise utilizing the most favourable private sector comparators, and an in-built 2 percent annual increment for more than one-half of the public servants who are yet to reach at the top of their salary scales. The public servants' real salary enhancements have been buttressed too, by changes in the rate of taxation for all personal income earners. At the top, the marginal tax rate has been reduced from 40 percent to 30 percent, a decrease in the personal income tax rate of 25 percent; and at the bottom, an increase in the income threshold from $12,000 to $20,000 annually below which no personal income tax is assessed to be paid.

Further, public servants have very generous study leave provisions, maternity and sick leave provisions;, 100 percent house mortgages (no down-payment mortgages), good prospects for advancement, and, generally speaking, good conditions of work.

In the 1950s and 1960s, the principal working class leader, Ebenezer Joshua, invariably denounced public servants as "the gentry" who did not have the interest of the labouring masses at heart. This rhetoric of Joshua was highly overblown, stylized. and inaccurate. He verbally attacked public servants because he was satisfied that politically they were aligned against him and were partial to the decaying colonial order; but Joshua's accusations and fulminations were grounded on a grain of truth about the public servants' elevated role in the social organisation of labour, their status, their material benefits, comparatively. Of course, the material benefits for the public servants today far exceed, in real terms, those of Joshua's era.

Still, the bulk of the public servants today are the sons and daughters of the lower-strata working class and the peasantry. No one can reasonably begrudge them the material benefits of their jobs or their social status. Further, the majority of them are progressive, social democratic and in solidarity with their other "brothers and sisters" among the broad mass of the working people. Moreover, overwhelmingly, they are appreciative of their material benefits, prospects for advancement and social status. They are also very reasonable in their demands for further enhancements to their salaries, allowances and working conditions. They realise too, that the current pension arrangements are not sustainable and unfair to their counterparts in the working class who, objectively, will be required to fund these unsustainable pensions.

But a very small section of the public servants, agitated by partisan opposition politics, by some leaders in the public service unions who are motivated by personal agendas or partisan political preferences, and a profound sense of entitlement grounded in the philosophy or idea of the creation or consolidation of a "labour aristocracy." pursue wholly selfish aims against the interest of the bulk of public servants, the working people and the nation. This tiny section of public servants, inclusive of a few in the leadership of public sector trade unions, embrace some of the more backward ideas in the political economy of neo-liberalism and monopoly capitalism. Objectively, in their undeveloped political consciousness, they side with those who are bent on curtailing or reversing the tremendous gains of the social democratic revolution, despite its limitations, spearheaded by successive "labour" political leaderships: Mc Intosh, Joshua, Cato, and Gonsalves. Unwittingly or not, this backward section of the leadership of the public sector unions find common ground with those who hanker at a renewed counter-revolution against their own interests, against social democracy in St. Vincent and the Grenadines and the region. This is where the reactionary spirits of a "labour aristocracy" find comfort, against the interests of the working class and the nation. They have even reached the stage of urging the ULP government to sell this country's citizenship and passports in order to fund the unsustainable pension arrangements and further salary enhancements beyond the level of any increase in national production!

Today, the overwhelming majority of the progressive movement in St. Vincent and the Grenadines is located within the ULP either as members or supporters. It remains the most popular political entity. A recent public opinion poll conducted in July 2018 by the reputable pollster, CADRES of Barbados, found, among other things, that there is a further swing to the ULP since the general elections of December 2015.

The ULP has been in governance for some 18 years continuously, thus far, since March 29, 2001. Its Political Leader, Ralph Gonsalves, was first elected as such on December 6, 1998, some twenty years ago. He has been the country's longest serving Prime Minister, from March 29, 2001, continuously until the present time. No other Head of Government in the Caribbean has retained his or her office, uninterruptedly, since 2001. He is now 72 years of age. For two years now, he has been articulating his preference to demit, voluntarily, the offices of Political Leader of the ULP and Prime Minister of St. Vincent and the Grenadines, hopefully before the expiration of his current Prime Ministerial term in December 2020. He and the ULP have already embarked upon the preparation of an orderly transition to younger leadership. Still, the overwhelming majority of the ULP supporters prefer him not to demit as yet. Recently, in December 2018, the ULP at its Annual Convention re-elected him as its Political Leader. It is not yet certain that he would lead the ULP in the next general elections, constitutionally due by December 2020.

It is important that the ULP avoids the political error of Joshua's PPP, Cato's SVLP, and Mitchell's NDP of not preparing carefully an appropriate transition to a new generation of leaders. The failure and/or refusal of these three parties to plan efficaciously for meaningful succession contributed significantly to their demise or "wilderness years" after the exhaustion of the respective leaderships of Joshua, Cato, and Mitchell.

The ULP's transition has the equally challenging task of finding a possible replacement for Julian Francis, as General Secretary. Francis has held that party position since October 16, 1994, and has been distinguished in that role. Moreover, he was the Campaign Manager for the ULP in the general elections of 1998, 2001, 2005, 2010, and 2015. In each of these elections, the ULP won the popular vote and on the last four occasions it triumphed in winning the most seats, thus forming the government. He has been a Senator in the Parliament since 2001 and has been the country's most successful Minister of Works ever. He has been a commanding presence on the platform and a major voice on "Star Radio", the ULP's radio station, of which he is the Managing

Director. He is five or so years Gonsalves' junior, but the ULP has to line up possible replacements for him, too.

In the changing of the leadership guard in the party and the government, the ULP has been emphasising the attractive rubric of "Continuity and Change" — continuing, and building upon, the advanced social democratic gains for the people and embracing change as the circumstances demand. A refreshing of personnel, policies, and organisation in the new period are necessary and desirable requisites.

The future progress and advance of the labour movement depend centrally on the following: the continuation of a Labour government dedicated to the further development of the social democratic revolution, inclusive of a programme focused on the interests of the working people and their trade unions; an increase in membership of trade unions in both the public and private sectors; the deepening of internal democracy in trade unions; the further ramping-up of targeted specific interventions for those disadvantaged on grounds of economic hardship, status or gender; the lifting of the political consciousness of the working people from a partial, trade union consciousness to a more developed political consciousness to advance the interests of the working people and the nation as a whole; the necessity and desirability of the leadership of trade unions to be responsible and responsive to their members and to avoid opportunism based on their personal or partisan political agendas which run counter to their members' interests, welfare and empowerment.

One final matter for concluding reflections touches and concerns the origin, nature, character, and functioning of the State. Historically, the wholly unrepresentative nature of the imposed colonial state for some 200 years, from 1763 until the unfolding of the gradualist process of constitutional independence in 1979, ensured a disconnect between the rulers and the governed. One consequence of this was that the people as a whole viewed the State as an alien power, which they did not own, standing over them. To be sure, the unrepresentative State provided basic functions particularly in relation to order and coercion, deliverer of certain elemental services and securing allegiance to the British sovereign. From 1951, universal adult suffrage accorded the people a vote which they used to create a political space in their interests. In time, more political authority was devolved to the people's elected representatives. At constitutional independence in 1979, the political umbilical cord of colonialism was formally severed.

Still, the people doubted they owned the state apparatuses: The Executive, the Legislature, the Judiciary, the Public Administration, and the coercive

Police Force. Increasingly, that ownership is becoming evident but there is more popular commitment to and connection with the landscape and seascape of St. Vincent and the Grenadines than to the composite of the State and its formal apparatuses. Themes such as "Land of Our Birth", "Vincy Life", the invisible aspects of the nation's culture, and a sense of belonging to the Vincentian component of the Caribbean civilisation, are far more resident in the population's consciousness than any real sense of ownership of the formal state institutions.

The colonial imposition of the state, its unrepresentativeness for so long and the failure of the colonial state to deliver a sufficiency or adequacy of benefits for the people, restrained the populace from truly embracing the State in its formal aspects. Indeed, the people have often devised ways and means to use, and even misuse, the State and its resources for their own personal or immediate community benefit. This colonial overhang still holds some sway in the people's perception or imagination of the State in independent St. Vincent and the Grenadines. This non-commitment to, and utilitarian view of the State in independent St. Vincent and the Grenadines remains a drag on the country's developmental prospects. The labour movement — trade unions and the Labour government — and nationalist civil society have vital roles to play in engendering a sense of national collective ownership of the State.

A second feature of the independent State in St. Vincent and the Grenadines, another inheritance from its colonial predecessor, has been its wont to act autonomously of contending classes within the country. This tendency of a seeming autonomy arises from the nature of the State's imposition originally — it did not grow out of, or evolve from any internal class contradictions in the society as happened in Europe — and the fact that the colonial State in St. Vincent fundamentally represented the economically-dominant class in Britain and not necessarily the planter-merchant elite — a relatively unformed class — in the country, save and except when and where their interests coincided, which was almost always; but undoubtedly the interests of the domestic planter-merchant elite were subordinate to those of the industrial-finance-monopoly capitalists in Britain and the requisites of the British Empire.

The history of the Caribbean, including St. Vincent and the Grenadines, is replete with examples of the colonial State acting as an autonomous entity, and even contrary to the interests of the planter-merchant elite. This was done, at times decisively, by the Colonial Governor. This gubernatorial inheritance from the colonial State has seeped into the State's activism in the period after internal self-government and independence. It has buttressed the constitutional and political praxis of Cabinet and Prime Ministerial governance in a context where the State is the single largest employer of labour and a provider of substantial patronage. Further, the size and range of the State's activities compared to the rest of the economy and society prompt it to create objective conditions for acting autonomously of the major contending classes or groups. Unless restrained, it becomes a consolidated power standing over society, even though based on popular democracy.

The undeveloped condition of the contending classes in St. Vincent and the Grenadines constitutes the material foundation for the "independent" or autonomous activism of the contemporary State. To be sure, democratic imperatives in the State's functioning demand that it acts popularly and not in the interest of the dominant economic class of capitalists but its gubernatorial inheritance enables it to do so easily and frequently if its political leadership is so inclined. The bourgeoisie (national and foreign) in St. Vincent and the Grenadines, and similarly-evolved Caribbean societies, cannot insist that the State be the official expression of its *exclusive* power simply, even though the State may accord the economic dominant class political recognition of its *specific* interests and may define them as consistent, at least for the present and immediate future, with the interests of the working people and nation as a whole. The only way in which the bourgeoisie can insist on the enthronement of its exclusive power is if it controls, indirectly, the executive and legislative arms of the State either through its ideological/programmatic symmetry with the government or strong financial support to the political party and leading individuals within it. The labour movement must thus be alert to any ideological/programmatic affinity of the government or political party with the economically dominant class, and the financial support from anti-national forces to the political party (in or out of government) especially for on-going organisational work and the conduct of election campaigns. In this regard, the working people and the nation as a whole must reject the ideological backwardness of neo-liberalism and the party financing by international operatives who seek to sell the country's passports and citizenship.

The undeveloped character and the limitations in the levels of political consciousness of the working people and their petit-bourgeois allies constrain them from fully representing themselves in the State. Trade unions, by their very nature, are unable to represent the working people in a thoroughly political manner. A political party, grounded in the working people and their class allies, avowedly "labour" in its instincts and orientation, philosophically or ideologically committed to advanced social democracy, steeped in nationalism and anti-imperialism, committed to and organised among the people and led by an appropriately-shaped leadership, has been shown to be the vehicle to represent optimally the working people and the nation in St. Vincent and the Grenadines.

At the same time, the political party representing, in the State, the working people, its allies and the nation as a whole, is required to ensure a deepening of popular democracy, transparency, responsiveness, and responsibility. The political party must be protective of the working people from the anti-labour pursuits of other classes or groups and it must always derive its political energy, spirit and direction from the working people and its allies so as not to appear as though the party is the source of the delivery of metaphoric "rain and sunshine" from above. Always, the people are the masters. Properly led, organised and represented, they, in communion with their government, are likely further to deliver prosperity and opportunity, equity and solidarity, freedom and justice, peace and the rule of law, in their interest and that of the nation as a whole.

Fundamental in all this, is the quest to uplift and transform the working people's consciousness and understanding as a class for themselves and the nation. In this process, the everyday struggles of workers for the improvement of their condition under capitalism and the raising of their total class consciousness to push, in their interest, for alterations, to contemporary monopoly capitalism, are inextricably inter-connected. They are part of the entire enterprise of advancing the interests of the working people and the nation. Thus, neither bundle of activity must undermine the other. They go hand in hand. On all these matters, and more, the labour movement needs further clarity, wisdom, maturity, and understanding.

Hopefully, this book contributes to this necessary quest of the working people, their organisations and the nation as a whole.

BIBLIOGRAPHY

Anderson, Perry. "The Limits and Possibilities of Trade Union Action." R. Blackburn and A. Cockburn: *The Incompatibles: Trade Union Militancy and the Consensus*. London. Penguin, 1965.

Best, Lloyd. "A Model of Pure Plantation Economy." *Social and Economic Studies*, Volume 87, No. 3. September 1968.

Brathwaite, Lloyd. "Social Stratification and Cultural Pluralism." *Annals of the New York Academy of Social Sciences*, Volume 83, January 1960.

Cesaire, Aimé. *Discourses on Colonialism*. Monthly Review Press. New York, 2000.

Čakardić, Ankica. "Rosa Luxemburg's Critique of Bourgeois Feminism as Early Reproduction Theory." Internet. February 25, 2018.

Craton, Michael. "Changing Patterns of Slave Families in the British West Indies." *Journal of Interdisciplinary History*. Volume X, No. 1, 1979.

Davis, Angela. "The Black Women's Role in the Community of Slaves." *The Black Scholar*. December 1971.

Depres, Leo. "Anthropological Theory, Cultural Pluralism, and the Study of Complex Societies." *Current Anthropology*. February 1968.

Engels, Frederick. "The Origin of the Family, Private Property and the State," *Karl Marx and Fredrick Engels: Selected Works*. London. Lawrence and Wishart, 1950.

Gonsalves, Ralph. "The Role of Labour in the Political Process of St. Vincent, 1935 – 1970." M.Sc Thesis. UWI, Mona, 1971.

Gonsalves, Ralph. *The Non-Capitalist Path to Development: Africa and the Caribbean*. London. One Caribbean Publishers, 1981.

Gonsalves, Ralph. *History and the Future: A Caribbean Perspective*. St. Vincent and the Grenadines. Great Works Depot, 1994.

Gonsalves, Ralph. *The Politics of Our Caribbean Civilisation: Essays and Speeches*. St. Vincent and the Grenadines. Great Works Depot, 2001.

Gonsalves, Ralph. *The Diary of a Prime Minister: Ten Days Among Benedictine Monks*. St. Vincent and the Grenadines. Strategy Forum Inc., 2010.

Gonsalves, Ralph. *The Making of 'The Comrade': The Political Journey of Ralph Gonsalves.* St. Vincent and the Grenadines. Strategy Forum Inc., 2010.

Gonsalves, Ralph. *Our Caribbean Civilisation and Its Political Prospects.* St. Vincent and the Grenadines. Strategy Forum Inc., 2014.

Gonsalves, Ralph. *The Case for Caribbean Reparatory Justice.* St. Vincent and the Grenadines, Strategy Forum Inc., 2017.

Gonsalves, Ralph. *The Making of a National Hero: Law and Practice in SVG, including The Trial of George Mc Intosh and the 1935 Uprising.* St. Vincent and the Grenadines. Strategy Forum Inc., 2018.

Hallam, Jennifer. "The Slave Experience: Men, Women, and Gender." Internet, undated.

Higman, B.W. "Household Structure and Fertility in Jamaican Slave Plantations: A Nineteenth-Century Example." *Population Studies.* Volume 27, Part 3, November 1973.

Hobsbawm, Eric. "The Labour Aristocracy in Nineteenth Century Britain." *Labouring Men: Studies in History of Labour.* London, 1964.

Hobsbawm, Eric. "Lenin and the Aristocracy of Labour." *Monthly Review.* December 2012.

Hobsbawm, Eric. *Revolutionaries.* London. Abacus, 2017)

Hobsbawm, Eric. *How to Change the World: Tales of Marx and Marxism.* London. Abacus, 2011.

James, CLR. *Black Jacobins: Toussaint L'Ouverture and the San Domingo Revolution.* New York. Vantage Books, 1963.

John, Kenneth. "St. Vincent: A Political Kaleidoscope." *Flambeau.* Number 6, July 1966.

Jonasdottier, Anna G. *Why Women are Oppressed.* Philadelphia, Penn.,Temple University Press, 1991.

Lenin, V.I. *Selected Works.* London. Lawrence and Wishart, 1969.

Lewis, Arthur. *Labour in the West Indies: The Birth of a Workers' Movement.* London. Victor Gollancz Ltd. and the Fabian Society, 1939)

Lewis, Gordon. *The Growth of the Modern West Indies.* London. Mc Kibbon and Kec Limited, 1968.

Lewis, Gordon. *Slavery, Imperialism and Freedom.* New York. *Monthly Review Press,* 1978.

Lewis, Rupert. *Walter Rodney's Intellectual and Political Thought.* Detroit, Mich. Wayne State University Press, 1998.

Marshall, Bernard. *Slavery, Law and Society in the British Windward Islands, 1763 – 1823.* Jamaica. Arawak Publications, 2007.

Martin, C.I. "The Role of Government in the Agricultural Development of St. Vincent." Unpublished M.Sc Thesis, UWI, St. Augustine, Trinidad, 1967.

Marx, Karl. *Karl Marx and Fredrick Engels: Selected Works.* London. Lawrence and Wishart, 1950.

Mitchell, James. *Beyond The Islands: An Autobiography.* Oxford. Macmillan Publishers, 2007.

Morgan, Lewis. *Ancient Society, Researchers in the Lines of Human Progress from Savagery through Barbarism to Civilisations.* London. Macmillan and Company, 1877.

Myers, Gordon. *Banana Wars: The Price of Free Trade – A Caribbean Perspective.* London. Zed Books Ltd., 2004.

Nieholt, Geertje Lycklama à. "Women and Development: Some Theoretical and Practical Considerations." *Gender: A Caribbean Multi-Disciplinary Perspective,* edited by Elsa Leo-Rhymie, Barbara Bailey, Christine Barrow. Kingston, Jamaica. Ian Randle Publishers, 1997.

Reddock, Rhoda. *Women, Labour and Politics in Trinidad and Tobago: A History.* Kingston, Jamaica. Ian Randle Publishers, 1994.

Rodney, Walter. *How Europe Underdeveloped Africa.* London. Bogle-L'Ouverture Publications, 1973.

Rottenberg, Catherine. "Feminists Must Reject Neo-Liberalism If We Want to Sustain the Me Too Movement." *The Independent.* United Kingdom, May 29, 2018.

Saffioti, Heleith. "Women in Class Society." *Monthly Review Press.* New York, 1978.

Schifrin, Anya. "Disinformation and Democracy: The Internet Transformed Protest But Did Not Improve Democracy." *Journal of International Affairs.* Fall/Winter, Volume 71, 2017.

Sewell, William G. *The Ordeal of Free Labour in the British West Indies.* London. Low, 1862.

Shils, Edward. "Demagogues and Cadres in the Political Development of the New States." *Communications and Political Development,* edited by Lucian W. Pye. New Jersey. Princeton University Press, 1963.

Singham, A.W. *The Hero and the Crowd in a Colonial Polity.* New Haven. Yale University Press, 1968.

Smith, M.G. *The Plural Society in the British West Indies.* Berkeley. University of California Press, 1965.

Smith, R.T. "Social and Cultural Pluralism in the Caribbean." *American Anthropologist.* Volume 63, Number 1, February 1961.

Spinelli, Joseph. "Land Use and Population in St. Vincent, 1763 – 1960: A Contribution to the Study of Patterns of Economic and Geographic Change in a Small West Indian Island." Unpublished PhD Thesis. University of Florida, 1973.

Trotz, Alicia. "Gender, Generation and Memory: Remembering a Future Caribbean." Working Paper No. 14, 2008. Centre for Gender and Development, UWI, Cave Hill, Barbados.

Unity Labour Party. "Election Manifesto for the years 1998, 2001, 2005, 2010, 2015." (ULP, Kingstown, SVG)

YULIMO. *Independence: The Beginning, Not the End.* St. Vincent and the Grenadines. YULIMO Publications, 1979.

REPORTS AND PUBLIC DOCUMENTS

United Kingdom

The Colonial Office. "West India Royal Commission Report." *HMSO.* London, 1897.

"Report by the Honourable E.F.L Wood on his visit to the West Indies and British Guiana, December 1921-February 1922". Cond. 1679. *HMSO.* London, 1922.

"Labour Conditions in the West Indies." Report by Major G. St. J. Orde Browne. Cond. 6070. *HMSO.* London, 1939.

"West India Royal Commission, 1938–39." Report by Lord Moyne. Cond. 6607. *HMSO.* London, 1945.

"Parliamentary Debates (Commons), Volume 312, Session 1935 – 1936"

"Colonial Office Annual Reports on St. Vincent for the years 1946 – 1956"

St. Vincent and the Grenadines

Agreements of Trade Unions with various Employers

Chenery, Justice J.W.B. "Award Concerning the Dispute Between the Board of the St. Vincent Arrowroot Association and the FIAWU, 1959." St. Vincent Government Printery, 1959.

Civil Service Associations Files

Commercial, Technical and Allied Workers Union's Files

Glasgow, E. "Report of the Tribunal Appointed to Determine a Dispute Between CTAWU and the Sanitary Department of the Government of St. Vincent, 1966." Kingstown. Mimeograph, 1966)

The Government Gazette. Volume for years 1901-2018.

Hansard of Legislature, 1942-2018. St. Vincent. Office of Clerk of House of Assembly.

Jolly, A.L. "Report of Commission of Enquiry on the Sugar Industry of St. Vincent, April 1965." St. Vincent Government Printery, 1965.

Joshua, Ebenezer. Personal Files from 1951 – 1970.

Malone, Sir Clement. "Report of the Commission of Enquiry into Wages and Other Conditions of Employment of Agriculture Workers in St. Vincent, January 1956." St. Vincent Government Printery, 1956

St. Vincent Workers Union's Files

Government of St. Vincent and the Grenadines

Various national and sectoral reports on different aspects of the economy, polity and society.

Registrar of Trade Unions Files.

Trade Union and Labour Laws. Attorney General's Chambers.

Newspapers

The Investigator. 1937-1947.

The Times. 1935-1948.

The Vincentian. 1946-present.

The Voice. 1962-1970.

Freedom and *Justice.* Organs of YULIMO and UPM respectively.

The Star. Organ of former SVGLP.

Unity. Organ of the former MNU.

The News

Searchlight

Periodicals and Magazines

Flambeau. Kingstown study group/EFP.

Touli. Periodical of the CSA.

Beacon. Theoretical Journal of YULIMO.

Various mimeographed publications of MNU, ULP, and NDP.

GENERAL INDEX

A

Agriculture, 35, 42–43, 45, 79, 87, 145, 172–73, 194, 201, 217, 251, 267, 325–26
plantation, 46, 71, 123–24, 126, 173, 275, 316
workers, 39, 43, 69, 79, 91, 95, 101, 131, 147–48, 179–80, 207, 339
All of Us. See ARWEE
American Institute of Free Labour Development (AIFLD), 139, 142
Anti-colonial uprisings, 24–25, 27, 66, 68, 314
Antigua, 28, 36, 56–57, 118, 133, 142, 206
Arrowroot, 35, 37–39, 41–42, 44, 97, 122–23, 273, 314
ARWEE (All of Us), 161, 163, 180, 183, 193, 196, 248, 317–18

B

Banana Growers' Association, 41, 147, 150, 239
Bananas, 35, 37, 39–43, 122–24, 134, 148, 165, 232, 273, 275, 316–17, 319
cultivation, 41, 126, 134
industry, 41–42, 121–23, 316
Barbados, 57, 133, 135, 182, 189, 195, 206, 253
government, 189
independence, 155
Labour Party, 80, 164, 203
legislation, 56
wages in, 133
Bequia, 17, 188, 191, 229, 243
Big Four, 23, 90–92
BLAC (Black Liberation Action Committee), 163, 317
Bourgeois feminism, 292–93, 302, 305, 307, 335
Britain, 18, 23, 86, 311, 314, 322, 331
Associate Statehood, 151, 154, 158
bananas, 248, 319
Colonial Office, 27
conquest and settlement, 18, 22, 47
emigration, 49
foreign affairs, 23
independence from, 17
Privy Council, 96
British colonialism, 19, 22, 26, 65, 68, 102, 298
British government, 37, 71, 110, 114, 145–46, 154, 266
British Guiana, 109, 114, 314, 338
By-elections, 198–200, 206, 263, 283, 285
Central Leeward, 198, 200, 202–4, 206, 249, 284
East Kingstown, 206, 271
East St. George, 205–6
Grenadines, 191–92, 212, 269, 284
Kingstown, 185
North Leeward, 98–99, 110
North Windward, 68
South Windward, 99

C

Callinago and Garifuna people, 18, 36, 50, 54, 255, 298
arrowroot cultivation, 37
genocide, 47
mode of production, 34
religion and the, 312
resistance to colonial domination, 19, 24, 26, 28
war with the British, 36
Capitalism, 13, 27–28, 31, 34, 50–51, 53, 55–56, 58–59, 294, 300–301, 323, 333
Caribbean civilisation, 54, 225, 229, 234, 255, 277, 306–7, 321, 331, 335–36
Caribbean Congress of Labour. See CCL
Caribbean Democratic Union (CDU), 278
Caribbean Free Trade Area (CARIFTA), 157, 173, 269
CARIFTA. See Caribbean Free Trade Area
CCL (Caribbean Congress of Labour), 131, 138–41, 146, 150, 156, 167, 188
CDU (Caribbean Democratic Union), 278
Central Government, 45, 77, 167, 176, 237, 239–41, 243, 257, 316, 324, 326
Central Kingstown, 209, 214, 219, 226–28, 231–32, 235, 271
Central Leeward, 172, 175, 199–200, 203–4, 206, 210, 214–15, 220, 228, 231, 234–36, 270–71, 275, 284
Central Windward, 88–89, 94, 99–101, 104,

107, 109–10, 119, 125, 143, 151, 155, 184, 284

Children, 71, 241–43, 245–46, 253, 291, 295–98, 308, 322

Civil Service Association. *See* CSA

Class struggles, 31, 33, 54, 94, 292–93

Coalition Governments, 161, 171, 173, 260–61

Colonial administration, 61–66, 68–72, 83, 90, 97–98, 314

  Administrator, 23, 69–70, 83, 88, 94, 96, 103–6, 120–21, 128–29, 131, 143, 146

  clashes with, 96, 98, 113, 128, 171

  cooperating with, 91, 93, 96

  disdain for unionism, 86, 91

  expansion of Westminster-style democracy, 102

  labour representation, 79

  land settlements, 275

  Mt. Bentinck work stoppage, 100

  social legislation, 83

Colonialism, 21–22, 24, 26–27, 49, 51, 61, 65–66, 68, 86, 91, 93, 103, 107, 116, 182, 260, 262, 274, 295, 315–16

  danger of trade unions under, 86

  failure of, 331

  land settlement under, 275

  limited secondary education, 26

  militance against, 315

  oppression of the working class, opp, 96

  radical attacks against, 93

  repression, 68, 73, 77

  repressive nature of, 65

  suffrage, 49, 84

  taxation, 70

  threats against workers, 132

Commercial Technical and Allied Workers' Union. *See* CTAWU

Cotton, 35, 37, 40–42, 314

CSA (Civil Service Association), 121, 128, 150, 156, 159, 162, 168–71, 177, 188, 196–97

CTAWU (Commercial Technical and Allied Workers' Union), 9, 141, 144–46, 148–50, 153, 155–59, 166, 176–77, 180, 195, 217, 236–37, 239, 250, 252, 259, 272, 286

  affinity with SVLP, 165–66

  battle for registration, 142

  challenges, 162

  dominance, 188

  and Geest Industries, 148, 158

and "Public Order" legislation, 196

recognition of, 147

D

Democratic Freedom Movement. *See* DFM

Democratic Labour Party. *See* DLP

DFM (Democratic Freedom Movement), 161, 163, 175, 177, 180–81, 183, 185, 193–96, 276, 317

DLP (Democratic Labour Party), 118, 164, 195, 203

E

Economic unionism, 75–76

Education Forum of the People. *See* EFP

EFP (Education Forum of the People), 9, 163, 169–72, 175, 177, 185

Electoral politics, 184, 270–71

Emancipation, 22, 38, 50, 53, 162, 292, 299, 301

Employers' and Employees Association. *See* (SVEEA)

Employment, 49, 78, 101, 103, 141, 144, 148–50, 171, 177, 186, 241, 288–89, 301, 312, 321, 324, 326, 339

Estates, 38, 40, 63, 68, 70, 73, 80, 97, 100–106, 108, 116, 124, 132, 134, 179, 275

  workers, 70–71, 103

Executive Councils, 23, 79, 94–95, 97, 107, 113, 116, 120, 146, 281

F

Factories, 39, 69, 94–95, 103, 105, 133–35, 249

Families, 34, 41, 51–52, 68, 116, 134, 246, 286, 294, 296–97, 299–300, 304, 308, 335

Farmers, 40–41, 102, 106, 123–24, 134, 179, 211

Farmers and National Workers' Union. *See* FNWU

Federated Industrial Agricultural Workers' Union. *See* FIAWU

Female candidates, 99–100, 271, 283–85, 287

Feminism, 305–9

FIAWU (Federated Industrial Agricultural Workers' Union), 43, 46, 91, 93, 101, 107–8, 116, 118, 126, 139–42, 144, 150, 167, 272, 275, 286

  challenges, 148

decline, 162, 176
dissension in, 119, 121
Geest Industries, 142, 149, 158
Job actions at Mt. Bentinck Estates, 95,
    100–101, 104–6, 128–29
Jolly Commission, 97
PPP and, 152, 155–56, 167
strike at Kingstown Banana Depot, 116
See also Mt. Bentinck Estates
FNWU (Farmers and National Workers'
    Union), 9, 179–80
Foreign policy, 217, 241, 250, 255, 269,
    278–79

G

Garifuna. *See* Callinago and Garifuna People
GAWU (Guyana Agricultural Workers'
    Union), 165
GDP (Gross Domestic Product), 43, 240–41,
    246–48, 327
Geest Industries, 41, 142, 148–50, 155, 158,
    166
General Workers' Union. *See* SVGWU
Georgetown, 61, 95, 100, 104, 106, 136–37,
    211, 214, 243–44
Governmental authority, 117, 140, 152,
    155–56, 250
Government Printery, 339
Gross Domestic Product. *See* GDP
Guyana Agricultural Workers' Union
    (GAWU), 165

H

HMSO (Report of Labour Conditions in the
    West Indies), 68, 338
House of Assembly, 24, 151, 164, 187, 192,
    196–97, 216–17, 220, 223, 225, 229,
    291, 339

I

ICFTU (International Confederation of
    Free Trade Unions), 140, 153, 156
ILO (International Labour Organisation),
    143, 145–46, 149, 157
Incumbents, 109–10, 125, 151, 155, 198,
    215–16, 234
Independence, 17, 22, 25, 143, 151, 155, 163,
    180–83, 185–86, 194, 229, 248, 259,
    273–74, 306, 317–18, 331, 338
Indigence, 244–45, 247, 251, 319

Internal self-government, 20, 49, 114, 151,
    158–59, 161, 182, 274, 331
International Confederation of Free Trade
    Unions. *See* ICFTU
International Democratic Union (IDU), 278
International Labour Organisation. *See* ILO

K

Kingstown, 61–63, 78, 80, 89–90, 92–94,
    98–99, 107–11, 116, 121, 124–26, 140,
    148, 150–51, 155, 178, 185, 206, 214,
    222, 224, 243, 268, 316, 338, 340
Kingstown Banana Depot, 116, 119, 148. *See
    also* bananas

L

Labour, 20, 32, 36, 47, 52, 54, 58, 79, 123,
    155, 157, 179, 191, 254, 286, 292, 294,
    298, 300–301, 304, 313
cocoa company and, 42
conditions, 27, 69, 338
exploitation of, 26
federation of, 10, 150, 156, 179
legislative council and, 72
minimum wage, 68–69
Labour Aloners, 211–12
Labour aristocracy, 321–23, 327–28, 336
Labour Commissioner, 69–70, 88, 94, 96,
    104–5, 132, 157–58
Labour Conditions in the West Indies. *See*
    HMSO
Labour Department, 27, 69, 78, 82, 95–96,
    101, 146, 253
Labour disputes, 104–5, 116, 120, 130–31,
    147, 149–50, 260, 339
Labourers, 69, 104, 132–33, 142, 295, 312
indentured, 20, 24, 37, 50, 312–13
See also labour
Labour force, 44–45, 77, 122, 148, 286,
    288–89, 313
Labour-MNU Unity, 215, 217, 250
Land Owners Association. *See* SVLOA
Laws, 22–23, 33, 52, 55, 67, 92, 111, 130,
    171, 178, 185, 191, 194, 196, 254,
    267–68, 282, 286, 291, 302–3, 315, 337
Legislative Council, 22–23, 61–62, 67, 72–
    73, 79, 84, 91–93, 95, 97–98, 100, 102,
    104, 107, 125–26, 128–30, 144, 154
Legislature, 23, 27, 67, 69, 72, 80, 84, 88,
    93–94, 97, 99, 102, 104, 107, 125, 132,
    144, 172, 176, 187, 263–64, 272, 330

London, 111, 180, 182, 272, 303, 305, 318, 336, 338

M

Marriaqua, 125, 172, 175, 188, 204, 209, 214, 219, 221, 226–27, 231, 234, 236, 270–71, 284
Mitchell-Sylvester Party. *See* MSP
MNU (Movement of National Unity), 15, 198–99, 201–3, 206, 208–9, 211–17, 248–50, 259, 265, 285, 320, 340
Modes of production, 25, 28, 30, 32–33, 35, 50, 52–55, 58, 124, 165, 282, 294–97, 299–300, 302–3, 305, 316
Monopoly capitalism, 20, 24, 28–29, 34, 55, 59, 71, 74, 165, 207, 248, 259–60, 276, 286, 293, 300–301, 305–7, 309, 311, 315, 317, 319–21, 328
Movement of National Unity. *See* MNU
MSP (Mitchell-Sylvester Party), 174–75, 214, 264, 266, 285, 318
Mt. Bentinck Estates, strikes at, 70, 96–97, 103, 105–6, 108, 130–32, 136
Mt. Bentinck Estates *See also* FIAWU

N

National Farmers' Union (NFU), 207
National Independence Committee (NIC), 181–82
National Insurance Services. *See* NIS
National Provident Fund (NPF), 170, 194
National Union of Progressive Workers. *See* NUPW
National Workers' Movement. *See* NWM
National Workers Union. *See* NWU
NDP (New Democratic Party), 25, 119, 161, 170, 176, 184–89, 191, 194, 196–200, 202–6, 209–20, 222, 224–32, 234, 236, 239, 248–51, 263–66, 271–72, 276, 278, 284–85, 287, 317–18, 340
NDP government, 189, 207, 209–10, 217–24, 239, 245, 249–51, 268, 271–72, 320
NEMO (National Emergency Management Organisation), 246
New Democratic Party. *See* NDP
New Jewel Movement. *See* NJM
NFU (National Farmers' Union), 207
NIC (National Independence Committee), 181–82
NIS (National Insurance Services), 45, 170, 194, 239–40, 252, 267, 326–27

NJM (New Jewel Movement), 165, 193, 198
North Central Windward, 15, 172, 175, 202, 204, 209, 215, 219, 225–27, 231, 234–36, 269–70, 316
Northern Grenadines, 214, 219, 226, 228, 231, 235, 269
North Leeward, 43, 89–90, 94, 97–99, 107, 109–10, 118–19, 121, 125–26, 151, 154–55, 172, 174, 187, 195, 197, 202, 204, 214, 219, 226, 228, 231, 235–36, 275, 316
NPF (National Provident Fund), 170, 194
NUPW (National Union of Progressive Workers), 10, 43, 162, 179–80, 259
NWM (National Workers' Movement), 162, 188, 195–96, 207, 216, 236–37, 250, 252
NWU (National Workers Union), 119

O

OBCA, 10, 163, 317
OECS, 10, 159, 208, 224, 240, 244, 246, 251, 269, 291, 321
Old Representative System. *See* ORS
Organisation for Black Cultural Awareness. *See* OBCA
Organisation of Eastern Caribbean States. *See* OECS
ORS (Old Representative System), 22, 27

P

Parliament, 43, 174, 176, 191, 193, 200, 205, 218, 221, 223–24, 229, 243, 267, 269–71, 278, 284, 286–87, 329
PDM (People's Democratic Movement), 183, 196–98, 203, 271, 317–18
Peasant Cultivators' Union. *See* SVPCU
Pensions, 170, 218, 223, 239–40, 327
People's Democratic Movement. *See* PDM
People's Democratic Party (PDP), 10, 197, 202
People's Liberation Movement. *See* PLM
People's Political Party. *See* PPP
People's Revolutionary Government. *See* PRG
Plantations, 71, 124, 162, 274, 295, 297, 312, 316
Planter-merchant elites, 22, 27, 70–71, 73, 79–81, 83, 88, 94, 97, 107, 115, 122, 136, 274, 296, 312, 314–15, 331
PLM (People's Liberation Movement), 109,

111, 117, 120, 283

Police, 23, 62, 95–97, 104, 107–8, 110, 113, 119, 131–32, 137, 178, 189, 212

Political unionism, 57, 75–77, 86, 106, 121, 142

Popular votes, 110, 125–26, 151–52, 154–55, 161, 173, 186, 188, 198, 202, 204, 209, 220, 222, 226, 228, 232, 251, 263–65, 320, 329

PPP (People's Political Party), 25, 91–92, 98–100, 109–11, 114–15, 118, 120, 122, 124–28, 140–41, 150–52, 154–56, 161, 164, 167–69, 171–75, 184–88, 197, 203, 214, 249, 263–66, 283, 285, 315–16

PRG (People's Revolutionary Government), 58, 189

Private sectors, 35, 77, 117, 156, 158, 176, 195, 211, 249, 251–52, 276–77, 288, 321, 323–24, 330

Protests, 28, 57, 63–64, 68, 167, 178, 188–89, 195, 216–18, 223, 233

PSU (Public Service Union), 217–18, 236–38, 241, 250

Public servants, 24, 98, 115–16, 121, 124, 168, 170–71, 173, 186–87, 237, 252, 287, 316, 327–28

Public service, 23, 110, 113, 128, 168–69, 238, 286, 292

Public Service Union. *See* PSU

R

Registrar of Trade Unions, 86–87, 92, 94, 119, 142, 150

S

Salaries, 28, 122, 174, 177, 207, 222–23, 238, 240, 326–28

Sanitation Department, 144–46, 149, 153, 156

Sanitation workers, 144–47, 149

Schools, secondary, 222, 237, 242–43, 267, 291

SCL (Strategic Communications Laboratories), 229, 232, 235, 278

SDGs (Sustainable Development Goals), 245, 256, 321

Senators, 23–24, 193, 205, 209, 285, 287, 329

Slaves, 18, 20, 22, 24–28, 31, 34–36, 47, 50, 53, 55, 61, 66, 104, 282, 295–99, 303–4, 311–12, 335, 337

communities, 297–98, 335

South Central Windward, 161, 172, 174, 184–85, 188, 204, 214–15, 219, 226–27, 231, 234–36, 262–63, 269–70, 316

Southern Grenadines, 188, 209, 212, 215, 219, 225–26, 228, 231, 235, 284

South Leeward, 89, 98–99, 109–11, 117–18, 121, 125, 151–53, 155, 172, 174, 204, 209, 214, 219, 226, 228, 231, 235–36, 266

Soviet Union, 57–58, 73, 140, 186, 195, 207, 260, 315

St. Lucia, 17, 41, 56–57, 132, 181–82, 203, 206, 208

Strategic Communications Laboratories. *See* SCL

Strikes, 24, 37, 70, 82, 96–97, 103–8, 116–17, 127, 129–31, 134, 136–40, 144, 150, 167, 177–79, 185, 195, 216, 218, 222

St. Vincent Electricity Services, 140–43, 150, 166, 180, 195, 206, 210, 249–50, 292

St. Vincent Employers' Federation, SVEF, 166

St. Vincent Federation of Labour, SVFL, 150, 156

St. Vincent Labour Party. *See* SVLP

St. Vincent National Movement (SVNM), 10, 198

St. Vincent Representative Government Association (SVRGA), 25, 63

St. Vincent Workers' Union. *See* SVWU

Sugar, 20, 35–38, 41–42, 47, 81, 95, 97, 101, 106, 122–23, 132–36, 148, 194, 201, 207, 249–50, 267, 273–75

Sugar production, 36–37, 134

Supervisor of Elections, 180, 291

Sustainable Development Goals (SDGs), 245, 256, 321

SVEEA (St. Vincent Employers' and Employees Association), 68

SVGTU, 121, 127, 150, 156, 159, 162, 171, 177–80, 188, 196, 200, 216, 218, 236–38, 241, 250, 285

SVGU, 77, 79

SVGWU (St. Vincent General Workers' Union), 57, 75, 77–79, 82–83

SVLOA (St. Vincent Land Owners Association), 68

SVLP (St. Vincent Labour Party), 25, 46, 66–67, 75, 78–80, 82, 109–11, 117–22, 124–29, 140, 142–44, 148–49, 151–59, 161, 165–78, 180, 184–88, 191, 194,

197–202, 204–6, 208–17, 239, 248–50, 263–66, 270–72, 314, 316–18, 320

SVLP Governments, 44, 46, 158–59, 165, 167–72, 177–78, 181, 183, 185–86, 188–89, 192, 194–97, 201, 218, 249, 273

SVLP/ULP, 265–66, 285

SVNM (St. Vincent National Movement), 10, 198

SVPCU (St. Vincent Peasant Cultivators' Union), 75, 77–79, 82, 315

SVRGA (St. Vincent Representative Government Association), 25, 63

SVTUC (St. Vincent Trade Union Congress), 86, 156–57, 179, 259

SVWA (St. Vincent Workingmen's Association), 25, 57, 66–68, 72–73, 75, 78–79, 82, 87, 272, 314

SVWU (St. Vincent Workers' Union), 127, 150, 162, 165–66, 180, 259, 314

T

Teachers, 98, 108, 121, 124, 127, 129, 170–71, 177–79, 185–86, 195, 216, 218, 222–24, 226, 237–38, 242, 252, 279, 316, 327

Teachers Union. *See* SVGTU

Technology, 32, 51, 123, 254, 273, 279, 307

Telecommunications Act, 247

Trade Union Congress. *See* SVTUC

Trade unions, 25, 43, 46, 49, 57, 86–88, 91–92, 94–95, 97–98, 103, 106, 116–17, 119–21, 123, 127–28, 140–43, 145, 150, 156–57, 164–66, 171, 176, 179–81, 194, 196, 206–7, 209, 217, 224, 227, 236–37, 251–54, 259, 273, 277, 286–87, 322, 330–32, 338

active, 162, 179

activism, 144, 148, 195

agricultural sector and, 43

capitalism and, 55, 59

function of, 54

future of, 330

Grenadines, 43

leaders, 59, 76, 82, 147, 252

legislative reform, 84

membership, 44, 46, 158, 187, 237, 252, 322, 330

ordinances, 69, 84, 315

political unionism and, 75–76

recognition, 95, 179, 195

registered, 54, 56, 93

regulation of, 67, 84

relelvant law, 55

relevant law, 55

rise of capitalism and, 50

women in, 286

See also unions

U

ULP (Unity Labour Party), 15, 19, 25, 46, 170–71, 212, 216–17, 219–36, 238, 245–46, 250–51, 255–56, 265, 270–71, 275, 279, 284, 287, 306, 320–21, 329–30, 338, 340

ULP governments, 43, 227–28, 238, 242, 244–47, 251–52, 254–55, 279, 286–87, 290, 302, 321, 328

Unions, 59, 67, 75–79, 82, 84–88, 92–93, 95, 100–101, 104–6, 116, 118–21, 126–31, 140–43, 145, 148–50, 152–55, 158, 165–67, 169, 177, 179–80, 188, 206–7, 209, 223, 237–39, 250–53, 259, 289

affiliated, 91, 121

blanket, 78, 85, 143, 150, 165, 252

leaders, 98, 178, 224, 252–53, 272

members, 120, 143, 148, 165, 209

political, 208, 212

politics and trade, 35, 46, 49, 77, 165, 286

public sector, 177, 224, 236–37, 251–52, 321, 328

See also Trade Unions

United People's Movement. *See* UPM

United Workers, Peasants, and Ratepayers' Union. *See* UWPRU

Unity Labour Party. *See* ULP

UPM (United People's Movement), 15, 161, 183–88, 193, 196–99, 201–3, 206, 213, 250, 259, 264, 271, 285, 317, 320

attack against, 186

candidates, 209

coalition, 271

cooperation with NDP, 200

criticism of Government, 195

demise of, 209, 211, 248

dissension in, 193, 198

Dread Bills, 197

Dread Bills and, 196

transformation, 197

unification, 194

and Union Island Uprising, 189

Uprisings, 26–27, 57, 61–66, 68, 71, 73, 75,

85, 87, 188–89, 191–92, 260, 273, 314, 336

UWPRU (United Workers, Peasants, and Ratepayers' Union), 11, 77, 84–89, 91–95

V

VINLEC. *See* St. Vincent Electricity Services

W

West Kingstown, 172, 175, 204, 206, 215–16, 219, 226–28, 231, 235, 284

West St. George, 125, 129, 151, 155, 167, 172, 174–75, 184–86, 204, 214, 219, 226–28, 231, 234, 236, 270–71, 284, 316

WFTU (World Federation of Trade Unions), 97, 140

Windward Islands Banana Growers' Association, 41, 268

Workingmen's Association. *See* SVWA

World Federation of Trade Unions. *See* WFTU

WPJ (Workers' Party of Jamaica), 164, 197

Y

Youlou United Liberation Movement. *See* YULIMO

YULIMO (Youlou United Liberation Movement), 14, 161, 163, 179–80, 182–83, 185–86, 196, 248, 317–18
  constitutional reform, 180
  inter-organizational dissension and, 193
  membership, 177, 259
  teachers union and, 185

NAME INDEX

A

Abbott, Vin, 216
Adams, Emmanuel F., 151, 155, 167
Adams, Grantley, 118
Adams, J.M. "Tom", 189, 195
Adams, Leroy, 118–19, 189
Allen, Alphaeus, 80, 118, 125
Allen, Alpian, 210, 216, 219
Allen, Oscar, 163, 183, 200, 202, 209, 211, 320
Anderson, Sydney, 104, 118, 335
Ash, Valcina, 198–99, 201, 284–85
Ashton, Carlisle, 193

B

Bailey, Barbara, 308, 337
Bailey, George, 178
Ballantyne, Peter, 187, 204, 284
Baptiste, Anesia, 285
Baptiste, René, 225–27, 284–85, 287
Barnard, Cyril, 128, 130
Barrow, Christine, 308, 337
Barrow, Errol W., 164, 189, 195, 203
Bascombe, Basil, 275
Baynes, Julian, 80, 89–91, 99, 102, 107, 109–10, 125, 151
Baynes, Rudolph, 89–90, 92, 99, 102–3, 107, 109, 111, 151, 206
Beache, Glen, 227
Beache, Vincent, 175–76, 204–5, 209–17, 219–21, 223, 225–27, 250, 270
Belmar, Herman, 234–35
Bennett, Advira, 285, 287
Bentick, Olivia "Yvette", 212, 215, 284–85
Best, Lloyd, 163
Bird, Vere Cornwall, 118, 203
Bishop, Clive, 203
Bishop, Maurice, 198, 200–201
Black, Natasha, 285
Bonadie, Joseph "Burns", 80, 85, 147, 150, 153–54, 156–57, 188, 201–2, 204, 206, 208–9, 226, 272
Bonadie, St. Clair, 67, 79–80, 84, 88–89, 98, 272
Boyea, Julian, 193, 203–4
Boyea, Ken, 220–22, 226

Brisbane, O.D., 84–85, 272
Browne, Glenroy, 164, 202
Browne, Joy, 285
Browne, Ken, 188, 204, 214
Browne, Luke, 235
Browne, Maurice, 118
Browne, Michael, 118, 162, 177–79, 184–85, 195, 202, 206, 213–14, 216, 219, 225–27, 270–72, 284
Browne, Stephanie, 212, 216, 284–85
Burgin, Clayton, 225–27, 231, 235, 271
Burnham, Forbes, 164, 203
Bustamante, Alexander, 80, 203
Butler, Solomon, 163
Butler, Tubal Uriah "Buzz", 85, 88
Bynoe, Wendy, 285

C

Caesar, Saboto, 231, 234
Cain, Ella, 285
Campbell, Parnel, 162–63, 169, 171, 183–84, 196, 210, 216, 219, 271, 312, 318
Campbell, Stinson, 109–10, 118–20, 125, 169, 171, 183–85, 193, 198, 205–6, 218–19, 271
Caruth, Marsha, 285
Castro, Fidel, 162–63, 285
Cato, John, 168–71
Cato, Robert Milton, 25, 102, 109–11, 117–18, 125, 127, 140, 144, 150–51, 155–56, 159, 162, 168–72, 174–76, 181, 183, 192, 195, 201, 203–5, 209, 211, 249–50, 257, 259–60, 262, 264, 266, 269, 273–77, 279, 281–82, 312, 315–20, 328–29
Charles, Deborah, 234–35, 285, 287
Charles, Elvis, 235
Charles, George Hamilton, 78, 84–94, 97, 99–100, 102–4, 107, 109–10, 125, 143, 147, 175, 189, 272, 315
Charles, Lennox "Bumba", 188
Charles, Maxwell, 235
Chatoyer, Joseph, 19, 36
Chenery, J.W.B., 120, 339
Child, Frank, 71
Child, Ian, 131, 134
Child, Sonny, 131, 137

Coard, Bernard, 165, 197–98
Commissiong, Leroy, 116, 118–19, 121, 126
Compton, John, 203, 208
Coombs, Venold, 214
Cordice, Gideon, 198
Cottle, Junior "Spirit", 163
Cozier, Cosmos, 184, 187–88, 191–92
Cruickshank, Allan, 203–4, 216, 219
Cuffy, Eli, 87
Cuffy, Victor, 172–74, 193, 202, 262
Cummings, Daniel, 231

D

Dacon, St. Clair, 172, 175
Daize, Nicola, 285
Daniel, Montgomery, 225–27, 231, 234, 270
Davis, H.A., 272
Davy, Celithia, 285
De Freitas, Marcus, 203–4
Dennie, Alphonso, 167, 172–75, 203, 261–62
Dennie, Olin, 203–4
De Roche, Orit, 285
Dougan, Carlyle, 183, 216
Duncan, Ebenezer, 67, 77–80, 84–85, 88, 272
Dyce, Osmond, 131, 138–39, 146

E

Ellis, Frank, 89
Els, Sabrina, 285
Eustace, Arnhim, 92, 153, 168–71, 177,
    219–20, 222–26, 228–29, 231, 236, 260,
    271–72
Eustace, Joseph L., 92, 151–53, 155

F

Fife, Michelle, 235, 285, 287
Forbes, Conrad, 100
Forde, Gabriel, 100, 283
Francis, Julian, 211, 217, 225, 234, 250, 329
Francis-Gibson, Yvonne, 177-78, 200, 216,
    272, 284–85
Fraser, Adrian, 260
Frederick, Vynette, 285, 287
Friday, Lorraine Godwin, 226, 228, 231, 272

G

Gairy, Eric, 115, 203, 280–81
Garvey, Marcus Mosiah, 25
Gaymes, Dennis, 218
George, Juliette, 225

George, Oswald, 203–4
Gibbs, Bernard, 81, 92, 94
Giles, Alexander F., 119, 128, 131
Glasgow, F.E., 149
Gonsalves, Camillo, 234–35
Gonsalves, Ralph, 25, 162, 164, 166, 181,
    183–85, 189, 193, 197–98, 200, 202–3,
    208–9, 211–17, 219–27, 230–31, 233–
    35, 250, 253, 256–60, 265, 269–70, 272,
    282, 306, 313, 318, 320, 328–29, 335–36
Gordon, Samuel "Kala", 178
Grant, Laverne, 285
Greene, Simeon, 163, 178, 183–84
Grier, Selwyn, 62, 64, 73
Griffith, Charles, 100, 206, 272
Griffith, Edward, 163, 171, 175, 203–4, 206,
    271

H

Haddaway, Verold, 193
Hadley, Eric, 80
Hadley, William, 68, 84–85
Hallam, Jennifer, 297, 336
Hamlett, Michael, 216, 225–26
Haynes, Afflick, 109, 120, 125, 128
Hazell, Earl, 191–92
Hector, Tim, 208
Horne, Earlene, 163
Horne, John, 203–4, 210, 216, 219
Hughes, E.A.C., 84–85, 103, 105, 116, 131,
    133
Hunte, Julian, 208
Hutchinson, Mary, 212, 284–85
Hutchinson, Sardine, 212

I

Ince, Alexander, 92
Isaacs, Grafton, 175–76, 201, 204
Israel, Edmond M., 147, 153

J

Jack, Cecil "Pa", 178
Jack, David, 203–4
Jackson, Angie, 15
Jackson, Glen, 218, 228
Jackson, Noel, 215–16, 272
Jagan, Cheddi, 109, 114, 164, 203
James, Carlos, 234–35
James, Duff, 13–14, 131, 139–47, 149–50,
    152–54, 157, 165–66, 180, 201, 336–37

Jenkins, A.H., 97
Joachim, Edmund, 80, 84–85, 89, 98–99, 110, 263
John, Cedney, 285
John, Kenneth, 154, 163, 175, 183–84
John, Pearlina, 285
John, Relton, 222
John, Stanley "Stalky," 205, 214, 216, 219–22, 226, 251, 336
Jones, Louis, 203–5, 210, 216, 219
Jones-Morgan, Judith, 287
Joseph, Carl, 219
Joseph, Roy, 85
Joshua, Ebenezer Theodore, 25, 46, 78, 84–85, 88–110, 113–22, 124–34, 136–40, 142–44, 146–51, 153, 155–57, 159, 161, 167–68, 172–76, 181–82, 184, 203, 259–64, 272–77, 279, 281–84, 312, 315–20, 327–29, 339
Joshua, Ivy, 104, 109–10, 119–20, 125, 130, 151, 155, 172, 174, 176, 184, 187, 272, 284–85

K

King, George, 109, 118
Knight, John Derek, 146
Kwayana, Eusi, 164

L

La Borde, Ernest, 157
Lashley, Amor, 222, 285
Latham, Levi, 99, 102, 107, 109–11, 118, 120, 125, 127, 151, 155, 166–67, 172, 175, 188
Leacock, St. Clair, 231
Lewis, Gordon, 63, 81, 85, 260, 281, 336–37
London, Caspar, 15, 43, 154, 163, 165–66, 179–81, 187, 195, 197–98, 203, 272, 320
Lucas, B.J., 213
Lumumba Warjabi. See Cato, Milton, 170

M

Maloney, Albert, 203
Maloney, Jim, 163
Mandeville, Alice, 188, 286
Manley, Norman, 118
Marksman, Roderick, 151, 155, 167
Martin, C.I., 39
Martin, Leopold, 143, 272
Matthews, Roland, 231

Mc Intosh, George Augustus, 25, 57, 62–67, 71–73, 77–78, 80, 82–85, 87–90, 93, 109, 117, 131, 143, 147, 257, 259–60, 272–77, 279, 281–82, 312, 314–15, 317–20, 328
Mc Kie, Cecil, 234–35
Miguel, Girlyn, 219, 221, 225–27, 231, 235, 270–71, 284–85, 287
Milette, James, 163
Mitchell, Cyril, 99, 283
Mitchell, James, 151–52, 155, 161–62, 170–74, 176, 181–84, 187, 191–93, 196–97, 199–205, 208–10, 213–14, 216, 218–19, 221–24, 248–50, 257–65, 269, 272, 274–79, 281–83, 317–19, 329, 337
Morgan, Evans, 89–90, 93, 99
Morris, Kerwyn, 163, 169, 171
Morris, Offord, 187, 204
Munroe, Trevor, 163–64, 197–98
Mutt, Bertha, 63

N

Naipaul, V.S., 163
Nanton, Newton, 129
Nanton, Stewart, 205, 218
Neehall, Cyp, 206
Neverson, Richard, 153

O

Odlum, George, 208
O'Garro, Robert, 178
Ollivierre, Frederick, 222
Ollivierre, Johnny, 214
Ollivierre, Terrance, 226, 228, 231
O'Neal, Ivan, 222, 228
Ottley, Timothy, 178

P

Parris, Karima, 285
Parris, Terrance, 213
Parris, Thaddeus, 87
Peters, Jonathan, 209
Prince, St. Clair "Jimmy", 234–35
Punnett, J., 68

Q

Quammie, Stanley, 216

R

Ragguette, Hugh, 163
Richards, Edgerton, 167, 198
Richardson, Clive, 87
Roberts, Cyril, 147, 153, 188, 196
Roberts, Monty, 216, 219
Robertson, Emery, 193, 206
Robinson, Nelcia, 203, 209, 285
Robinson, St. Clair, 193
Rodney, Walter, 14, 22, 163–64, 185
Rose, Cecil, 148
Rose, Renwick, 162–63, 181, 183, 186,
    195–96, 200, 223, 318, 320
Russell, Randolph, 172, 175, 192–93, 197,
    202, 204, 213–14
Ryan, Cecil, 202

S

Samuel, Adella, 285
Samuel, George, 87
Saunders, Adrian, 163, 202
Saunders, Thomas M., 98
Sayers, Conrad, 225–27, 272
Scott, Jeremiah, 193, 203–4, 210, 216
Simmonds, Floris, 99–100, 283, 285
Simmons, Alphine, 285
Simon, Yvonne, 285
Slater, Douglas, 225–26, 228
Slater, Samuel, 89–90, 98–99, 102, 107,
    109–11, 118, 120, 125, 151, 154–55, 263
Small, Rennie, 116, 119
Snagg, Edwin, 225, 235
Squires, Herbert, 142
Stephens, Percy, 68
Stephenson, Frederick, 234–35
Stephenson, Nigel, 231
Stewart, Curtis B., 146
Stewart, Glenford, 219
St. Hillaire, Henry, 214
Straker, Louis, 214–15, 220–21, 225, 228,
    231, 235, 250, 270
Sylvester, Othneil, 167, 172–74, 182, 214,
    262

T

Tannis, Clive, 89–90, 95, 99, 102–3, 107,
    109–11, 120, 125, 127, 151–52, 172–75,
    184, 186, 283
Tannis, Hudson, 125, 127, 152, 155, 166,
    172, 175, 201, 205, 211

Thomas, Jomo, 164, 234–35
Thomas, Matthew, 215
Thompson, Jerrol, 225–26, 228, 231, 235
Thompson, John, 175–76, 204, 214

W

Walker, Owen, 198–99
Williams, Arthur, 175, 178, 201, 204
Williams, Burton, 203–4, 215, 219
Williams, Calder, 43, 187, 192, 196–97, 202,
    272
Williams, Cecil "Blazer", 178, 198, 203, 209,
    215, 272
Woods, Arthur, 172, 175, 198–99, 271, 338
Woods, Ruth, 285, 287
Wyllie, Bernard, 210, 216, 219

Y

Young, Herbert, 199, 203–4, 210, 215, 285
Young, Herman, 89–90, 95, 98–99, 102, 107,
    109, 111, 117, 120, 125, 127, 151, 263,
    272

Made in the USA
Columbia, SC
20 April 2019